주한미군지위협정(SOFA)

한 · 미
합동위원회 1

주한미군지위협정(SOFA)

한·미
합동위원회 1

| 머리말

　미국은 오래전부터 우리나라 외교에 있어서 가장 긴밀하고 실질적인 우호 · 협력관계를 맺어온 나라다. 6 · 25전쟁 정전 협정이 체결된 후 북한의 재침을 막기 위한 대책으로서 1953년 11월 한미 상호방위조약이 체결되었다. 이는 미군이 한국에 주둔하는 법적 근거였고, 그렇게 주둔하게 된 미군의 시설, 구역, 사업, 용역, 출입국, 통관과 관세, 재판권 등 포괄적인 법적 지위를 규정하는 것이 바로 주한미군지위협정(SOFA)이다. 그러나 이와 관련한 협상은 계속된 난항을 겪으며 한미 상호방위조약이 체결로부터 10년이 훌쩍 넘은 1967년이 돼서야 정식 발효에 이를 수 있었다. 그럼에도 당시 미군 범죄에 대한 한국의 재판권은 심한 제약을 받았으며, 1980년대 후반 민주화 운동과 함께 미군 범죄 문제가 사회적 이슈로 떠오르자 협정을 개정해야 한다는 목소리가 커지게 되었다. 이에 1991년 2월 주한미군지위협정 1차 개정이 진행되었고, 이후에도 여러 사건이 발생하며 2001년 4월 2차 개정이 진행되어 현재에 이르고 있다.

　본 총서는 외교부에서 작성하여 최근 공개한 주한미군지위협정(SOFA) 관련 자료를 담고 있다. 1953년 한미 상호방위조약 체결 이후부터 1967년 발효가 이뤄지기까지의 자료와 더불어, 이후 한미 합동위원회을 비롯해 민 · 형사재판권, 시설, 노무, 교통 등 각 분과위원회의 회의록과 운영 자료, 한국인 고용인 문제와 관련한 자료, 기타 관련 분쟁 자료 등을 포함해 총 42권으로 구성되었다. 전체 분량은 약 2만 2천여 쪽에 이른다.

2024년 3월
한국학술정보(주)

| 일러두기

· 본 총서에 실린 자료는 2022년 4월과 2023년 4월에 각각 공개한 외교문서 4,827권, 76만 여 쪽 가운데 일부를 발췌한 것이다.

· 각 권의 제목과 순서는 공개된 원본을 최대한 반영하였으나, 주제에 따라 일부는 적절히 변경하였다.

· 원본 자료는 A4 판형에 맞게 축소하거나 원본 비율을 유지한 채 A4 페이지 안에 삽입 하였다. 또한 현재 시점에선 공개되지 않아 '공란'이란 표기만 있는 페이지 역시 그대로 실었다.

· 외교부가 공개한 문서 각 권의 첫 페이지에는 '정리 보존 문서 목록'이란 이름으로 기록물 종류, 일자, 명칭, 간단한 내용 등의 정보가 수록되어 있으며, 이를 기준으로 0001번부터 번호가 매겨져 있다. 이는 삭제하지 않고 총서에 그대로 수록하였다.

· 보고서 내용에 관한 더 자세한 정보가 필요하다면, 외교부가 온라인상에 제공하는 『대한 민국 외교사료요약집』 1991년과 1992년 자료를 참조할 수 있다.

| 차례

분류번호	729.41 1968 20-21차	등록번호	243	보존기간	영구乙
기능명칭	SOFA 한미 합동위원회 회의록, 제20-21차. 1968				
생 산 과	안보담당관실		생산년도	1968	

주;
1. 제20차.   1968. 1. 18
2. 제21차.   1968. 2. 21

1

		M/F No.		

729.41
1968
20-21차

SOFA 한미합동위원회 회의록, 제20-21차. 1968.

〈미국·유(UN) - 1227〉

1. 68.1.12   utilities & Services. (공익용역)
2. 68.1.18   20차 회의록.
3. 68.1.18   공익용역 분과위원회 신설.

1. 제 20 차. 1968. 1. 18

2

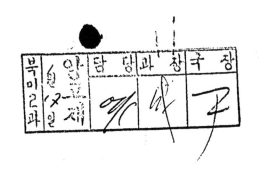

한.미 합동위원회
제20차 회의

한 국 대 표
발언요지 (안)

(의제 1 - 분과위원회 건의)

1. 시설구역 분과위원회

　가. 한국측 설명 10건

　　　(미국대표, 한국대표 제안 설명 요청)

　　　시설구역 분과위원회는 ~~주한 미군의 소요를 초과한다고 인정되거나~~ ~~또는 일정한 조건에 따라~~ 다음 10건의 토지에 대하여 그 취득 해제를 건의하고 있읍니다. 즉,

　　　(1) 취득번호 SAC-658　　　의 0.94 에이커

　　　(2) 　"　　 IC-221　　　 의 2.54 에이커

　　　(3) 　"　　 IC-37　　　　의 2.65 에이커

　　　(4) 　"　　 IC-1066　　　의 3.52 에이커

　　　(5) 　"　　 IC-194　　　 의 1.99 에이커

　　　(6) 　"　　 IC-118　　　 의 일부인 3.27 에이커

　　　(7) 　"　　 SAC-683　　　의 일부인 1.571 에이커

　　　(8) 　"　　 K-D-808　　　의 27.19 에이커

　　　(9) 　"　　 SAC-XC-160 의 일부인 4.59 에이커

　　　(10) 　"　 SAC-728　　　의 일부인 0.0601 에이커

에 관한 것입니다.

　　　한국 대표는 합동위원회가 이들 취득 해제에 관한 시설구역 분과위원회의 건의를 승인할 것을 제의합니다.

　　　(미국대표 동의를 표시)

4.

(의제 1 - 분과위원회 건의)

1. 시설구역 분과위원회

　　가. 미측설명 - 11건

　　　(미국대표, 분과위 건의 설명하고 이의 승인을 제의)

　　한국 대표는 신규취득, 임시 사용허가 연장 및 제한 지역권을 전속 지역권으로 변경하는등 11개 건의 채택에 동의합니다.

5

(의제 1안 - 상무 분과위원회 건의)

(미국대표 한국 대표의 설명을 요청)

감사합니다.

합동위원회는 1967년 9월 28일 개최됨 제15차 회의에서 상무 분과위원회에 대하여 대한민국 정부가 결정한 미군에게 적용되는 공익사업 및 용역의 우선권, 조건 및 요율의 변경에 관하여 제6조 합의의사록 1항이 규정한 합동위원회 협의 절차를 건의하는 과제를 부여한바 있읍니다.

동 분과위원회는 상당한 예비심의 끝에 배부한바와 같은 각서를 제출하여 왔읍니다.

동 분과위원회 건의 내용은 다음과 같읍니다.

(1) 제6조 공익사업 및 용역에 관한 책임으로 부터 상무분과위원회를 해제하고 동조 책임을 앞으로 조직하게될 가칭 공익용역 분과위원회에 재 배정한다.

(2) 협의절차를 안출하는 과제는 이 새 분과위원회에 재 부여한다.

(3) 이 새 분과위원회는 합동위원회 감독하에 제6조 합의의사록 제1항 규정 협의를 행하는 기관으로서의 기능을 다한다.

본 건의는 다음 두개의 고려 요소를 반영하는 것입니다.
즉, 과거 경험에 의하면 공공요율 변경에 관한 대한민국 정부의 정식 결정과 신요율 시행 일자간에는 극히 짧은 시일 여유밖에 없고 또 이러한 사력를 불가피하게하는 여건은 앞으로도 부정기간 존속할 것으로 보입니다. 장차의 가능한 요율 변경을 가급 장기간의 사전 예고를 받아야하는 미국측의 행정상 필요와 곧게 결정을 위요하는 현실 여건간의 접충조화를 이룩하기 위하여 주관 부처인 경제기획원에 의하여 본 건 문제에 관하여 주요역할을 할 것을 청하므로서 비공식 비밀 정보 및 의견교환을 최대한으로 이용하여야 한다는 것입니다.

둘째는 관계사항의 고도로 기술적인 성질과 협의에 사용할 수 있는 제한된 시간 요소를 감안하여 앞으로 설치될 위원회로 하여금 소정 협의를 행하는 주 기관이 되겠금 하고 합동위원회는 최종적 호소기관으로 존속게 하는 구상입니다. 이러한 사고방식이 상무분과위원회 각서 2b 항에 반영되고 있으며, 이 사고방식에 의하면 각 분과위원회의 권한을 합동위원회가 부여한 과제 취급에 한정한다는 현재 책택되고 있는 분과위원회 운영 일반원칙에 대한 예외 설정을 불가피하게 할 것입니다.

대한민국 대표는 상무분과위원회 건의에 대한 합동위원회 승인을 제의하며, 또한 설치 건의된 분과위원회 위원 명단은 한.미 양측 간사를 통하여 교환하되 신 분과위원회가 기능을 발휘하는 것과 동시에 상무 분과위원회에 부여됨 원 과제 심의를 시작할 것을 제의합니다.

(미국측 반응)

7

(의제 2 - 시설구역 분과위원회 신규과제 부여)

1. 한국측 설명 - 4건

　　　(미국대표, 한국대표의 설명 요청)

　　한국 대표는 해제요청에 관한 다음 4건을 시설구역 분과위원회에 신규
과제로서 부여할 것을 제의합니다.

즉, 취득번호 IC-134 의 일부인 9.01 에이커

　　" SAC-CS-283 의 0.23 에이커

　　" IC-97 의 약 1.79 에이커

　　" PAC-134 하이아틱 기지 등입니다.

8

(의제 2 - 시설구역 분과위원회 추가 과제 부여)

2. 미국측 설명 - 9건

   (미국대표 제안 설명, 동의요청)

   한국 대표는 지금 제안하신 9개의 신규과제를 시설구역 분과위원회에
부여하는데 동의합니다.

9

(의제 3 - 1967. 2. 9. SOFA 발효전 시설 및 구역의 취득과 해제에
   대한 합동위원회 승인)

미국측 설명

   (미국대표 설명하고 승인 제안)

   프리드만 장군 감사합니다. 동의하는 바입니다.

10

(의제 4 - 안전에 관한 범죄 목록에 대한 미국 대표 발언)

미국측 설명

(미국대표 발언)

지난번 합동위원회에서 수교한바 있는 본 건 목록에 대하여 친절하고 주의 깊게 검토해 주신데 대하여 대단히 감사합니다.

귀하의 발언 내용은 명백합니다. 한국측 관계위원들이 주의깊게 그리고 성실히 검토 해보겠으며, 이에 관한 한국측 견해는 다음 회의에서 알려 드리겠습니다.

11

(의제 5 - 미 초청계약자 지명)

(미국대표 각서 내용을 설명)

한국 대표는 지금 말씀하신 초청계약자 지명에 있어 합의한바 있는
협의절차를 완전히 거쳤다는 사실과 지명통고 각서 접수를 확인합니다.

12

(의제 6 - 협정시행상 미측이 한국 정부에 전달한 문서)

(미국대표는 지난 회의후 한국측 감사에게 전달한 문서를 열거)

진달 문서를 일일히 열거하여 주서서 감사합니다. 한국 대표는 지금 열거하신 문서를 한국측 사무국이 접수하였음을 확인합니다.

13

(의제 7 - 1967. 12. 28. 자 주한미군 소속 한국인 노무자 임금에 관한 합의와
특정 주한 미군 비세출기관 종업원의 퇴직금에 관한 수정의 기록)

미국측 설명

(미국대표 제안)

대한민국 대표는 이 기회에 한.미 양측 노무분과위원들이 주한 미군
소속 노무자들의 임금과 퇴직금에 관하여 만족할만한 해결을 짓는데 기여한
그들의 노고에 대하여 심심한 사의를 표하는 바입니다.

한국 대표는 전기 2개 양해가서 즉,

1967. 12. 28. 자 주한 미군 소속 한국인 노무자 임금과 특정 주한 미군
비세출 기관 종업원의 퇴직금에 관한 수정, 을 공식 회의록에 첨부 시키자는
귀하의 제의에 동의하는 바 입니다.

14

(의제 8 - 다음회의 예정)

　(미국대표 다음회의 일자를 제안)

　한국측 대표단은 오늘회의와 다음회의 사이에 보통보다 장기간의 시일을 두는 것을 제의하는 이유를 충분히 양해합니다.

　한국 대표는 다음회의 예정일자 전에 현재로는 예견할 수 없는 긴급한 중요문제가 발생하는 경우에는 특별 회의를 소집할 수 있으며 급한 사항은 양대표 또는 각기 교체 대표의 서명으로 처리할 수 있되 이러한 결정은 서명과 동시에 발효하며 다음회의에서 추인한다는 양해하에 제안을 수락하고자 합니다.

15

(의제 9 - 공동발표문 채택)

(미국 대표 양측 감사가 작성한 문안의 채택을 제의)

한국 대표는 작성된 문안을 그대로 채택하는데 동의합니다.

16

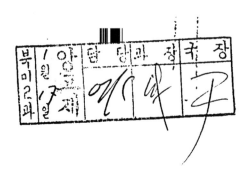

THE TWENTIETH MEETING

ROK-US JOINT COMMITTEE

NOTES

for

The Republic of Korea Representative

[?]

(Agenda I - Recommendations of Subcommittees)

1. Facilities and Areas Subcommittee

    a. ROK presentation - 10 Recommendations

    (The US Representative invites the ROK representative to
    present 10 recommendations)

    The Facilities and Areas Subcommittee has submitted
recommendations to release the following 10 acquisitions ~~of~~ *certain areas*

~~which were found in excess of USFK requirements, or within~~

~~certain conditions.~~   They are:

      (1) acquisition No. SAC 658, containing 0.94 acres.

      (2)   "   IC-221, containing 2.54 acres.

      (3)   "   IC-37, containing 2.65 acres

      (4)   "   IC-1066, containing 3.52 acres

      (5)   "   IC-194, containing 1.99 acres

      (6) a portion of IC-118, containing 3.27 acres

      (7) a portion of SAC-683, containing 1.571 acres

      (8) K-D-808, containing 27.19 acres

      (9) a portion of SAC-XC-160, containing 4.59 acres

      (10) a portion of SAC-728, involving 0.0601 acres

The Republic of Korea Representative is happy to propose
Joint Committee approval of those recommendations for release
of acquisitions.

    (U.S. Representative expresses his concurrence)

18

(Agenda I - Recommendations of Subcommittees)

1. Facilities and Areas Subcommittee

    b. U.S. presentation - 11 recommendations.

    (U.S. Representative presents 11 recommendations and
    proposes approval)

        The Republic of Korea Representative is pleased
to concur in the approval of 11 recommendations concerning
new acquisitions, extension of temporary use permit and
conversion of a restricted easement to an ~~exclusion~~ exclusive use
acquisition.

(Agenda I-2 - Recommendation of the Commerce Subcommittee)

(US Representative invites ROK presentation)

Thank you.

The Joint Committee at its fifteenth meeting on 28 September 1967, ~~has~~ assigned a task to the Commerce Subcommittee of recommending Joint Committee consultation procedures as provided for in the Agreed Minutes one to Article VI, with regard to changes determined by the Republic of Korea Government in priorities, conditions, rates or tariffs of utilities and services applicable to the United States armed forces.

The Subcommittee, after considerable preliminary deliberation, is ~~in~~ now submitting a Memorandum as distributed. The Subcommittee recommends: in substance

(1) that the Commerce Subcommittee be relieved from the responsibility for Article VI, Utilities and Services and the responsibility be reassigned to a new Sub-committee to be organized and tentatively called Utilities Subcommittee;

(2) that the task of formulating consultation procedures be transferred to this new Subcommittee, and

20

(3) that this new Subcommittee serve under Joint Committee
supervision as the agency to effect the consultation
provided in Agreed Minute 1 to Article VI.

This recommendation reflects the following two considerations:

Past experience indicates that very little time is
left between the formal decisions of the Republic of Korea
Government with regard to changes in utilities charges and
their effective dates, and ~~the~~ conditions *such deemed to* ~~which necessitate~~
~~such state of affairs will~~ continue ~~to prevail~~ for an indefinite
period. In order to reconcile U.S. administrative requirements
for being informed of possible future changes as far in
advance as possible and the conditions surrounding decisions
under discussion, maximum use should be made of informal and
confidential exchange of information and views by ~~asking~~ *letting*
the principally concerned organ, the Economic Planning Board,
to assume a major role in this question.

Secondly, in view of the highly technical nature of
the question involved and the limited time available for the
consultation, the new Subcommittee is envisaged to become
the principal organ to effect the provided consultation, and the
Joint Committee itself will remain as the organ of last
resort. This thinking is reflected in the wording of paragraph
2 (b) of the Subcommittee Memorandum. This line of thinking

will necessitate providing for an exception to the ~~adopted~~ *existing* general rule of Subcommittee operation, ~~that of limiting their competence to handle only tasks assigned~~ *so that the said Sub-committee may submit its recommendation* by the Joint Committee. *without being assigned* / *the task thereof* / *handle the problem and*

The Republic of Korea Representative proposes Joint Committee approval of the Commerce Subcommittee recommendation, and further suggest that list**s** of full memberships of the proposed Subcommittee be exchanged through two Secretaries and the new Subcommittee will proceed to consider the task originally given to the Commerce Subcommittee as soon as it becomes operational.

(U.S. response)

(Agenda II - Assign~~ed~~ ^ment^ of Additional Tasks to Facilities
and Areas Subcommittee)

1. ROK presentation - 4 tasks

    (U.S. Representative invites the ROK Representative to
    present 4 tasks)

    The ~~Republic of Korea~~ *Korean Representative* now wishes to propose new assignments
of the following 4 tasks pertaining to requests for release *of*
to the Facilities and Areas Subcommittee.   *certain areas*
                                                    now in use 중 by
    They are: (*acquisition No.*   *U.S.F.K.*
    (1) a portion of IC-134, consisting of 9.01 acres
    (2) *(Acquisition No.)* SAC-CS-283, containing 0.23 acres
    (3) " IC-97, containing approximately 1.79 acres
    (4) a small portion at Hialeah Compound PAC-134.
                        aquired under ~~upon~~ acquisition No.

    (U.S. Representative expresses concurrence)

2. U.S. presentation - 9 tasks

    (U.S. Representative presents and proposes approval)
    The Republic of Korea Representative is pleased to
agree to the assignment of the 9 tasks proposed by the
U.S. Representative to the Facilities and Areas Subcommittee.

23

(Agenda III - Joint Committee approval of acquisition and
           release of Facilities and Areas pre-dating
           the 9 February 1967 entry into force of the
           SOFA

U.S. presentation

    (U.S. Representative presents and proposes approval)

    Thank you General Friedman, I am happy to concur
to the proposal.

24

(Agenda IV - Statement with regard to the list of security
            offenses)

U.S. presentation

(U.S. Representative reads the statement)

Thank you very much, for your kind and careful examination
on the list which I transmitted at the other meeting of
the Joint Committee. Your comment is clear, and will be
carefully and sincerely studied by the members concerned
of the Korean component:

The Republic of Korea Representative, in this connection,
wishes to present his views at the later meeting with your kind
understanding.

25

(Agenda V - Designation of US Invited Contractor)

(US Representative presents the Memorandum)

The Republic of Korea Representative is happy to
confirm that the agreed procedures for the designation
have been fully adhered to and the receipt of the notifying
memorandum.

26

(Agenda VI - Memoranda presented to the ROK Government by
the U.S. in the implementation of the SOFA.)

(The US Representative enumerates the documents transferred
to the ROK Secretary since the last meeting)

Thank you, General Friedman, for the enumeration. The
Republic of Korea Representative is pleased to confirm the
receipt by the ROK Secretariat of the doduments as enumerated.

27

(Agenda VII - Recording of Agreement of 28 December 1967
            concerning USFK's Korean Employees Wages and
            Modification of Severance pay for Employees of
            certain USFK Nonappropriated Fund Activities)

U.S. presentation

    (U.S. Representative proposes approval)

    The Republic of Korea Representative wishes to take this
opportunity to express his sincere appreciation to ~~the~~
members ~~of~~ both the U.S. and Korean Labor Subcommittee for
their substantial contribution made in the satisfactory
settlements concerning wages and severance pay for USFK's
Korean employees.

    I am now happy to agree to your proposal that those
two memoranda of understanding, namely, Agreement of 28
December 1967 concerning USFK's Korean Employees Wages
and Modification of Severance pay for Employees of Certain
USFK Nonappropriated Fund Activities, be included in the
official minutes.

(Agenda VIII - Proposed Time of Next Meeting)

(U.S. Representative proposes the date)

Korean Component fully understands the reason for proposing to place a longer than normal interval between this meeting and the next meeting.

The Republic of Korea Representative accepts the proposal with the understanding that if any problem unforeseen at this time, important and pressing arises before the proposed next meeting, an emergency session may be called and that ~~for~~ pressing matters may be handled by signatures of two representatives or respective alternate, such decisions becoming effective immediately upon signatures and to be confirmed by the full meeting.

(Agenda IX - Agreement on Joint Press Release)

(U.S. Representative proposes adoption of text prepared
by the two Secretaries)

The Representative is happy to concur in the adoption
of the text as prepared.

30

한.미 합동위원회
제20차 회의
의 제

1968. 1. 18. 15:00시

미측 SOFA 회의실

1. 구 분과위원회 건의

　가. 시설구역 분과위원회

　　(1) 한국측 상정 - 10건

　　(2) 미국측 상정 - 11건

　나. 상무분과위원회 - 한국측 설명

2. 시설구역 분과위원회에 대한 추가 과제 부여

　가. 한국측 상정 - 4건

　나. 미국측 상정 - 9건

3. 1967년 2월 9일 군대지위협정 발효 이전부터 계류중인 시설구역 취득 및 해제에 대한 합동위원회 승인 - 미측 상정

4. 국가 안전관계 범죄 목록에 대한 발언 - 미측 상정

5. /초청계약자 지명에 관한 각서 - 미측 상정

6. 군대지위협정 시행을 위하여 미측와 한국 정부에 관련한 문서 - 미측 상정

7. 1967. 12. 28. 자 미군 고용 한국인 종업원에 대한 임금에 관한 합의 및 미군 일부 비세출 기관 고용원 퇴직금 급여 방식 변경에 관한 기록 삽입 - 미측 상정

8. 차기회의 예정 - 제안) 1968. 2. 21. (수) 15:00시 공상성 회의실에서

9. 공동발표문 채택

10. 폐 회

These minutes are considered as official documents pertaining to both Governments and will not be released without mutual agreement.

JOINT COMMITTEE
UNDER
THE REPUBLIC OF KOREA AND THE UNITED STATES
STATUS OF FORCES AGREEMENT

MINUTES OF THE TWENTIETH MEETING

18 January 1968
Headquarters
U.S. Forces, Korea
Seoul, Korea

1. The meeting was convened at 1500 hours by Lieutenant General Robert J. Friedman, the US Representative, who presided at the meeting. A copy of the agenda is attached as Inclosure 1.

2. The following were in attendance:

ROK	US
Mr. YOON Ha Jong	LTG Robert J. Friedman, USAF
Mr. LEE Sun Jung	CAPT M. R. Massie, USN
Mr. KIM Il Doo	COL Walter V. Gresham, USAF
Maj Gen KIM, Mook	COL Gerald W. Davis, USA
Mr. HUH Seung Joon	Mr. P. Wesley Kriebel, US Embassy
Mr. KIM Wan Soo	Mr. Robert A. Kinney, HQ USFK
Mr. SHIN Chung Sup	LTC Paul Jones, USAF
Mr. PARK Noh Soo	
Mr. OH Myong Too	

3. The US Representative called the meeting to order and invited the ROK Representative to present ten recommendations of the Facilities and Areas Subcommittee. The ROK Representative stated that the Facilities and Areas Subcommittee had submitted recommendations to release the following ten acquisitions; areas involved in the of certain areas:

a. Acquisition No. SAC 658, containing 0.94 acre (Inclosure 2).

b. Acquisition No. IC-221, containing 2.54 acres (Inclosure 3).

c. Acquisition No. IC-37, containing 2.65 acres (Inclosure 3).

20th JC
18 Jan 68

d. Acquisition No. IC-1066, containing 3.52 acres (Inclosure 3).

e. Acquisition No. IC-194, containing 1.99 acres (Inclosure 3).

f. A portion of IC-118, containing 3.27 acres (Inclosure 3).

g. A portion of SAC-683, containing 1.571 acres (Inclosure 3).

h. ~~Acquisition No.~~ K-D-808, containing 27.19 acres (Inclosure 4).

i. A portion of SAC-XC-160, containing 4.59 acres (Inclosure 4).

j. A portion of SAC-728, involving 0.0601 acres (Inclosure 5).

4. The Republic of Korea Representative proposed Joint Committee approval of these recommendations for release of acquisitions and the US Representative concurred.

5. The US Representative presented the following eleven recommendations of the Facilities and Areas Subcommittee:

a. Acquisition of 125 acres at Uijongbu City, Kyonggi-do (Inclosure 6). Of this acreage, 3.59 acres are for an indefinite period and the remaining 121.41 acres are for temporary use from 1 December 1967 through 30 November 1968.

b. Acquisition of 0.092 acre of land at Pochon-gun, Kyonggi-do, required for widening the road along MSR 33N and 1X (Inclosure 11).

c. Acquisition of an easement involving 2.72 acres of land at Yangju-gun, Kyonggi-do, required to construct a bridge on Route 2XE and realign the road (Inclosure 11).

d. Acquisition of an easement involving 2.82 acres of land at Paju-gun, Kyonggi-do, required for the construction of a bridge on Route 23 (Inclosure 11).

2

e. Acquisition of an easement involving 0.0023 acre of land at
Sochon-gun, Chungchongnamedo for construction of a water well and
pump shed (Inclosure 10).

f. Acquisition of 0.454 acre of land at Kimjae-gun, Chollapukedo
(Inclosure 10). Of this acreage, 0.446 acre is required for exclusive use
for construction of a barracks and 0.008 acre is required for an easement
for a sewer line.

g. Extension of temporary use permit 7X-T-17 for 2,400 acres
of land from 21 September 1967 to 20 September 1968. This land is required for a training area (Inclosure 7).

h. Extension of temporary use permit K-C-T-26 for 20.117
acres of land from 1 November 1967 to 31 October 1968 (Inclosure 7).
This land is required for a field storage area.

i. Extension of temporary use permit SAC-T-48 for 250 acres
of land from 1 November 1967 to 31 October 1968 (Inclosure 11). This
land is required for a training area.

j. Withdrawal of a request for conversion of a restricted easement (PAC-179) to an exclusive use acquisition (Inclosure 8). This involved 5.51 acres in Taegu City.

k. Withdrawal of a request for acquisition of 7.48 acres of land
at Kwangju-gun, Kyonggi-do (Inclosure 9).

6. The United States Representative proposed Joint Committee
approval of these eleven recommendations and the Republic of Korea
Representative concurred.

3

7. The ROK Representative stated that ~~just~~ the Joint Commi:tee at its fifteenth meeting on 28 September 1967, had assigned a task to the Commerce Subcommittee. This task was to recommend to the Joint Committee consultation procedures as provided for in the Agreed Minute 1 of Article VI, with regard to changes determined by the Republic of Korea Government in priorities, conditions, rates or tariffs of utilities and services applicable to the United States armed forces. The Subcommittee, after considerable preliminary deliberation, has submitted recommendations as follows (Inclosure 12):

a. The Commerce Subcommittee be relieved from the responsibility for Article VI, Utilities and Services and the responsibility be reassigned to a new Subcommittee to be organized and ~~tentatively called~~ designated as the Utilities Subcommittee.

b. The task of formulating consultation procedures be transferred to this new Subcommittee.

c. This new Subcommittee serve under Joint Committee supervision as the agency to effect the consultation provided in Agreed Minute 1, Article VI.

8. The ROK Representative stated that:

a. Past experience indicated that very little time is left between the formal decisions of the Republic of Korea Government with regard to changes in utilities charges and their effective dates, and such conditions will continue for an indefinite period. In order to reconcile US administrative requirements for being informed of possible future changes as far in

4

advance as possible ● the conditions surrounding de●ions under discussion, maximum use should be made of informal and confidential exchange of information and views by asking the principally concerned organ, the ROK Economic Planning Board, to assume a major role in this question.

b. In view of the highly technical nature of the question involved and the limited time available for the consultation, the new Subcommittee is envisaged to become the principal organ to effect the provided consultation, and the Joint Committee itself would remain as the organ of final authority. This thinking is reflected in the wording of paragraph 2(b) of the Subcommittee recommendations. This line of thinking would necessitate providing for an exception to the existing general rules for Subcommittee operations, so that the said Subcommittee could handle the problems and submit recommendations without being assigned tasks by the Joint Committee. The ROK Representative proposed Joint Committee approval of the Commerce Subcommittee recommendation, and further suggested that lists of full memberships of the proposed Subcommittee be exchanged through the two SOFA Secretaries. He proposed that the new Subcommittee should proceed to consider the task originally assigned to the Commerce Subcommittee as soon as it becomes operational (see Inclosure 8 of the minutes of the fifteenth meeting of the Joint Committee, 28 September 1967).

9. The US Representative concurred in the recommendation of the Commerce Subcommittee and stated that a new Utilities Subcommittee should be established expeditiously. This new Subcommittee should

5

proceed immediately ⬤ develop recommendations for ⬤ rly presentation to the Joint Committee regarding the consultation procedures necessary to implement paragraph 2 and Agreed Minute 1 of Article VI. The US Representative proposed early exchange of membership lists for the new Subcommittee between the ROK and US SOFA Secretariats. The US Representative commented that the direct involvement of the Economic Planning Board in the problem appeared to be a step in the right direction and that inclusion of representation from the US Operations Mission would be equally beneficial to both sides. He expressed the hope for an early agreement on recommendations to complete this assignment by the new Utilities Subcommittee.

10. The ROK Representative proposed four new assignments to the Facilities and Areas Subcommittee, pertaining to requests for release of areas held by the USFK, as follows:

a. A portion of IC-134, consisting of 9.01 acres (Inclosure 13). The remaining portion of IC-134, containing 0.15 acre of land is to be converted from an exclusive use acquisition to an easement.

b. *Acquisition No.* SAC-CS-283, containing 0.23 acre of land (Inclosure 13).

c. *Acquisition No.* IC-97, containing approximately 1.79 acres (Inclosure 14).

d. A small portion of Hialeah Compound in Pusan, PAC-134 (Inclosure 14).

11. The US Representative stated that he was happy to concur in the assignment of these four tasks to the Facilities and Areas Subcommittee.

12. The US Representative presented nine new tasks for assignment to the Facilities and Areas Subcommittee. These assignments involve;

6

a. Acquisition of 0.248 acre of land of which 0.223 acre is for exclusive use and 0.025 acre is for an easement in Kapyong-gun, Kyonggi-do (Inclosure 15).

b. Acquisition of 15.867 acres of land, of which 1.116 acres are for exclusive use and 14.751 acres are for an easement, in Seoul City for a transmitter site for the American Forces Korea Network (Inclosure 15).

c. Acquisition of 2.85 acres of land in Taegu City to provide additional storage area for Camp Walker (Inclosure 15).

d. Acquisition of 5.89 acres of land in Yangsan-gun, Kyongsang-namdo, for widening the access road to the Brooklyn VHF site (Inclosure 15).

e. Acquisition of a perpetual restrictive easement for 1.625 acre of land required for the construction of an underground cable line (Inclosure 15).

f. Acquisition of 0.41 acre of land for an easement for relocation of overhead power lines (portion of 7X-24) (Inclosure 15).

g. Extension of Temporary Use Permit SAC-T-18 from 16 December 1967 to 15 December 1968 (Inclosure 15).

h. Extension of Temporary Use Permit SAC-T-6 from 16 December 1967 to 15 December 1968 (Inclosure 15).

13. The US Representative proposed assignment of these new tasks to the Facilities and Areas Subcommittee and the ROK Representative concurred.

7

14. The US Representative stated that, at the thirteenth meeting of the Joint Committee on 31 August 1967, the Joint Committee approved three real estate transactions proposed by the Facilities and Areas Subcommittee. Processing of documentation on these transactions had begun prior to the entry into force of the SOFA. As a consequence, these actions were not assigned as tasks by the Joint Committee to the Facilities and Areas Subcommittee. The Facilities and Areas Subcommittee has now completed documentation on the last three tasks in this same category. These involve:

    a. Acquisition of 2.33 acres of land located in Subinggo-dong, Yongsan-ku, Seoul City, for expansion of the Yongsan Water System, construction of wells, and installation of water supply lines.

    b. Release of 0.36 acre of land (as cited in paragraph 14.a, above) which was acquired as an easement area. This area is now to be included in the 2.33 acres cited in paragraph 14.a.

    c. Acquisition of 1.20 cares of land in Byukkae-ri, Hongsung-gun, Chungchongnamdo for the expansion of Site 75, Tactical Facility 5.

15. The US Representative proposed approval by the Joint Committee of these three real estate transactions. This approval completes Joint Committee authentication of all specific actions on facilities and areas undertaken prior to 9 February 1967. The ROK Representative concurred in Joint Committee authentication of the documentation in the foregoing three specific actions.

8

16. The US Representative stated that he would like again to thank the Republic of Korea Representative for the list of security offenses under the laws of the Republic of Korea, which (ep) so kindly transmitted at the seventeenth meeting of the Joint Comittee. In the meantime, this list has been examined by various members of the US component with great interest. This list will be extremely valuable, should the need arise, in determining the security implications of cases as they occur. Because of the broad language that necessarily must be used in describing offenses that could possibly affect the security of a nation, the US Representative believes that the security implications of certain of the offenses listed can only be determined on a case by case basis. Examples of such offenses are those dealing with the organization of criminal bodies, with riot, with the unlawful use of explosives, and with actions directed against the flag. Reprehensible as such offenses are, they do not in all circumstances have security implications. It is noted that such implications may, under the SOFA, affect the right to exercise jurisdiction over the offense, the right of pre-trial custody, or the determination of the particular importance of the case.

17. The US Representative stated that because of the need for a case by case determination in these matters, the Republic of Korea and the United States lists can serve as extremely useful guides as to which offenses are likely to have security implications. The employment of these lists as guides, will not, he was certain, work to the detriment of the prompt and adequate disposition of offenses which are found to have security implications.

9

18.   The ROK Representative thanked the US Representative for his kind and careful examination of the list of security offenses, which he had transmitted at the seventeenth meeting of the Joint Committee.   He stated that the US Representative's comments were clear, and would be carefully and sincerely studied by the members of the Korean component concerned with this problem.   The Republic of Korea Representative stated that, in this connection, he wished to present his views at a later meeting, with the kind understanding of the US Representative.   The US Representative thanked the ROK Representative and assured his Korean colleagues on the Joint Committee that the security of both the Republic of Korea and the United States is the primary mission and concern of the United States armed forces present within ROK territory.   He did not believe that the utilization of these lists as guides will adversely affect the security of either the Republic of Korea or the United States.   The ROK Representative stated that the list of security offenses, as transmitted, was prepared by competent individuals in the field of ROK law. ~~He stated that the final~~ outcome of this matter, he was sure, would not be detrimental to the security of either country.   He indicated that he would express the point of view of his Government on this question at a later meeting.   The US Representative thanked the ROK Representative for the kind consideration which his Government will give to these US comments on the question of the exchange of security lists.

19. The US Representative presented a memorandum to the Joint Committee informing the Republic of Korea Government of the designation of a new invited contractor under Article XV of the Status of Forces Agreement. After consultation with personnel of the Republic of Korea Commerce Subcommittee, the United States Forces, Korea, had designated Adrian Wilson Associates as a US Invited Contractor for the execution of contract #DACA-81-68-C-0038 for architect-engineer services in connection with the Korean Joint Construction Agency. Pertinent (Inclosure 16). data concerning employees of this invited contractor will be provided to the Government of the Republic of Korea in accordance with mutually approved procedures.

20. The Republic of Korea Representative confirmed that the agreed procedures for the designation had been fully adhered to and he acknowledged receipt of the notifying memorandum.

21. The US Representative noted for the record that the United States SOFA Secretary had furnished the following information to the ROK SOFA Secretary since the last meeting of the Joint Committee. This material was presented for appropriate distribution within the Republic of Korea Government in the implementation of United States-Republic of Korea Status of Forces Agreement.

a. Five copies of reports on the United States armed forces disposition of cases for the month of November 1967, in accordance with Article XXII, paragraph 6(b), and United States-Republic of Korea Joint Committee Agreed View No. 5.

11

b. Twenty copies of a report listing arrivals, departures, and address changes of United States invited contractor personnel and their dependents, dated 31 December 1967, and twenty copies of the quarterly consolidated list of invited contractor personnel and their dependents for 31 December 1967. These reports are made in accordance with the procedures approved by the Joint Committee at its ninth meeting on 5 June 1967.

c. Twenty copies of the report of United States armed forces personnel, the civilian component, invited contractors, and dependents, entering or departing the Republic of Korea during the month of December 1967. This report was made in accordance with procedures adopted by the Joint Committee at its sixth meeting on 28 April 1967 and amended by the Joint Committee at its fourteenth meeting on 14 September 1967.

22. The ROK Representative stated that he was pleased to confirm the receipt by the ROK Secretariat of the documents, as enumerated by the US Representative.

23. The US Representative proposed that two recent Memoranda of Understanding relating to two significant labor problems, be recorded in the official minutes of the ROK-US Joint Committee. The Memorandum of Understanding of 28 December 1967 (Inclosure 17) terminated a labor dispute which the Foreign Organization Employees Union had filed. This dispute had been referred to the Office of Labor Affairs of the Government of the Republic of Korea for conciliation in accordance with paragraph 4 of

12

of Article XVII of the SOFA. The Memorandum of Understanding of 16 January 1968 resolved a question relating to severance pay for employees of certain USFK nonappropriated fund activities. Recently, problems developed in the administration of severance pay for Korean employees of certain non-appropriated fund activities of the Eighth US Army. This prompted a special study by Eighth US Army, including negotiations with the Foreign Organization Employees Union. In view of legal questions and the labor problem, consultation was held with the ROK Government officials of the Office of Labor Affairs, in accordance with Article XVII of the SOFA. The Eighth US Army plan provides for a major change in severance pay for certain nonappropriated fund employees. This change provided for changes in severance rates, for a lump sum payment of severance credits to employees based upon a separation and reappointment personnel action, and the deposit of such severance credits in individual employee accounts in one or more Korean banks. The Director, Office of Labor Affairs, Mr. LEE Sung Tack, had reviewed and approved this plan, as indicated in Inclosure 18. Mr. Lee advised that the proposed plan, with union acceptance, was considered by the Government of the Republic of Korea to be an appropriate action and met requirements of Republic of Korea labor law. The Foreign Organization Employees Union reviewed this proposal in detail and a union-management understanding was reached on the provisions of the plan. The Memorandum of Understanding of 16 January 1968 (Inclosure 19) contained the statement that the new plan

13

would be validated and recorded by the US-ROK SOFA Joint Committee.
Pertinent changes to Eighth US Army Regulation 690-1, relating to severance
pay procedures, is included as Inclosure 20.

24. The US Representative proposed that all of the four inclosures
on this subject be included in the minutes of the twentieth meeting of the
Joint Committee. He stated that he believed that official recording of
these understandings, worked out in accordance with provisions of
Article XVII of the SOFA, are ~~believed to be~~ in the mutual interests of
both the Governments of the Republic of Korea and of the United States.

25. The US Representative stated that he would like to take this
opportunity to express the appreciation of the United States Forces,
Korea, to the officials of the Government of the Republic of Korea, whose
devoted and effective work greatly assisted in achievement of the foregoing Memoranda of Understanding. He particularly expressed his
appreciation to a member of the Republic of Korea component of the
Joint Committee, Mr. HUH Seung Joon, Chief, Labor Affairs Bureau,
Office of Labor Affairs, and Chairman of the Labor Subcommittee. Mr.
Huh demonstrated deep understanding and great skill in his conciliation
role between the US Forces, Korea and the Foreign Organization Employees
Union.

26. The ROK Representative stated that he was happy to agree to the
US proposal to include in the Joint Committee minutes the Memoranda of
Understanding of 28 December 1967 concerning USFK's Korean employees

14

wages and the Memorandum of Understanding of 16 January 1968 regarding the modification of severance pay for employees of certain USFK nonappropriated fund activities, and related documents. (Inclosures 17, 18, 19, and 20)

27. The ROK Representative stated that he wished to take this opportunity to express his sincere appreciation to the members of both the United States and the Republic of Korea components of the Labor Subcommittee, and especially to Mr. Huh and Mr. Ogden C. Reed, Director of Civilian Personnel, Eighth US Army, for their substantial contributions made in the settlement of problems concerning wages of USFK's Korean employees and severance pay for certain of USFK's Korean nonappropriated fund employees.

28. The US Representative proposed that the next meeting of the US-ROK Joint Committee be held at 1500 hours on Wednesday, 21 February, at the ROK Capitol Building. In this connection, Joint Committee procedures provide for exigency actions to be accomplished without a formal Joint Committee meeting, by mutual agreement of the ROK and US Representatives; therefore, the US Representative proposed that, if any subcommittees with important pending projects reach signed agreements on recommendations for resolution of their assignments, that the ROK and US Representatives may review and approve these agreements prior to the next Joint Committee meeting. This would enable any urgent subcommittee recommendations to be approved and implemented as soon as possible. Joint Committee procedures provide that, in the

46

15

event of such contingency actions, the actions will be recorded in the official minutes of the next US-ROK Joint Committee meeting.

29. The ROK Representative stated that the ROK component fully understands the reason for proposing to place a longer than normal interval between this meeting and the next meeting. The ROK Representative accepted the proposal, with the understanding that:

a. If any problem unforeseen at this time, important and pressing, should arise before the proposed next meeting, an emergency session may be called.

b. That pressing matters between the two meetings may be handled by signatures of two Representatives or their respective Alternates, with such decisions becoming effective immediately upon signing by the two Representatives or their Alternates. These decisions would be confirmed at the next meeting of the Joint Committee.

30. The US Representative proposed approval of the proposed ROK-US joint press release for the twentieth Joint Committee meeting, as prepared by the ROK and US SOFA Secretaries (Inclosure 21). The ROK Representative indicated that he approved the joint press release as presented.

31. The meeting was adjourned at 1620 hours.

21 Inclosures

ROBERT J. FRIEDMAN   YOON HA JONG

47

16

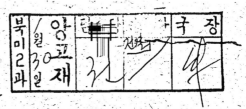

외   무   부

미이 720-   1968. 1. 30.

수 신 : 내 부처 참조

참 조 :

제 목 : 한.미 합동위원회 회의록 송부

　　　1. 한.미간 군대지위협정에 의하여 1968. 1. 18.에
개최된 한.미 합동위원회 제 20 차 회의의 회의록을 별첨 송부하오니
참고 하시기 바랍니다.

　　　2. 본 회의록은 한.미 양측의 합의에 의하여서만 공개할
수 있는 문서이오니 유념하시기 바랍니다.

　　　첨부 : 합동위원회 제 20 차 회의록 18 부.   끝

　　　　　　　　　　외 무 부 장 관

　　　　　　　　　　　　3 부

배부처 : 법무부장관 (법무실장, 검찰국장), 국방부장관 (기획국장,
　　　　시설국장), 재무부장관 (세관국장, 세제국장),
　　　　상공부장관 (상역국장), 노동청장 (노정국장),
　　　　교통부장관 (항공국장), 내무부장관 (치안국장), 주미
　　　　주일, 주중, 주비대사, 경제기획원장관 (경제기획국장,
　　　　물가정책과장)

48

결 번

넘버링 오류

결 번

넘버링 오류

한.미 합동위원회 제20차 회의 회의록 (요약)

일 시 : 1968. 1. 18.

장 소 : 미8군 사령부 회의실

1. 시설구역 분과위원회의 건의 21건과 동 분과위원회에 대한 13건의 과제부여를 승인했다.

　　내용 : (1) 건 의

종 별	건 수	면 적 (단위 : 에이커)
취 득	3	125.546
반 환	10	48.3211
지역권 취득	3	5.5423
임시사용허가연장	3	2670.117
취득취소	1	7.48
변경취소	1	5.51
계	21	

　　　　(2) 과제부여

종 별	건 수	면 적 (단위 : 에이커)
취 득	4	24.855
반 환	4	11.03
지역권취득	1	0.41
영구제한지역권취득	1	1.625
임시사용허가연장	3	2,818
계	13	

51

√ 2. 대한민국 대표는 협정 제6조 합의의사록 1에 규정되어 있는 공공용역에 관한 협의절차를 규제하기 위한 제1차적 기관으로 "공공용역 분과위원회" 를 설치할 것과 요율변경에 관하여 비공식적으로 정보 및 의견교환을 위하여 경제기획원을 최대한 이용할 것을 제안하였다. 미측 대표는 이에 동의하고 조속한 시일내에 동 분과위원회의 양측 위원명단을 교환 할것을 제의하였다.

3. 합동위원회는 1967년 2월 9일 협정 발효이전 부터 계류중인 3개의 시설구역 의 취득 및 반환을 승인하였다.

4. 미국 대표는 17차 회의에서 교환한바 있는 한.미 양국의 안전에 관한 법죄 목록중 한국의 안전법죄 목록에 관하여 그의 의견을 표명하고 한국 대표는 미국의 안전 법죄 목록에 관하여 차기회의에서그의 의견을 제시하겠다고 말하였다.

5. 합동위원회는 미국측 대표가 제출한 "Adrian Wilson Associates" 에 대한 미국 초청계약자로서의 지명을 승인했다.

√ 6. 합동위원회는 1967년 12월 28일자 외국기관 노동조합 종업원에 대한 임금 에 관한 합의와 1968년 1월 16일자 미군 일부 비세출 자금기관의 고용원에 대한 퇴직금 급여방식 변경에 관한 2개의 기록을 회의록에 삽입할 것을 승인했다.

7. 차기회의는 1968년 2월 21일 (수) 15:00시 중앙청회의실에서 개최키로 합의하고 본 회의의 공.동 발표문을 채택하였다.

52

*. These minutes are considered as official documents pertaining to both
Governments a██ ██ not be released without mu██ ██greement.

JOINT COMMITTEE
UNDER
THE REPUBLIC OF KOREA AND THE UNITED STATES
STATUS OF FORCES AGREEMENT

MINUTES OF THE TWENTIETH MEETING

18 January 1968
Headquarters
U.S. Forces, Korea
Seoul, Korea

1. The meeting was convened at 1500 hours by Lieutenant General
Robert J. Friedman, the US Representative, who presided at the meeting. A copy of the agenda is attached as Inclosure 1.

2. The following were in attendance:

ROK	US
Mr. YOON Ha Jong	LTG Robert J. Friedman, USAF
Mr. LEE Sun Jung	CAPT M. R. Massie, USN
Mr. KIM Il Doo	COL Walter V. Gresham, USAF
Maj Gen KIM, Mook	COL Gerald W. Davis, USA
Mr. HUH Seung Joon	Mr. P. Wesley Kriebel, US Embassy
Mr. KIM Wan Soo	Mr. Robert A. Kinney, HQ USFK
Mr. SHIN Chung Sup	LTC Paul Jones, USAF
Mr. PARK Noh Soo	
Mr. OH Myong Too	

3. The US Representative called the meeting to order and invited
the ROK Representative to present ten recommendations of the Facilities and Areas Subcommittee. The ROK Representative stated that the
Facilities and Areas Subcommittee had submitted recommendations to
release the areas involved in the following ten acquisitions:

a. Acquisition No. SAC-658, containing 0.94 acre (Inclosure 2).

b. Acquisition No. IC-221, containing 2.54 acres (Inclosure 3).

c. Acquisition No. IC-37, containing 2.65 acres (Inclosure 3).

d.. Acquisition No. IC-1066, containing 3.52 acres (Inclosure 3).

e. Acquisition No. IC-194, containing 1.99 acres (Inclosure 3).

f. A portion of IC-118, containing 3.27 acres (Inclosure 3).

20th JC
18 Jan 68

63

These minimes ~~considered~~ as official docume ~~pertaining~~ to both Governments ~~and will~~ not be released without ~~mutual~~ agreement.

    g. A portion of SAC-683, containing 1.571 acres (Inclosure 3).

    h. Acquisition No. K-D-808, containing 27.19 acres (Inclosure 4).

    i. A portion of SAC-XC-160, containing 4.59 acres (Inclosure 4).

    j. A portion of SAC-728, involving 0.0601 acres (Inclosure 5).

4. The Republic of Korea Representative proposed Joint Committee approval of these recommendations for release of acquisitions and the US Representative concurred.

5. The US Representative presented the following eleven recommendations of the Facilities and Areas Subcommittee:

    a. Acquisition of 125 acres at Uijongbu City, Kyonggi-do (Inclosure 6). Of this acreage, 3.59 acres are for an indefinite period and the remaining 121.41 acres are for temporary use from 1 December 1967 through 30 November 1968.

    b. Acquisition of 0.092 acre of land at Pochon-gun, Kyonggi-do, required for widening the road along MSR 33N and 1X (Inclosure 11).

    c. Acquisition of an easement involving 2.72 acres of land at Yangju-gun, Kyonggi-do, required to construct a bridge on Route 2XE and realign the road (Inclosure 11).

    d. Acquisition of an easement involving 2.82 acres of land at Paju-gun, Kyonggi-do, required for the construction of a bridge on Route 23 (Inclosure 11).

    e. Acquisition of an easement involving 0.0023 acre of land at Sochon-gun, Chungchong-namdo for construction of a water well and pump shed (Inclosure 10).

    f. Acquisition of 0.454 acre of land at Kimjae-gun, Chollapuk-do (Inclosure 10). Of this acreage, 0.446 acre is required for exclusive use for construction of a barracks and 0.008 acre is required for an easement for a sewer line.

    g. Extension of temporary use permit 7X-T-17 for 2.400 acres of land from 21 September 1967 to 20 September 1968. This land is required for a training area (Inclosure 7).

20th JC
18 Jan 68

These minutes are considered as official documents pertaining to both Governments a███ not be released without m███ agreement.

h. Extension of temporary use permit K-C-T-26 for 20.117 acres of land from 1 November 1967 to 31 October 1968 (Inclosure 7). This land is required for a field storage area.

i. Extension of temporary use permit SAC-T-48 for 250 acres of land from 1 November 1967 to 31 October 1968 (Inclosure 11). This land is required for a training area.

j. Withdrawal of a request for conversion of a restricted easement (PAC-179) to an exclusive use acquisition (Inclosure 8). This involved 5.51 acres in Taegu City.

k. Withdrawal of a request for acquisition of 7.48 acres of land at Kwangju-gun, Kyonggi-do (Inclosure 9).

6. The United States Representative proposed Joint Committee approval of these eleven recommendations and the Republic of Korea Representative concurred.

7. The ROK Representative stated that the Joint Committee, at its fifteenth meeting on 28 September 1967, had assigned a task to the Commerce Subcommittee. This task was to recommend to the Joint Committee consultation procedures as provided for in the Agreed Minute 1 of Article VI, with regard to changes determined by the Republic of Korea Government in priorities, conditions, rates or tariffs of utilities and services applicable to the United States armed forces. The Subcommittee, after considerable preliminary deliberation, has submitted recommendations as follows (Inclosure 12):

a. The Commerce Subcommittee be relieved from the responsibility for Article VI, Utilities and Services, and the responsibility be reassigned to a new Subcommittee to be organized and designated as the Utilities Subcommittee.

b. The task of formulating consultation procedures be transferred to this new Subcommittee.

c. This new Subcommittee serve under Joint Committee supervision as the agency to effect the consultation provided in Agreed Minute 1, Article VI.

8. The ROK Representative stated that:

20th JC
18 Jan 68

3

These minutes ███ considered as official docum ███ ertaining to both Governments a ███ not be released without m ███ agreement.

      a. Past experience indicated that very little time is left between the formal decisions of the Republic of Korea Government with regard to changes in utilities charges and their effective dates, and such conditions will continue for an indefinite period. In order to reconcile US administrative requirements for being informed of possible future changes as far in advance as possible and the conditions surrounding decisions under discussion, maximum use should be made of informal and confidential exchange of information and views by asking the principally concerned organ, the ROK Economic Planning Board, to assume a major role in this question.

      b. In view of the highly technical nature of the question involved and the limited time available for the consultation, the new Subcommittee is envisaged to become the principal organ to effect the provided consultation, and the Joint Committee itself would remain as the organ of final authority. This thinking is reflected in the wording of paragraph 2(b) of the Subcommittee recommendations. This line of thinking would necessitate providing for an exception to the existing general rules for Subcommittee operations, so that the said Subcommittee could handle the problems and submit recommendations without being assigned tasks by the Joint Committee. The ROK Representative proposed Joint Committee approval of the Commerce Subcommittee recommendation, and further suggested that lists of full memberships of the proposed Subcommittee be exchanged through the two SOFA Secretaries. He proposed that the new Subcommittee should proceed to consider the task originally assigned to the Commerce Subcommittee as soon as it becomes operational (see Inclosure 8 of the minutes of the fifteenth meeting of the Joint Committee, 28 September 1967).

9. The US Representative concurred in the recommendation of the Commerce Subcommittee and stated that a new Utilities Subcommittee should be established expeditiously. This new Subcommittee should proceed immediately to develop recommendations for early presentation to the Joint Committee regarding the consultation procedures necessary to implement paragraph 2 and Agreed Minute 1 of Article VI. The US Representative proposed early exchange of membership lists for the new Subcommittee between the ROK and US SOFA Secretariats. The US Representative commented that the direct involvement of the Economic Planning Board in the problem appeared to be a step in the right direction and that inclusion of representation from the US Operations Mission would be equally beneficial to both sides. He expressed the hope for an early agreement on recommendations to complete this assignment by the new Utilities Subcommittee.

20th JC
18 Jan 68

56

4

These minutes ●● considered as official docum●● ertaining to both Governments and will not be released without mutual agreement.

10. The ROK Representative proposed four new assignments to the Facilities and Areas Subcommittee, pertaining to requests for release of areas held by the USFK, as follows:

a. A portion of IC-134, consisting of 9.01 acres (Inclosure 13). The remaining portion of IC-134, containing 0.15 acre of land is to be converted from an exclusive use acquisition to an easement.

b. Acquisition No. SAC-CS-283, containing 0.23 acre of land (Inclosure 13).

c. Acquisition No. IC-97, containing approximately 1.79 acres (Inclosure 14).

d. A small portion of Hialeah Compound in Pusan, PAC-134 (Inclosure 14).

11. The US Representative stated that he was happy to concur in the assignment of these four tasks to the Facilities and Areas Subcommittee.

12. The US Representative presented nine new tasks for assignment to the Facilities and Areas Subcommittee. These assignments involve:

a. Acquisition of 0.248 acre of land of which 0.223 acre is for exclusive use and 0.025 acre is for an easement in Kapyong-gun, Kyonggi-do (Inclosure 15).

b. Acquisition of 15.867 acres of land, of which 1.116 acres are for exclusive use and 14.751 acres are for an easement, in Seoul City for a transmitter site for the American Forces Korea Network (Inclosure 15).

c. Acquisition of 2.85 acres of land in Taegu City to provide additional storage area for Camp Walker (Inclosure 15).

d. Acquisition of 5.89 acres of land in Yangsan-gun, Kyongsang-namdo, for widening the access road to the Brooklyn VHF site (Inclosure 15).

e. Acquisition of a perpetual restrictive easement for 1.625 acre of land required for the construction of an underground cable line (Inclosure 15).

f. Acquisition of 0.41 acre of land for an easement for relocation of overhead power lines (portion of 7X-24) (Inclosure 15).

20th JC
18 Jan 68

5

These minutes ⬤ onsidered as official docum⬤ ertaining to both Governments and will not be released without mutual agreement.

g. Extension of Temporary Use Permit SAC-T-18 from 16 December 1967 to 15 December 1968 (Inclosure 15).

h. Extension of Temporary Use Permit SAC-T-6 from 16 December 1967 to 15 December 1968 (Inclosure 15).

13. The US Representative proposed assignment of these new tasks to the Facilities and Areas Subcommittee and the ROK Representative concurred.

14. The US Representative stated that, at the thirteenth meeting of the Joint Committee on 31 August 1967, the Joint Committee approved three real estate transactions proposed by the Facilities and Areas Subcommittee. Processing of documentation on these transactions had begun prior to the entry into force of the SOFA. As a consequence, these actions were not assigned as tasks by the Joint Committee to the Facilities and Areas Subcommittee. The Facilities and Areas Subcommittee has now completed documentation on the last three tasks in this same category. These involve:

a. Acquisition of 2.33 acres of land located in Subinggo-dong, Yongsan-ku, Seoul City, for expansion of the Yongsan Water System, construction of wells, and installation of water supply lines.

b. Release of 0.36 acre of land (as cited in paragraph 14.a, above) which was acquired as an easement area. This area is now to be included in the 2.33 acres cited in paragraph 14.a.

c. Acquisition of 1.20 acres of land in Byukkae-ri, Hongsung-gun, Chungchongnam-do for the expansion of Site 75, Tactical Facility 5.

15. The US Representative proposed approval by the Joint Committee of these three real estate transactions. The ROK Representative concurred in Joint Committee authentication of the documentation in the foregoing three specific actions. (This approval completes Joint Committee authentication of all specific actions on facilities and areas undertaken prior to 9 February 1967.)

16. The US Representative stated that he would like again to thank the Republic of Korea Representative for the list of security offenses under the laws of the Republic of Korea, which he so kindly transmitted at the seventeenth meeting of the Joint Committee. In the meantime, this list has been examined by various members of the US component

20th JC
18 Jan 68

_6

These minutes ⬤ onsidered as official docum ⬤ ertaining to both Governments and will not be released without mutual agreement.

with great interest. This list will be extremely valuable, should the need arise, in determining the security implications of cases as they occur. Because of the broad language that necessarily must be used in describing offenses that could possibly affect the security of a nation, the US Representative believes that the security implications of certain of the offenses listed can only be determined on a case by case basis. Examples of such offenses are those dealing with the organization of criminal bodies, with riot, with the unlawful use of explosives, and with actions directed against the flag. Reprehensible as such offenses are, they do not in all circumstances have security implications. It is noted that such implications may, under the SOFA, affect the right to exercise jurisdiction over the offense, the right of pre-trial custody, or the determination of the particular importance of the case.

17. The US Representative stated that because of the need for a case by case determination in these matters, the Republic of Korea and the United States lists can serve as extremely useful guides as to which offenses are likely to have security implications. The employment of these lists as guides, will not, he was certain, work to the detriment of the prompt and adequate disposition of offenses which are found to have security implications.

18. The ROK Representative thanked the US Representative for his kind and careful examination of the list of security offenses, which he had transmitted at the seventeenth meeting of the Joint Committee. He stated that the US Representative's comments were clear, and would be carefully and sincerely studied by the members of the Korean component concerned with this problem. The Republic of Korea Representative stated that, in this connection, he wished to present his views at a later meeting, with the kind understanding of the US Representative. The US Representative thanked the ROK Representative and assured his Korean colleagues on the Joint Committee that the security of both the Republic of Korea and the United States is the primary mission and concern of the United States armed forces present within ROK territory. He did not believe that the utilization of these lists as guides will adversely affect the security of either the Republic of Korea or the United States. The ROK Representative stated that the list of security offenses, as transmitted, was prepared by competent individuals in the field of ROK law. He observed that, since internal legal system of each country is based on different concept and doctrine and has separate criteria for classification of offenses, US concepts may not always be applicable

20th JC
18 Jan 68

7

59

These minutes ⬤ onsidered as official docum ⬤ ertaining to both Governments and will not be released without mutual agreement.

to Korean legal system, and the question should be referred back to the authorities in the field who had originally prepared the list. He further stated that the concept of security itself is quite clear and the final out-come of this matter, he was sure, would not be detrimental to the secu-rity of either country. He indicated that he would express the point of view of his Government on this question at a later meeting. The US Representative thanked the ROK Representative for the kind considera-tion which his Government will give to these US comments on the ques-tion of the exchange of security lists.

19. The US Representative presented a memorandum to the Joint Committee informing the Republic of Korea Government of the designa-tion of a new invited contractor under Article XV of the Status of Forces Agreement. After consultation with personnel of the Republic of Korea Commerce Subcommittee, the United States Forces, Korea, had desig-nated Adrian Wilson Associates as a US invited contractor for the execu-tion of contract #DACA-81-68-C-0038 for architect-engineer services in connection with the Korean Joint Construction Agency (Inclosure 16). Pertinent data concerning employees of this invited contractor will be provided to the Government of the Republic of Korea in accordance with mutually approved procedures.

20. The Republic of Korea Representative confirmed that the agreed procedures for the designation had been fully adhered to and he acknowl-edged receipt of the notifying memorandum.

21. The US Representative noted for the record that the United States SOFA Secretary had furnished the following information to the ROK SOFA Secretary since the last meeting of the Joint Committee. This material was presented for appropriate distribution within the Republic of Korea Government in the implementation of United States-Republic of Korea Status of Forces Agreement.

   a. Five copies of reports on the United States armed forces dis-position of cases for the month of November 1967, in accordance with Article XXII, paragraph 6(b), and United States-Republic of Korea Joint Committee Agreed View No. 5.

   b. Twenty copies of a report listing arrivals, departures, and address changes of United States invited contractor personnel and their dependents, dated 31 December 1967, and twenty copies of the quarterly

20th JC
18 Jan 68

60

8

These minutes ●●onsidered as official docum●● ertaining to both Governments and will not be released without mutual agreement.

consolidated list of invited contractor personnel and their dependents for 31 December 1967. These reports are made in accordance with the procedures approved by the Joint Committee at its ninth meeting on 5 June 1967.

     c. Twenty copies of the report of United States armed forces personnel, the civilian component, invited contractors, and dependents, entering or departing the Republic of Korea during the month of December 1967. This report was made in accordance with procedures adopted by the Joint Committee at its sixth meeting on 28 April 1967 and amended by the Joint Committee at its fourteenth meeting on 14 September 1967.

     22. The ROK Representative stated that he was pleased to confirm the receipt by the ROK Secretariat of the documents, as enumerated by the US Representative.

     23. The US Representative proposed that two recent Memoranda of Understanding, relating to two significant labor problems, be recorded in the official minutes of the ROK-US Joint Committee. The Memorandum of Understanding of 28 December 1967 (Inclosure 17), terminated a labor dispute which the Foreign Organization Employees Union had filed. This dispute had been referred to the Office of Labor Affairs of the Government of the Republic of Korea for conciliation in accordance with paragraph 4 of Article XVII of the SOFA. The Memorandum of Understanding of 16 January 1968 resolved a question relating to severance pay for employees of certain USFK nonappropriated fund activities. Recently, problems developed in the administration of severance pay for Korean employees of certain nonappropriated fund activities of the Eighth US Army. This prompted a special study by Eighth US Army, including negotiations with the Foreign Organization Employees Union. In view of legal questions and the labor problem, consultation was held with the ROK Government officials of the Office of Labor Affairs, in accordance with Article XVII of the SOFA. The Eighth US Army plan provides for a major change in severance pay for certain nonappropriated fund employees. This change provided for changes in severance rates, for a lump sum payment of severance credits to employees based upon a separation and reappointment personnel action, and the deposit of such severance credits in individual employee accounts in one or more Korean banks. The Director, Office of Labor Affairs, Mr. LEE Sung Tack, had reviewed and approved this plan, as indicated in Inclosure 18. Mr. Lee advised that the proposed plan, with union acceptance, was considered by the Government of the Republic of Korea to be an appropriate action and met requirements of Republic of Korea labor law. The Foreign Organization Employees Union reviewed this proposal in detail and a union-management understanding was

9

6(

These minutes ●considered as official docum●●pertaining to both Governments and wi● not be released without mutual●agreement.

reached on the provisions of the plan. The Memorandum of Understanding of 16 January 1968 (Inclosure 19) contained the statement that the new plan would be validated and recorded by the US-ROK SOFA Joint Committee. Pertinent changes to Eighth US Army Regulation 690-1, relating to severance pay procedures, is included as Inclosure 20.

24. The US Representative proposed that all of the four inclosures on this subject be included in the minutes of the twentieth meeting of the Joint Committee. He stated that he believed that official recording of these understandings, worked out in accordance with provisions of Article XVII of the SOFA, are in the mutual interests of both the Governments of the Republic of Korea and of the United States.

25. The US Representative stated that he would like to take this opportunity to express the appreciation of the United States Forces, Korea, to the officials of the Government of the Republic of Korea, whose devoted and effective work greatly assisted in achievement of the foregoing Memoranda of Understanding. He particularly expressed his appreciation to a member of the Republic of Korea component of the Joint Committee, Mr. HUH Seung Joon, Chief, Labor Affairs Bureau, Office of Labor Affairs, and Chairman of the Labor Subcommittee. Mr. Huh demonstrated deep understanding and great skill in his conciliation role between the US Forces, Korea and the Foreign Organization Employees Union.

26. The ROK Representative stated that he was happy to agree to the US proposal to include in the Joint Committee minutes the Memorandum of Understanding of 28 December 1967 concerning USFK's Korean employees' wages and the Memorandum of Understanding of 16 January 1968 regarding the modification of severance pay for employees of certain USFK nonappropriated fund activities, and related documents (Inclosures 17, 18, 19, and 20).

27. The ROK Representative stated that he wished to take this opportunity to express his sincere appreciation to the members of both the United States and the Republic of Korea components of the Labor Subcommittee, and especially to Mr. Huh and Mr. Ogden C. Reed, Director of Civilian Personnel, Eighth US Army, for their substantial contributions made in the settlement of problems concerning wages of USFK's Korean employees and severance pay for certain of USFK's Korean nonappropriated fund employees.

20th JC
18 Jan 68

10

62

These minutes ████ considered as official docum████ pertaining to both Governments a██ ████ not be released without m█████ agreement.

28. The US Representative proposed that the next meeting of the US-ROK Joint Committee be held at 1500 hours on Wednesday, 21 February, at the ROK Capitol Building. In this connection, Joint Committee procedures provide for exigency actions to be accomplished without a formal Joint Committee meeting, by mutual agreement of the ROK and US Representatives; therefore, the US Representative proposed that, if any subcommittees with important pending projects reach signed agreements on recommendations for resolution of their assignments, that the ROK and US Representatives may review and approve these agreements prior to the next Joint Committee meeting. This would enable any urgent subcommittee recommendations to be approved and implemented as soon as possible. Joint Committee procedures provide that, in the event of such contingency actions, the actions will be recorded in the official minutes of the next US-ROK Joint Committee meeting.

29. The ROK Representative stated that the ROK component fully understands the reason for proposing to place a longer than normal interval between this meeting and the next meeting. The ROK Representative accepted the proposal, with the understanding that:

a. If any problem unforeseen at this time, important and pressing, should arise before the proposed next meeting, an emergency session may be called.

b. That pressing matters between the two meetings may be handled by signatures of the two Representatives or their respective Alternates, with such decisions becoming effective immediately upon signing by the two Representatives or their Alternates. These decisions would be confirmed at the next meeting of the Joint Committee.

30. The US Representative proposed approval of the proposed ROK-US joint press release for the twentieth Joint Committee meeting, as prepared by the ROK and US SOFA Secretaries (Inclosure 21). The ROK Representative indicated that he approved the joint press release as presented.

31. The meeting was adjourned at 1620 hours.

21 Inclosures

YOON HA JONG
Republic of Korea Representative

ROBERT J. FRIEDMAN
Lieutenant General
United States Air Force
United States Representative
20th JC
18 Jan 68

11

These minutes are considered as official documents pertaining to both Governments and shall not be released without mutual agreement.

AGENDA FOR THE TWENTIETH MEETING
OF THE ROK-US JOINT COMMITTEE
1500 HOURS, 18 JANUARY 1968 - US SOFA CONFERENCE ROOM

  I   Recommendations of Subcommittees:

      1. Facilities and Areas Subcommittee

          a. Ten Recommendations - ROK Presentation

          b. Eleven Recommendations - US Presentation

      2. Recommendation of the Commerce Subcommittee - ROK Presentation

  II   Assignment of Additional Tasks to Facilities and Areas Subcommittee:

      1. Four Tasks - ROK Presentation

      2. Nine Tasks - US Presentation

  III Joint Committee approval of acquisition and release of facilities
        and areas pre-dating the 9 February 1967 entry into force
        of the SOFA - US Presentation

  IV   Statement with regard to the list of security offenses - US Presentation

   V   Memorandum on the designation of a US invited contractor -
        US Presentation

  VI   Memoranda presented to the ROK Government by the US, in the
        implementation of the SOFA Agreement - US Presentation

  VII Recording of Memoranda of Understanding of 28 December 1967
        and of 16 January 1968, which resolved labor disputes in
        accordance with the procedures of SOFA Article XVII -
        US Presentation

 VIII Proposed Time of Next Meeting - 1500 hours, Wednesday,
        21 February 1968, in the ROK Capitol Building

  IX   Agreement on Joint Press Release

   X   Adjourn

20th JC (Incl 1)
18 Jan 68

64

These minutes are considered as official documents pertaining to both Governments and will not be released without mutual agreement.

REPUBLIC OF KOREA - UNITED STATES
FACILITIES AND AREAS SUBCOMMITTEE

29 November 1967

MEMORANDUM FOR: THE JOINT COMMITTEE

1. Subcommittee members:

United States	Republic of Korea
COL I. M. Rice, Chairman	MG KIM Mook, Chairman
LTC J. B. Carrick, USAFCSK	Mr. SONG Yong Tai
LTC Robert E. Graf, J4, USFK	Mr. SHIN Chung Sup
LTC Alvin J. Collins, USAF	Mr. NO Yong Goo
LCDR Joe T. Patterson, Jr., USNAG	Mr. LEE Kihl Choo
Mr. Francis K. Cook, J5, USFK	Mr. LEE Soon Dong
Mr. Richard Rose, USAEDFE	Mr. KIM Hwan Soo
Mrs. Betty H. Bowman, 8th Army	Mr. SEO Yong Kwan
	Mr. LEE Moon Sup
	Mr. CHANG Kyong Shik
	Mr. CHA Sang Chun
	Mr. OH, Myong Too
	Mr. YONG, Young Hoon
	LTC KANG Jong Kuk
	Mr. KANG Hong Suk

2. Subject of Recommendation: Request for Release of Real Estate (SAC-658). (Reference Joint Committee Memorandum, same subject, dated 14 September 1967).

3. Recommendation: Request for release of 0.94 acre, USFK Acquisition No. SAC-658, at Songsu-dong, Songdong-ku, Seoul, in connection with a project of the Seoul City authorities to build drainage facilities has been approved by the Ministry of National Defense with the condition that an alternate site be provided for AFKN. The Ministry of National Defense and the Far East District Engineer have been requested to prepare the necessary document. It is recommended that the Joint Committee approve this release and that the ROK and US Representatives, Joint Committee, SOFA, authenticate this document when it has been completed.

20th J.C (Incl 2) /
18 Jan 68

4. Security Classification:

   Unclassified.

_____
COLONEL I. M. RICE
Chairman, United States Component
Facilities and Areas Subcommittee

_____
MAJOR GENERAL KIM Mook
Chairman, Republic of Korea Component
Facilities and Areas Subcommittee

APPROVED BY THE JOINT COMMITTEE ON
18 JANUARY 1968 AT TWENTIETH MEETING

_____
YOON HA JONG
Republic of Korea Representative

_____
ROBERT J. FRIEDMAN
Lieutenant General
United States Air Force
United States Representative

2

99-1E
20th JC (Incl 2)
18 Jan 68

66

These minutes ⬤⬤nsidered as official docum⬤⬤ertaining to both Governments and w⬤ not be released without mutual agreement.

E.GG-EN   24 October 1967

MEMORANDUM FOR: THE FACILITIES AND AREA SUBCOMMITTEE, SOFA

SUBJECT: Report of Joint Working Committee on Release of Real Estate to City of Seoul for Development (SAC-658 (KS 787)

   1. As directed by letter file EAGL-SIM, Headquarters, Eighth United States Army, dated 7 October 1967, subject "Request for Release of Real Estate (SAC-658)" a working committee was formed comprised of the following US and ROK (City of Seoul) personnel:

       a. US

           LTC Gromme, HQ EASCOM (Chairman)
           MAJ Malmer, HQ 19th GSG
           Mr. Chun, HQ 19th GSG
           Mr. Barr, AFKN
           Mr. Brummett, HQ 19th GSG

       b. ROK (City of Seoul)

           Mr. Kim, Chief, Regional Adjustment Division
           Mr. Lee, Assistant

   2. An initial meeting was held on 20 October 1967, and final meeting on 23 October 1967.

   3. Release of subject real estate was agreed upon by the US component subject to the requirements listed in the inclosed conditions of r ease. The conditions were accepted by the City of Seoul representative. It is therefore recommended that proposal be forwarded to the Joint committee for approval.

KIM / SOON CHANG   J. W. CROMME, JR.
ROK (City of Seoul)   LTC, USA
Co-Chairman   Chairman

                                           20th JC (Incl 1 to Incl 2)
                                           18 Jan 68

67

These minutes ●● ●nsidered as official docum●●●ertaining to both
Governments and will not be released without mutual agreement.

CONDITIONS OF RELEASE

1. The United States agrees to release to the City of Seoul the
parcel of real estate known as USFK Acquisition No. SAC-656 subject to
the following conditions:

    a. Phase I

        (1) The City of Seoul agrees to dismantle all real property
facilities listed below, with the real property facility components being
stored in close proximity to present location until Phase II:

BLDG	USE	SQ FT	TYPE CONST
T-1	Operations	1,188	Wood
T-2	Barracks	2,115	Quonset
T-3	Generator Shed	375	CIS
T-4	Water Storage	90	CIS
T-5	Storage	228	Wood
S-9	Underground Fuel Tank	1,500	Steel
T-210	Electric Line	900 LF Gal cap	Steel
T-211	Water Storage Tank	4,200 Gal cap	Steel
T-212	Security Fence	780 LF	Barbea Wire

        (2) The City of Seoul agrees to provide a temporary fence,
security lights, guard shelter, and a generator shed for security of dis-
mentled real property.

        (3) The US agrees to continue providing security guard.

    b. Phase II - To be accomplished upon completion of acquisition
of new US real estate.

        (1) The City of Seoul will reerect the 24'x49½' wood frame
structure, Bldg#T-1, in the same dimensions as the one dismantled. The
concrete floor is to be installed in the same configuration as the present floor with materials provided by the City of Seoul. Construction
plans, specifications, and site plans will be provided by the Post
Engineer, Yongsan District.

        (2) Reerect quonset Bldg# T-2, plus approximate floor area
of Bldg #T-3, T-4, and T-5 for a total floor area of approximately 2,400
sq ft. Materials to be provided by City of Seoul. The quonset will be
erected in accordance with construction plans, specifications, and site
plan to be provided by the Post Engineer, Yongsan District.

20th JC (Incl 1 to Incl 2)
18 Jan 68

68

These minutes ●● considered as official docum●● ●●rtaining to both Governments and wi● not be released without mutual ●greement.

(3) Relocate security fence and security light poles in accordance with plans, specifications, and siting to be provided by Post Engineer, Yongsan District.

(4) Relocate fuel and water tanks in accordance with plans, ●●●cations, and siting to be provided by the Post Engineer, Yongsan District.

2. It is mutually agreed that upon completion of dismantling of the real property facilities and the provision of storage area security by the City of Seoul, the US will permit the city to undertake whatever construction on present site as is necessary without restraint.

3. The City of Seoul agrees that the reerection at the new site will begin not later than thirty days from the date of receipt of a notice to proceed from the Post Engineer, Yongsan District. In addition, the City of Seoul agrees to complete the reerection work in 45 working days or sooner as conditions permit.

4. The City of Seoul also agrees that the construction inspectors of the Yongsan District Post Engineer will periodically inspect construction and reerection work. In this regard, the City of Seoul agrees to promptly correct all construction deficiencies noted.

KIM, SOON CHANG
ROK (City of Seoul)
CO-Chairman

J. W. GROMME, JR.
LTC, USA
Chairman

5. 상기 각항중 철거 제 운반에 있어 한 차량은 미군측이 지천한다.

6. 철거는 년내에 하고 새로운 장소의 건립은 FY. 68.3 월 후로 한다.

20th JC (Incl 1 to Incl 2)
18 Jan 68

69

REPUBLIC OF KOREA - UNITED STATES
FACILITIES AND AREAS SUBCOMMITTEE

26 December 1967

MEMORANDUM FOR: THE JOINT COMMITTEE

1. Subcommittee members:

United States	Republic of Korea
COL I. M. Rice, Chairman	MG KIM Mook, Chairman
LTC J. B. Carrick, USAFCSK	Mr. SONG Yong Tai
LTC Robert E. Graf, J5, USFK	Mr. SHIN Chung Sup
LTC Alvin J. Collins, USAF	Mr. NO Yong Goo
LCDR Joe T. Patterson, J5, USNAG	Mr. LEE Kihl Choo
Mr. Francis K. Cook, J5, USFK	Mr. LEE Soon Dong
Mr. Richard Rose, USAEDFE	Mr. KIM Hwan Soo
Mrs. Betty H. Bowman, 8th Army	Mr. SEO Yong Kwan
	Mr. LEE Moon Sup
	Mr. CHA Sang Chun
	Mr. CHANG Kyong Shik
	Mr. OH Myong Too
	Mr. CHUNG Young Hoon
	LTC KANG Jong Kuk
	Mr. KANG Hong Suk

2. Subject of Recommendation: Requests for Release of Real Estate (Reference Joint Committee Memorandum, same subject, dated 30 November 1967).

3. Recommendations:

a. Request for release of IC-221, containing 2.54 acres of mainly non-arable land at Kosan-ni, Pyollae-myon, Yangju-gun, Kyonggi-do which is excess to USFK requirements and has been approved by the Ministry of National Defense. The Ministry of National Defense and the Far East District Engineer have been requested to prepare necessary documents. It is recommended that the Joint Committee approve this release, and that the ROK and US Representatives, Joint Committee, SOFA, authenticate these documents when they have been completed.

20th JC (Incl 3)
18 Jan 68

70

b. Request for release of IC-37, containing 2.65 acres of land at Sanbung-ni, Chunae-myon, Yangju-gun, Kyonggi-do which is excess to USFK requirements and has been approved by the Ministry of National Defense. The Ministry of National Defense and the Far East District Engineer have been requested to prepare necessary documents. It is recommended that the Joint Committee, SOFA, approve this release and that the ROK and US Representatives, Joint Committee, SOFA, authenticate these documents when they have been completed.

c. Request for release of IC-1066, containing 3.52 acres of land at Kosan-ni, Pyollae-myon, Yangju-gun, Kyonggi-do which is excess to USFK requirements and has been approved by the Ministry of National Defense. The Ministry of National Defense and the Far East District Engineer have been requested to prepare necessary documents. It is recommended that the Joint Committee, SOFA, approve this release and that the ROK and US Representatives, Joint Committee, SOFA, authenticate these documents when they have been completed.

d. Request for release of IC-194, containing 1.99 acres of land at Kanung-dong, Uijongbu-si, Kyonggi-do which is excess to USFK requirements and has been approved by the Ministry of National Defense. The Ministry of National Defense and the Far East District Engineer have been requested to prepare necessary documents. It is recommended that the Joint Committee, SOFA, approve this release and that the ROK and US Representatives, Joint Committee, SOFA, authenticate these documents when they have been completed.

e. Request for release of a portion of IC-118, containing 3.27 acres of land at Kumo-dong, Uijongbu-si, Kyonggi-do which is excess to USFK requirements and has been approved by the Ministry of National Defense. The Ministry of National Defense and the Far East District Engineer have been requested to prepare necessary documents. It is recommended that the Joint Committee approve this release and that the ROK and US Representatives, Joint Committee, SOFA, authenticate these documents when they have been completed.

f. Request for release of a portion of SAC-683, containing 1.571 acres of land at No. 39-1 Suhyang-ri, Sunghwan-myon, Chunwon-gun, Chungchongnam-do which is excess to USFK requirements and has been approved by the Ministry of National Defense. The Ministry of National Defense and the Far East District Engineer have been requested to prepare necessary documents. It is recommended that the Joint Committee, SOFA, approve this release and that the ROK and US Representatives, Joint Committee, SOFA, authenticate these documents when they have been completed.

20th JC (Incl 3)
18 Jan 68

2

These minutes a█████nsidered as official docume█████rtaining to both
Governments and wi██ not be released without mutual agreement.

4. Security Classification:

   Unclassified.

_____   _____
COLONEL I. M. RICE   MAJOR GENERAL KIM Mook
Chairman, United States Component   Chairman, Republic of Korea Component
Facilities and Areas Subcommittee   Facilities and Areas Subcommittee

APPROVED BY THE JOINT COMMITTEE ON
18 JANUARY 1968 AT TWENTIETH MEETING

_____   _____
YOON HA JONG   ROBERT J. FRIEDMAN
Republic of Korea Representative   Lieutenant General
                                          United States Air Force
                                          United States Representative

3

20th JC (Incl 3)
18 Jan 68

72

REPUBLIC OF KOREA - UNITED STATES
FACILITIES AND AREAS SUBCOMMITTEE

12 January 1968

MEMORANDUM FOR: THE JOINT COMMITTEE

1. Subcommittee members:

United States	Republic of Korea
COL I. M. Rice, Chairman	MG KIM Mook, Chairman
LTC J. B. Carrick, USAFCSK	Mr. SONG Yong Tai
LTC Robert E. Graf, J4, USFK	Mr. SHIN Chung Sup
LTC Alvin J. Collins, USAF	Mr. LEE Soon Dong
LCDR Joe T. Patterson, Jr., USNAG	Mr. LEE Kihl Choo
Mr. Francis K. Cook, J5, USFK	Mr. LEE Moon Sup
Mr. Richard Rose, USAEDFE	Mr. CHANG Kyong Shik
Mrs. Betty H. Bowman, 8th Army	Mr. CHA Sang Chun
	Mr. SEO Yong Kwan
	Mr. CHONG Young Hoon
	Mr. CHOI Chung Hwan
	Mr. NO Yong Goo
	Mr. LEE Chung Do
	Mr. PARK Noh Soo
	LTC KANG Jong Kuk
	Mr. KANG Hong Suk

2. Subject of Recommendations: Requests for Release of Real
Estate (Reference Joint Committee Memorandum, same subject, dated 21
December 1967).

3. Recommendations:

a. Request for release of K-D-808, containing 27.19 acres
of land and two buildings located at Hwajon-ni, Sindo-myon, Koyang-gun,
Kyonggi-do which is excess to USFK requirements and has been approved
by the Ministry of National Defense. The Ministry of National Defense
and the Far East District Engineer will be requested to prepare
necessary documents. It is recommended that the Joint Committee approve
this release and that the ROK and US Representatives, Joint Committee,
SOFA, authenticate these documents when they have been completed.

20th JC (Incl 4)
18 Jan 68

73

b. Request for release of a portion of SAC-XC-160, containing 4.59 acres of land located at Kwandae-ri, Nam-myon, Injae-gun, Kangwon-do which is excess to USFK requirements and has been approved by the Ministry of National Defense. The Ministry of National Defense and the Far East District Engineer will be requested to prepare necessary documents. It is recommended that the Joint Committee approve this release and that the ROK and US Representatives, Joint Committee, SOFA, authenticate these documents when they have been completed.

4. Security Classification: Unclassified.

COLONEL I. M. RICE
Chairman, United States Component
Facilities and Areas Subcommittee

MAJOR GENERAL KIM Mook
Chairman, Republic of Korea Component
Facilities and Areas Subcommittee

APPROVED BY THE JOINT COMMITTEE ON 18 JANUARY 1968 AT TWENTIETH MEETING

YOON HA JONG
Republic of Korea Representative

ROBERT J. FRIEDMAN
Lieutenant General
United States Air Force
United States Representative

2

20th JC (Incl 4)
18 Jan 68

#130

REPUBLIC OF KOREA - UNITED STATES
FACILITIES AND AREAS SUBCOMMITTEE

12 January 1968

MEMORANDUM FOR: THE JOINT COMMITTEE

1. Subcommittee members:

United States	Republic of Korea
COL I. M. Rice, Chairman	MG KIM Mook, Chairman
LTC J. B. Carrick, USAFCSK	Mr. SONG Yong Tai
LTC Robert E. Graf, J4, USFK	Mr. SHIN Chung Sup
LTC Alvin J. Collins, USAF	Mr. LEE Soon Dong
LCDR Joe T. Patterson, Jr., USNAG	Mr. LEE Kihl Choo
Mr. Francis K. Cook, J5, USFK	Mr. LEE Moon Sup
Mr. Richard Rose, USAEDFE	Mr. CHANG Kyong Shik
Mrs. Betty H. Bowman, 8th Army	Mr. CHA Sang Chun
	Mr. SEO Yong Kwan
	Mr. CHONG Young Hoon
	Mr. CHOI Chung Hwan
	Mr. NO Yong Goo
	Mr. LEE Chung Do
	Mr. PARK Noh Soo
	LTC KANG Jong Kuk
	Mr. KANG Hong Suk

2. Subject of Recommendation: Request for Release of Real Estate
(Joint Committee Memorandum, same subject, dated 21 December 1967).

3. Recommendation: Request for release of a portion of SAC-728,
involving 0.0601 acre of land which is excess to USFK requirements and
has been approved by the Ministry of National Defense. The Ministry of
National Defense and the Far East District Engineer have been requested
to prepare necessary documents. It is recommended that the Joint
Committee approve this release and that the ROK and US Representatives,
Joint Committee, SOFA, authenticate these documents when they have been
completed.

20th JC (Incl 5)
18 Jan 68

4. Security Classification: Unclassified.

COLONEL I. M. RICE
Chairman, United States Component
Facilities and Areas Subcommittee

MAJOR GENERAL KIM Mook
Chairman, Republic of Korea Component
Facilities and Areas Subcommittee

**APPROVED BY THE JOINT COMMITTEE ON
18 JANUARY 1968 AT TWENTIETH MEETING**

YOON HA JONG
Republic of Korea Representative

ROBERT J. FRIEDMAN
Lieutenant General
United States Air Force
United States Representative

2

20th JC (Incl 5)
18 Jan 68

REPUBLIC OF KOREA - UNITED STATES
FACILITIES AND AREAS SUBCOMMITTEE

2 January 1968

MEMORANDUM FOR: THE JOINT COMMITTEE

1. Subcommittee members:

United States	Republic of Korea
COL I. M. Rice, Chairman	MG KIM Mook, Chairman
LTC J. B. Carrick, USAFCSK	Mr. SONG Yong Tai
LTC Robert E. Graf, J5, USFK	Mr. SHIN Chung Sup
LTC Alvin J. Collins, USAF	Mr. NO Yong Goo
LCDR Joe T. Patterson, J5, USNAG	Mr. LEE Kihl Choo
Mr. Francis K. Cook, J5, USFK	Mr. LEE Soon Dong
Mr. Richard Rose, USAEDFE	Mr. KIM Hwan Soo
Mrs. Betty H. Bowman, 8th Army	Mr. SEO Yong Kwan
	Mr. LEE Moon Sup
	Mr. CHA Sang Chun
	Mr. CHANG Kyong Shik
	Mr. OH Myong Too
	Mr. CHUNG Young Hoon
	LTC KANG Jong Kuk
	Mr. KANG Hong Suk

2. Subject of Recommendation: Request for Acquisition and Release
of Real Estate and for Extension of Temporary Use Permit (Reference para 2a,
Joint Committee Memorandum, same subject, dated 22 June 1967).

3. Recommendation: Request for acquisition of 125 acres at Singong-
dong, Uijongbu City, Kyonggi-do for an indefinite period for field training
has been revised by the using agency for acquisition of 3.59 acres for an
indefinite period and the remaining 121.41 acres for temporary use from
1 December 1967 through 30 November 1968. This request has been approved
by the Ministry of National Defense. The Ministry of National Defense and
the Far East District Engineer will be requested to prepare the necessary
documents. It is recommended that the Joint Committee, SOFA, approve this
acquisition and that the ROK and US Representatives, Joint Committee, SOFA,
authenticate the documents when they have been completed.

77

20th JC (Incl 6)
18 Jan 68

4. Security Classification:

   Unclassified.

_____
COLONEL I. M. RICE
Chairman, United States Component
Facilities and Areas Subcommittee

_____
MAJOR GENERAL KIM Mook
Chairman, Republic of Korea Component
Facilities and Areas Subcommittee

**APPROVED BY THE JOINT COMMITTEE ON
18 JANUARY 1968 AT TWENTIETH MEETING**

_____
YOON HA JONG
Republic of Korea Representative

_____
ROBERT J. FRIEDMAN
Lieutenant General
United States Air Force
United States Representative

2

20th JC (Incl 6)
18 Jan 68

These minutes a█████nsidered as official documen██████ertaining to both Governments and w██ not be released without mut███ greement.

#12~-121

REPUBLIC OF KOREA - UNITED STATES
FACILITIES AND AREAS SUBCOMMITTEE

26 December 1967

MEMORANDUM FOR: THE JOINT COMMITTEE

1. Subcommittee members:

United States	Republic of Korea
COL I. M. Rice, Chairman	MG KIM Mook, Chairman
LTC J. B. Carrick, USAFCSK	Mr. SONG Yong Tai
LTC Robert E. Graf, J5, USFK	Mr. SHIN Chung Sup
LTC Alvin J. Collins, USAF	Mr. NO Yong Goo
LCDR Joe T. Patterson, J5, USNAG	Mr. LEE Kihl Choo
Mr. Francis K. Cook, J5, USFK	Mr. LEE Soon Dong
Mr. Richard Rose, USAEDFE	Mr. KIM Hwan Soo
Mrs. Betty H. Bowman, 8th Army	Mr. SEO Yong Kwan
	Mr. LEE Moon Sup
	Mr. CHA Sang Chun
	Mr. CHANG Kyong Shik
	Mr. OH Myong Too
	Mr. CHUNG Young Hoon
	LTC KANG Jong Kuk
	Mr. KANG Hong Suk

2. Subject of Recommendation: Requests for Extension of Temporary Use Permits (Reference Joint Committee Memorandum, same subject, dated 30 November 1967).

3. Recommendations:

a. Request for extension of temporary use permit 7X-T-17 for 2,400 acres of land located in Taehoesan-ni and Sohesan-ni, Yongbung-myon, Pochon-gun, Kyonggi-do from 21 September 1967 to 20 September 1968 has been approved by the Ministry of National Defense. The land is required for a training area. The Ministry of National Defense and the Far East District Engineer have been requested to prepare the necessary documents. It is recommended that the Joint Committee, SOFA, approve this permit and that the ROK and US Chairmen of the Facilities and Areas Subcommittee be authorized to authenticate these extension documents when they have been completed.

20th JC (Incl 7)
18 Jan 68

79

RESTRICTED OF KOREA - UNITED STATES

b. Request for extension of temporary use permit K-C-T-26 for 20.117 acres of land located in Chosong-ni, Chongson-myon, Pochon-gun, and in Chongong-ni, Chongong-myon, Yonchong-gun, Kyonggi-do from 1 November 1967 to 31 October 1968 has been approved by the Ministry of National Defense. The land is required for field storage area for construction of a road between the Hantan River and the town of Chongong-ni. The Ministry of National Defense and the Far East District Engineer have been requested to prepare the necessary documents. It is recommended that the Joint Committee, SOFA, approve this permit and that the ROK and US Chairmen of the Facilities and Areas Subcommittee be authorized to authenticate these extension documents when they have been completed.

4. Security Classification: Unclassified.

COLONEL I. M. RICE
Chairman, United States Component
Facilities and Areas Subcommittee

MAJOR GENERAL KIM Mook
Chairman, Republic of Korea Component
Facilities and Areas Subcommittee

**APPROVED BY THE JOINT COMMITTEE ON
18 JANUARY 1968 AT TWENTIETH MEETING**

YOON HA JONG
Republic of Korea Representative

ROBERT J. FRIEDMAN
Lieutenant General
United States Air Force
United States Representative

2

20th/JC (Incl 7)
18 Jan 68

REPUBLIC OF KOREA - UNITED STATES
FACILITIES AND AREAS SUBCOMMITTEE

5 January 1968

MEMORANDUM FOR: THE JOINT COMMITTEE

1. Subcommittee members:

United States	Republic of Korea
COL I. M. Rice, Chairman	MG KIM Mook, Chairman
LTC J. B. Carrick, USAFCSK	Mr. SONG Yong Tai
LTC Robert E. Graf, J5, USFK	Mr. SHIN Chung Sup
LTC Alvin J. Collins, USAF	Mr. NO Yong Goo
LCDR Joe T. Patterson, J5, USNAG	Mr. LEE Kihl Choo
Mr. Francis K. Cook, J5, USFK	Mr. LEE Soon Dong
Mr. Richard Rose, USAEDFE	Mr. KIM Hwan Soo
Mrs. Betty H. Bowman, 8th Army	Mr. SEO Yong Kwan
	Mr. LEE Moon Sup
	Mr. CHA Sang Chun
	Mr. CHANG Kyong Shik
	Mr. OH Myong Too
	Mr. CHUNG Young Hoon
	LTC KANG Jong Kuk
	Mr. KANG Hong Suk

2. Subject of Recommendation: Request for Real Estate Actions
(Reference para 2d, Joint Committee Memorandum, same subject, dated
31 August 1967).

3. Recommendation: Request for conversion of a restricted easement
(PAC-179) to an exclusive use acquisition of 5.51 acres at #91-1, Taemyung-
dong, Taegu City, Kyongsang Pukto for expansion of Camp Walker has been
withdrawn by the United States agency originating the request and selection
of another site will be considered. It is therefore recommended that no
further action be taken on this task.

20th JC (Incl 8)
18 Jan 68

4. Security Classification:

    Unclassified.

_____   _____
COLONEL I. M. RICE   MAJOR GENERAL KIM Mook
Chairman, United States Component   Chairman, Republic of Korea Component
Facilities and Areas Subcommittee   Facilities and Areas Subcommittee

APPROVED BY THE JOINT COMMITTEE ON
18 JANUARY 1968 AT TWENTIETH MEETING

_____   _____
YOON HA JONG   ROBERT J. FRIEDMAN
Republic of Korea Representative Lieutenant General
                                 United States Air Force
                                 United Stated Representative

                    2

                                    20th JC (Incl 8)
                                    18 Jan 68

ㅁ 79

REPUBLIC OF KOREA - UNITED STATES
FACILITIES AND AREAS SUBCOMMITTEE

29 December 1967

MEMORANDUM FOR: THE JOINT COMMITTEE

1. Subcommittee members:

United States	Republic of Korea
COL I. M. Rice, Chairman	MG KIM Mook, Chairman
LTC J. B. Carrick, USAFCSK	Mr. SONG Yong Tai
LTC Robert E. Graf, J5, USFK	Mr. SHIN Chung Sup
LTC Alvin J. Collins, USAF	Mr. NO Yong Goo
LCDR Joe T. Patterson, J5, USNAG	Mr. LEE Kihl Choo
Mr. Francis K. Cook, J5, USFK	Mr. LEE Soon Dong
Mr. Richard Rose, USAEDFE	Mr. KIM Hwan Soo
Mrs. Betty H. Bowman, 8th Army	Mr. SEO Yong Kwan
	Mr. LEE Moon Sup
	Mr. CHA Sang Chun
	Mr. CHANG Kyong Shik
	Mr. OH Myong Too
	Mr. CHUNG Young H$_o$on
	LTC KANG Jong Kuk
	Mr. KANG Hong Suk

2. Subject of Recommendation: Request for Real Estate Actions (Reference para 2a Joint Committee Memorandum, same subject, dated 31 August 1967).

3. Recommendation: Request for acquisition of 7.48 acres (6.72 acres for exclusive use and 0.76 acre for easement (SAC-772)) at Hasangkok-ni, Tongbu-myon, Kwangju-gun, Kyonggi-do for expansion of Camp William H. Colbern has been withdrawn by the United States agency originating the request. It is therefore recommended that no further action be taken on this task.

20th JC (Incl 9)
18 Jan 68

4. Security Classification: Unclassified.

_____   _____
COLONEL I. M. RICE   MAJOR GENERAL KIM Mook
Chairman, United States Component   Chairman, Republic of Korea Component
Facilities and Areas Subcommittee   Facilities and Areas Subcommittee

APPROVED BY THE JOINT COMMITTEE ON
18 JANUARY 1968 AT TWENTIETH MEETING

_____   _____
YOON HA JONG   ROBERT J. FRIEDMAN
Republic of Korea Representative   Lieutenant General
                                            United States Air Force
                                            United States Representative

2

REPUBLIC OF KOREA - UNITED STATES
FACILITIES AND AREAS SUBCOMMITTEE

12 January 1968

MEMORANDUM FOR: THE JOINT COMMITTEE

1. Subcommittee members:

United States	Republic of Korea
COL I. M. Rice, Chairman	MG KIM Mook, Chairman
LTC J. B. Carrick, USAFCSK	Mr. SONG Yong Tai
LTC Robert E. Graf, J4, USFK	Mr. SHIN Chung Sup
LTC Alvin J. Collins, USAF	Mr. LEE Soon Dong
LCDR Joe T. Patterson, Jr., USNAG	Mr. LEE Kihl Choo
Mr. Francis K. Cook, J5, USFK	Mr. CHANG Kyong Shik
Mr. Richard Rose, USAEDFE	Mr. CHA Sang Chun
Mrs. Betty H. Bowman, 8th Army	Mr. SEO Yong Kwan
	Mr. CHONG Young Hoon
	Mr. CHOI Chung Hwan
	Mr. NO Yong Goo
	Mr. LEE Chung Do
	LTC KANG Jong Kuk
	Mr. PARK Noh Soo
	Mr. KANG Hong Suk
	Mr. LEE Moon Sup

2. Subject: Requests for Acquisition of Real Estate (Joint Committee Memorandum, same subject, dated 21 December 1967).

3. Recommendations:

a. Request for acquisition of an easement involving 0.0023 acre of land at Piin-myon, Sochon-gun, Chungchongnam-do for construction of a water well and pump shed has been approved by the Ministry of National Defense. The Ministry of National Defense and the Far East District Engineer will be requested to prepare necessary documents. It is recommended that the Joint Committee, SOFA, approve this acquisition and that the ROK and US Representatives, Joint Committee, SOFA, authenticate these documents when they have been completed.

20th JC (Incl 10)
18 Jan 68

   b. Request for acquisition of 0.454 acre of land at Hwangsan-ri, Hwangsan-myon, Kimjae-gun, Chollapuk-do has been approved by the Ministry of National Defense. Of the total acreage, 0.446 acre is required for exclusive use for construction of a barracks and 0.008 acre is required as an easement for a sewer line to the barracks. The Ministry of National Defense and the Far East District Engineer will be requested to prepare necessary documents. It is recommended that the Joint Committee, SOFA, approve this acquisition and that the ROK and US Representatives, Joint Committee, SOFA, authenticate these documents when they have been completed.

   4. Security Classification: Unclassified.

COLONEL I. M. RICE	MAJOR GENERAL KIM Mook
Chairman, United States Component	Chairman, Republic of Korea Component
Facilities and Areas Subcommittee	Facilities and Areas Subcommittee

**APPROVED BY THE JOINT COMMITTEE ON
18 JANUARY 1968 AT TWENTIETH MEETING**

YOON HA JONG	ROBERT J. FRIEDMAN
Republic of Korea Representative	Lieutenant General
	United States Air Force
	United States Representative

2

20th JC (Incl 10)
18 Jan 68

86

124-127

REPUBLIC OF KOREA - UNITED STATES
FACILITIES AND AREAS SUBCOMMITTEE

12 January 1968

MEMORANDUM FOR: THE JOINT COMMITTEE

1. Subcommittee members:

United States	Republic of Korea
COL I. M. Rice, Chairman	MG KIM Mook, Chairman
LTC J. B. Carrick, USAFCSK	Mr. SONG Yong Tai
LTC Robert E. Graf, J4, USFK	Mr. SHIN Chung Sup
LTC Alvin J. Collins, USAF	Mr. LEE Soon Dong
LCDR Joe T. Patterson, Jr., USNAG	Mr. LEE Kihl Choo
Mr. Francis K. Cook, J5, USFK	Mr. LEE Moon Sup
Mr. Richard Rose, USAEDFE	Mr. CHANG Kyong Shik
Mrs. Betty H. Bowman, 8th Army	Mr. CHA Sang Chun
	Mr. SEO Yong Kwan
	Mr. CHONG Yong Hoon
	Mr. CHOI Chung Hwan
	Mr. NO Yong Goo
	Mr. LEE Chung Do
	Mr. PARK Noh Soo
	LTC KANG Jong Kuk
	Mr. KANG Hong Suk

2. Subject: Requests for Acquisition of Real Estate and Extension of Temporary Use Permit (Joint Committee Memorandum, same subject, dated 21 December 1967).

3. Recommendations:

a. Request for acquisition of 0.092 acre of land at Chosong-ni, Chongsan-myon, Pochon-gun, Kyonggi-do has been approved by the Ministry of National Defense. This land is required for widening the road along MSR 33N and 1X to Babicz Bridge. The road widening will require the removal of two houses situated on this real estate. The Ministry of National Defense and the Far East District Engineer will be requested to prepare necessary documents. It is recommended that the Joint Committee, SOFA, approve this acquisition and that the ROK and US Representatives, Joint Committee, SOFA, authenticate these documents when they have been completed.

20th JC (Incl 11)
18 Jan 68

87

b. Request for acquisition of an easement involving 2.72 acres of land at Chonghang-ni, Pyollac-myon, Yangju-gun, Kyonggi-do has been approved by the Ministry of National Defense. This property is required to construct a bridge on Route 2XE and to realign the existing road. Of the total acreage, 0.47 acre is required for a main road and bridge site and 2.09 acres for a streambed, both for indefinite periods, while 0.16 acre is required for a by-pass road until 31 December 1968. The Ministry of National Defense and the Far East District Engineer will be requested to prepare necessary documents. It is recommended that the Joint Committee, SOFA, approve this acquisition and that the ROK and US Representatives, Joint Committee, SOFA, authenticate these documents when they have been completed.

c. Request for acquisition of an easement involving 2.82 acres of land located at Daenung-ni, Chonhyon-myon, Paju-gun, Kyonggi-do has been approved by the Ministry of National Defense. This real estate is required for the construction of a bridge on Route 23 and realignment of the existing road. Of the total acreage, 2.75 acres are required to realign Route 23 and 0.07 acre is required for a by-pass and bivouac area. The Ministry of National Defense and the Far East District Engineer will be requested to prepare necessary documents. It is recommended that the Joint Committee, SOFA, approve this acquisition and that the ROK and US Representatives, Joint Committee, SOFA, autenticate these documents when they have been completed.

d. Request for extension of temporary use permit (SAC-T-48) containing 250 acres at Changwoo-ri, Chunhyon-ri, and Hasangok-ri, Tongbu-myon, Kwangju-gun, Kyonggi-do from 1 November 1967 to 31 October 1968 has been approved by the Ministry of National Defense. This land has been used as a training area since 1964 and renewed on a yearly basis. The Ministry of National Defense and the Far East District Engineer will be requested to prepare necessary documents. It is recommended that the Joint Committee, SOFA, approve this permit and that the ROK and US Chairmen of the Facilities and Areas Subcommittee be authorized to authenticate these extension documents when they have been completed.

4. Security Classification: Unclassified.

COLONEL I. M. RICE
Chairman, United States Component
Facilities and Areas Subcommittee

MAJOR GENERAL KIM Mook
Chairman, Republic of Korea Component
Facilities and Areas Subcommittee

APPROVED BY THE JOINT COMMITTEE ON 18 JANUARY 1968 AT TWENTIETH MEETING

YOON HA JONG
Republic of Korea Representative

ROBERT J. FRIEDMAN
Lieutenant General
United States Air Force
United States Representative

2

20th JC (Incl 11)
18 Jan 68

These minutes are ████ nsidered as official document ████ ertaining to both Governments and ████ not be released without mutu ████ agreement.

THE REPUBLIC OF KOREA AND THE UNITED STATES
STATUS OF FORCES AGREEMENT
COMMERCE SUBCOMMITTEE

USFK DJ   12 January 1968

MEMORANDUM FOR: The Joint Committee

SUBJECT: Article VI, Utilities and Services

1. It is recommended that the Commerce Subcommittee be relieved from responsibility for Article VI, Utilities and Services, and that this responsibility be reassigned to a new subcommittee to be organized and designated as the Utilities Subcommittee.

2. It is further recommended that the Utilities Subcommittee:

a. Be transferred responsibility for recommending to the Joint Committee the consultation procedures necessary to implement Article VI, paragraph 2, and Agreed Minute 1 of Article VI. This task was assigned by Joint Committee memorandum of 28 September 1967 to the Commerce Subcommittee, but has not been completed.

b. Serve under Joint Committee supervision as the agency to effect the consultation provided in Agreed Minute 1 of Article VI.

SHIM UI HWAN   FLOYD R. WALTZ, JR.
Chairman, Republic of Korea Component   Chairman, United States Component
Commerce Subcommittee   Commerce Subcommittee

APPROVED BY THE JOINT COMMITTEE ON
18 JANUARY 1968 AT TWENTIETH MEETING

YOON HA JONG   ROBERT J. FRIEDMAN
Republic of Korea Representative   Lieutenant General
                                          United States Air Force
                                          United States Representative

89

20th JC (Incl 12)
18 Jan 68

These minutes are considered as official documents pertaining to both Governments and ⬛ not be released without mutual ⬛ agreement.

JOINT COMMITTEE
UNDER
THE REPUBLIC OF KOREA AND THE UNITED STATES
STATUS OF FORCES AGREEMENT

18 January 1968

MEMORANDUM FOR: Chairmen, Facilities and Areas Subcommittee

SUBJECT: Requests for Release of Real Estate

    1. SOFA provides, in Article II, paragraph 2, that the Governments of the Republic of Korea and the United States may agree that facilities and areas or portions thereof shall be returned to the Republic of Korea or that additional facilities and areas may be provided.

    2. Pursuant to paragraph 1 above, it is requested that recommendations be presented to the Joint Committee concerning requests for the following releases:

        a. Release of a portion of IC-134, consisting of 9.01 acres of land located at Howon-dong, Uijongbu-si, Kyonggi-do. It is further requested that the remaining portion of IC-134, containing 0.15 acre of land, be converted from an exclusive use acquisition to an easement (right-of-way) and transferred to Acquisition No. IC-168 for electric power pole lines for I Corps (Group) Rear Area.

        b. Release of 0.23 acre of land, originally acquired under SAC-CS-283, and located at Kyongban-ni, Kapyong-myon, Kapyong-gun, Kyonggi-do. The area contains two USFK constructed buildings which are to be abandoned in place.

YOON HA JONG
Republic of Korea Representative

ROBERT J. FRIEDMAN
Lieutenant General
United States Air Force
United States Representative

APPROVED BY THE JOINT COMMITTEE ON
18 JANUARY 1968 AT TWENTIETH MEETING

20th JC (Incl 13)
18 Jan 68

These minutes are considered as official documents pertaining to both Governments and ~~will~~ not be released without mutual agreement.

JOINT COMMITTEE
UNDER
THE REPUBLIC OF KOREA AND THE UNITED STATES
STATUS OF FORCES AGREEMENT

18 January 1968

MEMORANDUM FOR: Chairmen, Facilities and Areas Subcommittee

SUBJECT; Requests for Release of Real Estate

      1. SOFA provides, in Article II, paragraph 2, that the Governments of the Republic of Korea and the United States may agree that facilities and areas or portions thereof shall be returned to the Republic of Korea or that additional facilities and areas may be provided.

      2. Pursuant to paragraph 1 above, it is requested that recommendations be presented to the Joint Committee concerning requests for the following releases:

      a. Release of approximately 1.79 acres of land (IC-97) at Uijongbu in connection with plans for construction of a highway to Seoul City.

      b. Release of a small portion (exact area not yet determined) at Hialeah Compound (PAC-134) at Pusan. The Special City of Pusan requires a small area along the rear boundary of this facility for use in connection with an urban development project.

YOON HA JONG
Republic of Korea Representative

ROBERT J. FRIEDMAN
Lieutenant General
United States Air Force
United States Representative

APPROVED BY THE JOINT COMMITTEE ON
18 JANUARY 1968 AT TWENTIETH MEETING

20th JC (Incl 14)
18 Jan 68

91

**JOINT COMMITTEE
UNDER
THE REPUBLIC OF KOREA AND THE UNITED STATES
STATUS OF FORCES AGREEMENT**

18 January 1968

MEMORANDUM FOR: Chairmen, Facilities and Areas Subcommittee

SUBJECT: Requests for Acquisitions of Real Estate and Extension of Temporary Use Permits

1. SOFA provides, in Article II, paragraph 2, that the Governments of the Republic of Korea and the United States may agree that facilities and areas or portions thereof shall be returned to the Republic of Korea or that additional facilities and areas may be provided.

2. Pursuant to paragraph 1 above, it is requested that recommendations be presented to the Joint Committee concerning requests for the following acquisitions:

a. Acquisition of 0.248 acre of non-arable land located at Hwaak-san, Buk-myon, Kapyong-gun, Kyonggi-do. Of the total acreage, 0.223 acre is required for exclusive use and 0.025 acre is required for an easement. Since SAC-789 was cancelled and redocumented under amendment No. 1 to SAC-755, the 0.14 acre of easement area presently held under SAC-755 is included in the above requested exclusive use area. This real estate is required for a facility for housing the 508th US Army Security Agency Group.

b. Acquisition of approximately 15.867 acres of land located at Bange-dong and Songpa-dong, Sungdong-ku, Seoul City. Of this total acreage, 1.116 acres are required for exclusive use and 14.751 acres are required for an easement. This real estate is required to provide a transmitter site for the American Forces Korea Network.

c. Acquisition of 2.85 acres of land located at Bongduk-dong, Taegu City, Kyongsang-bukdo. The real estate is required for the expansion of Camp Walker to provide additional storage area.

d. Acquisition of 5.89 acres of largely non-arable land located at Tae-ri, Wodong-myon, Yangsan-gun, Kyongsang-namdo. This real estate is required for widening the existing access road leading to Brooklyn VHF Site (Acquisition No. PAC-54).

20th JC (Incl 15)
18 Jan 68

92

. These minutes are ~~considered~~ as official documen~~ts~~ ~~pertaining~~ to both Governments and ~~will~~ not be released without mut~~ual~~ agreement.

e. Acquisition of a perpetual restrictive easement for 1.625 acres of non-arable land located at Shihung-dong, Yongdungpo-ku, Seoul City, and at Suksoo-dong, Anyang-up, Shihung-gun, Kyonggi-do. This real estate is required for the construction of an underground cable line.

f. Acquisition of 0.41 acre of land for an easement for the relocation of existing overhead power lines (portion of 7X-24).

3. Pursuant to paragraph 1 above, it is requested that recommendations be presented to the Joint Committee concerning requests for extensions of temporary use permits, as follows:

a. Temporary Use Permit SAC-T-18, involving 421 acres of land located at Wonchang-ni, Dongsan-myon, Chunsung-gun, Kangwon-do. Extension is requested from 16 December 1967 to 15 December 1968. This area has been used for tactical training and practice alert dispersal by the 4th US Army Missile Command since 1961 and renewed on an annual basis.

b. Temporary Use Permit SAC-T-6, involving 338 acres of land located at Sanchon-ni, Shinbuk-myon, Chunsung-gun, Kangwon-do. Extension is requested from 16 December 1967 to 15 December 1968. This real estate has been used for tactical training and practice alert dispersal by the 4th US Army Missile Command since 1961 and renewed on an annual basis.

c. Temporary Use Permit PAC-T-8, involving 2,059 acres of sand areas along Naktong River. Extension is requested from 1 January 1968 to 31 December 1968. This land has been used as drop zones for airborne training since 1963 and renewed on an annual basis.

YOON HA JONG
Republic of Korea Representative

ROBERT J. FRIEDMAN
Lieutenant General
United States Air Force
United States Representative

APPROVED BY THE JOINT COMMITTEE ON
18 JANUARY 1968 AT TWENTIETH MEETING

20th JC (Incl 15)
18 Jan 68

2

These minutes are ●onsidered as official document●●ertaining to both
Governments and ●● not be released without mutu●●agreement.

JOINT COMMITTEE
UNDER
THE REPUBLIC OF KOREA AND THE UNITED STATES
STATUS OF FORCES AGREEMENT

USFK DJ-O   10 January 1968

MEMORANDUM TO: The Joint Committee

SUBJECT: Designation of US Invited Contractor under Article XV,
          Status of Forces Agreement

    1. References:

        a. Paragraph 2, Article XV, Status of Forces Agreement.

        b. US Commerce Subcommittee Memorandum of Consultation,
dated 20 Nov 67, subject as above. (Incl 1)

        c. ROK Commerce Subcommittee Memorandum of Consultation,
dated 27 Nov 67, subject as above. (Incl 2)

    2. The United States, after consultation with the ROK Commerce
Subcommittee and after having duly considered their views, has designated
Adrian Wilson Associates as a US Invited Contractor, for the execution of
contract #DACA-81-68-C-0038 for architect-engineer services, accomplish-
ing engineering and consulting services in connection with the Korean
Joint Construction Agency administered by Commander, U. S. Forces, Korea.

    3. Pertinent data concerning U.S. citizen employees will be
provided to the Joint Secretariat in the established periodic arrival
and departure format.

2 Incl   ROBERT J. FRIEDMAN
  as   Lieutenant General, USAF
                                 Chief of Staff

                                                    20th JC (Incl 16)
                                                    18 Jan 68

APPROVED BY THE JOINT COMMITTEE ON
18 JANUARY 1968 AT TWENTIETH MEETING

94

These minutes ar⬤nsidered as official document⬤ertaining to both Governments a⬤d will not be released without m⬤tual agreement.

SUBJECT: Designation of US Invited Contractor under Article XV, Status of Forces Agreement

TO: Chairman, ROK Commerce Subcommittee

1. Reference: Paragraph 2, Article XV of the Status of Forces Agreement.

2. The Government of the Republic of Korea is informed through this written consultive process that the United States Forces, Korea, proposes to extend invited contractor status to the successful negotiated bidder among qualified US firms on the contract described in paragraph 3 below.

3. The following data is provided:

    a. Company Names:

        (1) Adrian Wilson Associates
        (2) Daniel Mann Johnson Mendenhall
        (3) Pacific Architects and Engineers, Inc.

    b. Local Addresses:

        (1) #1, 5-ka, Namdaemun-ro, Chung-Ku, Seoul, Korea
        (2) Seoul Shinmoon Annex, 30 Taipyong-ro, Chung-Ku, Seoul, Korea
        (3) APO San Francisco 96302

    c. Identification of U.S. Citizen Employees: to be supplied on conclusion of negotiations.

    d. Number of US and ROK Employees: It is estimated that 7 US citizens and 15 Koreans will be employed under this contract.

    e. Reasons for Designation of an Invited Contractor: Open competitive bidding is not practicable due to the following:

        (1) Restrictions imposed by United States law, specifically the Armed Services Procurement Regulation, paragraph 6-703.2, which states, in part "...Procurement for the Military Assistance Program shall be restricted to domestic concerns and to United States end products..."

20th JC (Incl 1 to Incl 16)
18 Jan 68

95

SUBJECT: Designation of US Invited Contractor under Article XV, Status
of Forces Agreement

    f. <u>Location of contracts</u>:

        Various locations, Korea (all elements of ROK Military
Construction Program)

    g. <u>Type of Contract</u>: Architect-engineer services for accomplish-
ing engineering and consulting services in connection with the Korean
Joint Construction Agency administered by Commander, U.S. Forces, Korea.

    h. <u>Length of Contract</u>: Estimated 12 months. (1 Jan 1968 thru
31 Dec 1968)

    i. <u>Sponsoring Component Command</u>: CGUSAEIGHT.

    4. The United States certifies that the successful bidder or named
contractors are present in the Republic of Korea solely for the purpose
of executing contracts with the United States, for the benefit of the
United States Armed Forces or other armed forces under the Unified
Command receiving logistical support from the United States Forces.

    5. The views of the Government of the Republic of Korea are earnestly
solicited prior to United States selection and designation of an invited
contractor to perform the work outlined above. You may be assured that
your views will be considered carefully.

    6. Your early reply will be greatly appreciated.

FLOYD R. WALTZ, JR.
Colonel, GS
Chairman, US Commerce Subcommittee

These minutes are considered as official documents pertaining to both Governments and will not be released without mutual agreement.

MINISTRY OF COMMERCE AND INDUSTRY
REPUBLIC OF KOREA
SEOUL, KOREA

27 November 1967

SUBJECT: Designation of US Invited Contractor under Article XV, Status of Forces Agreement.

TO : Chairman, US Commerce Subcommittee

1. References:

a. Paragraph 2, Article XV, Status of Forces Agreement.

b. US Commerce Subcommittee Memorandum of Consultation, dated 20 November 1967, subject as above, pertaining to a contract for architect-engineer services for accomplishing engineering and consulting services in connection with the Korean Joint Construction Agency administered by Commander, U.S. Forces, Korea.

2. The US memorandum, reference 1b above, has been reviewed and the Government of the Republic of Korea fully understands the requirement for an invited contractor in this instance.

Chairman
ROK Commerce Subcommittee

20th JC (Incl 2 to Incl 16)
18 Jan 68

97

Incl 2

These minutes are considered as official documents pertaining to both Governments and ▓▓ not be released without mut▓▓ greement.

DEC 2 8 1967

<u>Memorandum of Understanding</u>

1. With regard to issues in the current labor dispute, USFK advises FOEU that actions set forth in paragraphs 2-6 have or are being taken:

2. New wage schedules approved by the Army-Air Force Wage Board (Incl 1) will be effected for appropriated fund (direct-hire and invited contractors), JAKOR-PAGEX, and NAF Special Services on 1 January 1968. KSC wage schedules based upon Army-Air Force Wage Board rates will be offensive also on 1 January. Effective date for other NAF activities will be 1 February, with possible extension for serious financial reasons to 1 March for messes operated by voluntary contributions of military personnel. Extensions will be individually approved by headquarters-level determinations in each USFK component. (NOTE: CCP, 8th U.S. Army will inform FOEU on such extensions prior to 1 February 1968.) (NOTE: FOEU expresses its regret regarding the relatively low rate of increase for the lowest three grades of each schedule.)

3. Two additional one-day holidays are approved for Lunar New Year and for Chusuk.

4. In line with the general intent of Article 19, Labor Standards Act, severance pay will be computed on the basis of average base wages during the last three months rather than the last six months.

5. USFK advises that a review is underway on current policy which requires complete forfeiture of severance (retirement) credits in case of removals resulting from "felony or grave misconduct." Changes in policy will be the subject of later discussions between USFK and FOEU, assisted by OLA.

6. USFK advises that Driver (Light) jobs are being upgraded by A-AF Wage Board determination. Actions will be effected by 1 February 1968. (NOTE: FOEU recommends that the Driver (Heavy) grade also be raised.)

7. USFK and FOEU agree that this year's time schedule for the annual review of wages is, generally speaking, satisfactory.

8. The issues of additional time-off (excused absence) for certain union officials and the status of management officials have been deferred. They will be considered, along with other labor relations issues, during discussions planned to take place prior to expiration of the current USFK-FOEU labor-management agreement.

9. FOEU agrees to support management efforts to increase employee productivity, with particular reference to high employee performance, skills and supervisor training, Zero Defects and the suggestion program. USFK-Eighth U.S. Army will work with FOEU in establishing supporting activities in each of these areas.

10. FOEU advises that it will fully support USFK efforts to reduce pilferage of supplies and to eliminate black-marketing. FOEU will take

20th JC (Incl 17)
18 Jan 68

98

These minutes a█ ██sidered as official documen█ ██rtaining to both Governments and w██ not be released without mutua█ agreement.

Memorandum of Understanding-

various actions in support of these objectives. In addition, Eighth U.S. Army (and other military services as indicated) will coordinate with FOEU in specific measures to enlist employee cooperation in these efforts.

11. FOEU and USFK agree that a major future objective is to maintain and further develop cooperative and responsible labor relations, thus helping to promote effective manpower support to USFK missions and an effective sharing of responsibilities in support of joint ROK-US security objectives. Included in this objective are appropriate improvements in employee welfare and working conditions and positive employee relations and Korean-American relations at work sites.

12. The labor dispute initiated by FOEU has been terminated.

1 Incl
New Wage Schedules

OGDEN C. REED
Civilian Personnel Director
Eighth U.S. Army

LEE KWANG CHO
President
Foreign Organizations Employees Union

JOHN K. RITTENHOUSE
Civilian Personnel Officer
314th Air Division

HAN UNG HUI
Secretary General
Foreign Organizations Employees Union

HUH SEUNG JOON
Chief, Labor Affairs Bureau
Office of Labor Affairs
ROKG

20th JC (Incl 17)
18 Jan 68

99

ARMY-AIR FORCE WAGE BOARD
WASHINGTON, D. C. 20310

KOREA
NON-MANUAL WAGE SCHEDULE
KOREAN EMPLOYEES

HOURLY STEP RATES (LOCAL CURRENCY--WON)

KGS GRADE	STEP A	STEP B	STEP C	STEP D	STEP E	STEP F	STEP G	STEP H	STEP I	STEP J
KGS-1	46	48	50	52	54	56	58	60	63	66
KGS-2	62	65	68	71	74	77	80	83	86	89
KGS-3	79	82	85	89	93	97	101	105	109	113
KGS-4	96	100	104	108	113	118	123	128	133	138
KGS-5	112	117	122	127	132	137	142	147	152	158
KGS-6	127	133	139	145	151	157	163	169	175	181
KGS-7	144	150	157	164	171	178	185	192	199	206
KGS-8	165	172	180	188	196	204	212	220	228	236
KGS-9	186	195	204	213	222	231	240	249	258	267
KGS-10	207	217	227	237	247	257	267	277	287	297
KGS-11	229	240	251	262	273	284	295	306	317	328
KGS-12	251	263	275	287	299	311	323	335	347	359
KGS-13	272	285	298	311	324	337	350	363	376	389

BY AUTHORITY OF THE SECRETARIES OF THE ARMY AND THE AIR FORCE:

Army-Air Force Wage Board

Per:

s/ Raymond J. Braitsch
t/ RAYMOND J. BRAITSCH
Chief, Technical Staff

EFFECTIVE: 1 January 1968

Incl 1

ARMY-AIR FORCE WAGE BOARD
WASHINGTON, D. C. 20310

KOREA
MANUAL WAGE SCHEDULE
KOREAN EMPLOYEES

HOURLY STEP RATES (LOCAL CURRENCY--WON)

KWB GRADE	STEP A	STEP B	STEP C	STEP D	STEP E	STEP F	STEP G	STEP H	STEP I	STEP J
KWB-1	51	53	55	57	59	61	64	67	70	73
KWB-2	59	62	65	68	71	74	77	80	83	86
KWB-3	71	74	77	80	83	86	90	94	98	102
KWB-4	79	83	87	91	95	99	103	107	111	115
KWB-5	91	95	99	103	107	111	116	121	126	131
KWB-6	99	104	109	114	119	124	129	134	139	144
KWB-7	111	116	121	126	131	136	141	147	153	159
KWB-8	119	125	131	137	143	149	155	161	167	173
KWB-9	131	137	143	149	155	161	167	173	179	185
KWB-10	141	147	153	160	167	174	181	188	195	202
KWB-11	151	158	165	172	179	186	193	200	207	214
KWB-12	161	168	175	183	191	199	207	215	223	231
KWB-13	172	180	188	196	204	212	220	228	236	245

BY AUTHORITY OF THE SECRETARIES OF THE ARMY AND THE AIR FORCE:

Army-Air Force Wage Board

Per:

s/ Reymond J. Braitsch
t/ RAYMOND J. BRAITSCH
Chief, Technical Staff

EFFECTIVE: 1 January 1968

101
Incl 2

ARMY-AIR FORCE WAGE BOARD
WASHINGTON, D. C. 20310

KOREA
MARINE WAGE SCHEDULE
KOREAN EMPLOYEES

JOB TITLE	STEP A	STEP B	STEP C	STEP D	STEP E	STEP F	STEP G	STEP H	STEP I	STEP J
Deckhand Wiper	71	74	77	80	83	86	89	92	96	100
Fireman Assistant Cook	75	79	83	87	91	95	99	103	107	111
Able Seaman	84	88	92	96	100	104	108	112	116	120
Oiler Cook	93	97	101	105	109	113	117	121	126	131
Radio Operator Boatswain	105	110	115	120	125	130	135	140	145	150
Crane Operator Engineer (Small Boat) 3rd Assistant Engineer	119	124	129	134	140	146	152	158	164	170
Second Mate Small Boat Operator 2nd Assistant Engineer	140	146	152	159	166	173	180	187	194	201
1st Assistant Engineer First Mate Crane Engineer	162	169	176	184	192	200	208	216	224	232
Crane Master Chief Engineer	192	201	210	219	228	237	246	255	264	274
Master	221	231	241	251	261	271	281	292	303	314

BY AUTHORITY OF THE SECRETARIES OF THE ARMY AND THE AIR FORCE.

Army-Air Force Wage Board

Per:

s/ Raymond J. Braitsch
t/ RAYMOND J. BRAITSCH
Chief, Technical Staff

EFFECTIVE: 1 January 1968

Incl 3

These minutes are considered as official documents pertaining to both
Governments and ▮▮ not be released without mutu▮▮greement.

Memorandum of Understanding

1. Problems have developed in administration of severance pay in
certain nonappropriated fund (NAF) activities of Eighth U.S. Army. Severance
reserves for around 5,900 employees are held by over 200 separate nonappropriated fund organizations. Fund problems primarily result from the requirement to recompute and build up severance reserves at the time of each pay
increase.

2. These financial problems have reached a point where major employee
reductions are likely, particularly in units financed by voluntary contributions. As a result, the Eighth U.S. Army has conducted a study on severance
reserves and the possible use of Korean banking facilities, as a means of
minimizing costs and stabilizing employment. This has included negotiations
with the FOEU and consultation with the Office of Labor Affairs, ROK Government.

3. As a result, a plan has been developed which modifies the severance
pay provisions for NAF units and provides for individual employee deposits
at high interest rates in Korean banking facilities. These changes in the
severance pay plan are outlined in the inclosed change to Eighth Army Regulation 690-1. This plan is subject to extension to Air Force, JAKOR/PACEX
and Navy.

4. FOEU agrees to changes in current NAF severance policy set forth
in Appendix L, EA Reg 690-1, Incl 1. Office of Labor Affairs, ROKG has
concurred in general features of the plan by letter of 11 January 1967.

5. Selection of a Korean bank or banks for individual employee severance
deposits will be made by 18 January 1968. Initial bank deposits will be at

103

20th JC (Incl 18)
18 Jan 68 Incl 2

These minutes are ● ●sidered as official document ● ●rtaining to both Governments and w●● not be released without mutual agreement.

Memorandum of Understanding

the standard interest rate for an 18-month term account with reinvestment of interest. Withdrawal of any portion of the severance account by an employee will be considered as a de facto notice of resignation. No other controls over such deposits or use of deposits will be exercised by any party. Employees will be assured that deposits are their property without qualification. Designation of a bank or banks will be made by Eighth U.S. Army, after full coordination with FOEU.

 6. Eighth U.S. Army advises that it will undertake special efforts to minimize reductions-in-force actions, as specified in para 2f, Appendix L, EA Reg 690-1.

 7. The new plan will be validated and recorded by the U.S.-ROK SOFA Joint Committee.

OGDEN C. REED
Civilian Personnel Director
Eighth U.S. Army

LEE KWANG CHO
President
Foreign Organizations Employees Union

HAN UNG HUI
Secretary General
Foreign Organizations Employees Union

2

20th JC (Incl 18)
18 Jan 68

104

These minutes ar█████sidered as official documen██████rtaining to both
Governments and wil██ot be released without mutual a█reement.

OFFICE OF LABOR AFFAIRS

FILE NO. 130-167   11 January 1968

TO: Civilian Personnel Director
        Headquarters Eighth US Army

SUBJECT: Letter

1. This is reply to your letter, dated 5 January 1968.

2. In reviewing the agreement between your command and the Foreign
Organizations Employees Union concerning payment of severance pay for Korean
employees of certain nonappropriated fund activities of the Eighth US Army,
it is considered to be an appropriate action for the maintenance of Korean
employment level and to alleviate problems caused by payment of severance
pay, and in terms of reviewing this agreement against provisions of the
ROK Labor Standards Law:

    a. The plan in the agreement for payment and deposit of severance
pay earned by employees for continuous service prior to 21 January 1968 is
satisfactory in as much as the amount of severance pay exceeds legal requirements. With regard to payment of severance pay for continuous service
after 21 January 1968, payment is to be made in accordance with the law.

    b. Use of the Korean bank in the plan is to be decided at your
discretion; however, there should be provisions to assure that individual
employees are paid directly in the full amount as entitled when eligible
for payment.

3. In reference to your request that this matter be submitted to the
ROK-US Joint Committee for recording, I have no objection and agree to this.

        Director, Office of Labor Affairs   Lee, Sung Taek (Chop)

Dispatched 5 o'clock, 11 Jan 68   20th JC (Incl 19)
                                                   18 Jan 68

APPENDIX L - EIGHTH ARMY REGULATION 690-1

SEVERANCE PAY FOR EMPLOYEES OF CERTAIN
NONAPPROPRIATED FUND ACTIVITIES

1. Applicability. Special severance pay provisions are hereby established for NAF employees paid from Open Mess funds, Central and Command Locker funds, Supplemental Field Ration Mess funds and other Sundry funds deriving revenue solely from membership contributions or service charges. Effective date is 27 January 1968, except for earlier date applicable to NAF units of the 7th Infantry Division. (See para 3b, below.)

2. Program Requirements. a. Each such NAF activity will make lump-sum severance pay deposits to individual employee accounts in a designated Korean bank(s) between 22 January and 5 February 1968. Deposits will be based upon a combined Separation-Appointment personnel action and will comprise the total amount of severance pay credit earned to include the last full month of service prior to 27 January 1968. As provided in the Eighth US Army agreement with the receiving bank, each employee will be issued an 18-month term time deposit certificate and a bank book for posting of monthly earned interest. (See para 3a, below, for exception to requirement for initial full pay-off.)

b. The lump-sum payment by bank deposit fulfills the severance pay obligation for prior service pursuant to the ROKG Office of Labor Affairs letter dated 11 January 1968, Articles 5 and 13 of the USFK/Eighth Army-FOEU Labor-Management Agreement, and US-ROK SOFA Joint Committee validation on __ January 1968.

c. Severance pay entitlement will be determined as follows:

(1) For NAF employees paid from Open Mess funds and Central and Command Locker funds - continuous service between 30 April 1956 and 26 January 1968 constitutes creditable service.

(2) For NAF employees paid from Supplemental Field Ration Mess funds and other Sundry funds deriving revenue solely from membership contributions or service charges - continuous service between 30 April 1961 and 26 January 1968 constitutes creditable service.

(3) A table for use in calculating lump-sum payments is shown at Inclosure 1. Credits represent the midpoint between voluntary and involuntary rates established in Schedules I and II (App E) of the current USFK/Eighth Army Severance Pay Plan.

(4) Amount of severance pay is computed by multiplying the number of months' credit for employee's period of service by his average normal wage during the previous full 6 months (July - December 1967). Guidance as to "normal wage" provided in paragraph 60c(1) of basic regulation applies.

20th JC (Incl 20)
18 Jan 68

d. Withdrawal of any portion of the severance pay deposit by the employee will constitute advance notice of resignation and his separation 30 days after notification of his withdrawal is mandatory. Consistent with paragraph 115d(2)(d), basic regulation, any employee separated on this basis will not be eligible for reemployment for a year following his separation. In individual cases where a bona fide emergency was the cause for deposit withdrawal, waiver of the established waiting period for rehire is authorized to permit reemployment after a minimum of 1 month break in service, based on recommendation of Fund Custodian, supported by documentary evidence of emergency, and concurred in by the servicing CPO. Examples of such emergencies are: (1) critical illnesses within immediate family involving large expenditures, and (2) destruction of home by fire or flood.

e. Each employee will be requested by letter (Inclosure 2) to sign in triplicate the bilingual Statement attached thereto, acknowledging that the lump-sum bank deposit constitutes the full amount of severance pay due employee as of 26 January 1968, and that later withdrawal of deposit will constitute a de facto notice of resignation. Original of signed Statement will be forwarded to servicing CPO for filing in Official Personnel Folder (201 file). The employee will receive one copy and the other copy will be retained by the Fund Custodian or equivalent official.

f. In any case where the employee refuses to sign the Statement, the Fund Custodian will annotate all copies to that effect, showing date of employee's refusal to sign. The Fund Custodian or equivalent official will then prepare a Request for Personnel Action (SF 52), in triplicate, with the nature of action as Separation-Failure to Accept Change in Employment Conditions. The SF 52 will be approved by the servicing CPO and will serve as an advance notice of separation. The effective date for all such separation actions will be 31 March 1968. "App L, EA Reg 690-1" will be cited as authority for the separation. A copy of the unsigned and annotated Statement will be attached as an inclosure to each SF 52. The employee will then receive his lump-sum severance pay in cash, based on the "Separation-Appointment" action of 26 January 1968 and computed at the midpoint, as in the case of other employees. The employee will be permitted to change his original decision refusing the deposit by signing the Statement at any time prior to receipt of his severance pay in cash.

g. Starting 27 January 1968 (date of new appointment), severance pay entitlement will be 1 month for each full year of continuous service.

h. Any employee involuntarily separated on or before 30 June 1968 will receive an additional payment constituting the difference between the amount of his severance pay deposit and the amount of severance pay for which he was eligible on 26 January 1968 computed at the involuntary separation rate as shown in Schedule II, Appendix E.

i. Beginning on 1 July 1968, employees who are separated involuntarily will receive an additional payment equal to 1 month's normal wage at the time they draw their final pay. New employees hired on or after the effective date of this Appendix will be entitled to the additional payment if they have had one full year of service at time of separation.

2

20th JC (Incl 20)
18 Jan 68

These minutes are considered as official documents pertaining to both Governments and ▓▓ not be released without mutu ▓▓ reement.

Appendix L - Eighth Army Regulation 690-1 (Cont'd)

    j. Employees removed for felony or grave misconduct (e.g., theft, collusion, bribery) will be required to forfeit lump-sum payment for any unused annual leave as well as any future severance pay earnings which would otherwise be due on date of removal.

    k. In addition to normal contacts with the union as required by basic regulation (para 16c), the following will pertain whenever dissolution of a Supplemental Field Ration Mess fund or a significant RIF is under consideration by the membership: Fund management will advise the servicing CPO at an early date; CPO will undertake discussions with fund management and with union representatives; alternate work arrangements will be considered and explored with the objective of offsetting possible RIFs.

    l. The minimum workday of 8 hours will be applied except where parttime employment is justified by reference to paragraph 34g, basic regulation, or where 6-day work weeks with 40 or more hours of work are individually established by this headquarters.

    3. Exceptions. a. Individual NAF activities without sufficient funds to make the lump-sum payment in full by 5 February 1968 may request authorization, through channels, from Eighth US Army, ATTN: G-1 to deposit (or pay in cash) by 5 February 1968, as a minimum portion of the severance pay obligation, 1 month's pay for each year of the employee's service in each case. Where such initial partial payment is authorized, the remainder of the obligation will be paid at the earliest possible date and not later than 5 August 1968. Employees separated on 31 March 1968 as a result of failure to sign Statement (para 2f) will be paid the remaining severance pay obligation with their final pay.

    b. For NAF activities in 7th Infantry Division units, effective date optionally may be 21 January 1968. Dates for dual personnel action will then be as follows: Separation (Severance Pay) will be effective on 20 January 1968, with Appointment (Indefinite) effective on 21 January 1968. Creditable service (para 2c, above) will extend through 20 January 1968. New severance pay entitlement (para 2g, above) will start as of 21 January 1968. Date shown in reference to Statement in paragraph 2e, above, will be 20 January 1968. Payment of wages due (paras 4a and 5e) will cover period ending 20 January 1968; payment of wages for remainder of January, under the new appointment, will be on a separate payroll at end of January. Employees who received severance pay in cash in late December 1967 and early January 1968 on the basis of resignation actions, will be paid the additional portion by bank deposit following rules set forth in this Appendix.

    4. Procedures for Implementation. a. Servicing CPOs will prepare a dual personnel action document to effect Separation (Severance Pay) on 26 January 1968, and Appointment (Indefinite) on 27 January 1968, for each NAF employee. Either individual Notification of Personnel Action (SF 50) or Mass Change procedure may be used. This Appendix (App L, EA Reg 690-1) will be cited as authority for the dual action. The following information will be shown under REMARKS on the SF 50: "Separation action authenticates payment of severance pay. Employee is entitled to ___ months of severance pay. Employee will receive payment of wages due him through 26 January 1968 on the basis of the separation action. Personnel benefits which depend upon

(08

3

20th JC (Incl 20)
18 Jan 68

continuity of service, other than severance pay credit, are not affected."
If Mass Change procedure is used, the number of months' severance pay due
each employee will be shown in a separate column. The same REMARKS will be
entered over signature of Appointing Officer except that the second sentence
will read: "Employee is entitled to the number of months' severance pay
indicated beside his name."

b. For any activity authorized (under provisions of para 3a, above)
to make only a partial severance payment as of 26 January 1968, the use of
SF 50s is required, and the following statement will be added to the REMARKS:
"Severance pay in the amount of __ months' pay represents the initial payment. The balance of __ months' severance pay will be paid within 6 months."

5. Banking Procedures. a. The NAF payroll will be prepared in accordance with normal procedure, with one additional copy for the bank. The payroll will list each employee and specify amount of severance pay to be
transferred to the bank. Names of employees who have refused to sign the
Statement accepting severance pay by bank deposit (para 2f) will be "red-
lined" on bank copy of payroll and appropriate adjustment in severance pay
total will be entered.

b. The Fund Custodian (pay agent) will transfer the total amount of
severance pay as shown on the payroll to the bank by Won or Won check, together with bank's copy of the payroll. The Custodian will obtain a receipt
from the bank for the transaction.

c. By terms of Eighth Army agreement with receiving bank(s), the
bank will prepare an individual 18-month term bank deposit certificate and
bank book for each employee listed on the payroll, within 5 days of receipt.

d. Servicing CPO will advise the bank as to place and time for de-
livery of the deposit certificates and bank books to individual employees.
Any final processing required for the deposit will be accomplished at this
time. Fund Custodians will advise employees that each individual must have
his seal (chop) with him when he receives his deposit certificate and bank
book.

e. Wages through 26 January 1968 will be disbursed at the same
time and the employee will sign the payroll for receipt of both wages and
severance pay.

f. Term certificates and bank books will be renewed at the expiration of 18 months. Procedures will be developed at a later date.

4

20th JC (Incl 20)
18 Jan 68

NAF LUMP-SUM SEVERANCE PAY CHART
JANUARY 1968

Service	Mo. Pay	Service	Mo. Pay	Service	Mo. Pay	Service	Mo. Pay
Less than							
1 mo	0	3 Years	3.5	6 Years	8.50	9 Years	15.25
1 mo	0	1 mo	3.6	1 mo	8.65	1 mo	15.40
2 mo	0	2 mo	3.7	2 mo	8.80	2 mo	15.55
3 mo	0.1	3 mo	3.8	3 mo	8.95	3 mo	15.70
4 mo	0.2	4 mo	3.9	4 mo	9.10	4 mo	15.85
5 mo	0.3	5 mo	4.0	5 mo	9.25	5 mo	16.00
6 mo	0.4	6 mo	4.5	6 mo	9.75	6 mo	16.50
7 mo	0.5	7 mo	4.5	7 mo	9.90	7 mo	16.65
8 mo	0.6	8 mo	4.5	8 mo	10.05	8 mo	16.80
9 mo	0.7	9 mo	4.5	9 mo	10.20	9 mo	16.95
10 mo	0.8	10 mo	4.5	10 mo	10.35	10 mo	17.10
11 mo	0.9	11 mo	4.5	11 mo	10.50	11 mo	17.25
1 Year	1.0	4 Years	4.5	7 Years	10.75	10 Years	17.50
1 mo	1.1	1 mo	4.6	1 mo	10.90	1 mo	17.65
2 mo	1.2	2 mo	4.7	2 mo	11.05	2 mo	17.80
3 mo	1.3	3 mo	4.8	3 mo	11.20	3 mo	17.95
4 mo	1.4	4 mo	4.9	4 mo	11.35	4 mo	18.10
5 mo	1.5	5 mo	5.0	5 mo	11.50	5 mo	18.25
6 mo	2.0	6 mo	5.5	6 mo	12.00	6 mo	19.25
7 mo	2.0	7 mo	5.6	7 mo	12.15	7 mo	19.25
8 mo	2.0	8 mo	5.7	8 mo	12.30	8 mo	19.35
9 mo	2.0	9 mo	5.8	9 mo	12.45	9 mo	19.45
10 mo	2.0	10 mo	5.9	10 mo	12.60	10 mo	19.55
11 mo	2.0	11 mo	6.0	11 mo	12.75	11 mo	19.65
2 Years	2.0	5 Years	6.25	8 Years	13.00	11 Years	19.75
1 mo	2.1	1 mo	6.35	1 mo	13.15	1 mo	19.90
2 mo	2.2	2 mo	6.45	2 mo	13.30	2 mo	20.05
3 mo	2.3	3 mo	6.55	3 mo	13.45	3 mo	20.20
4 mo	2.4	4 mo	6.65	4 mo	13.60	4 mo	20.35
5 mo	2.5	5 mo	6.75	5 mo	13.75	5 mo	20.50
6 mo	3.0	6 mo	7.50	6 mo	14.25	6 mo	21.50
7 mo	3.0	7 mo	7.60	7 mo	14.40	7 mo	21.50
8 mo	3.1	8 mo	7.70	8 mo	14.55	8 mo	21.60
9 mo	3.2	9 mo	7.80	9 mo	14.70	9 mo	21.70
10 mo	3.3	10 mo	7.90	10 mo	14.85	10 mo	21.80
11 mo	3.4	11 mo	8.00	11 mo	15.00	11 mo	21.90

Underlining indicates midpoint between Schedules I and II in USFK/Eighth Army Severance Pay Plan at 6-month intervals.

NOTE: See paragraph 2c(1) and (2), Appendix L, for beginning dates of creditable service.

Inclosure 1

20th JC (Incl 20)
18 Jan 68

– HEADING –

TO: (Name)
앞   성명   귀하
    (Position title & grade)
    직위 및 급수
    (Organization)
    소 속

Headquarters Eighth US Army, with agreement of the Foreign Organi-
미 8군 사령부는 외국기관 노동조합의 동의와 한국 정부의 승인을
zations Employees Union and approval of the ROK Government, has established
거쳐 새로운 비 세출기관 한국인 직원 퇴직금 제도를 설정 하였읍니다.
a new severance pay plan for nonappropriated fund Korean employees. This
이 제도는 한국인 직원의 직장 안정과 한국 일반은행을 효과적으로 이용하여
new plan is intended to support Korean employment and to effectively use
퇴직금 적립에 따르는 여러 문제점을 완화 시키는데 그 의도가 있는것 입니다.
Korean banks as a means of reducing the problem of severance pay reserves.
이 새 제도를 다음과 같이 설명 드리겠읍니다.
The plan is described below:

1. Each employee will receive a bank deposit (18-month term time
        1968년 1월   일 부 각 직원이 지급 받을수 있는 퇴직금을
deposit) in his account, the amount of deposit comprised of severance pay
각 직원의 개인 명의로 18개월 정기 예금으로 한국 일반 은행에 예금
earned as of __ January 1968, calculated at the midpoint between the
한다. 이 퇴직금율은 현 주한 미군 미 8군 한국인 퇴직금 제도의
voluntary and involuntary separation severance pay rates established in
사직율과 감원율의 중간선으로 한다. 퇴직금 수혜 근무 기간은
the current USFK/Eighth Army Severance Pay Plan. The total amount of
1개월 이상의 근무 기간도 포함한다. 퇴직금 산출 기준은 지난
severance pay credit will cover all of the employee's creditable service
6개월 (1967년 7월 에서 12월 까지의 기간)의 평균 임금으로 한다.
to include the last full month. Severance pay will be based on the em-

ployee's average wage for the last six months (July – December 1967).

Inclosure 2

20th JC (Incl 20)
18 Jan 68

2. The bank deposit in each individual employee's account represents
이 퇴직금 은행 예금은 1968년 1월   일 이전의 근무 기간에
severance pay for service prior to __ January 1968, and the employer ful-
대한 퇴직금으로서, 고용주는 한미 행정 협정 XVII 조 3항과 노사
fills severance pay obligation for prior service, under paragraph 3,
단체 협약에 의한 이전 근무 기간에대한 퇴직금 지급 의무를 완료 한다.
Article XVII, US-ROK SOFA, and the USFK/Eighth Army-FOEU Labor-Manage-

ment Agreement.

3. Each employee will receive a Separation (Severance Pay)-Appoint-
각 직원은 "해직 (퇴직금) 과 동시 채용 (무기한) " 인사
ment (Indefinite) personnel action--this is a special personnel action
조치를 받는다. 이 인사 조치는 현 고용 조건하에의 고용을
used to terminate employee service under current employment conditions
종료시키며 새로운 고용 조건하에 근무 중단 기간없이 재 채용하는
and to rehire, without break in service, under new employment conditions.
특별 인사 조치이다.

4. Severance pay rate for new appointment will be one month's pay
새로운 고용 조건 하에의 근무에대한 퇴직금율은 1년 근속에
for each year of service, and this amount will be retained by the employer
대하여 1개월분 급료로 하며 이 액수는 이후 해직시 지급되도록 고용주가
for payment at time of later separation. Each employee who is actually
보관한다. 퇴직금 은행 예치일로부터 5개월 이내에 타의 해직되는
involuntarily separated at any time up to five months subsequent to the
직원은 퇴직금 은행 예치일자에 현행 퇴직금 제도의 감원율에 따라
date of deposit will receive an additional payment which will make up the
받을수 있었던 금액과 중간선에 따라 은행에 예금된 액수의 차액을
difference between the midpoint payment and the involuntary separation rate
추가로 지급 받는다. 5개월의 기간이 경과한 이후에 타의로 해직되는
as of the date of deposit. After the 5-month period, each employee in-
직원은 해직 당시 퇴직금에 추가하여 1개월분 급료에 해당되는 액수
voluntarily separated will receive an additional one month's pay at the
를 추가로 지급 받는다.
time of separation.

2

20th JC (Incl. 20)
18 Jan 68

5. Any withdrawal of money deposited for severance pay purpose will
은행에 예치된 퇴직금의 인출은 사직으로 간주하며 이로서
be considered as a resignation and will serve as an automatic 30-day
직원이 이미 30일간의 사직 사전 통고를 한것으로 간주한다.
advance notice of resignation.

6. An employee removed for "felony or grave misconduct" will for-
중죄 및 중대 과실로 파면된 직원은 축적된 년가와 이후
feit accumulated annual leave and any future severance pay earned.
축적되는 퇴직금을 몰수한다.

7. The bank deposit will be made by _____ 1968. /Note to
은행 예금은 1968년 ————— 까지 완료한다. 기금
Fund Custodian: If the deposit is to be completed in two stages, that
관리인에게 알림; 만일 은행 예금을 2 차적으로 완료할 경우에는
will be explained to the employee in this paragraph.7
이 사실을 본항에 설명한다.

The plan described above will tend to support continued employment
위에 설명 드린 새 퇴직금 제도는 본 기금에 종사하고 있는 직원
of the employees of this fund, and will alleviate problems in administra-
들의 계속 근무와 본기금 한국인 직원 퇴직금 행정에 수반되고
tion of severance pay for Korean employees of this fund. The use of
있는 여러 문제점을 완화 시킬 것으로 생각 됩니다. 위에서 설명된바와
Korean banks, as stated, will also provide the employees the benefit of
같이 한국 일반은행의 이용은 또한 직원들로 하여금 은행이 지급하고
high interest rates paid by Korean banks.
있는 높은 이자율의 혜택을 받을수 있도록 할것입니다.

The attached is a statement for your consideration. You are requested
이 서한에 진술서를 3부 첨부 하오니 내용을 검토하시고 내용을
to examine the statement and sign all three copies if you understand and
이해하고 또한 동의 하시면 서명 하여 원본과 부본 1통은 본인에게
agree to its contents. Two signed copies (original and first copy) should
제출하여 주시고 부본 1통은 귀하가 보관 하여 주시기 바랍니다.

/13

20th JC (Incl 20)
18 Jan 68

be returned to the undersigned. The third copy should be retained by you

제출한 진술서의 1통은 귀하의 인사 기록철 (201 첩)에 보관하겠읍니다.

for your information. A signed copy will be placed in your 201 file.

                              Sincerely,
                              경   배,

                    _____
                              (Fund Custodian)
                              서   명

STATEMENT – SEVERANCE PAY

TO:

1. I, the undersigned, understand:

    a. That my employment under current employment conditions will be terminated as of __ January 1968 and that beginning __ January 1968, my employment under new employment conditions will begin.

    b. That the amount payable to me for severance pay as of __ January 1968, calculated at midpoint between the voluntary and involuntary separation severance pay schedules, will be deposited (18-month term time deposit) in my individual account at _____ Bank.

    c. That the deposit represents my severance pay for service prior to __ January 1968 and that my employer fulfills the severance obligation for service prior to this date, in view of ROKG approval and USFK/Eighth Army-FOEU memorandum of understanding, 16 January 1968.

    d. That the deposit can be withdrawn in accordance with the procedures of the bank in which the money is deposited. However, such withdrawal, either partial or total, constitutes my notice of resignation.

    e. That the bank deposit will be made by _____(date)_____. (That the initial deposit of (amount) will be made by _____(date)_____, and the remainder as soon as possible, with objective of full payment by _____(date) .)

2. In line with the above understanding, I, the undersigned, agree:

    a. That the amount payable to me for severance pay as of __ January 1968 for prior service, will be deposited (18-month term deposit) in my account at _____ Bank.

    b. That I have no further claim for severance pay for service prior to __ January 1968.

_____   _____
(Date)   (Signature)

                                 _____
                                    (Organization)

Witnessed above:

_____   _____
(Date)   (Signature of Witness)
                                 (Position Title & Grade)

Attachment to
Inclosure 2   (Korean Translation on Reverse Side)   **20th JC (Incl 20)**
                                                             18 Jan 68

진 술 서 — 퇴 직 금

앞: 귀하

1. 아래에 서명한 본인은 다음 사항을 충분히 이해함.

ㄱ. 현 고용 조건에 의한 고용은 1968년 1월___일 부로 종료됨과 동시 1968년 1월___일 부로 새로운 고용 조건에 의한 근무를 시작한다.

ㄴ. 1968년 1월___일자로 현행 퇴직금율의 사직율과 감원율의 중간선에 의하여 계산하여 본인이 받을 수 있는 퇴직금을_____ 은행에 18개월 만기 정기 예금으로 예치 한다.

ㄷ. 등 은행 예금은 1968년 1월___일 이전의 근무 기간에 대한 본인의 퇴직금이며, 이로서 1968년 1월 16일자 주한 미군 미8군과 외국기관 노동조합 사이의 협정 및 한국 정부의 승인에 따라 고용주는 이전 근무 기간에 대한 퇴직금 지급 의무를 완료한다.

ㄹ. 예금의 인출은 예금된 은행절차에 따라 할 수 있다. 단 이와같은 인출은 일부거나 또는 전액이거나를 막론코 사직 사전 통고로 간주한다.

ㅁ. 은행 예금은 1968년_____일까지 완료한다.
(1차 은행 예금은 1968년_____일까지 완료하며, 나머지는 1968년_____일을 목표로하여 가능한한 빠른 시일내에 예금 완료한다.)

2. 위의 사항을 이해함과 동시 아래에 서명한 본인은 다음과 같은 사항에 동의 한다.

ㄱ. 1968년 1월___일 이전의 근무기간에 대하여 본인에게 지급되는 퇴직금을_____ 은행에 본인의 개인 명의로 예금 (18개월 만기 정기 예금). 함.

ㄴ. 이로서, 1968년 1월___일 이전의 근무 기간에 대한 퇴직금 청구권이 없음.

_____
(서명 일자)

위를 보증한다:

_____
(서명 일자)

_____
(직원의 서명)

_____
(소 속)

(보증인의 서명과 직위 및 급수)

116

ㅅ209   20th JC (Incl 20)
         18 Jan 68

JOINT ROK - US PRESS RELEASE
TWENTIETH ROK-US JOINT COMMITTEE MEETING
18 JANUARY 1968

The ROK-US Joint Committee, at its twentieth formal meeting on 18 January, approved 21 recommendations of its Facilities and Areas Subcommittee. These recommendations related to the acquisition and release of facilities and areas by the US armed forces in Korea. The Joint Committee also assigned 13 new tasks to the Facilities and Areas Subcommittee.

The Joint Committee also agreed to establish a new Utilities Sub-committee and assigned it the responsibility of developing procedures for ROK-US consultation regarding changes in priorities, conditions, and rates for utilities and services used by the US armed forces in Korea, in accordance with the provisions of Article VI of the SOFA.

The US Representative, Lieutenant General Robert J. Friedman, Chief of Staff, USFK, presided at this meeting held at the US SOFA Conference Room. He presented several memoranda to the Joint Committee relating to various aspects of the implementation of the SOFA.

The Joint Committee decided that the next meeting of the Committee will be held on Wednesday, 21 February, at the Republic of Korea Capitol Building.

20th JC (Incl 21)
18 Jan 68

117

한.미 합동위원회 제20차 회의 공동 발표문

1968. 1. 18. (목)

한.미 합동위원회는 지난 18일 제20차 공식 회의를 열고 시설 구역 분과위원회의 건의 21개를 승인했다. 이들 건의는 주한 미군에 의한 시설과 구역의 취득과 반환에 관계되는 것이다. 또한 동 합동위원회는 시설구역 분과위원회에 13개의 과제를 부여하였다.

한.미 합동위원회는 또한 공의 용역 분과위원회의 신설에 동의 하고 군대지위협정 제6조의 규정에 따라 주한 미군에 의하여 사용 되고 있는 공의물과 용역에 대한 우선권, 조건 및 요율변경에 관한 한.미간의 협의 절차를 규제할 임무를 부여하였다.

미측 대표 주한 미군 참모장 프리드만 중장이 미8군 회의실 에서 열린 동 회의를 주재하고 여러가지 면에 걸쳐 군대 지위협정의 운영에 관한 제 각서를 제출했다.

한.미 합동위원회는 차기회의를 2월 21일 (목) 중앙청에서 개최 키로 합의 하였다.

118

ㅈ. 제 21차. 1968. 2. 21

21. 사전준비.

119

공 란

공 란

공 란

공   란

(의제 1 - 2 - 재무분과위원회 과제부여)

그러면 의제 1 - 2 재무분과위원회에 대한 과제부여를 상정하겠읍니다.
프리드맨 장군께서 설명해 주실것으로 믿읍니다.

(미측 설명)

감사합니다. 미군 고용 한국인에 대한 소득세, 원천징수의 실시가 막대한
행정부담과 비용을 수반하므로 한국측 대표단은 이러한 부담을 담당한 미국 정부의
호의 표시와 더불어 이러한 부담을 인식하여야 한다고 생각하며 따라서 지금
설명하신 과제는 극히 타당하다고 보고있읍니다.

그러나 현재로서는 예견됨 재정상 보상에 대한 법적 근거가 없다는 사실에
유의할 필요가 있음니다. ~~따라서 본 과제는 신속히 완결할 수 있는 성질의 것이~~
~~아닙니다.~~ 이러한 양해하에 한국 대표는 재무분과위원회에 대하여 동 재정보상의
가능을 모색하고 동 보상의 범위를 결정하는 과제를 부여하는데 전적으로 동의합니다.

124

(의제 1 - 3 - 상무분과위원회 추가과제 부여)

다음의제로 넘어가 상무분과위원회에 부여할 과제를 설명하겠읍니다.

이것 또한 회의중간에 상호 합의하여 처리한 양식절차에 관한 것입니다.

즉, 2월 6일 양측 수석대표가 각서에 서명하여 과제가 이미 끝난것인 미국 초청계약자인 Trans-Asia Engineering Associates, Inc. 를 협정 제5조 제2 (나)항의 규정에도 불구하고 군대지위협정에 따라 부여한 특권과 면제를 해제함이 없이 서울 특별시와 같이 특별한 경우 계약업무를 집행할 수 있는지의 여부를 결정하고저 했던 것입니다.

대한민국 대표는 상무분과위원회의 과제 부여를 정식으로 제안하는 바이며 미국측의 동의를 구하는 바입니다.

125

(의제 1 - 4 - 형사관할권 분과위원회에 대한 과제 부여)

가. 협조절차

다음의제는 형사관할권 분과위원회에 대한 2개 과제부여인바 미국대표께서 협조 절차에 관한 제1 과제를 설명하여 주실것을 청하고저 합니다.

(미측 설명)

한국 대표는 미국대표께서 설명하신 과제 부여에 동의하는 바입니다.

나. 화기통제

그러면 형사관할권 분과위원회에 부여할 나머지 1개 과제를 설명하고저 합니다.

군대지위협정 규제대상인원이 사용하는 화기통제에 관한 상호 합의된 절차의 필요성을 자명하다고 생각됩니다.

관계한국 법규에 합치하지 않는 화기 소유는 해당자에 대하여 중대한 법률문제를 초래할 것이며 통일적이고 효과적인 화기통제는 일반 공공안전상 극히 필요합니다. 따라서 형사관할권 분과위원회에 대하여 공동절차를 작성하여 합동위원회에 건의하는 과제를 부여할 것을 제안하며 이에 대한 미국대표의 동의를 청하고저 합니다.

126

(의제 1 - 5 - 출입국 임시분과위원회 추가과제 부여)

　　다음 의제는 출입국 임시분과위원회에 대한 과제부여 문제입니다.
미국대표께서 설명해 주시리라 믿읍니다.

　　(미국측 설명)

　　대한민국 대표는 출입국 임시분과위원회의 부활과 과제 부여에 동의
하는 바입니다.

127

공 란

(의제 2 (2) - 재무분과위원회 건의 소득세 원천 징수)

　　그러면 다음 의제를 상정하여 재무분과위원회의 미군 고용 한국인 소득세 원천징수에 관한 건의를 설명하고저 합니다.

　　1967년 2월 19일 개최된 제2차 실무자 예비회의는 긴급 최초 과제의 일부로서 제17조 합의의사록 3항 시행에 필요한 절차를 안출하는 과제를 재무분과위원회에 부여하였읍니다.

　　동 규정 시행을 위하여 관계 소득세법의 개정이 필요하였는바 소요입법은 행정부로서는 어절수 없는 사정에 의하여 지난 11월까지 지연되었으며 이에 따라 본 과제완결에 상당한 지연이 불가피하였읍니다.

　　본 과제는 한국 소득세법의 복잡한 구조 주한 미군의 규모 및 관련 피고용원의 수로 인하여 대단한 행정 세부 문제를 포함하였으며 개정 세법은 금년 년초부터 시행하기로 규정되어 있었으나 신세법 통과와 시행 일자 사이의 시간제약과 특히 관련된 기술적 문제의 복잡성으로 인하여 동 분과위원회 주동위원들의 필사적인 작업 강행에도 불구하고 전기 마감일자를 지키지 못하였읍니다. 동 분과위원회는 2월 6일 건의를 제출하였고 같은날 양국 대표가 승인하여 이미 합동위원회가 합의한바에 따라 즉시 효력을 발생하였읍니다. 동 절차 골자는 동 분과위원회 양측 위원단 대표가 서명한 2월 6일자 합의각서에 기재되어 있는바 그 요점은 다음과 같읍니다.

　　(1) 합의의사록의 "고용자"라는 어구는 비세출기관 및 초청계약자를 포함한 주한 미군을 의미한다.

　　(2) "피고용자"라는 어구는 KSC 인원을 포함한 "고용자"가 고용한 모든 민간인을 의미하되 지위협정 규제대상인원이 사적으로 고용하는 하인을 포함하지 않는다.

129

(3) 원천징수는 관계 한국 법규소정의 세율에 의하여 2월 1일 이후에 시작되는 봉급기간부터 실시하며 납부는 해당 급여 지급 다음 달 월말까지 행하되 한국 은행에 설치된 용산 세무서 구좌에 예입한다.

(4) 고용자는 계산확인, 통제 책임을 진다. 한국 대표는 한국 위원단을 대표하여 동 분과위원들의 노고에 사의를 표 하고 복잡하고 어려운 본 과제완결을 진심으로 축하하고저 하며 또한 이러한 성과에 대한 양 간사의 역할과 공헌도 인정되어야 할것으로 생각합니다. 그리고 특히 한국 대표는 본 건에 게재하는 막대한 행정부담을 담당하므로서 표시한 미국 정부의 호의에 대하여 재차 심심한 사의를 표하고저 합니다.

이제 한국 대표는 동 건의에 대한 합동위원회 승인의 공식 지 확인을 제의하고저 합니다.

(미측 대답)

130

(3. 상무분과위원회 건의 Trans-Asia Engineering 한국측 설명)
                              Associates, Inc.

의제의 다음 항으로 넘어가서, 대한민국 대표는 현재 주한미군 초청계약자로

체결중인 Trans-Asia Engineering 의 용역을 제공받고저하는
                  Associates, Inc.

한국정부 요청에 관련됨 상무분과위원회 건의를 설명하겠읍니다. Trans-Asia

Engineering Associates, Inc.하여금 한국에서 한국정부에 직접적으로

관련되는 제업무를 수행케 하는것은 군대지위협정의 관계조문에 위배되는 것은

아니라고 봅니다. 왜냐하면 협정정신이나 특수한 경우를 감안해서라도, 조문

해석은 여사한 업무수행은 미국군대에 간접적으로 그리고 아주 밀접한 관계를

내포하고 있는것으로 보아야 하기 때문입니다.

따라서 대한민국 대표는 상무분과위원회가 건의한대로 Trans-Asia Engineering

Associates, 가 추가인원을 고용해서 한국정부와의 계약업무를 수행한다
        Inc.

하더라도 군대지위협정에 따라 부여받고 있는 제특권과 면제를 계속

향유할수 있도록 건의하는바 입니다.

그러나 군대지위협정에 따르는 이 초청계약자의 제특권과 면제가 한국정부와의

계약집행을 위하여 특별히 추가적으로 고용한 고용원들에게는 적용되지는

않는 것으로 이해합니다.

171

공 란

(의제 4 - 안전관계법회 한국측 목록에 대한 견해 표시)

　　한국 대표는 미국 대표가 합동·위원회 제20차 회의에서 한국의 안전
관계 법회 세목과 관계되는 법규에 관하여 희한 발언에 언급코저 합니다.
본 건에 관하여 미국 대표가 표시한 미측 견해를 한국측 대표단은 심중히
검토하였읍니다. 한국 대표단을 대표하여 미측위원단의 관심과 심중한 검토
에 대하여 재차 사의를 표하면서 한국측의 견해를 표명하고저 합니다.

　　개별사건이 안전관계 법회이냐 아니냐의 여부가 관계법회의 성질
과 내용에 따라 결정됨은 자명합니다.

　　그러나 제22조 2 (다)항에 관한 합의의사록의 취지는 각기 법 체계
하에서의 안전관계 법회 세목의 상호 룽보를 요구하는 것으로 결코 어떠한
안전관계 법회 정의의 "지침" 교환을 요구하는 것이 아닌 것으로 해석됩니다.

　　또한 안전관계 법회는 당해국이 정하여야 하는 것도 명백합니다.
한국측이 작성한 목록은 제22조 2 (다)항의 예시와 한국 법규에 규정됨
안전개넘을 기초로 침법기본법의이나 범회 구성요건에 있어 대한민국 안전
에 관계되는 요소를 포함하는 범회만을 수록한 것입니다.
동 목록 작성에서 주력한바는 안전관계법회의 범위를 제한하는 것이었고,
이점은 미측 목록작성에 있어서도 동일한 것으로 믿읍니다.

　　요컨대, 한국 정부의 입장은 한국측 목록은 확정적인 것으로 간주하여야
하며 동 목록 소재 종류에 속하는 범회가 발생하면 일단 이를 안전에 관한
법회로 간주하고 이에 따라 수사가 진행되어야 한다는 것입니다.

　　그러지않고 동 목록을 단순한 "지침" 으로 간주하는 경우 사건이 발생
할때마다 그 범회가 안전관계법회인자 아닌지에 관하여

(133)

한.미 당국간에 수사 첫단계에서부터 이견과 마찰을 야기하여 신속하고 효율적인 수사진행을 크게 조해할 우려가 있는것입니다. 또한 범죄의 진상은 수사 완결후에야 판정할 수 있음을 지적하여야 할 것입니다.

이에 관련하여 대한민국 정부는 개별사건을 안전관계범죄로 취급함을 결정함에 있어 신중을 다하는 것이라는 명백한 보장을 미 당국에 하고저 합니다. 대한민국 정부는 개별사건의 안전범죄적 성거이 없음이 판명되는 즉시, 자발적으로 또는 요청에 의하여 구금을 이관할 용의가 있으며 제22조 3 (나) 항에 대한 합의의사록에 관한 양해사항 1 (가) 항에 관련한 "특별 중요성" 결정에서 신중을 다할 것입니다. 이러한 보장은 여기서 자발적으로 행하는 것인바 그 이유는 이에 반대되는 조치가 우리 양국 이익에 배치될 것임이 명백하기 때문입니다.

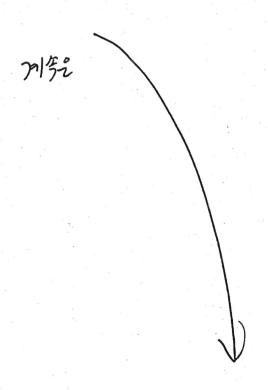

계속은

134

군대지위협정 받은 전후를 통하
여 상군 비록인원이 관련된
안전관계 범죄가 발생한
예가 없으며, 장차에 있어서도
딸히 발생하는 것이라고 예건
하여야할 아무런 이유가 없다
는 점에 유의하여야 하는 것 입니다.
    따라서 이문제는 별다른
권선적 중요성이 없다고도 볼수있
읍니다.
    불행히도 차종 사건이 발생
하는 경우는 지위협정에 ①그해
결상 중대한문제 발생을 방지
하는 여러 규정이 준비되아 있
읍니다.

125

한국대표는 미측에서 전술한 한국측 입장을 적어도 발분간 수락 하는것을 권하고자합니다.

시간이 경과하고, 시행 경험을 쌓은 후, 동 목록에 관련 한 여 용에 한 문제 가 발생 하는 경우 에는 한국 대표 단은 항시 현실 적 해결 책 발 견 에 협력 할 용 의 가 있읍니다~

136

(의제 5 - 미국 초청계약자 지명에 관한 각서 - 2건 - 미국측 설명)

의제 5 입니다. 미국 대표께서 미국 초청계약자 지명에 관한 2건을 설명하여 주시기 바라고 믿읍니다.

(미국대표 설명)

프리드만 장군 감사합니다. 미국 초청계약자로서 "스미쇼니안 인스티류트" 와 "바클레이 오바써스"를 지명한 사실 정히 접수하는 바입니다.

137

(의 제6 - 한.미 통신관계 당국자 지명)

　　의제 다음 사항으로 넘어가서 대한민국 대표는　협정 제3조 제3 (나) 항
에 따라 지명하는 통신관계 당국자에 관하여 한.미 양측 간사간에 교환된
문서의 내용을 공식회의록에 포함시키고저 합니다.
한국측 간사는 1968년 1월 29일자 서한으로 상기협정에 따른 당국자로서
체신부 전무국장 진 근 현 씨를 지명하였음을 통고하였습니다.
미국측 간사는 또한 1968년 2월 12일자 서한으로 미군측 상대자로서 주한 미군
통신부장 잭크. 콜 대령과 미국측 전파협조관 및 연락관으로서
콜 대령의 참모인 리챠드 드웨일 지명하였음을 통고하여 왔습니다.

1328

(의제 VII 대한민국 정부가 재판권 행사한 사건의 처리결과에 관하여 대한민국정부가 미국정부에 제출한 각서 - 한국측 설명)

의제 7로 넘어가서, 대한민국 대표는 군대지위협정 한국측 간사가, 대한민국정부가 주한미군의 범죄에 대하여 재판권을 행사한 사건 처리 결과의 1967년 12월분 통보를 미국측 간사를 통하여 미국정부에 전달했음을 알려드리는 바이며, 이 사실을 공식 회의록에 수록하도록 제안하는 바입니다.

(미국 대표 동의)

139

(의제 8 - 군대지위협정 시행에 있어서 미국측에서 한국측에 제출하는 각서)

다음의 의제 8입니다. 미국 대표께서 군대지위협정 시행상의 각서에 관하여 설명해 주실것으로 생각합니다.

(미국대표 설명)

합동위원회 한국측 사무국에 전달한 문서를 일일히 얼거해 주신데 대하여 감사하면서 지금 얼거하신 문서의 접수를 확인하는 바입니다.

140

공 란

(의제 10 은 차기회의 일시)

　　다음 의제로 넘어가서 이 합동위원회의 차기 회의를 관례에 따라
1968년 3월 14일 목요일 15:00시 주한 미군 사령부 회의실에서 개최하도록
건의하는 바입니다.

　　(미국대표 동의)

142

(의제 11 - 공동발표문)

이제 마지막 의제로 공동발표문 채택문제입니다.

양측 간사들이 작성하였고, 여러분에게 이미 배부되어 있는 공동발표문, 여기서는 전문 낭독을 생략하겠읍니다마는, 채택하도록 건의하는 바입니다.

(미국측 동의)

이제는 의제에 있는 모든 사항을 전부 토의한 것 같읍니다. 프리드만 장군, 혹시 폐회하기전에 다른 안건이 없읍니까?

(미국측 반응 보임.)

폐   회

143

(Agenda IV - Comments with regard to the ROK list of
        security offenses.)

        The Republic of Korea Representative wishes to refer

to the statement made by the United States Representative

at the twentieth meeting of the Joint Committee with regard

to the ~~ROK list~~ *details* of security offenses *of the Republic of Korea* and related provisions *thereto.*

The U.S. view expressed by the US Representative in this matter ~~which~~ was most carefully studied by the Korean Component.

Expressing once again the deep appreciation on behalf of

the Korean component for the keen interest and thoughtful

consideration of the U.S. counterpart, he wishes now to

clarify the position of the Korean component on the question.

        There is no doubt that the question as to whether a

particular offense constitutes a security offense or not

should be decided by the nature and content of the offense

in question. ~~under consideration.~~ However, the intent of the Agreed

Minutes Regarding Article XXII, paragraph 2(c) is understood

to require mutual notification of the details of security

offenses under respective legislation, *but* ~~and~~ in no way to demand

exchange of "guidelines," *for defining such security offense.*

        It is also obvious that the definition of security

offenses is a matter to *be* decided by the country *in a manner* ~~in question;~~

~~and not by any other country, and the word "inform" in the~~

~~said Agreed Minutes is understood to mean unilateral~~

~~notification not involving the consent of the other party.~~

The list prepared by the Korean side includes only those offenses which involve elements affecting the security of the Republic of Korea either by reason of the basic interest affected or the ~~offense-constituting~~ elements the ~~based on the types of offenses~~ enumerated in paragraph 2(c), Article XXII, which is ~~as examples~~ not limitative but inclusive, and the concept of national security set forth in Korean legislation. The primary concern in preparation of the list was to limit ~~strictly~~ the extent of security offenses, and it is believed that the same care was applied to the preparation of the U.S. list.

In short the position of the Korean Government is that the Korean list should be considered definitive, and that if a suspected the offense falls within category listed, the case should be considered in the first instance constituting a security offense and the investigation should proceed accordingly. However, If the list is considered otherwise as mere "guidelines" ~~it will not only not conforming to the original purpose of the list, but~~ it is ~~also~~ feared that it may cause disagreement and friction between ROK and U.S. authorities or not as to whether a particular case constitutes a security offense ~~or not~~ every time a case occurs even at the initial stages of investigation and thereby greatly hinder rapid and efficient progress of investigation. It should be pointed out that the true mature of an offense cannot be determined until

152 주한미군지위협정(SOFA) 한·미 합동위원회 1

after ~~successful~~ conclusion of investigation.

In this connection the Republic of Korea Government
gives a clear and definite assurances to the United States
authorities that it will be most restrictive in its
determination of security implications of individual cases.
~~It is not in its intention to insist to classify cases as security offenses despite contrary findings;~~ The K.G ~~It~~ is prepared
to transfer custody(voluntarily)or upon request, as soon as
it becomes cl~~ear~~ that there is no security implications in
particular case; it will be most ~~liberal~~ discreet in the judgment
of "particular importance" in connection with paragraph 1(a),
Agreed Understanding Re Agreed Minute Re paragraph 3, b,
Article XXII~~, it will make best use of waiver of jurisdiction provisions, both for exclusive and primary jurisdiction, in connection with the offense in the ROK list.~~ These assurances
are willingly given here, because we know that actions
contrary to these assurances will not serve the mutual
interests of our two countries.

It is to be noted that so far, both before and after
the entry into force of the Status of Forces Agreemnt, we
have had no case of security offenses involving U.S. personnel,
and we ~~cannot~~ do not forsee any change of circumstances ~~whereby~~ and see no reason to ~~entertain~~ we that
will have many such ~~cases, so~~ offenses in future. the whole question may not be
Such being the case,
of a great practical significanc'e. And if unfortunately there

146

occur some such cases, there are so many mechanisms in the

SOFA which will prevent serious difficulties ~~from being~~

~~created.~~ *in solving these cases to the mutual satisfaction.*

the US component

The Republic of Korea Representative wishes to ask ∧

to accept the foreging Korean position, at least for the

time being. If, after passage of time and experience of

actual implementation, there arise serious problems ~~with~~

connected with

~~regard~~ ∧ the list of security offenses, the Korean component

will always be ready to cooperate to find a workable solution.

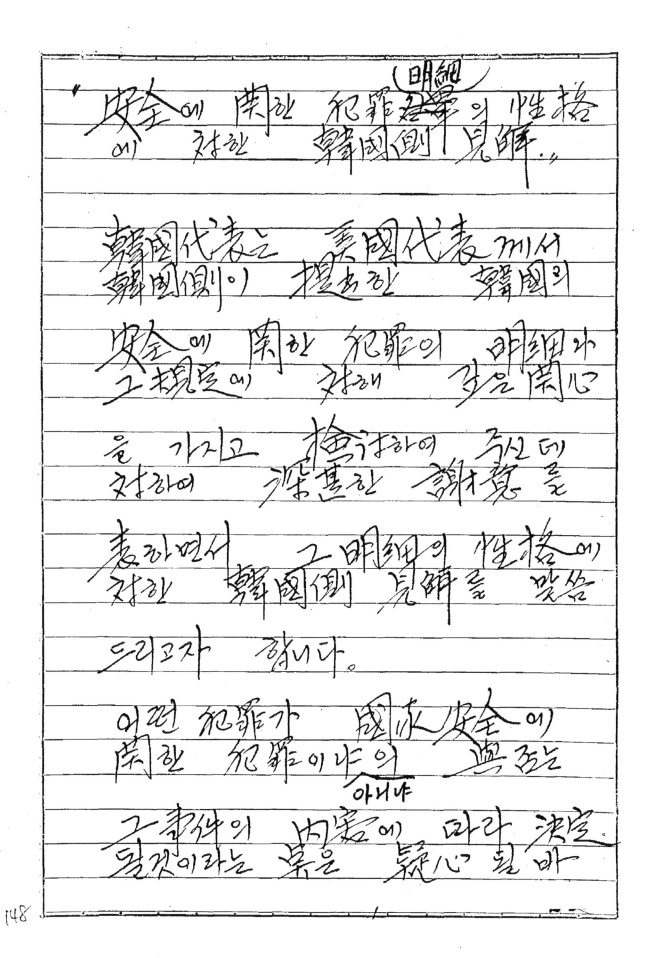

"安全에 關한 犯罪 (明細) 의 性格
에 對한 韓國側 見解.."

韓國代表는 美國代表께서
韓國側이 提出한 韓國의

安全에 關한 犯罪의 明細와
그 根據에 對해 깊은 關心

을 가지고 檢討하여 우리 側에
對하여 深重한 謝意 를

表하면서 그 明細의 性格에
對한 韓國側 見解를 말씀

드리고자 합니다.

어떤 犯罪가 國家安全에
關한 犯罪이냐의 與否는
아니냐

그 事件의 內容에 따라 決定
될것이라는 點은 疑心 할 바

148

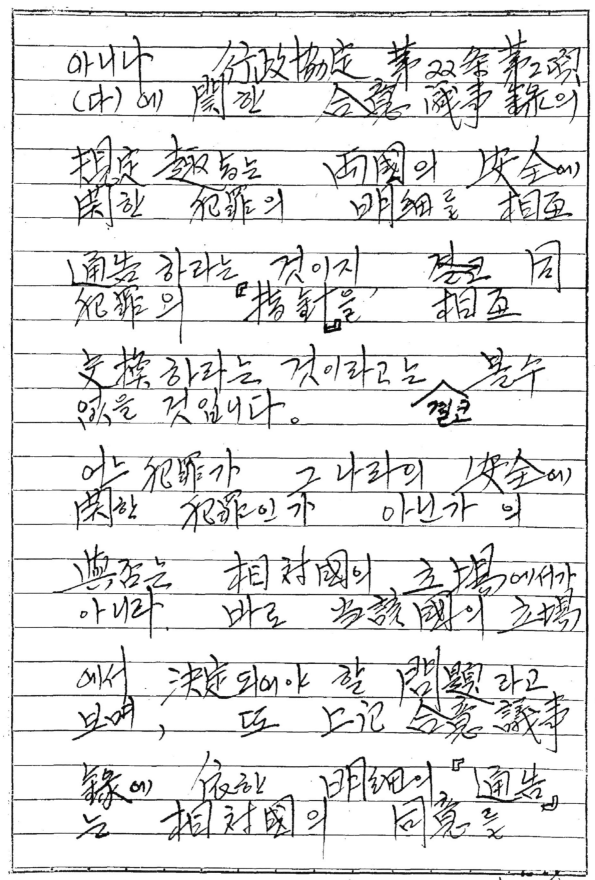

아니나 行政協定 第22條 第2項
(다)에 關한 合意議事錄의

規定 趣旨는 兩國의 安全에
關한 犯罪의 明細를 相互

通告 하라는 것이지 各 同
犯罪의 「措置를」 相互

交換 하라는 것이라고는 볼수
없을 것입니다. 결코

어느 犯罪가 그 나라의 安全에
關한 犯罪인가 아닌가 의

與否는 相對國의 立場에서가
아니라 바로 当該國의 立場

에서 決定되어야 할 問題라고
보며, 또 上記 合意議事

錄에 依한 明細의 「通告」
는 相對國의 同意를

149

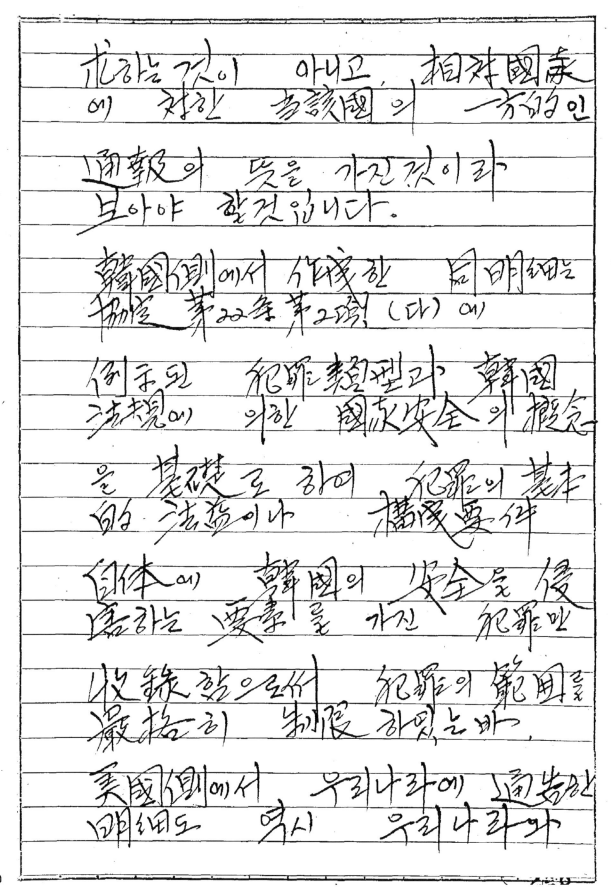

北하는 것이 아니고, 相对國家
에 对한 当該國 의 一方的인

通報의 뜻을 가진것이라
보아야 할것입니다.

韓國側에서 作成한 同 明細는
協定 第22条 第2項 (다) 에

例示되 犯罪 類型과 韓國
法規에 의한 國家安全 의 槪念
을 基礎로 하여 犯罪의 基本
的 法益이나 構成要件

自体에 韓國의 安全을 侵
害하는 要素를 가진 犯罪만
收錄함으로서 犯罪의 範囲를
嚴格히 制限 하있는바.

美國側에서 우리나라에 通告한
明細도 역시 우리나라와

150

同一한 基準에서 嚴格하게
作成 된것으로 믿습니다.
그러므로 (또 말씀드린 바에 依하여) 어떤 特定 事件 이
同 明細 에 該當 되는 限,

一應 이를 安全에 關한 犯罪
로 取扱 하여 搜査를 遂行

하여야 할것으로 생각하는 것
입니다.   그렇지 않고

만일 同 明細를   어떤 事件의
國家 安全 關聯 與否를 判斷

하기 為한 指針 으로서만 適用하게
되면   同 明細를 通告 한

趣旨에   違反 되는 理論
事件이 發生 할때 마다 搜查

當初부터   同 事件의 國家安全
關聯 與否를   둘러 싸고

韓美 兩國間에 意見対立을
가져와 도리혀 事件処理의

(와 適正
公正와 迅速을 達할 念意가
적지 아니 할것 입니다.

그렇다고 하여 韓國側이 捜査
終結 後에도 安全에 関한

犯罪가 아닌 것을 安全에 関한
犯罪 라고 고집 한다거나, 専属

犯罪가 專屬的 裁判権이
屬하는 것이건, 第一次的 裁判権
的
이 屬하는 것이건 間에 美合衆
國의 要請에 의하여 刑事

裁判 管轄権 行使 를 抛棄할수
있다는 協定 條項 을 受諾 看過
우리나라가
하려는것은 결코 아닙니다.

157 「

외 무 부

미이 723-   1968. 2. 9.

수 신 : 배부처 참조

참조 :

제 목 : 한미합동위원회 회의 개최 통지

　　1. 오는 1968년 2월 21일 (수요일) 15.00시에 중앙청 5층
~~각요회의실, 주한미군사령부 회의실~~ 에서 한미합동위원회 제 21 차
회의가 개최될 예정이오니 각 위원의 참석을 바랍니다.

　　2. 한편, 동 회의에 대비한 한국 대표단의 대책회의를 오는
2 월 20일 (화요일) 10.00 시에 외무부 회의실에서 개최하오니 참석
하시기바랍니다.　끝.

	담 당	과 장	국 장
북미2과 2월 9일 기재	양요	전결	

외　무　부　장　관

배부처 : 법무부 장관 (법무실장, 검찰국장), 국방부장관 (기획국장,
　　시설국장), 재무부장관 (~~새겸국장~~ (세겸국장)), 상공부장관 (상역국장),
　　~~교통부장관 (항공국장)~~, 노동청장 (노정국장).
　　경제기획원 (경제기획국장)

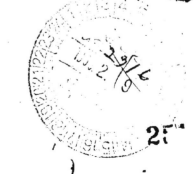

공 란

공   란

공   란

9. The US Representative proposed inclusion in the minutes of the twenty-first Joint Committee meeting, the task assigned to the Financial Affairs Subcommittee by the Republic of Korea and US Representatives on 6 February 1968 (Inclosure 11). The United States Representative stated that he was happy to note that this newly assigned task was related to the concurrent agreement to have the US armed forces in Korea begin income tax withholdings of their Korean employees, effective 1 February 1968. He stated that the withholding of these income taxes was in accordance with the provisions of Agreed

4

Minute III of Article XVII of the SOFA (Inclosure 11): These income taxes

of USFK's approximately 40,000 Korean employees, will be deposited by

the US armed forces directly into designated bank accounts of the Govern-

ment of the Republic of Korea. The new task provided that, in view of

the administrative burden entailed in the withholding of such income taxes,

mutual consultations were required to formulate agreed recommendations

concerning appropriate reimbursement to the US Forces, Korea, for the

expenses incurred in connection with the withholding of income taxes of

USFK's Korean employees.

10. The ROK Representative stated that, inasmuch as the actual

withholding of income taxes of the USFK-employed Korean personnel

involved tremendous administrative burden and costs, the Korean com-

ponent believed that recognition should be given to this burden, and to

the gesture of goodwill on the part of US authorities in undertaking to

assume this burden. Therefore, the task as formulated was considered

most appropriate. However, it should be noted that there was, at present,

and therefore the task was not one to be solved no legal basis for the envisioned financial compensation. The ROK Repre- _quickly_

sentative indicated that, with this understanding, the ROK Representative

whole-heartedly agreed to assigning to the Financial Affairs Subcommittee

the task of exploring the possibility and determining the extent of the

financial compensation. The US Representative stated that he felt con-

fident that resolution of this task could be achieved in a spirit of mutual

understanding.

158

5

11.   The ROK Representative stated he would like to present a task to be assigned to the Commerce Subcommittee.   He stated that this was another example of assignment of a task agreed upon since the last Joint Committee meeting.   The memorandum (Inclosure 12) assigning the task was signed on 6 February 1968, by the two Representatives and the task has (already) been completed.   The task assigned was to determine if the Trans-Asia Engineering Associates, Inc. , a US invited contractor, could also perform a proposed contract with a ROK Government Agency (in this particular case the City of Seoul), ~~The Trans-Asia Engineering invited contractor personnel would continue to enjoy~~ (without forfeiting) the privileges and immunities granted under the SOFA, notwithstanding the provisions of paragraph 2(b), Article XV.   ~~However, the additional employees of Trans-Asia, working for the City of Seoul, would not have SOFA rights and privileges.~~   The ROK Representative proposed ~~the inclusion of~~ that the assignment of this task to the Commerce Subcommittee be included in the minutes of the twenty-first Joint Committee meeting.   The US Representative concurred.

12.   The US Representative proposed assignment of a new task to the Criminal Jurisdiction Subcommittee (Inclosure 13).   Under the provisions of paragraph 6(b), of Article XXII, and Agreed View Number 5, the US authorities have been reporting the disposition of cases of US armed forces personnel suspected of offenses against the Republic of Korea and Korean nationals.   No Joint Committee procedures, however, have yet been adopted for cooperation in regard to the disposition of cases in which Korean nationals were

159

6

suspected of the commission of offenses against US armed forces in Korea, or against United States personnel assigned to such forces. The Criminal Jurisdiction Subcommittee is being assigned this new task (Inclosure 13) under the provisions of Articles XXII and XXV of the SOFA. The Criminal Jurisdiction Subcommittee was requested to recommend establishment of procedures which would enhance the mutual cooperation required to protect US armed forces personnel, US property, and US installations within the Republic of Korea. The US Representative, in proposing this important new task to the Criminal Jurisdiction Subcommittee, expressed the hope that the procedures recommended would enhance mutual understanding and thus promote ROK-US friendship and understanding. The ROK Representative concurred in this assignment.

13. The ROK Representative presented another task to be assigned to the Criminal Jurisdiction Subcommittee (Inclosure 14). He stated that the need for mutually agreed procedures pertaining to the control of privately owned firearms of personnel covered by the SOFA was self-evident. Possession of firearms not conforming to pertinent Korean regulations may cause serious legal problems for the individual concerned and uniform and effective control of firearms was highly desirable for general public safety. The ROK Representative proposed that the Criminal Jurisdiction Subcommittee be assigned the task of formulating mutually agreed procedures on this subject and of recommending them to the Joint Committee. The US Representative concurred.

7.

14. The US Representative stated that the Joint Committee Ad Hoc Subcommittee on Entry and Exit completed all of the tasks assigned to it expeditiously in the Spring of 1967. These procedures have been in effect ~~now~~ for many months and have generally worked very well. Experience over the past months, however, has indicated a possible need for minor modifications in some of the procedures. The ~~Joint Committee~~ *US Representative,* therefore, proposed that the Ad Hoc Entry and Exit Subcommittee review the agreements that it developed in 1967 and recommend to the Joint Committee any revisions in these procedures which would improve their effectiveness (Inclosure 15).

15. The ROK Representatived indicated that he concurred in the reactivation of the Ad Hoc Subcommittee and to the assignment of the proposed task (Inclosure ~~15~~). In a discussion of the task, Mr. LEE Sun Jung, who is Chairman of the ROK component of the Ad Hoc Subcommittee, commented on paragraph 2 of the task relating to application of entry and exit procedures to US invited contractor personnel. *ROK Representative* ~~He~~ stated *Noting that the previous ~~request~~ proposal by the had remained unanswered by the US side,* that it was the ROK position that the entry and exit procedures apply not only to USFK personnel, but also to US invited contractor personnel, *who are not covered by the previously adopted procedures.* ~~it.~~ After further discussion, it was agreed that the Ad Hoc Entry and Exit Subcommittee would make specific recommendations of this point in the light of provisions of Article VIII and Article XV of the SOFA, as well as the previous decisions of the Joint Committee on the entry and exit of personnel covered by the SOFA.

161

공   란

공   란

19. The ROK Representative presented the recommendations of the Financial Affairs Subcommittee, relating to withholding income taxes of USFK-employed Koreans (Inclosure 22). The ROK Representative explained that the second meeting of the Preliminary Working Group, on 19 January 1967, had assigned the task of devising procedures to implement the provisions of paragraph 3, Agreed Minutes to Article XVII. The implementation of the said provisions required the revision of pertinent ROK income tax legislation. The necessary legislation was delayed until last November due to circumstances beyond the control of the Execu-

10

tive branch of the Government. Hence, the considerable delay for the conclusion of the task in question. The task involved tremendous administrative details because of the complicated structure of Korean income tax legislation, the size of the USFK organization, and the number of employees affected. The revised legislation was to become effective on 1 January 1968. However, due to the limited time available between the passage of the revised legislation and its effective date, and above all, the tremendous technical problems involved, the Subcommittee failed to meet the deadline despite frantic hard work by members of the Subcommittee. The Subcommittee submitted its recommendations on 6 February 1968. They were approved on the same day by the two Representatives and became effective immediately, in pursuant to the previous agreement of the Joint Committee. The recommendations stipulated that:

a. The expression "employer" refers to the USFK, including nonappropriated fund organizations and US invited contractors.

b. The expression "employee" refers to any civilian employed by an "employer," including Korean Service Corps personnel, but excluding a domestic employed privately by the personnel covered by the SOFA.

c. Withholdings will be effected in accordance with rates established by pertinent ROK legislation, without modification, starting with the full pay period beginning on or after 1 February 1968. Tax remittances will be made not later than the end of the following month of pay period, to the Bank of Korea, in the account of the Yongsan Internal Revenue Office.

11

d.   Employer has the responsibility for controlling the compu-
tation, withholding, and remittances of income taxes of employees.

20.   The ROK Representative, on behalf of the Korean component,
expressed his deep appreciation for the hard work of the Subcommittee
members and his whole-hearted congratulations for the successful completion of this complicated and difficult task. He stated that a word of
recognition was due also to the active role and contributions of the two
SOFA Secretaries in this happy result. The ROK Representative expressed again his deep appreciation for the gesture of good will on the
part of the United States Government in assuming the tremendous administrative burden involved. The ROK Representative proposed formal
confirmation of the Joint Committee approval of the Subcommittee's
recommendations.

21.   The United States Representative stated he was happy to agree,
to the inclusion of the recommendations of the Financial Affairs Subcommittee, which were approved by the United States and Republic of Korea
Representatives on 6 February 1968, in the minutes of this Joint Committee meeting. He joined with the ROK Representative in congratulating
all ROK and US personnel involved in the achievement of agreement on
this important task.

22.   The ROK Representative presented the recommendation of the
Commerce Subcommittee (Inclosure 23), relating to the request of the
ROK Government to obtain the services of the Trans-Asia Engineering

12

Associates, Inc., currently an invited contractor of USFK. The Subcommittee recommended that the Joint Committee agree that Trans-Asia Engineering Associates, Inc., may engage in business activities in the Republic of Korea pertaining immediately and directly to the Government of the Republic of Korea, ~~and not be in~~ violation of the relevant provisions of the SOFA. The ROK Representative agreed that, in this instance and under the special facts appearing, the SOFA provisions may and should be construed so as to favor those certain business activities which bear an indirect, yet reasonably close, relationship to the mission of the US armed forces. The ROK Representative therefore proposed acceptance of the recommendations of the Commerce Subcommittee, to permit Trans-Asia Engineering Associates, Inc., to retain the privileges and immunities granted under the SOFA, even though it performed certain contracts with additional personnel for the Government of the Republic of Korea. The ROK Representative stated he understood that invited contractor privileges and immunities granted under the SOFA will not be extended to the additional personnel of the Trans-Asia Engineering Associates, Inc., employed on the contract with the Government of the Republic of Korea.

23. The US Representative stated he was happy to approve the recommendations of the Commerce Subcommittee, concerning Trans-Asia Engineering Associates, Inc. The US Representative confirmed that this US invited contractor was authorized to perform his contracts for the Republic of Korea Government, with the understanding that the additional

13

US personnel employed on these Republic of Korea contracts will not be
extended the privileges and immunities of the SOFA.

14

26.   The ROK Representative stated that he wished to refer to the
statement made by the US Representative at the twentieth meeting of the
Joint Committee, with regard to the details of security offenses of the
Republic of Korea and related provisions thereto.   The US view expressed
by the US Representative in this matter was most carefully studied by the
ROK component.   Expressing once again, on behalf of the ROK component,
his deep appreciation for the keen interest and thoughtful consideration
of the US component, the ROK Representative stated he wished to clarify
the position of the ROK component on the question.   There is no doubt
that the question as to whether a particular offense constitutes a security

15

offense or not should be decided by the nature and content of the offense in question. However, the intent of the Agreed Minutes Regarding Article XXII, paragraph 2(c), is understood to require mutual notification of the details of security offenses under respective legislation but in no way to demand exchange of "guidelines" for defining such security offenses.

27. The ROK Representative stated that it is also obvious that the definition of security offenses was a matter to be decided by the country concerned. The list prepared by the ROK side included only those offenses which involved elements affecting the security of the Republic of Korea (either by reason of the basic interests affected or the offense-constituting elements), based on the enumeration in paragraph 2(c), Article XXII, which is not limitative but inclusive, as well as the concept of national security set forth in ROK legislation. The primary concern in preparation of the list was to limit the extent of security offenses, and it was believed that the same care was applied to the preparation of the US list. In short, the position of the ROK Government was that the Korean list should be considered definitive, and that if a suspected offense fell within the category listed, the case should be considered in the first instance constituting a security offense and the investigation should proceed accordingly. However, if the list were to be considered otherwise (as mere "guidelines"), it was feared that it could cause disagreement and friction between ROK and US authorities. Such disagreement could develop over

16

whether or not a particular case constituted a security offense. Such a disagreement could arise every time a case occurred even at the initial stages of investigation, and thereby greatly hinder rapid and efficient progress of the investigation. It should be pointed out, the ROK Representative emphasized, that the true nature of an offense cannot be determined until after conclusion of the investigation.

28. The ROK Representative stated that, in this connection, the Government of the Republic of Korea gave clear and definite assurances to the United States authorities that it will be most restrictive in its determination to treat individual cases as security offenses. The Government of the Republic of Korea was prepared to transfer custody, voluntarily or upon request, as soon as it became clear that there was no security implications in a particular case; it will be most discreet in its decisions relating to the term "of particular importance," in connection with paragraph 1(a), Agreed Understanding Re Agreed Minute Re Paragraph 3(b) of Article XXII. These assurances were willingly given here, because the ROK authorities knew that actions contrary to these assurances would not serve the mutual interests of the ROK and US. The ROK Representative stated that it should be noted that so far, both before and after the entry into force of the Status of Forces Agreement, there have been no cases of security offenses involving US personnel. No changes in these circumstances were foreseen and there is no reason to anticipate that there will be many such offenses in the future. Such

being the case, the whole question may not be of a great practical significance.
such
Even if, unfortunately, some cases occur, there are many mechanisms in

the SOFA which would prevent serious difficulties from arising in solving

these cases to the mutual satisfaction.

    29. The ROK Representative stated that he wished to ask the US

component to accept the foregoing Korean position, at least for the time

being. If, after passage of time and experience in actual implementation,

there should arise serious problems in connection with the list of secu-

rity offenses, the ROK component will always be ready to cooperate to

find a workable solution.

    30. The US Representative thanked the ROK Representative for

his extremely thoughtful reply to the United States Representative's

comments in regard to the list of security offenses of the Republic of

Korea, which were made at the twentieth meeting of the Joint Committee.

A comparison of the comments of the US Representative and the reply of

the ROK Representative indicated that the basic views of both countries

appeared indeed very similar. However, the US component was unable

to accept the ROK position at this time and wished to consider the matter

further. For example, it was noted that the matter of pre-trial custody

of a suspect was involved. In this regard, the Agreed Understanding to

Paragraph 5, Article XXII, provided in connection with security offenses,

that there must be mutual United States-Republic of Korea agreement as

to the circumstances in which such custody was appropriate. The US

18

Representative stated that the US component would like to consider the ROK position further and comment at a later meeting. In the meantime, the US component suggested that if an offense occurred which was suspected of having security implications, the suspected offender should remain in the custody of the US authorities pending the conclusion of an investigation which substantiated the security implications of the offense.

31. The US Representative presented a memorandum to the Joint Committee informing the Republic of Korea Government of the designation of two new invited contractors under Article XV of the Status of Forces Agreement. After consultation with Republic of Korea Commerce Subcommittee personnel, the US Forces, Korea designated Barclay Overseas, Inc. (Inclosure 24), and the Smithsonian Institution (Inclosure 25), as US invited contractors. Pertinent data concerning employees of these invited contractors will be provided to the Government of the Republic of Korea, in accordance with mutually approved procedures.

32. The ROK Representative stated that the designation of the Smithsonian Institute and Barclay Overseas, Inc., as US invited contractors, was duly noted.

33. The ROK Representative stated that he wished to include in the official Joint Committee minutes the substance of correspondence between the two SOFA Secretaries with regard to designation of the communications authorities, in accordance with Article III, paragraph 2(b). The ROK Secretary informed the US Secretary by his letter, dated 29 January

193

1968, of the designation of the Ministry of Communications represented by Mr. JIN Keun Hyun, Director, Bureau of Telecommunications, as the ROK communications authorities referred to by the said SOFA Article. On his part, the US SOFA Secretary, in his letter dated 12 February 1968, confirmed that Colonel Jack N. Cole, Assistant Chief of Staff, J-6, US Forces, Korea, continued to be the designated US communications authority in accordance with Article III. Mr. Richard W. DeWeil, a part of the staff of Colonel Cole, continued to be the US Frequency Coordinator and US liaison with the ROK Government in matters concerning radio frequencies.

34. The US Representative acknowledged that the information set forth by the ROK Representative concerning designated United States and Republic of Korea communications authorities, in accordance with paragraph 2(b) of Article III, had been exchanged. The US Representative agreed that this information should be incorporated into the minutes of this Joint Committee meeting.

35. The ROK Representative noted for the record that the ROK SOFA Secretary had transmitted to the US SOFA Secretary, the Republic of Korea Government report on the disposition of offenses, in which the Republic of Korea exercised jurisdiction over US Forces, Korea personnel, for the month of December 1967. The ROK Representative proposed that this transmittal be recorded in the Joint Committee minutes.

21

36. The US Representative acknowledged receipt of the Republic of Korea Government report for December 1967, on the disposition of offenses in which the Republic of Korea exercised jurisdiction over USFK personnel.

~~37. The ROK Representative confirmed the receipt of the documents, as enumerated by the ROK SOFA Secretary.~~

37-38. The US Representative noted for the record that the US SOFA Secretary had furnished the following information to the ROK SOFA Secretary, in the implementation of United States - Republic of Korea Status of Forces Agreement:

a. Five copies of reports on the US armed forces disposition of cases for the month of December 1967.

b. Twenty copies of a report listing arrivals, departures, and address changes of US invited contractor personnel and their dependents, dated 31 January 1968.

c. Twenty copies of the report of US armed forces personnel, the civilian component, invited contractors, and dependents entering or departing the Republic of Korea during the month of January 1968.

38-39. The ROK Representative confirmed the receipt by the ROK SOFA Secretary of the documents enumerated by the US Representative.

39-40. The ROK Representative stated that he would like to make a statement with regard to past increases in utility rates. He recalled that at the sixteenth meeting of the Joint Committee, on 19 October 1967, the ROK Representative proposed that since it may take some time for the Commerce Subcommittee to recommend consultation procedures provided for in paragraph 1 of the Agreed Minutes to Article VI, maximum use be made of the existing arrangements for revision of individual contracts necessitated by imminent increases in utility rates.   Subsequently, revised contracts contain a clause to the effect that the revision was subject to Joint Committee consultation.   It now appeared that the US agencies directly concerned have interpreted this clause as suspensive.   It was pointed out that, if the US agencies insisted on the suspensive nature of the clause, it would be equivalent to exercising a veto.   In that case, such action would not be consonant with the spirit of the SOFA provisions, which uses the expression "consultation," not implying "consent." It was feared that if strictly insisted upon, the new clause in the contracts could become a source of unnecessary friction, which obviously was not the intention of either Government.   The ROK Representative suggested that the USFK take action to prevent unnecessary misunderstanding.

4D.   The ROK Representative also stated he would like to refer to another aspect of the utility rates problem.   The said Agreed Minutes define the subject of Joint Committee consultation as "any changes determined by the authorities of the Republic of Korea..." The text is believed to exclude any contract not controlled by ROK Government authorities.   There has been a case involving water supply to the Kunsan Air Base, which has been effected by a local irrigation association.   The US contracting officer refused to negotiate a rate increase necessary to cover costs on the grounds of the lack of prior Joint Committee consultation. This necessitated a trip to Seoul by a representative of the Association, which was obviously absurd in view of the amount involved. The ROK Representative suggested that the USFK take action to clarify its views on the issue.

42. The US Representative assured the ROK Representative that early resolution of this Subcommittee task was urgent. He proposed that the Utility Subcommittee be urged to have its recommendations on the task assigned to it completed as soon as possible, and not later than the next Joint Committee meeting, tentatively scheduled for mid-March. The US Representative also reiterated his previous agreement, made at the sixteenth Joint Committee meeting, that simultaneous negotiations under applicable contracts should proceed. He emphasized that it was the desire of the US Representative that these questions be resolved on a mutually agreeable basis at the earliest possible date.

43. After further discussion of various aspects of this problem, it was agreed that the ROK and US Representatives would take under consideration the recommendations of the Utilities Subcommittee as soon as they were presented, hopefully within the next week or two and ~~by the next Joint Committee meeting at the latest~~. It was also agreed that the point brought up by the ROK Representative regarding the Korean contractor at the Kunsan Air Base would be taken up on the basis of the

private contracts, even if they pertain to utilities, could not be the subject of the Joint Committee consultation, and agreement reached at the sixteenth Joint Committee meeting. The US Representative emphasized that, in addition to expeditious action by the Utilities Subcommittee, simultaneous negotiations under applicable contracts should proceed, as previously agreed by the ROK and US Government Representatives, at the 19 October 1967 Joint Committee meeting.

43.44. The ROK Representative proposed that, following the past practice, the next Joint Committee meeting be held at 1500 hours, on Thursday, 14 March 1968, in the US SOFA Conference Room, Yongsan. The US Representative concurred.

44.45. The ROK Representative proposed adoption of the joint press release, as prepared by the two SOFA Secretaries, (Inclosure 26). The US Representative concurred.

45.46. The meeting was adjourned at 1715 hours.

26 Inclosures

ROBERT J. FRIEDMAN   YOON HA JONG

공　　　란

공　　　란

공 란

공   란

공   란

공 란

공   란

공   란

공 란

공   란

공   란

공 란

공　　란

JOINT COMMITTEE
UNDER
THE REPUBLIC OF KOREA AND THE UNITED STATES
STATUS OF FORCES AGREEMENT

6 February 1968

MEMORANDUM FOR: Chairmen, ROK Finance Subcommittee/
US Financial Affairs Subcommittee

SUBJECT: Withholding Tax (Article XVII, para 3, Agreed Minutes)

REFERENCES: (a) Memorandum to Chairmen, Finance Subcommittee, subject: Withholding Tax, (Inclosure 9, Minutes of Second Meeting of the "Preliminary Working Group", 19 January 1967).
(b) Recommendations of the Financial Affairs Subcommittee, dated 6 February 1968, subject as above, approved by the ROK-US Representatives of the Joint Committee on 6 February 1968.

1. It is mutually recognized that the implementation of procedures embodied in reference (b) above, concerning the withholding of income taxes of USFK Korean employees in accordance with the provisions of Article XVII, paragraph 3, Agreed Minutes, will levy an administrative burden upon the "employer", as defined in Article XVII, paragraph 1 (a), ROK-US SOFA.

2. In view of the administrative burden entailed in the withholding of income taxes, mutual consultations are required to formulate agreed recommendations concerning appropriate reimbursement by the Government of the Republic of Korea to the "employer" for the expenses incurred by the "employer" in the process of withholding of income taxes of United States armed forces Korean employees.

ROBERT J. FRIEDMAN
Lieutenant General
United States Air Force
United States Representative

YOON HA JONG
Republic of Korea Representative

6 February 1968

MEMORANDUM FOR: Chairmen, Commerce Subcommittee

SUBJECT: Interpretation of Paragraph 2(b), Article XV, SOFA in Regard to the Trans-Asia Engineering Associates, Inc.

1. The Government of the Republic of Korea considers it to be in its best interests to have the services of the Trans-Asia Engineering Associates, Inc., an invited contractor of the US Forces, Korea, to perform certain contracts for the Government of the Republic of Korea with additional personnel.

2. Mutual consultations are requested to determine the applicability of the provisions of paragraph 2(b), of Article XV, if the agencies of the Government of the Republic of Korea entered into contracts with the Trans-Asia Engineering Associates, Inc., without causing the latter to lose the privileges and immunities granted to it under the SOFA.

YOON HA JONG
Republic of Korea Representative

ROBERT J. FRIEDMAN
Lieutenant General
United States Air Force
United States Representative

IP3

21 February 1968

MEMORANDUM FOR: Chairmen, Criminal Jurisdiction Subcommittee

SUBJECT: Cooperating Procedures on the Disposition of
Incidents Involving Korean Nationals

1. Under the provisions of Paragraph 6(b), Article XXII, and Agreed View No. 5, procedures have been adopted for United States authorities to report the disposition of cases of United States armed forces personnel suspected of offenses against the Republic of Korea and Korean nationals.

2. No procedures have been adopted for cooperation in regard to the disposition of cases in which Korean nationals were suspected of the commission of offenses against the United States armed forces in Korea, or against US personnel assigned to such forces. Under the provisions of Article XXV and the Agreed Understanding thereto, the establishment of such procedures would further that mutual cooperation required to protect United States armed forces personnel, United States property, and installations within the Republic of Korea.

3. Your recommendations on cooperating procedures in such dispositions are to be transmitted to the Joint Committee.

YOON HA JONG	ROBERT J. FRIEDMAN
Republic of Korea	Lieutenant General
Representative	United States Air Force
	United States Representative

ℓℓ4

21 February 1968

MEMORANDUM FOR: Chairmen, Criminal Jurisdiction Subcommittee

SUBJECT: Privately Owned Firearms

1. Mutual procedures pertaining to the control of privately owned firearms of members of the United States armed forces, members of the civilian component, invited contractors, and dependents of the foregoing are desirable.

2. Your recommendations on such procedures are to be transmitted to the Joint Committee.

YOON HA JONG
Republic of Korea
Representative

ROBERT J. FRIEDMAN
Lieutenant General
United States Air Force
United States Representative

185

21 February 1968

MEMORANDUM FOR: Chairmen, Ad Hoc Entry and Exit Subcommittee

SUBJECT: Request for Review of Procedures Established by the
Joint Committee Relative to Article VIII, US-ROK
Status of Forces Agreement

1. References:

a. Procedures for notifying the Government of the
Republic of Korea of numbers and categories of persons entering
and departing, approved by the Joint Committee on 28 April 1967
at its Sixth Meeting.

b. The meaning of the words "reasonable time" in
paragraph 4 of the Agreed Minute Re Article VIII, approved by the
Joint Committee on 23 March 1967 at its Fourth Meeting.

c. Procedures for notifying the authorities of the
Republic of Korea of a change in status of any person brought into
the ROK under paragraph 1, Article VIII, approved by the Joint
Committee on 28 April 1967 at its Sixth Meeting.

d. Determination of the meaning of the phrase "reasonable
time" as expressed in paragraph 5, Article VIII, approved by the
Joint Committee on 28 April 1967 at its Sixth Meeting.

e. Procedures and designation of ports of Entry and Exit
for the implementation of paragraph 4, Article VIII, approved by the
Joint Committee on 22 June 1967 at its Tenth Meeting.

f. Appropriate documentation and verification of status of
members of the civilian component, their dependents, and the dependents of members of the United States Armed Forces as provided for
in paragraph 4, Article VIII, approved by the Joint Committee on 25
May 1967 at its Eighth Meeting.

2. The agreements listed in paragraph 1 above govern various aspects of entry and exit procedures and change of status in accordance with the provisions of Article VIII, US-ROK Status of Forces Agreement. Experience over the past months in the implementation of these agreements has indicated the possible need to modify some of these procedures, and to consider the feasibility of applying such procedures to US invited contractor personnel. It is therefore requested that the Ad Hoc Entry and Exit Subcommittee review these agreements to determine desired changes in these procedures, and prepare and transmit to the Joint Committee recommendations embodying revisions to improve the effectiveness of these procedures.

ROBERT J. FRIEDMAN   YOON HA JONG
Lieutenant General   Republic of Korea Representative
United States Air Force
United States Representative

2

공　　　　란

공 란

공　　　란

공 란

공 란

공　　　　란

공 란

공 란

공 란

공   란

공   란

공   란

REPUBLIC OF KOREA - UNITED STATES
FINANCIAL AFFAIRS SUBCOMMITTEE

6 February 1968

MEMORANDUM FOR: THE JOINT COMMITTEE

1. Subcommittee members:

United States	Republic of Korea
COL Thomas A. Taylor, Jr., Chairman	Mr. CHOI Kack Kyu, Chairman
LTC Talmadge L. Bartelle, USFK	Mr. NAM Sang Chin
LTC John F. Rogan, 8th Army	Mr. KIM Thong Bin
LTC Paul V. Colaianni, USFK	Mr. PARK Bong Jin
LTC Mary C. Lane, 8th Army	Mr. PARK Joon Kyu
LCDR R. D. Webb, USFK	Mr. PARK Sang Woo
Mr. Francis K. Cook, USFK	Mr. LEE An Hae
Mr. Ogden C. Reed, 8th Army	Mr. YANG Bo Sung
Mr. Arthur Hopper, 8th Army	Mr. LEE Teak Nyung
	Mr. BAIK Nahk Jun
	Mr. KIM Tong Kyu
	Mr. OH Myong Too
	Mr. LEE Churl Hee

2. Subject: Withholding Tax (Joint Committee Memorandum, same subject, dated 19 January 1967).

3. Recommendation: It is recommended that the attached Memorandum of Agreement be approved.

210

4. Security Classification: Unclassified.

FoR: COLONEL THOMAS A. TAYLOR, JR.　　　MR. NAM SANG CHIN
Chairman, United States Component　　　Alternate Chairman
Financial Affairs Subcommittee　　　　 Republic of Korea Component
　　　　　　　　　　　　　　　　　　　　 Finance Subcommittee

APPROVED BY THE JOINT COMMITTEE

ROBERT J. FRIEDMAN　　　　　　　　　　YOON HA JONG
Lieutenant General　　　　　　　　　　 Republic of Korea Representative
United States Air Force
United States Representative

2

6 February 1968

M E M O R A N D U M   O F   A G R E E M E N T

1. Reference is made to:

    a. Article XVII of the Agreed Minutes to the Status of
Forces Agreement Between the United States of America and the Republic
of Korea, 9 July 1966.

    b. Article VIII of the Agreement Between the Republic of
Korea and the United States of America Regarding the Status of the
Korean Service Corps, 23 February 1967.

    c. Republic of Korea Income Tax Law No. 1966, promulgated on
29 November 1967.

    d. Republic of Korea Presidential Decree No. 3320, promulgated
on 30 December 1967.

2. In consonance with the foregoing references, it is agreed that:

    a. The expression "employer" refers to the United States
Armed Forces (including nonappropriated fund organizations and USFK
invited contractors). The expression "employee" refers to any civilian
(including personnel of the Korean Service Corps) employed by an employer
except a domestic employed by an individual member of the United States
Armed Forces, the civilian component, or dependents of the foregoing.
Such employees shall be nationals of the Republic of Korea.

    b. Employer will withhold income tax from the pay of his
employees effective with the first pay period beginning on or after
1 February 1968. Taxes will be withheld in accordance with the rates
established by reference 1c.

    c. Employer will forward tax remittances to the ROK Government
not later than the end of the month following the month in which salary
payment is made to the employee. Remittance may be in won, won check,

2/2

or U. S. dollar check. All remittances will be deposited in the account of the Yongsan Internal Revenue Office at the Bank of Korea, #110-3Ka, Namdaemun-Ro, Chung-Ku, Seoul, Korea. Remittances will be accompanied by 2 copies of each payroll which will include the employee's name, taxable income, tax amount, pay period covered, and unit designation.

     d. All employees will be granted a 40% discount in tax amount as provided by paragraph (3), Article 43, of ROK Income Tax Law No. 1966.

     e. Employer responsibility for the collection of taxes begins on the effective date of withholding, as stated in paragraph 2b above. Taxes levied by the ROK Government on an employee prior to that date will be a matter solely between the employee and the ROK Government.

     f. Employer has the responsibility for controlling the computation, withholding and remittance of income tax of employees, as provided for in this agreement.

COLONEL THOMAS A. TAYLOR, JR.
Chairman, United States Component
Financial Affairs Subcommittee

MR. NAM SANG CHIN
Alternate Chairman
Republic of Korea Component
Finance Subcommittee

2

JOINT COMMITTEE
UNDER
THE REPUBLIC OF KOREA AND THE UNITED STATES
STATUS OF FORCES AGREEMENT

8 February 1968

MEMORANDUM FOR: THE JOINT COMMITTEE

1. Subcommittee Members:

United States	Republic of Korea
Col Floyd R. Waltz, Jr. - J4, USFK	Mr. SHIM Ui Hwan
Col John T. Horrocks, Jr. - J4, USFK	Mr. HAN Byung Il
LTC Walter A. Brown, Jr. - J4, USFK	Mr. MOON Ki Sang
Col Norman I. Radin - 6314 Spt Wing	Mr. PARK Pil Soo
Osan AB, Korea	Mr. RHEE Eun Tak
LTC James A. Jolley - Eng Office, USFK	Mr. LEE Chang Ha
LTC Paul E. Jones - J5, USFK	Mr. LEE Woong Soo
Maj James L. Hicks - 6314 Spt Wing	Mr. IM Young Duk
Osan AB, Korea	Mr. NAMKOONG Chull
LCDR Raymond F. Milburn - USN	Mr. KIM Sae Kwon
Mr. Oliver Kennedy - KPA, EUSA	Mr. SONG Ju In
Mr. Charles E. Coleman - PACEX	Mr. DOKKO Young
Mr. Lawrence D. Hillyer, Jr. - USAEDFE	Mr. KIM Bong Kyun
Mr. Samuel Pollack - SJA, USFK	Mr. OH Myong Too

2. Subject of Recommendation. Interpretation of paragraph 2(b), Article XV, SOFA, in regard to the Trans-Asia Engineering Associates, Inc. Reference Minutes of Joint Committee Meeting 12, 14 August 1967, concerning Collins Radio Company.

3. Proposal that Trans-Asia Engineering Associates, Inc. engaged in business activities in the Republic of Korea pertaining immediately and directly to the Government of the Republic of Korea would not be in violation of paragraph 2(b), Article XV, SOFA, because in this instance and under the special facts appearing, the provision may and should be construed so as to favor those certain business activities which do also bear an indirect yet reasonably close pertaining relation to the United States Armed Forces. This construction of the provision will allow those Trans-Asia Engineering Associates, Inc. employees presently in the Republic of Korea for the purpose of performing contracts with the US Armed Forces to retain the privileges and immunities granted under SOFA even though the Trans-Asia Engineering Associates, Inc. is performing certain contracts with additional personnel, for the Republic of Korea. Invited Contractor privileges and immunities granted under SOFA will not be extended to the additional personnel of Trans-Asia Engineering Associates, Inc. employed on the contract with the Republic of Korea.

4. Recommandation. It is recommended that the construction as outlined in paragraph 3 above be adopted.

_____   _____
SHIM UI HWAN   COLONEL FLOYD R. WALTZ, JR.
Chairman, ROK Commerce   Chairman, US Commerce
Subcommittee   Subcommittee

APPROVED BY THE JOINT COMMITTEE ON

_____   _____
YOON HA JONG   ROBERT J. FRIEDMAN
Republic of Korea Representative   Lieutenant General
                                          United States Air Force
                                          United States Representative

215

12 February 1968

MEMORANDUM FOR: The Joint Committee

SUBJECT: Designation of US Invited Contractor under Article XV, Status
of Forces Agreement

1. References:

a. Paragraph 2, Article XV, Status of Forces Agreement.

b. US Commerce Subcommittee Memorandum of Consultation,
dated 24 Oct 67, subject as above (Inclosure 1).

c. ROK Commerce Subcommittee Memorandum of Consultation,
dated 13 Dec 67, subject as above (Inclosure 2).

2. The United States, after consultation with the ROK Commerce
Subcommittee and after having duly considered their views, has designated the Smithsonian Institution as a US invited contractor for
execution of contract number F44620-67-C-0013 for the purpose of
ecological study.

3. Pertinent data concerning US citizen employees will be
provided to the Joint Secretariat in the established periodic arrival
and departure format.

2 Incl
as

ROBERT J. FRIEDMAN
Lieutenant General
United States Air Force
United States Representative
Joint Committee

226

JOINT COMMITTEE
UNDER
THE REPUBLIC OF KOREA AND THE UNITED STATES
STATUS OF FORCES AGREEMENT

USFK DJ   24 October 1967

SUBJECT: Designation of US Invited Contractor under Article XV,
Status of Forces Agreement

TO: Chairman
           ROK Commerce Subcommittee

1. References: a. Paragraph 2, Article XV of the Status of Forces
Agreement.

        b. Memorandum to: Joint Committee, dated 30 June 1967, subject:
Report of invited contractors with contracts expiring after 30 June 1967.

2. The Government of the Republic of Korea is informed through this
written consultive process that the United States Forces, Korea, proposes
to extend the invited contractor status of the US firm listed below from
the original expiration date of 14 October 1967 through 30 June 1968.

3. The following data is provided:

        a. Company name: Smithsonian Institution.

        b. Local Address: In care of US Embassy, Seoul.

        c. Identification of US citizen employees: Provided to the
Joint Secretariat in the established periodic reporting procedures.

        d. Number of US and ROK employees: 1 US employee and no ROK
employees.

        e. Reasons for Designation of an Invited Contractor: Technical
qualifications of the contractor, in that Smithsonian Institution provides necessary training and guidance to ROK scientists.

        f. Location of Contract: Operations under this contract are
conducted primarily in uninhabited areas in and below the southern half
of the Demilitarized Zone.

        g. Type of Contract: Conducting an ecological study, i.e. to
study the adaptation made by plant and animal life in areas previously
inhabited by man as they revert to the natural wild state. This contract
is also assisting in tracking down causes of hemhorragic fever in the
Republic of Korea.

217

USFK DJ   24 October 1967
SUBJECT: Designation of US Invited Contractor under Article XV,
          Status of Forces Agreement

       h. Length of Contract: The contract extension is for the
period 15 October 1967 through 30 June 1968.

       i. Sponsoring Component Command: US Air Forces, Korea.

    4. The United States certifies that the Smithsonian Institution
is present in the Republic of Korea solely for the purpose of executing
contracts with the United States, for the benefit of the United States
Armed Forces or other armed forces under the Unified Command receiving
logistical support from the United States Forces.

    5. The view of the Government of the Republic of Korea are
earnestly solicited prior to United States extension of invited contractor status for the remainder of the contract in order that the work
outlined above may be efficiently performed. You may be assured that
your views will be considered carefully.

    6. Your early reply will be greatly appreciated.

                        FLOYD R. WALTZ, JR.
                        Colonel, United States Army
                        Chairman, US Commerce Subcommittee

2

218

MINISTRY OF COMMERCE AND INDUSTRY
REPUBLIC OF KOREA
SEOUL, KOREA

13 Dec. 1967

SUBJECT: Designation of US Invited Contractor under Article XV, Status of Forces Agreement

TO: Chairman, US Commerce Subcommittee

1. References:

    a. Paragraph 2, Article XV, Status of Forces Agreement.

    b. US Commerce Subcommittee Memorandum of Consultation, dated 24 October 1967, subject as above, pertaining to a contract for conducting an ecological study, ie, to study the adaptation made by plant and animal life in areas previously inhabited by man as they revert to the natural wild state.

    2. The US memorandum, reference 1b above, has been reviewed and the Government of the Republic of Korea fully understands the requirement for an invited contractor in this instance.

                                        Chairman
                                        ROK Commerce Subcommittee

219

USFK DJ-O   8 February 1968

MEMORANDUM FOR: The Joint Committee

SUBJECT: Designation of US Invited Contractor under Article XV,
          Status of Forces Agreement.

    1. References:

        a. Para 2, Article XV, Status of Forces Agreement.

        b. US Commerce Subcommittee Memorandum of Consultation,
dated 4 Jan 1968, subject as above. (Incl 1)

        c. ROK Commerce Subcommittee Memorandum of Consultation,
dated 1 Feb 1968, subject as above. (Incl 2)

    2. The United States, after consultation with the ROK Commerce
Subcommittee and after having duly considered their views, has designated Barclay Overseas, Inc. as a US Invited Contractor, for the
execution of contract F62562-67-C-0363 for furnishing and delivering
Minnesota Mining copying machines, thermofax brand copy paper, and
other copying products to the US Armed Forces in Korea.

    3. Pertinent data concerning US citizen employees will be
provided to the Joint Secretariat in the established periodic arrival
and departure format.

2 Incl   ROBERT J. FRIEDMAN
  as   Lieutenant General, USAF
                                          Chief of Staff

220

USFK DJ   4 January 1968

MEMORANDUM FOR: Chairman, ROK Commerce Subcommittee

SUBJECT: Designation of US Invited Contractors under Article XV,
Status of Forces Agreement

1. Reference: Paragraph 2, Article XV of the Status of Forces
Agreement.

2. The Government of the Republic of Korea is informed through
this written consultative process that the United States Forces, Korea
proposes to continue to extend invited contractor status to Barclay
Overseas, Inc. on the contract described in paragraph 3 below.

3. The following data is provided:

a. Company Name: Barclay Overseas, Inc.

b. Local Address: #50-2, Susomun-dong, Sudaemun-ku, Seoul,
Korea.

c. Identification of U.S. employee: Patrick E. O'Sullivan,
Manager, UN Village Apt D-2, Seoul, Korea.

d. Number of U.S. employees   _1_.
   Number of ROK employees   _3_.

e. Reasons for Designation of an Invited Contractor: Unavailability of materials and services required by U.S. standards. The contractor is required to furnish and deliver Minnesota Mining products of
copying machines, thermofax brand copy paper, and other copying products
to the U.S. Armed Forces in Korea. They are also required to provide
necessary maintenance on the copying machines involved.

f. Location of contract: Kimpo, Kunsan, and Osan Air Bases.
Also, all U.S. Army installations in Korea.

g. Type of Contract: Furnish and deliver Minnesota Mining
copying machines, thermofax brand copy paper and other copying products
to the U.S. Armed Forces in Korea. Also to provide necessary maintenance
on the copying machines involved.

USFK DJ
SUBJECT: Designation of US Invited Contractors under Article XV,
Status of Forces Agreement

h. Length of contract: 15 Jan 1967 to 5 April 1968.

i. Sponsoring Component Command: Commander, Air Forces Korea.

4. The United States certifies that the named contractor is present in the Republic of Korea solely for the purpose of executing a contract with the United States, for the benefit of the United States Armed Forces or other Armed Forces under the Unified Command receiving logistical support from the United States Forces.

5. The views of the Government of the Republic of Korea are earnestly solicited prior to United States continuation of invited contractor status to Barclay Overseas, Inc. to perform the work outlined above. You may be assured that your views will be considered carefully.

6. Your early reply will be greatly appreciated.

FLOYD R. WALTZ, JR.
Colonel   USA
Chairman, US Commerce Subcommittee

2

MINISTRY OF COMMERCE AND INDUSTRY
REPUBLIC OF KOREA
SEOUL, KOREA

1 February 1968

SUBJECT: Designation of US Invited Contractor under Article XV, Status of Forces Agreement.

TO   : Chairman, US Commerce Subcommittee.

1. References;

    a. Paragraph 2, Article XV, Status of Forces Agreement.

    b. US Commerce Subcommittee Memorandum of Consultation, Dated 4 January 1968, subject as above, pertaining to a contract for furnishing and delivering Minnesota Mining copying machine, thermofax brand copy paper and other copying products to the U.S. Armed Forces in Korea.

    2. The US memorandum, reference 1b above, has been reviewed and the Government of the Republic of Korea fully understands the requirement for an invited contractor in this instance.

for Chairman
ROK Commerce Subcommittee

JOINT ROK - US PRESS RELEASE
TWENTY-FIRST ROK-US JOINT COMMITTEE MEETING
21 FEBRUARY 1968

The ROK-US Joint Committee on 21 February approved procedures for the US armed forces in Korea to begin the withholding of income taxes of its Korean employees, as provided in the ROK-US SOFA. The United States armed forces will deduct ROK income taxes from the wages of its Korean employees. The income tax deductions will be at the rates established by recently revised ROK income tax legislation. The taxes collected will be deposited in the Bank of Korea by the US armed forces, to the account of the Government of the Republic of Korea.

The Joint Committee also approved eleven recommendations of its Facilities and Areas Subcommittee relating to acquisition and release of areas and facilities utilized by the US armed forces. It also assigned seventeen new tasks to the same Subcommittee. The Criminal Jurisdiction Subcommittee was assigned two new tasks, the first relating to procedures pertaining to the control of privately owned firearms of US Forces, Korea personnel. The second task relating to US-ROK cooperation with regard to offenses committed by Korean nationals against United States Forces, Korea personnel and property. The Ad Hoc Entry and Exit Subcommittee was assigned a new task concerning review and possible revision of certain entry and exit reporting procedures of USFK personnel.

In addition, the US and ROK Representatives exchanged several memoranda relating to various aspects of the implementation of the SOFA.

The ROK Representative, Mr. YOON Ha Jong, Director of the Europe and America Bureau of the Foreign Ministry, presided at this meeting which was held at the ROK Capitol Building. The next Joint Committee meeting is scheduled for 14 March, in the US SOFA Conference Room, Yongsan.

2

외 무 부

미이 720-   196 8 . 3 . 7 .

수 신 : 배북처참조

참 조 :

제 목 : 한.미 합동위원회 회의록 송부

　　　　1. 한.미간 군대지위협정에 의하여 196 8 . 2 . 21 .에
개최된 한.미 합동위원회 제 21 차 회의의 회의록을 별첨 송부하오니
참고 하시기 바랍니다.

　　　　2. 본 회의록은 한.미 양측의 합의에 의하여서만 공개될
수 있는 문서이오니 유념하시기 바랍니다.

첨부 : 합동위원회 제 21 차 회의록

　　　　　　　　　　　　　　　외 무 부 장 관

배부처 : 법무부장관 (법무실장, 검찰국장), 국방부장관 (기획국장,
　　　　시설국장), 재무부장관 (세관국장, 세제국장),
　　　　상공부장관 (상역국장), 노동청장 (노정국장),
　　　　교통부장관 (항공국장), 내무부장관 (치안국장), 주미
주일, 주중, 주비대사 경제기획원장관 (3)외국국장)

226

공   란

공 란

공   란

공   란

공   란

9. The US Representative proposed inclusion in the minutes of the twenty-first Joint Committee meeting, the task assigned to the Financial Affairs Subcommittee by the Republic of Korea and US Representatives on 6 February 1968 (Inclosure 11). The US Representative stated that he was happy to note that this newly assigned task was related to the concurrent agreement to have the US armed forces in Korea begin income tax withholdings of their Korean employees, effective 1 February 1968. He stated that the withholding of these income taxes was in accordance with

232

21st JC
21 Feb 68

3

These minutes are c●sidered as official documents p●taining to both Governments and will not be released without mutual agreement.

the provisions of Agreed Minute 3 of Article XVII of the SOFA. These income taxes of USFK's approximately 40,000 Korean employees will be deposited by the US armed forces directly into designated bank accounts of the Government of the Republic of Korea. The new task provided that, in view of the administrative burden entailed in the withholding of such income taxes, mutual consultations were required to formulate agreed recommendations concerning appropriate reimbursement to the US Forces, Korea, for the expenses incurred in connection with the withholding of income taxes of USFK's Korean employees.

10. The ROK Representative stated that, inasmuch as the actual withholding of income taxes of the USFK-employed Korean personnel involved a tremendous administrative burden and added costs, the Korean component believed that recognition should be given to this burden, and to the gesture of goodwill on the part of US authorities in undertaking to assume this burden. Therefore, the task as formulated was considered most appropriate. However, it should be noted that there was, at present, no legal basis for the envisioned financial compensation and, therefore, that the task was not one to be solved quickly. The ROK Representative indicated that, with this understanding, the ROK Representative whole heartedly agreed to assigning to the Financial Affairs Subcommittee the task of exploring the possibility and determining the extent of the financial compensation. The US Representative stated that he felt confident that resolution of this task could be achieved in a spirit of mutual understanding.

11. The ROK Representative stated he would like to present a task to be assigned to the Commerce Subcommittee. He stated that this was another example of assignment of a task agreed upon since the last Joint Committee meeting. The memorandum (Inclosure 12) assigning the task was signed on 6 February 1968 by the two Representatives and the Subcommittee has submitted its recommendations. The task assigned was to determine if the Trans-Asia Engineering Associates, Inc., a US invited contractor, could also execute a proposed contract with a ROK Government Agency (in this particular case, the City of Seoul), without forfeiting the privileges and immunities granted under the SOFA, notwithstanding the provisions of paragraph 2(b), Article XV. The ROK Representative proposed that the assignment of this task to the Commerce Subcommittee be included in the minutes of the twenty-first Joint Committee meeting. The US Representative concurred.

12. The US Representative proposed assignment of a new task to the Criminal Jurisdiction Subcommittee (Inclosure 13). Under the provisions of paragraph 6(b), of Article XXII, and Agreed View Number 5,

21st JC
21 Feb 68

4

These minutes are considered as official documents pertaining to both Governments and will not be released without mutual agreement.

the US authorities have been reporting the disposition of cases of US armed forces personnel suspected of offenses against the Republic of Korea and Korean nationals. No Joint Committee procedures, however, have yet been developed in regard to the disposition of cases in which Korean nationals were suspected of the commission of offenses against US armed forces in Korea, or against United States personnel assigned to such forces. The Criminal Jurisdiction Subcommittee is being assigned this new task under the provisions of Articles XXII and XXV of the SOFA. The Criminal Jurisdiction Subcommittee was requested to recommend establishment of procedures which would enhance the mutual cooperation required to protect US armed forces personnel, US property, and US installations within the Republic of Korea. The US Representative, in proposing this important new task to the Criminal Jurisdiction Subcommittee, expressed the belief that the procedures recommended would enhance mutual understanding and thus promote ROK-US friendship and understanding. The ROK Representative concurred in this assignment.

13. The ROK Representative presented another task to be assigned to the Criminal Jurisdiction Subcommittee (Inclosure 14). He stated that the need was self-evident for mutually agreed procedures pertaining to the control of privately owned firearms of personnel covered by the SOFA. Possession of firearms not conforming to pertinent Korean regulations could cause serious legal problems for the individual concerned and uniform and effective control of firearms was highly desirable for general public safety. The ROK Representative proposed that the Criminal Jurisdiction Subcommittee be assigned the task of formulating mutually agreed procedures on this subject and of recommending them to the Joint Committee. The US Representative concurred.

14. The US Representative stated that the Joint Committee Ad Hoc Subcommittee on Entry and Exit completed expeditiously all of the tasks assigned to it in the Spring of 1967. These procedures have been in effect for many months and have generally worked very well. Experience over the past months, however, has indicated a possible need for minor modifications in some of the procedures. The US Representative, therefore, proposed that the Ad Hoc Entry and Exit Subcommittee review the agreements that it developed in 1967 and recommend to the Joint Committee any revisions in these procedures which would improve their effectiveness (Inclosure 15).

15. The ROK Representative indicated that he concurred in the reactivation of the Ad Hoc Subcommittee and to the assignment of the proposed task. In a discussion of the task, Mr. LEE Sun Jung, who is Chairman of the ROK component of the Ad Hoc Subcommittee, commented on paragraph 2 of the task relating to application of entry and

234

21st JC
21 Feb 68

5

These minutes are considered as official documents pertaining to both Governments and will not be released without mutual agreement.

exit procedures to US invited contractor personnel. Noting that a previous proposal by the ROK Representative on this point had remained unanswered by the US side, he stated that it was the ROK position that the entry and exit procedures apply not only to USFK personnel, but also to US invited contractor personnel, who are not covered by previously adopted procedures. Further discussion brought out that the US component of the Joint Committee has been making regular reports on arrivals, departures, place of residence, and change of status of US invited contractor personnel, in accordance with Joint Committee-approved procedures recommended by the Commerce Sub-committee. Correlation of current entry and exit procedures for US invited contractor personnel, especially relating to change of status of such personnel in Korea, is desirable. It was agreed that the Ad Hoc Entry and Exit Subcommittee would make specific recommendations on these points, in the light of provisions of Article VIII and Article XV of the SOFA, as well as the previous decisions of the Joint Committee on the entry and exit of personnel covered by the SOFA.

235

21st JC
21 Feb 68

6

19. The ROK Representative presented the recommendations of the Financial Affairs Subcommittee, relating to withholding income taxes of USFK-employed Koreans (Inclosure 22). The ROK Representative explained that the second meeting of the Preliminary Working Group, on 19 January 1967, had assigned the task of devising procedures to implement the provisions of paragraph 3, Agreed Minutes to Article XVII. The implementation of the said provisions required the revision of pertinent ROK income tax legislation. The necessary legislation was delayed until last November due to circumstances beyond the control of the Executive branch of the Government. Hence, the considerable delay for the conclusion of the task in question. The task involved tremendous administrative details because of the complicated structure of Korean income

236

21st JC
21 Feb 68

7

These minutes are considered as official documents pertaining to both Governments and will not be released without mutual agreement.

tax legislation, the size of the USFK organization, and the number of employees affected. The revised legislation was to become effective on 1 January 1968. However, due to the limited time available between the passage of the revised legislation and its effective date, and above all, the tremendous technical problems involved, the Subcommittee failed to meet the deadline despite frantic hard work by members of the Subcommittee. The Subcommittee submitted its recommendations on 6 February 1968. They were approved on the same day by the two Representatives and became effective immediately, pursuant to the previous agreement of the Joint Committee. The recommendations stipulated that:

    a. The expression "employer" refers to the USFK, including nonappropriated fund organizations and US invited contractors.

    b. The expression "employee" refers to any Korean civilian employed by an "employer," including Korean Service Corps personnel, but excluding a domestic employed privately by the personnel covered by the SOFA.

    c. Withholdings will be effected in accordance with rates established by pertinent ROK legislation, without modification, starting with the full pay period beginning on or after 1 February 1968. Tax remittances will be made not later than the end of the following month of a pay period, to the Bank of Korea, in the account of the Yongsan Internal Revenue Office.

    d. The employer has the responsibility for controlling the computation, withholding, and remittances of income taxes of employees.

20. The ROK Representative, on behalf of the Korean component, expressed his deep appreciation for the hard work of the Subcommittee members and his whole-hearted congratulations for the successful completion of this complicated and difficult task. He stated that a word of recognition was due also to the active role and contributions of the two SOFA Secretaries in this happy result. The ROK Representative expressed again his deep appreciation for the gesture of good will on the part of the United States Government in assuming the tremendous administrative burden involved. The ROK Representative proposed formal confirmation of the Joint Committee approval of the Subcommittee's recommendations.

21. The US Representative stated he was happy to confirm Joint Committee approval of these recommendations and to agree to the

21st JC
21 Feb 68

8

These minutes are considered as official documents pertaining to both Governments and will not be released without mutual agreement.

inclusion of the recommendations of the Financial Affairs Subcommittee, which were approved by the United States and Republic of Korea Representatives on 6 February 1968, in the minutes of this Joint Committee meeting. He joined with the ROK Representative in congratulating all ROK and US personnel involved in the achievement of agreement on this important task.

22. The ROK Representative presented the recommendation of the Commerce Subcommittee (Inclosure 23), relating to the request of the ROK Government to obtain the services of the Trans-Asia Engineering Associates, Inc., currently an invited contractor of USFK. The Subcommittee recommended that the Joint Committee give its approval for Trans-Asia Engineering Associates, Inc., to engage in business activities in the Republic of Korea pertaining immediately and directly to the Government of the Republic of Korea, without constituting a violation of the relevant provisions of the SOFA. The ROK Representative agreed that, in this instance and under the special facts appearing, the SOFA provisions may and should be construed so as to favor those certain business activities which bear an indirect, yet reasonably close, relationship to the mission of the US armed forces. The ROK Representative therefore proposed acceptance of the recommendations of the Commerce Subcommittee to permit Trans-Asia Engineering Associates, Inc., to retain the privileges and immunities granted under the SOFA even though it performed certain contracts with additional personnel for the Government of the Republic of Korea. The ROK Representative stated he understood that invited contractor privileges and immunities granted under the SOFA would not be extended to the additional personnel of the Trans-Asia Engineering Associates, Inc., employed on the contract with the Government of the Republic of Korea.

23. The US Representative stated he was happy to approve the recommendations of the Commerce Subcommittee, concerning Trans-Asia Engineering Associates, Inc. The US Representative confirmed that this US invited contractor was authorized to perform contracts for the Republic of Korea Government, with the understanding that the additional US personnel employed on these Republic of Korea contracts would not be extended the privileges and immunities of the SOFA.

238

9

21st JC
21 Feb 68

26. The ROK Representative stated that he wished to refer to the statement made by the US Representative at the twentieth meeting of the Joint Committee, with regard to the details of security offenses of the Republic of Korea and related provisions thereto. The US view expressed by the US Representative in this matter was most carefully studied by the ROK component. Expressing once again, on behalf of the ROK component, his deep appreciation for the keen interest and thoughtful consideration of the US component, the ROK Representative stated he wished to clarify the position of the ROK component on the question. There is no doubt that the question as to whether a particular offense constitutes a security offense or not should be decided by the nature and content of the offense in question. However, the intent of the Agreed Minutes regarding Article XXII, paragraph 2(c), is understood to require mutual notification of the details of

21st JC
21 Feb 68

10

These minutes are considered as official documents pertaining to both Governments and wil● ●t be released without mutual ● eement.

security offenses under respective legislation but in no way to demand exchange of "guidelines" for defining such security offenses.

27. The ROK Representative stated that it is also obvious that the definition of security offenses was matter to be decided by the country concerned. The list prepared by the ROK side included only those offenses which involved elements affecting the security of the Republic of Korea (either by reason of the basic interests affected or the offense-constituting elements), based on the enumeration in paragraph 2(c), Article XXII, which is not limitative but inclusive, as well as the concept of national security set forth in ROK legislation. The primary concern in preparation of the list was to limit the extent of security offenses, and it was believed that the same care was applied to the preparation of the US list. In short, the position of the ROK Government was that the Korean list should be considered definitive, and that if a suspected offense fell within the category listed, the case should be considered in the first instance constituting a security offense and the investigation should proceed accordingly. However, if the list were to be considered otherwise (as mere "guidelines"), it was feared that it could cause disagreement and friction between ROK and US authorities. Such disagreement could develop over whether or not a particular case constituted a security offense. Such a disagreement could arise whenever a case occurred, even at the initial stages of investigation, and thereby greatly hinder rapid and efficient progress of the investigation. It should be pointed out, the ROK Representative emphasized, that the true nature of an offense cannot be determined until after conclusion of the investigation.

28. The ROK Representative stated that, in this connection, the Government of the Republic of Korea gave clear and definite assurances to the United States authorities that it would be most restrictive in its determination to treat individual cases as security offenses. The Government of the Republic of Korea was prepared to transfer custody, voluntarily or upon request, as soon as it became clear that there was no security implications in a particular case; it will be most discreet in its decisions relating to the term "of particular importance," in connection with paragraph 1(a), Agreed Understanding Re Agreed Minute Re Paragraph 3(b) of Article XXII. These assurances were willingly given here, because the ROK authorities knew that actions contrary to these assurances would not serve the mutual interests of the ROK and the US. The ROK Representative stated that it should be noted that so far, both before and after the entry into force of the Status of Forces Agreement, there have been no cases of security offenses involving US personnel. No changes in these circumstances

21st JC
21 Feb 68

240

11

These minutes are considered as official documents pertaining to both Governments and will not be released without mutual agreement.

were foreseen and there is no reason to anticipate that there will be many such offenses in the future. Such being the case, the whole question may not be of a great practical significance. Even if, unfortunately, some such cases occur, there are many mechanisms in the SOFA which would prevent serious difficulties from arising in solving these cases to the mutual satisfaction.

29. The ROK Representative stated that he wished to ask the US component to accept the foregoing Korean position, at least for the time being. If, after passage of time and experience in actual implementation, there should arise serious problems in connection with the list of security offenses, the ROK component will always be ready to cooperate to find a workable solution.

30. The US Representative thanked the ROK Representative for his extremely thoughtful reply to the US Representative's comments in regard to the list of security offenses of the Republic of Korea, which were made at the twentieth meeting of the Joint Committee. A comparison of the comments of the US Representative and the reply of the ROK Representative indicated that the basic views of both countries appeared indeed very similar. However, the US component was unable to accept the ROK position at this time and wished to consider the matter further. For example, it was noted that the matter of pre-trial custody of a suspect was involved. In this regard, the Agreed Understanding to Paragraph 5, Article XXII, provided that, in connection with security offenses, that there must be mutual United States - Republic of Korea agreement as to the circumstances in which such custody was appropriate. The US Representative stated that the US component would like to consider the ROK position further and comment at a later meeting. In the meantime, the US component suggested that if an offense occurred which was suspected of having security implications, the suspected offender should remain in the custody of the US authorities pending the conclusion of an investigation which substantiated the security implications of the offense.

31. The US Representative presented a memorandum to the Joint Committee informing the Republic of Korea Government of the designation of two new invited contractors under Article XV of the Status of Forces Agreement. After consultation with Republic of Korea Commerce Subcommittee personnel, the US Forces, Korea designated Barclay Overseas, Inc., (Inclosure 24), and the Smithsonian Institution (Inclosure 25), as US invited contractors. Pertinent data concerning employees of these invited contractors will be provided to the Government of the Republic of Korea, in accordance with mutually approved procedures.

21st JC
21 Feb 68

12

These minutes are c●idered as official documents p●taining to both Governments and will not be released without mutual agreement.

32. The ROK Representative stated that the designation of the Smithsonian Institute and Barclay Overseas, Inc., as US invited contractors, was duly noted.

33. The ROK Representative stated that he wished to include in the official Joint Committee minutes the substance of correspondence between the two SOFA Secretaries with regard to designation of the communications authorities, in accordance with Article III, paragraph 2(b). The ROK Secretary informed the US Secretary by his letter, dated 29 January 1968, of the designation of the Ministry of Communications, represented by Mr. JIN Keun Hyun, Director, Bureau of Telecommunications, as the ROK communications authority referred to by the said SOFA Article. On his part, the US SOFA Secretary, in his letter dated 12 February 1968, confirmed that Colonel Jack N. Cole, USA, Assistant Chief of Staff, J-6, US Forces, Korea, continued to be the designated US communications authority in accordance with Article III. Mr. Richard W. DeWeil, a member of the staff of Colonel Cole, continued to be the US Frequency Coordinator and US liaison with the ROK Government in matters concerning radio frequencies.

34. The US Representative acknowledged that the information set forth by the ROK Representative concerning designated United States and Republic of Korea communications authorities, in accordance with paragraph 2(b) of Article III, had been exchanged. The US Representative agreed that this information should be incorporated into the minutes of this Joint Committee meeting.

35. The ROK Representative noted for the record that the ROK SOFA Secretary had transmitted to the US SOFA Secretary, the Republic of Korea Government report on the disposition of offenses, in which the Republic of Korea exercised jurisdiction over US Forces, Korea personnel, for the month of December 1967. The ROK Representative proposed that this transmittal be recorded in the Joint Committee minutes.

36. The US Representative acknowledged receipt of the Republic of Korea Government report for December 1967, on the disposition of offenses in which the Republic of Korea exercised jurisdiction over USFK personnel.

37. The US Representative noted for the record that the US SOFA Secretary had furnished the following information to the ROK SOFA Secretary, in the implementation of United States - Republic of Korea Status of Forces Agreement:

21st JC
21 Feb 68

13

These minutes are considered as official documents pertaining to both Governments and will not be released without mutual agreement.

a. Five copies of reports on the US armed forces disposition of cases for the month of December 1967.

b. Twenty copies of a report listing arrivals, departures, and address changes of US invited contractor personnel and their dependents, dated 31 January 1968.

c. Twenty copies of the report of US armed forces personnel, the civilian component, invited contractors, and dependents entering or departing the Republic of Korea during the month of January, 1968.

38. The ROK Representative confirmed the receipt by the ROK SOFA Secretary of the documents enumerated by the US Representative.

39. The ROK Representative stated that he would like to make a statement with regard to past increases in utility rates. He recalled that at the sixteenth meeting of the Joint Committee, on 19 October 1967, the ROK Representative proposed that since it may take some time for the Commerce Subcommittee to recommend consultation procedures provided for in paragraph 1 of the Agreed Minutes to Article VI, maximum use be made of the existing arrangements for revision of individual contracts necessitated by imminent increases in utility rates. Subsequently, revised contracts contained a clause to the effect that the revision was subject to Joint Committee consultation. It now appeared that the US agencies directly concerned have interpreted this clause as suspensive. It was pointed out that, if the US agencies insisted on the suspensive nature of the clause, it would be equivalent to exercising a veto. In that case, such action would not be consonant with the spirit of the SOFA provisions, which uses the expression "consultation," not implying "consent." It was feared that if strictly insisted upon, the new clause in the contracts could become a source of unnecessary friction, which obviously was not the intention of either Government. The ROK Representative suggested that the USFK take action to prevent unnecessary misunderstanding.

40. The ROK Representative also stated he would like to refer to another aspect of the utility rates problem. The said Agreed Minutes define the subject of Joint Committee consultation as "any changes determined by the authorities of the Republic of Korea..." The text is believed to exclude any contract not controlled by ROK Government authorities. There has been a case involving water supply to the Kunsan Air Base, which has been effected by a local irrigation association. The US contracting officer refused to negotiate a rate increase necessary to cover costs on the grounds of the lack of prior Joint Committee consultation. This necessitated a trip

21st JC
21 Feb 68

14

These minutes are considered as official documents pertaining to both Governments and will not be released without mutual agreement.

to Seoul by a representative of the Association, which was obviously absurd in view of the amount involved. The ROK Representative suggested that the USFK take action to clarify its views on the issue.

41. The US Representative assured the ROK Representative that early resolution of this Utilities Subcommittee task was urgent. He proposed that the Utility Subcommittee be urged to have its recommendations on the task assigned to it completed as soon as possible, and not later than the next Joint Committee meeting, tentatively scheduled for mid-March. The US Representative also reiterated his previous agreement, made at the sixteenth Joint Committee meeting, that simultaneous negotiations under applicable contracts should proceed. He emphasized that it was the desire of the US Representative that these questions be resolved on a mutually agreeable basis at the earliest possible date.

42. After further discussion of various aspects of this problem, it was agreed that the ROK and US Representatives would take under consideration the recommendations of the Utilities Subcommittee as soon as they were presented, hopefully within the next week or two. It was also agreed that Joint Committee consultation pertained only to "utilities and services which are owned, controlled, or regulated by the Government of the Republic of Korea, or local subdivisions thereof." (Article VI, paragraph 1). Other private contracts, even if they pertained to utilities, would not be subject to Joint Committee consultation. It was agreed that the case concerning the Korean irrigation association supplying water to the Kunsan Air Base would be taken up on the basis of the agreement reached at the sixteenth Joint Committee meeting. The US Representative emphasized that, in addition to expeditious action by the Utilities Subcommittee, simultaneous negotiations under applicable contracts should proceed, as previously agreed by the ROK and US Government Representatives, at the 19 October 1967 Joint Committee meeting.

43. The ROK Representative proposed that, following the past practice, the next Joint Committee meeting be held at 1500 hours, on Thursday, 14 March 1968, in the US SOFA Conference Room, Yongsan. The US Representative concurred.

44. The ROK Representative proposed adoption of the joint press release, as prepared by the two SOFA Secretaries (Inclosure 26). The US Representative concurred.

21st JC
21 Feb 68

244

15

These minutes are c█idered as official documents p█taining to both Governments and will not be released without mutual agreement.

45. The meeting was adjourned at 1715 hours.

26 Inclosures

YOON HA JONG
REPUBLIC OF KOREA
REPRESENTATIVE

ROBERT J. FRIEDMAN
LIEUTENANT GENERAL
UNITED STATES AIR FORCE
UNITED STATES REPRESENTATIVE

245.

16

공   란

공　란

공   란

공 란

공   란

공   란

공　　　란

공   란

공   란

공   란

공 란

공   란

공   란

These minutes are considered as official documents pertaining to both Governments and w███not be released without mutual ███reement.

JOINT COMMITTEE
UNDER
THE REPUBLIC OF KOREA AND THE UNITED STATES
STATUS OF FORCES AGREEMENT

6 February 1968

MEMORANDUM FOR: Chairmen, ROK Finance Subcommittee/
US Financial Affairs Subcommittee

SUBJECT: Withholding Tax (Article XVII, para 3, Agreed Minutes)

REFERENCES: (a) Memorandum to Chairmen, Finance Subcom-
mittee, subject: Withholding Tax, (Inclosure 9,
Minutes of Second Meeting of the "Preliminary
Working Group", 19 January 1967).

(b) Recommendations of the Financial Affairs Subcommittee, dated 6 February 1968, subject as
above, approved by the ROK-US Representatives
of the Joint Committee on 6 February 1968.

    1. It is mutually recognized that the implementation of pro-
cedures embodied in reference (b) above, concerning the withholding
of income taxes of USFK Korean employees in accordance with the
provisions of Article XVII, paragraph 3, Agreed Minutes, will levy
an administrative burden upon the "employer", as defined in Article
XVII, paragraph 1 (a), ROK-US SOFA.

    2. In view of the administrative burden entailed in the with-
holding of income taxes, mutual consultations are required to
formulate agreed recommendations concerning appropriate reimbursement by the Government of the Republic of Korea to the "employer"
for the expenses incurred by the "employer" in the process of withholding of income taxes of United States armed forces Korean employees.

YOON HA JONG
Republic of Korea Representative

ROBERT J. FRIEDMAN
Lieutenant General
United States Air Force
United States Representative

APPROVED BY THE JOINT COMMITTEE ON
21 FEBRUARY 1968 AT TWENTY-FIRST MEETING

259

21st JC (Incl 11)
21 Feb 68

These minutes are considered as official documents pertaining to both
Governments and wi●●ot be released without mutual●reement.

JOINT COMMITTEE
UNDER
THE REPUBLIC OF KOREA AND THE UNITED STATES
STATUS OF FORCES AGREEMENT

6 February 1968

MEMORANDUM FOR: Chairmen, Commerce Subcommittee

SUBJECT: Interpretation of Paragraph 2(b), Article XV, SOFA in
Regard to the Trans-Asia Engineering Associates, Inc.

1. The Government of the Republic of Korea considers it to be in
its best interests to have the services of the Trans-Asia Engineering
Associates, Inc., an invited contractor of the US Forces, Korea, to
perform certain contracts for the Government of the Republic of Korea
with additional personnel.

2. Mutual consultations are requested to determine the applicability
of the provisions of paragraph 2(b), of Article XV, if the agencies of the
Government of the Republic of Korea entered into contracts with the
Trans-Asia Engineering Associates, Inc., without causing the latter to
lose the privileges and immunities granted to it under the SOFA.

_____   _____
YOON HA JONG   ROBERT J. FRIEDMAN
Republic of Korea Representative   Lieutenant General
                                United States Air Force
                                United States Representative

APPROVED BY THE JOINT COMMITTEE ON
21 FEBRUARY 1968 AT TWENTY-FIRST MEETING

21st JC (Incl 12)
21 Feb 68

These minutes are considered as official documents pertaining to both Governments and will not be released without mutual agreement.

**JOINT COMMITTEE
UNDER
THE REPUBLIC OF KOREA AND THE UNITED STATES
STATUS OF FORCES AGREEMENT**

21 February 1968

MEMORANDUM FOR: Chairmen, Criminal Jurisdiction Subcommittee

SUBJECT: Cooperating Procedures on the Disposition of Incidents Involving Korean Nationals

    1. Under the provisions of Paragraph 6(b), Article XXII, and Agreed View No. 5, procedures have been adopted for United States authorities to report the disposition of cases of United States armed forces personnel suspected of offenses against the Republic of Korea and Korean nationals.

    2. No procedures have been adopted for cooperation in regard to the disposition of cases in which Korean nationals were suspected of the commission of offenses against the United States armed forces in Korea, or against US personnel assigned to such forces. Under the provisions of Article XXV and the Agreed Understanding thereto, the establishment of such procedures would further that mutual cooperation required to protect United States armed forces personnel, United States property, and installations within the Republic of Korea.

    3. Your recommendations on cooperating procedures in such dispositions are to be transmitted to the Joint Committee.

YOON HA JONG
Republic of Korea
Representative

ROBERT J. FRIEDMAN
Lieutenant General
United States Air Force
United States Representative

APPROVED BY THE JOINT COMMITTEE ON
21 FEBRUARY 1968 AT TWENTY-FIRST MEETING

21st JC (Incl 13)
21 Feb 68

These minutes are considered as official documents pertaining to both Governments and will not be released without mutual agreement.

**JOINT COMMITTEE
UNDER
THE REPUBLIC OF KOREA AND THE UNITED STATES
STATUS OF FORCES AGREEMENT**

21 February 1968

MEMORANDUM FOR: Chairmen, Criminal Jurisdiction Subcommittee

SUBJECT: Privately Owned Firearms

    1. Mutual procedures pertaining to the control of privately owned firearms of members of the United States armed forces, members of the civilian component, invited contractors, and dependents of the fore-going are desirable.

    2. Your recommendations on such procedures are to be transmitted to the Joint Committee.

YOON HA JONG
Republic of Korea
Representative

ROBERT J. FRIEDMAN
Lieutenant General
United States Air Force
United States Representative

APPROVED BY THE JOINT COMMITTEE ON
21 FEBRUARY 1968 AT TWENTY-FIRST MEETING

21st JC (Incl 14)
21 Feb 68

These minutes are considered as official documents pertaining to both Governments and wi●●ot be released without mutual●●reement.

**JOINT COMMITTEE
UNDER
THE REPUBLIC OF KOREA AND THE UNITED STATES
STATUS OF FORCES AGREEMENT**

21 February 1968

MEMORANDUM FOR: Chairmen, Ad Hoc Entry and Exit Subcommittee

SUBJECT: Request for Review of Procedures Established by the Joint Committee Relative to Article VIII, US-ROK Status of Forces Agreement

1. References:

a. Procedures for notifying the Government of the Republic of Korea of numbers and categories of persons entering and departing, approved by the Joint Committee on 28 April 1967 at its Sixth Meeting.

b. The meaning of the words "reasonable time" in paragraph 4 of the Agreed Minute Re Article VIII, approved by the Joint Committee on 23 March 1967 at its Fourth Meeting.

c. Procedures for notifying the authorities of the Republic of Korea of a change in status of any person brought into the ROK under paragraph 1, Article VIII, approved by the Joint Committee on 28 April 1967 at its Sixth Meeting.

d. Determination of the meaning of the phrase "reasonable time" as expressed in paragraph 5, Article VIII, approved by the Joint Committee on 28 April 1967 at its Sixth Meeting.

e. Procedures and designation of ports of Entry and Exit for the implementation of paragraph 4, Article VIII, approved by the Joint Committee on 22 June 1967 at its Tenth Meeting.

f. Appropriate documentation and verification of status of members of the civilian component, their dependents, and the dependents of members of the United States Armed Forces as provided for in paragraph 4, Article VIII, approved by the Joint Committee on 25 May 1967 at its Eighth Meeting.

21st JC (Incl 15)
21 Feb 68

263.

These minutes are ●sidered as official documents ●rtaining to both Governments and will not be released without mutual agreement.

2. The agreements listed in paragraph 1 above govern various aspects of entry and exit procedures and change of status in accordance with the provisions of Article VIII, US-ROK Status of Forces Agreement. Experience over the past months in the implementation of these agreements has indicated the possible need to modify some of these procedures, and to consider the feasibility of applying such procedures to US invited contractor personnel. It is therefore requested that the Ad Hoc Entry and Exit Subcommittee review these agreements to determine desired changes in these procedures, and prepare and transmit to the Joint Committee recommendations embodying revisions to improve the effectiveness of these procedures.

YOON HA JONG
Republic of Korea Representative

ROBERT J. FRIEDMAN
Lieutenant General
United States Air Force
United States Representative

APPROVED BY THE JOINT COMMITTEE ON
21 FEBRUARY 1968 AT TWENTY-FIRST MEETING

공　　　란

공 란

공   란

공　　　란

공 란

공   란

공   란

공　　란

공   란

공　　　란

공   란

공　　　란

These minutes are considered as official documents pertaining to both Governments and will not be released without mutual agreement.

REPUBLIC OF KOREA - UNITED STATES
FINANCIAL AFFAIRS SUBCOMMITTEE

6 February 1968

MEMORANDUM FOR: THE JOINT COMMITTEE

1. Subcommittee members:

United States	Republic of Korea
COL Thomas A. Taylor, Jr., Chairman	Mr. CHOI Kack Kyu, Chairman
LTC Talmadge L. Bartelle, USFK	Mr. NAM Sang Chin
LTC John F. Rogan, 8th Army	Mr. KIM Thong Bin
LTC Paul V. Colaianni, USFK	Mr. PARK Bong Jin
LTC Mary C. Lane, 8th Army	Mr. PARK Joon Kyu
LCDR R. D. Webb, USFK	Mr. PARK Sang Woo
Mr. Francis K. Cook, USFK	Mr. LEE An Hae
Mr. Ogden C. Reed, 8th Army	Mr. YANG Bo Sung
Mr. Arthur Hopper, 8th Army	Mr. LEE Teak Nyung
	Mr. BAIK Nahk Jun
	Mr. KIM Tong Kyu
	Mr. OH Myong Too
	Mr. LEE Churl Hee

2. Subject: Withholding Tax (Joint Committee Memorandum, same subject, dated 19 January 1967).

3. Recommendation: It is recommended that the attached Memorandum of Agreement be approved.

21st JC (Incl 22)
21 Feb 68

These minutes are considered as official documents pertaining to both
Governments and will not be released without mutual agreement.

4. Security Classification: Unclassified.

_____
MR. NAM SANG CHIN
Alternate Chairman
Republic of Korea Component
Finance Subcommittee

By. COLONEL THOMAS A. TAYLOR, JR.
Chairman, United States Component
Financial Affairs Subcommittee

APPROVED BY THE JOINT COMMITTEE ON
21 FEBRUARY 1968 AT TWENTY-FIRST MEETING

_____
YOON HA JONG
Republic of Korea Representative

_____
ROBERT J. FRIEDMAN
Lieutenant General
United States Air Force
United States Representative

, These minutes are considered as official documents pertaining to both Governments and will not be released without mutual agreement.

REPUBLIC OF KOREA - UNITED STATES
FINANCIAL AFFAIRS SUBCOMMITTEE

6 February 1968

M E M O R A N D U M   O F   A G R E E M E N T

1. Reference is made to:

a. Article XVII of the Agreed Minutes to the Status of Forces Agreement Between the United States of America and the Republic of Korea, 9 July 1966.

b. Article VIII of the Agreement Between the Republic of Korea and the United States of America Regarding the Status of the Korean Service Corps, 23 February 1967.

c. Republic of Korea Income Tax Law No. 1966, promulgated on 29 November 1967.

d. Republic of Korea Presidential Decree No. 3320, promulgated on 30 December 1967.

2. In consonance with the foregoing references, it is agreed that:

a. The expression "employer" refers to the United States Armed Forces (including nonappropriated fund organizations and USFK invited contractors). The expression "employee" refers to any civilian (including personnel of the Korean Service Corps) employed by an employer except a domestic employed by an individual member of the United States Armed Forces, the civilian component, or dependents of the foregoing. Such employees shall be nationals of the Republic of Korea.

b. Employer will withhold income tax from the pay of his employees effective with the first pay period beginning on or after 1 February 1968. Taxes will be withheld in accordance with the rates established by reference 1c.

c. Employer will forward tax remittances to the ROK Government not later than the end of the month following the month in which salary payment is made to the employee. Remittance may be in won, won check,

21st JC (Incl 1 to Incl 22)
21 Feb 68

These minutes are considered as official documents pertaining to both Governments and will not be released without mutual agreement.

or U. S. dollar check. All remittances will be deposited in the account of the Yongsan Internal Revenue Office at the Bank of Korea, #110-3Ka, Namdaemun-Ro, Chung-Ku, Seoul, Korea. Remittances will be accompanied by 2 copies of each payroll which will include the employee's name, taxable income, tax amount, pay period covered, and unit designation.

     d. All employees will be granted a 40% discount in tax amount as provided by paragraph (3), Article 43, of ROK Income Tax Law No. 1966.

     e. Employer responsibility for the collection of taxes begins on the effective date of withholding, as stated in paragraph 2b above. Taxes levied by the ROK Government on an employee prior to that date will be a matter solely between the employee and the ROK Government.

     f. Employer has the responsibility for controlling the computation, withholding and remittance of income tax of employees, as provided for in this agreement.

MR. NAM SANG CHIN
Alternate Chairman
Republic of Korea Component
Finance Subcommittee

For: COLONEL THOMAS A. TAYLOR, JR.
Chairman, United States Component
Financial Affairs Subcommittee

2

21st JC (Incl 1 to Incl 22)
21 Feb 68

These minutes are considered as official documents pertaining to both Governments and will ●ot be released without mutual ●eement.

JOINT COMMITTEE
UNDER
THE REPUBLIC OF KOREA AND THE UNITED STATES
STATUS OF FORCES AGREEMENT

8 February 1968

MEMORANDUM FOR: THE JOINT COMMITTEE

1. Subcommittee Members:

United States	Republic of Korea
Col Floyd R. Waltz, Jr. - J4, USFK	Mr. SHIM Ui Hwan
Col John T. Horrocks, Jr. - J4, USFK	Mr. HAN Byung Il
LTC Walter A. Brown, Jr. - J4, USFK	Mr. MOON Ki Sang
Col Norman I. Radin - 6314 Spt Wing	Mr. PARK Pil Soo
Osan AB, Korea	Mr. RHEE Eun Tak
LTC James A. Jolley - Eng Office, USFK	Mr. LEE Chang Ha
LTC Paul E. Jones - J5, USFK	Mr. LEE Woong Soo
Maj James L. Hicks - 6314 Spt Wing	Mr. IM Young Duk
Osan AB, Korea	Mr. NAMKOONG Chull
LCDR Raymond F. Milburn - USN	Mr. KIM Sae Kwon
Mr. Oliver Kennedy - KPA, EUSA	Mr. SONG Ju In
Mr. Charles E. Coleman - PACEX	Mr. DOKKO Young
Mr. Lawrence D. Hillyer, Jr. - USAEDFE	Mr. KIM Bong Kyun
Mr. Samuel Pollack - SJA, USFK	Mr. OH Myong Too

2. **Subject of Recommendation.** Interpretation of paragraph 2(b), Article XV, SOFA, in regard to the Trans-Asia Engineering Associates, Inc. Reference Minutes of Joint Committee Meeting 12, 14 August 1967, concerning Collins Radio Company.

3. Proposal that Trans-Asia Engineering Associates, Inc. engaged in business activities in the Republic of Korea pertaining immediately and directly to the Government of the Republic of Korea would not be in violation of paragraph 2(b), Article XV, SOFA, because in this instance and under the special facts appearing, the provision may and should be construed so as to favor those certain business activities which do also bear an indirect yet reasonably close pertaining relation to the United States Armed Forces. This construction of the provision will allow those Trans-Asia Engineering Associates, Inc. employees presently in the Republic of Korea for the purpose of performing contracts with the US Armed Forces to retain the privileges and immunities granted under SOFA even though the Trans-Asia Engineering Associates, Inc. is performing certain contracts with additional personnel, for the Republic of Korea. Invited Contractor privileges and immunities granted under SOFA will not be extended to the additional personnel of Trans-Asia Engineering Associates, Inc. employed on the contract with the Republic of Korea.

21st JC (Incl 23)
21 Feb 68

These minutes are considered as official documents pertaining to both Governments and will not be released without mutual agreement.

    4. <u>Recommendation</u>. It is recommended that the construction as outlined in paragraph 3 above be adopted.

SHIM UI HWAN
Chairman, ROK Commerce
Subcommittee

COLONEL FLOYD R. WALTZ, JR.
Chairman, US Commerce
Subcommittee

APPROVED BY THE JOINT COMMITTEE ON
21 FEBRUARY 1968 AT TWENTY-FIRST MEETING

YOON HA JONG
Republic of Korea Representative

ROBERT J. FRIEDMAN
Lieutenant General
United States Air Force
United States Representative

21st JC (Incl 23)
21 Feb 68

HEADQUARTERS, UNITED STATES FORCES, KOREA
APO SAN FRANCISCO 96301

USFK DJ-O   8 February 1968

MEMORANDUM FOR: The Joint Committee

SUBJECT: Designation of US Invited Contractor under Article XV, Status of Forces Agreement.

1. References:

    a. Para 2, Article XV, Status of Forces Agreement.

    b. US Commerce Subcommittee Memorandum of Consultation, dated 4 Jan 1968, subject as above. (Incl 1)

    c. ROK Commerce Subcommittee Memorandum of Consultation, dated 1 Feb 1968, subject as above. (Incl 2)

2. The United States, after consultation with the ROK Commerce Subcommittee and after having duly considered their views, has designated Barclay Overseas, Inc. as a US Invited Contractor, for the execution of contract F62562-67-C-0363 for furnishing and delivering Minnesota Mining copying machines, thermofax brand copy paper, and other copying products to the US Armed Forces in Korea.

3. Pertinent data concerning US citizen employees will be provided to the Joint Secretariat in the established periodic arrival and departure format.

2 Incl
as

             ROBERT J. FRIEDMAN
             Lieutenant General, USAF
             Chief of Staff

**APPROVED BY THE JOINT COMMITTEE ON
21 FEBRUARY 1968 AT TWENTY-FIRST MEETING**

                          21st JC (Incl 24)
                          21 Feb 68

HEADQUARTERS, UNITED STATES FORCES, KOREA
APO SAN FRANCISCO 96301

USFK DJ   4 January 1968

MEMORANDUM FOR: Chairman, ROK Commerce Subcommittee

SUBJECT: Designation of US Invited Contractors under Article XV, Status of Forces Agreement

1. Reference: Paragraph 2, Article XV of the Status of Forces Agreement.

2. The Government of the Republic of Korea is informed through this written consultative process that the United States Forces, Korea proposes to continue to extend invited contractor status to Barclay Overseas, Inc. on the contract described in paragraph 3 below.

3. The following data is provided:

   a. Company Name: Barclay Overseas, Inc.

   b. Local Address: #50-2, Susomun-dong, Sudaemun-ku, Seoul, Korea.

   c. Identification of U.S. employee: Patrick E. O'Sullivan, Manager, UN Village Apt D-2, Seoul, Korea.

   d. Number of U.S. employees   1 .
       Number of ROK employees   3 .

   e. Reasons for Designation of an Invited Contractor: Unavailability of materials and services required by U.S. standards. The contractor is required to furnish and deliver Minnesota Mining products of copying machines, thermofax brand copy paper, and other copying products to the U.S. Armed Forces in Korea. They are also required to provide necessary maintenance on the copying machines involved.

   f. Location of contract: Kimpo, Kunsan, and Osan Air Bases. Also, all U.S. Army installations in Korea.

   g. Type of Contract: Furnish and deliver Minnesota Mining copying machines, thermofax brand copy paper and other copying products to the U.S. Armed Forces in Korea. Also to provide necessary maintenance on the copying machines involved.

                                        21st JC (Incl 1 to Incl 24)
                                        21 Feb 68

USFK DJ
SUBJECT: Designation of US Invited Contractors under Article XV,
Status of Forces Agreement

h. Length of contract: 15 Jan 1967 to 5 April 1968.

i. Sponsoring Component Command: Commander, Air Forces Korea.

4. The United States certifies that the named contractor is
present in the Republic of Korea solely for the purpose of executing a
contract with the United States, for the benefit of the United States
Armed Forces or other Armed Forces under the Unified Command receiving
logistical support from the United States Forces.

5. The views of the Government of the Republic of Korea are
earnestly solicited prior to United States continuation of invited
contractor status to Barclay Overseas, Inc. to perform the work outlined above. You may be assured that your views will be considered
carefully.

6. Your early reply will be greatly appreciated.

FLOYD R. WALTZ, JR.
Colonel   USA
Chairman, US Commerce Subcommittee

380-ㅏ E

MINISTRY OF COMMERCE AND INDUSTRY
REPUBLIC OF KOREA
SEOUL, KOREA

1 February 1968

SUBJECT: Designation of US Invited Contractor under Article XV, Status of Forces Agreement.

TO   : Chairman, US Commerce Subcommittee.

1. References;

    a. Paragraph 2, Article XV, Status of Forces Agreement.

    b. US Commerce Subcommittee Memorandum of Consultation, Dated 4 January 1968, subject as above, pertaining to a contract for furnishing and delivering Minnesota Mining copying machine, thermofax brand copy paper and other copying products to the U.S. Armed Forces in Korea.

    2. The US memorandum, reference 1b above, has been reviewed and the Government of the Republic of Korea fully understands the requirement for an invited contractor in this instance.

For Chairman
ROK Commerce Subcommittee

21st JC (Incl 2 to Incl 24)
21 Feb 68

286

These minutes are considered as official documents pertaining to both
Governments and will not be released without mutual agreement.

JOINT COMMITTEE
UNDER
THE REPUBLIC OF KOREA AND THE UNITED STATES
STATUS OF FORCES AGREEMENT

12 February 1968

MEMORANDUM FOR: The Joint Committee

SUBJECT: Designation of US Invited Contractor under Article XV, Status
of Forces Agreement

   1. References:

      a. Paragraph 2, Article XV, Status of Forces Agreement.

      b. US Commerce Subcommittee Memorandum of Consultation,
dated 24 Oct 67, subject as above (Inclosure 1).

      c. ROK Commerce Subcommittee Memorandum of Consultation,
dated 13 Dec 67, subject as above (Inclosure 2).

   2. The United States, after consultation with the ROK Commerce
Subcommittee and after having duly considered their views, has designated the Smithsonian Institution as a US invited contractor for
execution of contract number F44620-67-C-0013 for the purpose of
ecological study.

   3. Pertinent data concerning US citizen employees will be
provided to the Joint Secretariat in the established periodic arrival
and departure format.

2 Incl
   as

ROBERT J. FRIEDMAN
Lieutenant General
United States Air Force
United States Representative
Joint Committee

APPROVED BY THE JOINT COMMITTEE ON
21 FEBRUARY 1968 AT TWENTY-FIRST MEETING

21st JC (Incl 25)
21 Feb 68

These minutes are considered as official documents pertaining to both Governments and wi██not be released without mutua██reement.

**JOINT COMMITTEE
UNDER
THE REPUBLIC OF KOREA AND THE UNITED STATES
STATUS OF FORCES AGREEMENT**

USFK DJ   24 October 1967

SUBJECT: Designation of US Invited Contractor under Article XV, Status of Forces Agreement

TO: Chairman
             ROK Commerce Subcommittee

1. References: a. Paragraph 2, Article XV of the Status of Forces Agreement.

b. Memorandum to: Joint Committee, dated 30 June 1967, subject: Report of invited contractors with contracts expiring after 30 June 1967.

2. The Government of the Republic of Korea is informed through this written consultive process that the United States Forces, Korea, proposes to extend the invited contractor status of the US firm listed below from the original expiration date of 14 October 1967 through 30 June 1968.

3. The following data is provided:

a. Company name: Smithsonian Institution.

b. Local Address: In care of US Embassy, Seoul.

c. Identification of US citizen employees: Provided to the Joint Secretariat in the established periodic reporting procedures.

d. Number of US and ROK employees: 1 US employee and no ROK employees.

e. Reasons for Designation of an Invited Contractor: Technical qualifications of the contractor, in that Smithsonian Institution provides necessary training and guidance to ROK scientists.

f. Location of Contract: Operations under this contract are conducted primarily in uninhabited areas in and below the southern half of the Demilitarized Zone.

g. Type of Contract: Conducting an ecological study, i.e. to study the adaptation made by plant and animal life in areas previously inhabited by man as they revert to the natural wild state. This contract is also assisting in tracking down causes of hemhorragic fever in the Republic of Korea.

288

21st JC (Incl 1 to
21 Feb 68 Incl 25)

USFK DJ   24 October 1967
SUBJECT: Designation of US Invited Contractor under Article XV,
         Status of Forces Agreement

        h. Length of Contract: The contract extension is for the
period 15 October 1967 through 30 June 1968.

        i. Sponsoring Component Command: US Air Forces, Korea.

    4. The United States certifies that the Smithsonian Institution
is present in the Republic of Korea solely for the purpose of executing
contracts with the United States, for the benefit of the United States
Armed Forces or other armed forces under the Unified Command receiving
logistical support from the United States Forces.

    5. The view of the Government of the Republic of Korea are
earnestly solicited prior to United States extension of invited contractor status for the remainder of the contract in order that the work
outlined above may be efficiently performed. You may be assured that
your views will be considered carefully.

    6. Your early reply will be greatly appreciated.

                            FLOYD R. WALTZ, JR.
                            Colonel, United States Army
                            Chairman, US Commerce Subcommittee

                                2

MINISTRY OF COMMERCE AND INDUSTRY
REPUBLIC OF KOREA
SEOUL, KOREA

13 Dec. 1967

SUBJECT: Designation of US Invited Contractor under Article XV, Status of Forces Agreement

TO: Chairman, US Commerce Subcommittee

1. References:

    a. Paragraph 2, Article XV, Status of Forces Agreement.

    b. US Commerce Subcommittee Memorandum of Consultation, dated 24 October 1967, subject as above, pertaining to a contract for conducting an ecological study, ie, to study the adaptation made by plant and animal life in areas previously inhabited by man as they revert to the natural wild state.

2. The US memorandum, reference 1b above, has been reviewed and the Government of the Republic of Korea fully understands the requirement for an invited contractor in this instance.

Chairman
ROK Commerce Subcommittee

21st JC (Incl 2 to Incl 25)
21 Feb 68

JOINT ROK - US PRESS RELEASE
TWENTY-FIRST ROK-US JOINT COMMITTEE MEETING
21 FEBRUARY 1968

The ROK-US Joint Committee on 21 February approved procedures for the US armed forces in Korea to begin the withholding of income taxes of its Korean employees, as provided in the ROK-US SOFA. The United States armed forces will deduct ROK income taxes from the wages of its Korean employees. The income tax deductions will be at the rates established by recently revised ROK income tax legislation. The taxes collected will be deposited in the Bank of Korea by the US armed forces, to the account of the Government of the Republic of Korea.

The Joint Committee also approved eleven recommendations of its Facilities and Areas Subcommittee relating to acquisition and release of areas and facilities utilized by the US armed forces. It also assigned seventeen new tasks to the same Subcommittee. The Criminal Jurisdiction Subcommittee was assigned two new tasks, the first relating to procedures pertaining to the control of privately owned firearms of US Forces, Korea personnel. The second task relating to US-ROK cooperation with regard to offenses committed by Korean nationals against United States Forces, Korea personnel and property. The Ad Hoc Entry and Exit Subcommittee was assigned a new task concerning review and possible revision of certain entry and exit reporting procedures of USFK personnel.

21st JC (Incl 26)
21 Feb 68

In addition, the US and ROK Representatives exchanged several memoranda relating to various aspects of the implementation of the SOFA.

The ROK Representative, Mr. YOON Ha Jong, Director of the Europe and America Bureau of the Foreign Ministry, presided at this meeting which was held at the ROK Capitol Building. The next Joint Committee meeting is scheduled for 14 March, in the US SOFA Conference Room, Yongsan.

2

한.미 합동위원회 제21차 회의 공동발표문

1968.2. 21.

한.미 합동위원회는 2월 21일, 한.미 군대지위협정의 규정에 따라 주한 미군이 동 군대소속 한국 노무자에 대하여 소득세를 원천징수 하도록 하는 절차규정을 승인했다. 미군당국이 동 군대소속 한국인 노무자의 임금에서 대한민국 소득세를 공제하게되며 소득세의 공제는 최근 개정된 대한민국의 소득세법에 규정된 세율에 의하고 징수됨 세금은 주한 미군에 의하여 대한민국 정부 계정으로 한국 은행에 여치 된다.

또한 합동위원회는 미군에 의하여 사용되는 시설과 구역의 취득과 반환에 관한 시설 구역 분과위원회의 건의 11건을 승인했다. 합동위원회 는 또한 동 분과위원회에 17건의 신규과제를 부여하였다. 형사재판권 분과위원회는 2건의 신규과제를 부여받았는데 그 하나는, 주한 미군의 개인소유 총포에 대한 통제절차이고 또 다른 하나는, 주한 미국 군인 및 재산에 대하여 한국인이 범한 범죄에 대한 한.미간 협조문제에 관한 과제이다. 출입국 임시 분과위원회는 주한 미군에 대한 출입국 상황 보고절차의 재 검토와 수정에 관한 신규과제 1건을 부여 받았다. 아울러 한.미 양국 대표는 군대지위협정 운영에 있어 제반문제에 관련된 수개의 각서를 교환 했다.

본 회의는 한국측 대표인 외무부 구미국장이 중앙청 회의실에서 주재하였으며 차기회의는 3월 14일 미8군 회의실에서 개최될 예정이다.

243

분류번호	729.41 1968 25-27차	등록번호	245	보존기간	영구乙
기능명칭	SOFA-한미 합동위원회 회의록, 제25-27차 1968				
생 산 과	안보담당 관실	생산년도	1968		

주;

1. 제25차   1968. 5. 17
2. 제26차   1968. 6. 5
3. 제27차   1968. 6. 7

	M/F No.	2055

001

결 번

넘버링 오류

결 번

넘버링 오류

1. 제 25 차, 1968. 5. 17

4

외 무 부

원미이 723-   1968 . 5 . 6 .

수신 : 배부처 참조

참조 :

제목 : 한미합동위원회 회의 개최 통지

　　　　　1. 오는 1968년 5월 17일(금요일) 15.00 시에 중앙청
5층 회의실 (528호실)
~~제회의실, 주한미군사령부 회의실~~ 에서 한미합동위원회 제 25 차
회의가 개최될 예정이오니 각 위원의 참석을 바랍니다.

　　　　　2. 한편, 동 회의에 대비한 한국 대표단의 대책회의를 오는
5월 16일(목요일) 10.00시에 외무부 회의실에서 개최하오니 참석
하시기바랍니다. 끝.

북미2과	5월6일	양응재	담당	과장	국장

외　　무　　부　　장　　관

배부처 : 법무부 장관(법무심장, 검찰국장), 국방부장관(기획국장,
　　　　시설국장), 재무부장관(세관국장), 상공부장관(상역국장),
　　　　교통부장관(방공국장), 노동청장(노정국장).
　　　　경제기획원장관(경제기획국장).

5

한.미 합동위원회 제25차 회의 의제

1968. 5. 17. (금) 15:00시
외무부 회의실

1. 시설구역 분과위원회 추가 과제부여

    가. 미측 설명 4건

    나. 한국측 설명 3건

2. 시설구역 분과위원회 건의

    가. 미측 설명 23건

    나. 한국측 설명 2건

3. 미초청 계약자 지명 - 미측 설명

4. 협정시행상 미국측이 한국 정부에 제출하는 각서

5. 차기회의 6월 7일 (금) 15:00시 용산 SOFA 회의실

6. 공동발표문 채택

7. 폐 회

6

(개   회)

프리드만 장군 준비되었으면 회의를 개최하겠읍니다.

(의 제 1 - 추가과제부여 - 시설구역 분과위원회)

(미국측 설명 - 4건)

첫재 의제는 시설구역 분과위원회에 대한 추가 과제부여 입니다.

이제 미국 대표께서 시설구역 분과위원회에 부여할 4건의 과제를
설명하여 주시기 바랍니다.

(미국측 4건 설명)

감사합니다.

대한민국 대표는 4건의 과제를 시설구역 분과위원회에 부여하는데
동의하는 바입니다.

대한민국 대표는 시설구역 분과위원회에 부여할 다음 3건을 제시하고
귀하의 동의를 구하는 바입니다.

그중 2건은 이미 긴급과제로 양측 대표가 서명하여 시설구역 분과
위원회에 부여하였던 것입니다. 그것은 서울특별시의 도로 확장공사에
필요한 SAC-715, Section 2,3   과 715-A   및 D.E.F.G
의 지역권의 일부 해제이고 다음으로 경기도 수원시 파장동 소재 SAC-CS-198
의 해제요청입니다.

이 사실을 공식 기록에 남겨 놓기를 제안하는 바입니다.
다음 1건의 추가 과제는 용산역 구내 철로 공동사용에 관한 것입니다. 이 과제
를 시설구역 분과위원회에 부여하도록 제안하는 바입니다.

7

(의 제 2 - 시설구역 분과위원회 건의)

미국측 설명 - 23건

그러면 다음의제인 시설구역 분과위원회 건의를 토의하겠읍니다.
총 25건의 건의가 있는데 이는 분과위원회의 그대로 반영될것으로 봄니다.
미국 대표께서 시설구역 분과위원회가 합동위원회의 승인을 위하여

제출한 23건의 건의사항을 설명해 주시기 바랍니다.

(미국측 설명)

감사합니다.

대한민국 대표는 전기 건의사항의 승인에 동의하는 바입니다.

이제 대한민국 대표가 잔여 2건의 시설구역 분과위원회 건의를 설명

하겠읍니다. 즉, 그것은

　　PAC-67　　　의 일부인 1.2558 에이커의 해제요청과

　　SAC-685　　　의 일부인 1.571 에이커의 해제요청입니다.

대한민국 대표는 상기 2건의 건의를 합동위원회가 승인하도록

제안하는 바입니다.

8

(의 제 3 - 미국초청계약자 지명 - 6건)

다음의제는 미국 초청계약자 지명에 관한 것입니다.

미국대표께서 설명해 주시기 바랍니다.

(미국측 설명)

감사합니다.

대한민국 대표는 미국대표께서 설명하신 전기 6개 상사를 미국

초청계약자로 지명한 것을 확인하는 바입니다.

9

(의 제4 - 협정시행상 한국 정부에 제출하는 각서)

(미국측 설명)

관계문서를 엽기해 주신데 대하여 감사합니다.

대한민국 대표는 전기 문서를 한국측 간사가 정히 접수하였음을 확인하는 바입니다.

10

(의 제 5 - 차기회의)

　　　　다음 의제는 차기회의에 관한 것입니다.
　　　　차기회의를 1968. 6. 7.　15:00시 주한 미군사령부　SOFA　회의실
에서 개최토록 제안하는 바입니다.

11

(의 제 6 - 공동발표문)

감사합니다.

마지막 의제로 넘어가서 공동발표문 채택문제입니다.

양측 간사들이 합의 작성한 공동발표문은 이미 여러분에게 나누어준 자료에 첨부되어 있으리라 믿으며 따라서 전문 낭독을 생략하고 그대로 채택하기를 제안하는 바입니다.

(미국측 동의)

프리드만 장군, 기타 토의안건이 없으면 폐회 하겠읍니다.

12

THE ROK-US SOFA JOINT COMMITTEE
THE TWENTY-FIFTH MEETING
(17 May 1968)

NOTES
for
the Republic of Korea Representative

13

(Opening of the Meeting)

General Friedman, if you are ready I would call
the Meeting to order.

(Agenda I - Assignment of Additional Tasks to Facilities
and Areas Subcommittee)

1. Four Tasks - US Presentation

The first item of the agreed agenda is the assignment
of additional tasks to the Facilities and Areas Subcommittee,
and I believe the United States Representative would
please present four new tasks.

(US presentation of four tasks)

Thank you for the presentation.
The Republic of Korea Representative is happy to
concur in the assignment of the four tasks as presented
to the Facilities and Areas Subcommittee.

14

2. Three tasks - ROK Presentation

Now the Republic of Korea Representative wishes to present for formal concurrence of the United States Representative three (3) new tasks to be assigned to the Facilities and Areas Subcommittee.

The first two of the three tasks have already been signed by the two Representatives and assigned, as exigency measure, to the Subcommittee.

These two tasks are to prepare recommendations for the following requests:

1) Release of a portion of SAC-715, Section 2, 3 and 715-A, and a portion of Easement D.E.F and G which are required for urban development project of the Special City of Seoul.

2) Release of SAC-CS-198 located at Pajang-dong, Suwon, Kyonggi-do.

The Republic of Korea Representative wishes to propose that these two tasks be included in the official record of the Joint Committee.

The third and last task is related to the request for joint use of a railway side track at the Yongsan Railway Station.

The Republic of Korea Representative wishes to propose the formal assignment of these tasks to the Facilities and Areas Subcommittee.

(Agenda II - Recommendations of Facilities and Areas
　　　　　Subcommittee)

1. Twenty-three recommendations - US Presentation

　　　Now I suggest to move on to the next item on the
Agenda, recommendations of Facilities and Areas Subcommittee.
We have before us a total of twenty-five recommendations
reflecting much hard work of the Subcommittee, and I wish
to invite the United States Representative to present
twenty-three recommendations which the Facilities and
Areas Subcommittee has submitted for Joint Committee approval.

　　　(US Presentation)

　　　Thank you for the presentation.
　　　The Republic of Korea Representative is pleased to
concur in the approval the twenty-three recommendations
as presented.

2. Two recommendations - ROK Presentation

　　　Now the Republic of Korea Representative is pleased
to present the remaining two recommendations of the Facilities
and Areas Subcommittee.

16

The Subcommittee recommends:

1) Release of a portion of PAC-67, involving 1.2558 acres.

2) Release of a portion of SAC-685, involving 1.571 acres.

The Republic of Korea Representative wishes to propose the Joint Committee approval of these two recommendations.

(US Concurrence)

Thank you very much.

(Agenda III - Memoranda on designation of six USFK Invited
Contractors - US Presentation)

Next item on the Agenda concerns designation of
USFK Invited Contractors, and I wish to invite the United
States Representative to present the memoranda.

(US Presentation)

Thank you very much.

The Republic of Korea Representative is pleased to
take note of and acknowledge US notification on the
designation of these six USFK Invited Contractors.

18

(Agenda IV - Memoranda presented to the ROK Government by
the US in the Implementation of the SOFA
- US Presentation)

(ROK Representative invites US presentation)

(US Presentation)

Thank you very much for the enumeration of the documents transmitted. The Republic of Korea Representative is pleased to confirm the receipt by the ROK SOFA Secretariat of the documents as enumerated.

19

(Agenda V - Next Meeting)

The next item on the Agenda concerns the next meeting of the Joint Committee. In line with the past practice I would propose that the next meeting be held at 1500 hours, ~~Thursday~~ Friday, 7 June, in the US SOFA Conference Room, Yongsan.

(US Concurrence)

Thank you very much.

20

(Agenda VI - Agreement on Joint Press Release)

Now, I would like to suggest to move on to the next
and final item on the Agenda, Agreement on Joint Press
Release.

I believe that copies of the draft text of the Joint
Press Release prepared and agreed on by the two Secretaries
have been included in the papers distributed to you
beforehand, and therefore, I would omit to recite the
text and wish to propose adoption of the text as prepared.

(US Concurrence)

General Friedman, if you have no other subjects to
discuss, I would declare the meeting adjourned.

21

JOINT COMMITTEE
UNDER
THE REPUBLIC OF KOREA AND THE UNITED STATES
STATUS OF FORCES AGREEMENT

MINUTES OF THE TWENTY-FIFTH MEETING

17 May 1968
Capitol Building
Republic of Korea
Seoul, Korea

1. The meeting was convened at 1500 hours by Mr. YOON Ha Jong, the ROK Representative, who presided at the meeting. A copy of the agenda is attached as Inclosure 1.

2. The following were in attendance:

ROK	US
Mr. YOON Ha Jong	LTG Robert J. Friedman, USAF
Mr. HUH Seung Joon	CAPT M. R. Massie, USN
Mr. SHIN Chung Sup	COL Walter V. Gresham, USAF
Mr. PARK Noh Soo	COL Herbert C. Hicks, Jr. USA
Mr. OH Myong Too	COL Gerald W. Davis, USA
Mr. WHANG Kong Riol	Mr. P. Wesley Kriebel, US Embassy
	Mr. Robert A. Kinney, USFK
	LTC Paul E. Jones, USAF

3. The ROK Representative called the meeting to order and invited the US Representative to present four new tasks to the Facilities and Areas Subcommittee.

4. The US Representative proposed the assignment of four additional tasks to the Facilities and Areas Subcommittee, as follows:

a. Acquisition of a total of 16.455 acres of land in Paju-gun, Kyonggi-do (Inclosure 2).

b. Conversion of 0.014 acre in Kwangju-gun, Kyonggi-do, currently held as a perpetual restrictive easement, to an exclusive use basis (Inclosure 2).

c. Extension of Temporary Use Permit CAV-T-16 from 1 May 1968 to 30 April 1969 (Inclosure 2).

d. Conversion of 0.643 acre in Shihung-gun, Kyonggi-do, from a perpetual restrictive easement to an exclusive use basis (Inclosure 3).

5. The US Representative requested Joint Committee approval of the assignment of these four tasks to the Facilities and Areas Subcommittee and the ROK Representative concurred.

6. The ROK Representative presented for formal concurrence of the US Representative, three new tasks, to be assigned to the Facilities and Areas Subcommittee. The first two of the three tasks had already been signed by the two Representatives and assigned, as an exigency measure, to the Subcommittee. These two tasks were to prepare recommendations for the following requests (Inclosure 4):

a. Release of a portion of SAC-715, Sections 2 and 3; 715-A; and a portion of Easement D, E, F, and G, which were required for an urban development project of the Special City of Seoul.

b. Release of SAC-CS-198, located at Pajang-dong, Suwon, Kyonggi-do, in connection with an urban renewal project in the City of Suwon.

7. The ROK Representative proposed that these two tasks be included in the official record of the Joint Committee, and the US Representative concurred.

2

23

8. The ROK Representative stated that the third and last task related to the request for joint use of a railway side track at the Yongsan Railway Station (Inclosure 5). The ROK Representative proposed the formal assignment of this task to the Facilities and Areas Subcommittee, and the US Representative concurred.

9. The US Representative presented twenty-three recommendations of the Facilities and Areas Subcommittee, as follows:

a. That the record of facilities and areas in use by the United States armed forces as of 9 February 1967 be approved (Inclosure 6). The US Representative commented that the determination of format and compilation of this record represents another outstanding achievement of the Facilities and Areas Subcommittee.

b. The acquisition of the following land areas:

(1) 5.07 acres at Hasangok-ni, Kyonggi-do (Inclosure 7).

(2) 10.48 acres at Dongpa-ri, Kyonggi-do (Inclosure 8).

(3) 1.56 acres at Pobwon-ni, Kyonggi-do (Inclosure 8).

(4) 0.0103 acre at Samok-ni, Kyonggi-do (Inclosure 9).

c. The acquisition of a perpetual restrictive easement involving 0.16 acre of land at Majang-dong, Sungdong-ku, Seoul City (Inclosure 8)

d. The acquisition of the following easements:

(1) 1.1845 acres at 1004-6 Haemang-dong, Kunsan City and at 1501 Shinpung-ri, Chollapuk-do (Inclosure 9).

(2) 1.0 acre of land at Tonggi-ri, Kyonggi-do (Inclosure 9).

3

(3) 0.95 acre of existing road at Wonam-ni, Kangwon-do (Inclosure 10).

e. The acquisition of temporary use permits for:

(1) 59 acres of land at Toegyewon-ni, Kyonggi-do (Inclosure 11).

(2) 173.943 acres of land at Kawol-li and Chuwol-li, Kyonggi-do (Inclosure 11).

(3) 142.524 acres of land at Mapo-ri, Kyonggi-do (Inclosure 11).

(4) 12,720 acres at various locations in Kimpo-gun, Kyonggi-do (Inclosure 10).

f. The extension of the following Temporary Use Permits:

(1) IC-T-38 (Inclosure 8).

(2) 7X-T-3 (Inclosure 11).

(3) 7X-IC-T-5 (Inclosure 11).

(4) 7X-T-21 (Inclosure 10).

(5) 7X-T-22 (Inclosure 10).

(6) K-C-T-27 (Inclosure 10).

(7) K-C-T-36 (Inclosure 10).

(8) 7X-T-5 (Inclosure 10).

(9) 7X-T-7 (Inclosure 10).

g. The conversion of a portion of SAC-679B (23.50 acres) from an easement basis to an exclusive use basis (Inclosure 12).

10. The US Representative proposed Joint Committee approval of these 23 recommendations of the Facilities and Areas Subcommittee. He commended this Subcommittee for having completed 90% of the 199 tasks it had

4

been assigned prior to this twenty-fifth meeting. The ROK Representative concurred in the approval of these 23 recommendations, and also expressed the ~~gratitude~~ *satisfaction* of his Government for the good work of the Facilities and Areas Subcommittee.

11. The ROK Representative presented two recommendations of the Facilities and Areas Subcommittee, as follows:

    a. The release of a portion of PAC-67, involving 1.2558 acres (Inclosure 13).

    b. The release of a portion of SAC-685, involving 1.571 acres (Inclosure 14).

12. The US Representative concurred in Joint Committee approval of these two recommendations of the Facilities and Areas Subcommittee.

13. The US Representative presented memoranda to the Joint Committee informing the Republic of Korea Government of the designation of six new invited contractors under Article XV of the Status of Forces Agreement. After consultation with Republic of Korea Commerce Subcommittee personnel, the United States Forces, Korea, had designated the following as US invited contractors:

    a. Adrian Wilson Associates (Inclosure 15).

    b. Pacific Architects & Engineers, Inc (Inclosure 16).

    c. Vinnell Corporation (Inclosure 17).

    d. Barclay Overseas, Inc. (Inclosure 18).

    e. Daniel, Mann, Johnson & Mendenhall (Inclosure 19).

    f. Trans-Asia Engineering Associates, Inc. (Inclosure 20).

5

14. The US Representative stated that pertinent data concerning employees of these invited contractors would be provided to the Government of Korea in accordance with mutually approved procedures. The ROK Representative indicated that he was pleased to take note of and acknowledge US notification on the designation of these six USFK invited contractors.

15. The US Representative noted for the record that the US SOFA Secretary had furnished the following information to the ROK SOFA Secretary, in accordance with Joint Committee decisions:

a. Twenty copies of a report listing arrivals, departures, and address changes of United States invited contractor personnel and their dependents, dated 27 April 1968.

b. Twenty copies of the report of United States armed forces personnel, the civilian component, invited contractors, and dependents entering or departing the Republic of Korea during the month of April 1968.

16. The ROK Representative confirmed the receipt by the ROK SOFA Secretary of the documents as enumerated.

17. The ROK Representative proposed that the next meeting of the Joint Committee be held at 1500 hours, on Friday, 7 June, in the US SOFA Conference Room, Yongsan. He indicated that this was the usual three-week interval between meetings, and that it was being scheduled for Friday, 7 June, because the Korean Memorial Day was being observed on Thursday, 6 June. The US Representative agreed that the next Joint Committee meeting be scheduled for 1500 hours, on Friday, 7 June.

6

18. The ROK Representative ~~then proposed coordination of the final~~ ~~the~~ *after indicating* ~~item on the agenda, agreement on Joint Press Release. He stated~~ that copies of the draft text of the Joint Press Release, prepared and agreed upon by the two SOFA Secretaries (Inclosure 21), ~~the~~ proposed adoption *had been distributed beforehand,* of the text as prepared, and the US Representative concurred.

19. The meeting was adjourned at 1540 hours.

21 Inclosures

ROBERT J. FRIEDMAN
LIEUTENANT GENERAL
UNITED STATES AIR FORCE
UNITED STATES REPRESENTATIVE

YOON HA JONG
REPUBLIC OF KOREA
REPRESENTATIVE

7

AGENDA FOR THE TWENTY-FIFTH MEETING
OF THE ROK-US JOINT COMMITTEE
1500 HOURS, 17 MAY 1968, ROK CAPITOL BUILDING

I   Assignment of Additional Tasks to Facilities and Areas Subcommittee:

   1. Four tasks   -   US Presentation

   2. Three tasks   -   ROK Presentation

II   Recommendations of Facilities and Areas Subcommittee:

   1. Twenty-three recommendations   -   US Presentation

   2. Two recommendations   -   ROK Presentation

III   Memoranda on Designation of Six USFK Invited Contractors   -

      US Presentation

IV   Memoranda Presented to the ROK Government by the US, in the

      Implementation of the SOFA   -   US Presentation

V   Proposed Time of Next Meeting   -   1500 hours, Friday, 7 June,

      in the US SOFA Conference Room, Yongsan

VI   Agreement on Joint Press Release

VII   Adjourn

29

JOINT COMMITTEE
UNDER
THE REPUBLIC OF KOREA AND THE UNITED STATES
STATUS OF FORCES AGREEMENT

17 May 1968

MEMORANDUM FOR: Chairmen, Facilities & Areas Subcommittee

SUBJECT: Request to Convert to an Exclusive Use Basis Land
Currently Held as a Perpetual Restrictive Easement

1. SOFA provides, in Article II, paragraph 2, that the Governments of the Republic of Korea and the United States may agree that facilities and areas or portions thereof shall be returned to the Republic of Korea or that additional facilities and areas may be provided.

2. Pursuant to paragraph 1 above, it is requested that a recommendation be presented to the Joint Committee concerning a request to convert to an exclusive use basis 0.643 acre of land currently held as a perpetual restrictive easement (a portion of SAC-685). The real estate is located at Bakdal-ni, Anyang-up, Shihung-gun, Kyonggi-do. It is required to construct a helicopter landing pad.

ROBERT J. FRIEDMAN
Lieutenant General
United States Air Force
United States Representative

YOON HA JONG
Republic of Korea Representative

30

**JOINT COMMITTEE
UNDER
THE REPUBLIC OF KOREA AND THE UNITED STATES
STATUS OF FORCES AGREEMENT**

17 May 1968

MEMORANDUM FOR: Chairmen, Facilities & Areas Subcommittee

SUBJECT: Request for Acquisition of Real Estate and Extension
of Temporary Use Permit

1. SOFA provides, in Article II, paragraph 2, that the Governments
of the Republic of Korea and the United States may agree that
facilities and areas or portions thereof shall be returned to the
Republic of Korea or that additional facilities and areas may be
provided.

2. Pursuant to paragraph 1 above, it is requested that a recommendation be presented to the Joint Committee concerning a request for
the acquisition of a total of 16.455 acres of land at various locations
in Imjin-myon, Paju-gun, Kyonggi-do. Of this acreage, 3.76 acres
are required for exclusive use, and 12.695 acres of existing road
are required as an easement. The real estate is required as a
by-pass route for tracked vehicles.

3. Pursuant to paragraph 1 above, it is requested that a recommendation be presented to the Joint Committee concerning a request to
convert to an exclusive use basis 0.014 acre currently held as a
perpetual restrictive easement. The real estate is located at #142-1,
Hasangok-ni, Tongbu-myon, Kwangju-gun, Kyonggi-do. It is required
to construct a retaining wall to prevent erosion.

4. Pursuant to paragraph 1 above, it is requested that a recommendation
be presented to the Joint Committee concerning a request for extension of
Temporary Use Permit CAV-T-16, involving a total of 128,713.04 acres
of land. Of this acreage, 38,116.82 acres consist of arable land and
90,596.22 acres of non-arable land. The extension is requested from
1 May 1968 to 30 April 1969 for training purposes.

ROBERT J. FRIEDMAN
Lieutenant General
United States Air Force
United States Representative

YOON HA JONG
Republic of Korea Representative

3/

6 May 1968

MEMORANDUM FOR: Chairmen, Facilities & Areas Subcommittee

SUBJECT: Requests for Release of Real Estate

1. SOFA provides, in Article II, paragraph 2, that the Governments of the Republic of Korea and the United States may agree that facilities and areas or portions thereof shall be returned to the Republic of Korea or that additional facilities and areas may be provided.

2. Pursuant to paragraph 1 above, it is requested that recommendations be presented to the Joint Committee concerning requests for the following releases:

    a. Release of a portion of SAC-715, Section 2, 3, and 715-A, and a portion of Easement D, E, F, and G located at Siheung, Yongdongpo-ku, Seoul. This real estate is required for urban development projects of the Special City of Seoul.

    b. Release of SAC-CS-198, located at Pajong-dong, Suwon, Kyonggi-do. This real estate is required for an urban development project of the city of Suwon.

ROBERT J. FRIEDMAN
Lieutenant General
United States Air Force
United States Representative

YOON HA JONG
Republic of Korea Representative

17 May 1968

MEMORANDUM FOR: Chairmen, Facilities and Areas Subcommittee

SUBJECT: Request for Joint Use of a Railway Side Track

1. SOFA provides, in Article II, paragraph 2, that the Governments of the Republic of Korea and the United States may agree that facilities and areas or portions thereof shall be returned to the Republic of Korea or that additional facilities and areas may be provided.

2. Pursuant to paragraph 1 above, it is requested that a recommendation be presented to the Joint Committee concerning a request for joint use of a railway side track at the Yongsan Railway Station.

YOON HA JONG
Republic of Korea
Representative

ROBERT J. FRIEDMAN
Lieutenant General
United States Air Force
United States Representative

33

REPUBLIC OF KOREA - UNITED STATES
FACILITIES AND AREAS SUBCOMMITTEE

25 April 1968

MEMORANDUM FOR: THE JOINT COMMITTEE

1. Subcommittee members:

United States	Republic of Korea
COL I. M. Rice, Chairman	MG KIM Mook, Chairman
LTC J. B. Carrick, USAFCSK	Mr. SONG Yong Tai
LTC Robert E. Graf, J5, USFK	Mr. SHIN Chung Sup
MAJ James B. Hoodenpyle, USAF	Mr. LEE Soon Dong
LCDR Joe T. Patterson, J5, USNAG	Mr. LEE Kihl Choo
Mr. Francis K. Cook, J5, USFK	Mr. LEE Moon Sup
Mr. Richard Rose, USAEDFE	Mr. LEE Jong Do
Mrs. Betty H. Bowman, 8th Army	Mr. CHANG Kyong Shik
	Mr. CHA Sang Chun
	Mr. SEO Yong Kwan
	Mr. CHONG Young Hoon
	Mr. CHOI Chung Hwan
	Mr. NO Yong Goo
	Mr. PARK Noh Soo
	LTC KANG Jong Kuk
	Mr. KANG Hong Suk

2. Reference the Facilities and Areas Subcommittee memorandum to
the Joint Committee, 23 March 1967, subject: Determination of the
Format Involved in the Maintenance by the Joint Committee of Records
of Facilities and Areas in Use by the U. S. Armed Forces (Reference
Article II, para 1(b) of the SOFA).

3. Recommendation: It is recommended that the record of facilities
and areas in use by the U. S. Armed Forces as of 9 February 1967 as
enumerated on the attached Schedule of Facilities and Areas be approved.

34

4. Security Classification: Unclassified.

_____
COLONEL I. M. RICE
Chairman, United States Component
Facilities and Areas Subcommittee

_____
MAJOR GENERAL KIM Mook
Chairman, Republic of Korea Component
Facilities and Areas Subcommittee

2

35

REPUBLIC OF KOREA - UNITED STATES
FACILITIES AND AREAS SUBCOMMITTEE

25 April 1968

MEMORANDUM FOR: THE JOINT COMMITTEE

1. Subcommittee members:

United States	Republic of Korea
COL I. M. Rice, Chairman	MG KIM Mook, Chairman
LTC J. B. Carrick, USAFCSK	Mr. SONG Yong Tai
LTC Robert E. Graf, J4, USFK	Mr. SHIN Chung Sup
MAJ James B. Hoodenpyle, USAF	Mr. LEE Soon Dong
Mr. Francis K. Cook, J5, USFK	Mr. LEE Kihl Choo
Mr. Richard Rose, USAEDFE	Mr. LEE Moon Sup
Mrs. Betty H. Bowman, 8th Army	Mr. LEE Jong Do
	Mr. CHANG Kyong Shik
	Mr. CHA Sang Chun
	Mr. KIM Byoung Chan
	Mr. CHONG Young Hoon
	Mr. CHOI Chung Hwan
	Mr. NO Yong Goo
	Mr. PARK Moh Soo
	LTC KANG Jong Kuk
	Mr. KANG Hong Suk

2. Subject of Recommendations: Requests for Acquisition of Real Estate and Extension of Temporary Use Permits. (Reference Joint Committee Memorandum, same subject, dated 11 April 1968).

3. Recommendations:

a. The request for acquisition of a temporary use permit for a total of 59 acres of land, consisting of 25 acres of river bed and 34 acres of wooded land located at Toegyewon-ni, Pyollae-myon, Yangju-gun, Kyonggi-do, for the period 9-10 April 1968, has been accepted by the Ministry of National Defense. The real estate is required to conduct an operational readiness test. The Ministry of National Defense and the Far East District Engineer will be requested to prepare the necessary documents. It is recommended that the Joint Committee, SOFA, approve this acquisition.

36

b. The request for acquisition of a temporary use permit for 173.943 acres of river bed located at Kawol-li, and Chuwol-li, Choksong-myon, Paju-gun, Kyonggi-do, for the period 1 May 1968 to 30 April 1969, has been accepted by the Ministry of National Defense. The real estate is required for the conduct of firing tests and for training. The Ministry of National Defense and the Far East District Engineer will be requested to prepare the necessary documents. It is recommended that the Joint Committee, SOFA, approve acquisition of this temporary use permit.

c. The request for acquisition of a temporary use permit for 142.524 acres of river bed located at Mapo-ri, Chongong-myon, Yonchon-gun, Kyonggi-do, for the period 1 May 1968 to 30 April 1969, has been accepted by the Ministry of National Defense. The real estate is required for the conduct of firing tests and for training. The Ministry of National Defense and the Far East District Engineer will be requested to prepare the necessary documents. It is recommended that the Joint Committee, SOFA, approve acquisition of this temporary use permit.

d. The request for extension of temporary use permit 7X-T-3, involving 287 acres of forested land, from 14 April 1968 to 13 April 1969, has been accepted by the Ministry of National Defense. The real estate is required for continued use as a field training area. The Ministry of National Defense and the Far East District Engineer will be requested to prepare the necessary documents. It is recommended that the Joint Committee, SOFA, approve extension of this permit.

e. The request for extension of temporary use permit 7X-IC-T-5, involving 400 acres of forested land, from 14 April 1968 to 13 April 1969, has been accepted by the Ministry of National Defense. The real estate is required for continued use as a field training area. The Ministry of National Defense and the Far East District Engineer will be requested to prepare the necessary documents. It is recommended that the Joint Committee, SOFA, approve extension of this permit.

4. Security Classification: Unclassified.

COLONEL I. M. RICE
Chairman, United States Component
Facilities and Areas Subcommittee

MAJOR GENERAL KIM Mook
Chairman, Republic of Korea Component
Facilities and Areas Subcommittee

2

37

REPUBLIC OF KOREA – UNITED STATES
FACILITIES AND AREAS SUBCOMMITTEE

26 April 1968

MEMORANDUM FOR: THE JOINT COMMITTEE

1. Subcommittee members:

<u>United States</u>   <u>Republic of Korea</u>

COL I. M. Rice, Chairman   MG KIM Mook, Chairman
LTC J. B. Carrick, USAFCSK   Mr. SONG Yong Tai
LTC Robert E. Graf, J4, USFK   Mr. SHIN Chung Sup
MAJ James B. Hoodenpyle, USAF   Mr. LEE Soon Dong
Mr. Francis K. Cook, J5, USFK   Mr. LEE Kihl Choo
Mr. Richard Rose, USAEDFE   Mr. LEE Moon Sup
Mrs. Betty H. Bowman, 8th Army   Mr. LEE Jong Do
                                      Mr. CHANG Kyong Shik
                                      Mr. CHA Sang Chun
                                      Mr. KIM Byoung Chan
                                      Mr. CHONG Young Hoon
                                      Mr. CHOI Chung Hwan
                                      Mr. NO Yong Goo
                                      Mr. PARK Moh Soo
                                      LTC KANG Jong Kuk
                                      Mr. KANG Hong Suk

2. Subject of Recommendations: Requests for Acquisition of Real Estate.
(Reference Joint Committee Memorandum, same subject, dated 11 April 1968).

3. Recommendations:

    a. The request for acquisition of 0.0103 acre of nonarable land
located at Samok-ni, Imjin-myon, Paju-gun, Kyonggi-do, has been accepted
by the Ministry of National Defense. The real estate is required for the
erection of two observation towers to improve security. The Ministry of
National Defense and the Far East District Engineer will be requested to
prepare the necessary documents. It is recommended that the Joint
Committee, SOFA, approve this acquisition.

38

b. The request for acquisition of an easement for 1.1845 acres of land located at 1004-6 Haemang-dong, Kunsan City, and at 1501 Shinpung-ri, Mi-myon, Okku-gun, Chollapuk-do, has been accepted by the Ministry of National Defense. The real estate is required to install POL pipe line between two military installations. The Ministry of National Defense and the Far East District Engineer will be requested to prepare the necessary documents. It is recommended that the Joint Committee, SOFA, approve this acquisition.

c. The request for acquisition of an easement for 1.00 acre of land, consisting of 0.35 acre of stream bed and 0.65 acre of existing road located at Tonggi-ri, Kwangtan-myon, Paju-gun, Kyonggi-do, has been mutually agreed upon by the Ministry of National Defense and Eighth Army, in accordance with stipulations contained in the Kyonggi-do Governor's Instructions of 29 March 1968, attached. The real estate is required to construct a water pipe line connecting two military compounds. The Ministry of National Defense and the Far East District Engineer will be requested to prepare the necessary documents. It is recommended that the Joint Committee, SOFA, approve this acquisition.

4. Security Classification: Unclassified.

_____
COLONEL I. M. RICE
Chairman, United States Component
Facilities and Areas Subcommittee

_____
MAJOR GENERAL KIM Mook
Chairman, Republic of Korea Component
Facilities and Areas Subcommittee

1 Incl
as

2

Kyonggi-Const No. 21

        Sunyu-Ri, Imchin-Myon, Paju-Gun, Kyonggi-Do
        2d Infantry Division, MND RE Representative
        Park Kyong Man

In accordance with Article 40 of Road Law, the request for use of road site dated 19 March 1968 is approved with the following stipulations.

1. Location: Between Sinsan-Ri and Bangchu-Ri, Kwangtan-Myon, Paju-Gun, Kyonggi-Do.

2. Acreage: 796 pyong

3. Purpose and period: Installation of underground water pipe line (for ten (10) years)

4. Construction period: From 10 April to 30 June 1968.

5. The pipe line should be installed in road shoulder.

6. Man pwer (Labor) be utilized to dig out the roadsurface and traffic hindrance be prohibited.

7. Backfilling be accomplished with good soil and sand by labor after installation of pipe. The existing facilities be protected from the operation of heavy equipment.

8. If any road damages should occur from this project, it will be rehabilitated by using agency.

9. The cancellation of the approval will be possible if necessary by Road Management Office.

10. In case of above, road obtainer has a responsibility to rehabilitate the road and its necessary expense be made by using agency as per Road Management Office.

11. Within project area, a sign board indicating the followings be prepared.

    a. Date of approval and No.
    b. Location of acquired area.
    c. Period of acquisition.

29 March 1968

GOVERNER OF KYONGGIDO, PARK KYONG MON

REPUBLIC OF KOREA - UNITED STATES
FACILITIES AND AREAS SUBCOMMITTEE

26 April 1968

MEMORANDUM FOR: THE JOINT COMMITTEE

1. Subcommittee members:

United States	Republic of Korea
COL I. M. Rice, Chairman	MG KIM Mook, Chairman
LTC J. B. Carrick, USAFCSK	Mr. SONG Yong Tai
LTC Robert E. Graf, J4, USFK	Mr. SHIN Chung Sup
MAJ James B. Hoodenpyle, USAF	Mr. LEE Soon Dong
Mr. Francis K. Cook, J5, USFK	Mr. LEE Kihl Choo
Mr. Richard Rose, USAEDFE	Mr. LEE Moon Sup
Mrs. Betty H. Bowman, 8th Army	Mr. LEE Jong Do
	Mr. CHANG Kyong Shik
	Mr. CHA Sang Chun
	Mr. KIM Byoung Chan
	Mr. CHONG Young Hoon
	Mr. CHOI Chung Hwan
	Mr. NO Yong Goo
	Mr. PARK Moh Soo
	LTC KANG Jong Kuk
	Mr. KANG Hong Suk

2. Subject of Recommendations: Requests for Acquisition of Real Estate
and Extension of Temporary Use Permits. (Reference Joint Committee
Memorandum, para 2, same subject, dated 14 March 1968).

3. Recommendations: The request for acquisition of 5.07 acres of non-
arable land located at Hasangok-ni, Tongbu-myon, Kwangju-gun, Kyonggi-do,
(of this total acreage, 3.732 acres of land are required for exclusive use,
0.89 acre of land is required for an easement, and 0.448 acre of an existing easement is required for conversion to exclusive use land) has been
accepted by the Ministry of National Defense. The real estate is required
for the expansion of Camp Colbern. The Ministry of National Defense and
the Far East District Engineer will be requested to prepare the necessary
documents. It is recommended that the Joint Committee, SOFA, approve
this acquisition.

4. Security Classification: Unclassified.

COLONEL I. M. RICE   for MAJOR GENERAL KIM Rook
Chairman, United States Component   Chairman, Republic of Korea Component
Facilities and Areas Subcommittee   Facilities and Areas Subcommittee

2

42

13 May 1968

MEMORANDUM FOR: THE JOINT COMMITTEE

1. Subcommittee members:

United States	Republic of Korea
COL I. M. Rice, Chairman	MG KIM Mook, Chairman
LTC J. B. Carrick, USAFCSK	Mr. SONG Yong Tai
LTC Robert E. Graf, J4, USFK	Mr. SHIN Chung Sup
MAJ James B. Hoodenpyle, USAF	Mr. LEE Soon Dong
Mr. Francis K. Cook, J5, USFK	Mr. LEE Kihl Choo
Mr. Richard Rose, USAEDFE	Mr. LEE Moon Sup
Mrs. Betty H. Bowman, 8th Army	Mr. LEE Jong Do
	Mr. CHANG Kyong Shik
	Mr. CHA Sang Chun
	Mr. KIM Byoung Chan
	Mr. CHONG Young Hoon
	Mr. CHOI Chung Hwan
	Mr. NO Yong Goo
	Mr. PARK Moh Soo
	LTC KANG Jong Kuk
	Mr. KANG Hong Suk

2. Subject of Recommendations: Requests for Acquisition of Real Estate, Acquisition of Temporary Use Permit, and Extension of Temporary Use Permits. (Reference Joint Committee Memorandum, paras 2, 3a, and 4a-f, same subject, dated 25 April 1968).

3. Recommendations:

a. The request for acquisition of an easement for 0.95 acre of existing road located at Wonam-ni, Tosung-myon, Kosung-gun, Kangwon-do, has been accepted by the Ministry of National Defense. The real estate is required to connect an airfield operations area with MSR S 24. The Ministry of National Defense and the Far East District Engineer will be requested to prepare the necessary documents. It is recommended that the Joint Committee, SOFA, approve this acquisition.

43

b. The request for acquisition of a temporary use permit for 12,720 acres of land located at various locations in Kimpo-myon, Kumdan-myon, Yangchon-myon, and Daekot-myon, Kimpo-gun, Kyonggi-do, required for the conduct of field exercises by the 7th US Division, from 29 April through 25 May 1968, has been accepted by the Ministry of National Defense. The Ministry of National Defense and the Far East District Engineer will be requested to prepare the necessary documents. It is recommended that the Joint Committee, SOFA, approve acquisition of this temporary use permit.

c. Request for extension of temporary use permit 7X-T-21, involving 123.6 acres of land for training purposes for the period 1 March 1968 through 28 February 1969, has been accepted by the Ministry of National Defense. The Ministry of National Defense and the Far East District Engineer will be requested to prepare the necessary documents. It is recommended that the Joint Committee, SOFA, approve extension of this permit.

d. Request for extension of temporary use permit 7X-T-22, involving 10,946 acres of land for training purposes for the period 1 February 1968 through 31 January 1969, has been accepted by the Ministry of National Defense. The Ministry of National Defense and the Far East District Engineer will be requested to prepare the necessary documents. It is recommended that the Joint Committee, SOFA, approve extension of this permit.

e. Request for extension of temporary use permit K-C-T-27, involving 30 acres of stream bed for training purposes for the period 15 May 1968 through 14 May 1969, has been accepted by the Ministry of National Defense. The Ministry of National Defense and the Far East District Engineer will be requested to prepare the necessary documents. It is recommended that the Joint Committee, SOFA, approve extension of this permit.

f. Request for extension of temporary use permit K-C-T-36, involving 365 acres of land for training purposes for the period 1 May 1968 through 30 April 1969, has been accepted by the Ministry of National Defense. The Ministry of National Defense and the Far East District Engineer will be requested to prepare the necessary documents. It is recommended that the Joint Committee, SOFA, approve extension of this permit.

g. Request for extension of temporary use permit 7X-T-5, involving 7,972 acres of land for training purposes for the period 16 May 1968 through 15 May 1969, has been accepted by the Ministry of National Defense. The Ministry of National Defense and the Far East District Engineer will be requested to prepare the necessary documents. It is recommended that the Joint Committee, SOFA, approve extension of this permit.

h. Request for extension of temporary use permit 7X-T-7, involving 486 acres of hilly and forested land for training purposes for the period 10 March 1968 through 9 March 1969, has been accepted by the Ministry of National Defense. The Ministry of National Defense and the Far East District Engineer will be requested to prepare the necessary documents. It is recommended that the Joint Committee, SOFA, approve extension of this permit.

44

4. Security Classification: Unclassified.

_____
COLONEL I. M. RICE
Chairman, United States Component
Facilities and Areas Subcommittee

_____
MAJOR GENERAL KIM Hook
Chairman, Republic of Korea Component
Facilities and Areas Subcommittee

3

45

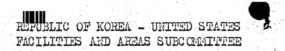

REPUBLIC OF KOREA — UNITED STATES
FACILITIES AND AREAS SUBCOMMITTEE

14 May 1968

MEMORANDUM FOR: THE JOINT COMMITTEE

1. Subcommittee members:

United States	Republic of Korea
COL I. M. Rice, Chairman	MG KIM Mook, Chairman
LTC J. B. Carrick, USAFCSK	Mr. SONG Yong Tai
LTC Robert E. Graf, J4, USFK	Mr. SHIN Chung Sup
MAJ James B. Hoodenpyle, USAF	Mr. LEE Soon Dong
Mr. Francis K. Cook, J5, USFK	Mr. LEE Kihl Choo
Mr. Richard Rose, USAEDFE	Mr. LEE Moon Sup
Mrs. Betty H. Bowman, 8th Army	Mr. LEE Jong Do
	Mr. CHANG Kyong Shik
	Mr. CHA Sang Chun
	Mr. KIM Byoung Chan
	Mr. CHONG Young Hoon
	Mr. CHOI Chung Hwan
	Mr. NO Yong Goo
	Mr. PARK Moh Soo
	LTC KANG Jong Kuk
	Mr. KANG Hong Suk

2. Subject of Recommendation: Request for Conversion of Real Estate to Exclusive Use. (Reference Joint Committee Memorandum, same subject, dated 14 March 1968).

3. Recommendation: The request for conversion of a portion of SAC-679B, located at Shindong-ni, Shinbuk-myon, Chunsung-gun, Kangwon-do, consisting of 23.50 acres of land from a perpetual restrictive easement basis to an exclusive use basis, has been accepted by the Ministry of National Defense. This conversion is required to establish a buffer area along the existing perimeter fence and for future erosion control. In addition, the area is required for construction of facilities for a Republic of Korea security guard assigned at the site. The Ministry of National Defense and the Far East District Engineer will be requested to prepare the necessary documents. It is recommended that the Joint Committee, SOFA, approve this conversion.

46

4. Security Classification: Unclassified.

_____   _____
COLONEL I. M. RICE   MAJOR GENERAL KIM Mook
Chairman, United States Component   Chairman, Republic of Korea Component
Facilities and Areas Subcommittee   Facilities and Areas Subcommittee

2

47

REPUBLIC OF KOREA - UNITED STATES
FACILITIES AND AREAS SUBCOMMITTEE

26 April 1968

MEMORANDUM FOR: THE JOINT COMMITTEE

1. Subcommittee members:

United States	Republic of Korea
COL I. M. Rice, Chairman	MG KIM Mook, Chairman
LTC J. B. Carrick, USAFCSK	Mr. SONG Yong Tai
LTC Robert E. Graf, J4, USFK	Mr. SHIN Chung Sup
MAJ James B. Hoodenpyle, USAF	Mr. LEE Soon Dong
Mr. Francis K. Cook, J5, USFK	Mr. LEE Kihl Choo
Mr. Richard Rose, USAEDFE	Mr. LEE Moon Sup
Mrs. Betty H. Bowman, 8th Army	Mr. LEE Jong Do
	Mr. CHANG Kyong Shik
	Mr. CHA Sang Chun
	Mr. KIM Byoung Chan
	Mr. CHONG Young Hoon
	Mr. CHOI Chung Hwan
	Mr. NO Yong Goo
	Mr. PARK Moh Soo
	LTC KANG Jong Kuk
	Mr. KANG Hong Suk

2. Subject of Recommendations: Request for Release of Real Estate.
(Reference Joint Committee Memorandum, same subject, dated 11 April 1968).

3. Recommendations: The request for release of a portion of PAC-67,
involving 1.2558, has been accepted by the Ministry of National Defense.
The Ministry of National Defense and the Far East District Engineer will
be requested to prepare the necessary documents. It is recommended that
the Joint Committee, SOFA approve this release.

48

4. Security Classification: Unclassified.

_____ _____
COLONEL I. M. RICE   MAJOR GENERAL KIM Mook
Chairman, United States Component Chairman, Republic of Korea Component
Facilities and Areas Subcommittee Facilities and Areas Subcommittee

2

49.

REPUBLIC OF KOREA - UNITED STATES
FACILITIES AND AREAS SUBCOMMITTEE

29 April 1968

MEMORANDUM FOR: THE JOINT COMMITTEE

1. Subcommittee members:

United States	Republic of Korea
COL I. M. Rice, Chairman	MG KIM Mook, Chairman
LTC J. B. Carrick, USAFCSK	Mr. SONG Yong Tai
LTC Robert E. Graf, J4, USFK	Mr. SHIN Chung Sup
MAJ James B. Hoodenpyle, USAF	Mr. LEE Soon Dong
Mr. Francis K. Cook, J5, USFK	Mr. LEE Kihl Choo
Mr. Richard Rose, USAEDFE	Mr. LEE Moon Sup
Mrs. Betty H. Bowman, 8th Army	Mr. LEE Jong Do
	Mr. CHANG Kyong Shik
	Mr. CHA Sang Chun
	Mr. KIM Byoung Chan
	Mr. CHONG Young Hoon
	Mr. CHOI Chung Hwan
	Mr. NO Yong Goo
	Mr. PARK Moh Soo
	LTC KANG Jong Kuk
	Mr. KANG Hong Suk

2. Subject of Recommendations: Requests for Release of Real
Estate. (Reference Joint Committee Memorandum, para 2f, same subject,
dated 30 November 1967.

3. Recommendations:

Request for release of a portion of SAC-685, containing 1.571
acres at No. 39-1 Suhyang-ri, Sunghwan-myon, Chunwon-gun, Chungchongnam-
do. Memorandum recommending approval of this release was submitted to
the Joint Committee, 26 December 1967. Release was approved by the
Joint Committee on 18 January 1968. Subsequently, it was determined
that retention of the area is required. Retention of the facility has
been accepted by the Ministry of National Defense. It is therefore
recommended that no further action be taken on this task.

4. Security Classification: Unclassified.

_____   _____
COLONEL I. M. RICE   for MAJOR GENERAL KIM Mook
Chairman, United States Component   Chairman, Republic of Korea Component
Facilities and Areas Subcommittee   Facilities and Areas Subcommittee

2

14 May 1968

MEMORANDUM FOR: The Joint Committee

SUBJECT: Designation of US Invited Contractor under Article XV,
Status of Forces Agreement

1. References:

a. Paragraph 2, Article XV, Status of Forces Agreement.

b. US Commerce Subcommittee Memorandum of Consultation, dated
9 May 1968, subject as above (Inclosure 1).

c. ROK Commerce Subcommittee Memorandum of Consultation, dated
10 May 1968, subject as above (Inclosure 2).

2. The United States, after consultation with the ROK Commerce Subcommittee and after having duly considered their views, has designated
Daniel, Mann, Johnson & Mendenhall as a US invited contractor for
execution of Contract #F62087-68-C-0095 for Architect and Engineering
services.

3. Pertinent data concerning US citizen employees will be provided to
the Joint Secretariat in the established periodic arrival and departure
format.

2 Incl
as

ROBERT J. FRIEDMAN
Lieutenant General
United States Air Force
United States Representative
Joint Committee

MINISTRY OF COMMERCE AND INDUSTRY
REPUBLIC OF KOREA
SEOUL, KOREA

10 May 1968

SUBJECT: Desingation of US Invited Contractor under Article XV,
Status of Forces Agreement.

TO   : Chairman, US Commerce Subcommittee

1. References:

   a. Paragraph 2, Article XV, Status of Forces Agreement.

   b. US Commerce Subcommittee Memorandum of Consultation, Dated
9 May 1968, subject as above, pertaining to contract for architect-
engineering service in the Kwangju, Kunsan, Osan and Taegu Air Base
construction projects.

2. The US memorandum, reference 1b above, has been reviewed and
the Government of the Republic of Korea fully understands the requirement for an invited contractor in this instance.

for Kil Yong Um
Chairman
ROK Commerce Subcommittee

53

REPUBLIC OF KOREA - UNITED STATES
COMMERCE SUBCOMMITTEE

9 May 1968

SUBJECT: Designation of US Invited Contractor under Article XV,
Status of Forces Agreement

ROK Chairman, Commerce Subcommittee

1. Reference: Paragraph 2, Article XV of the Status of Forces Agreement.

2. The Government of the Republic of Korea is informed through this written consultive process that the United States Forces, Korea, proposes to extend invited contractor status to the successful negotiated bidder among qualified US firms on the contract described in paragraph 3 below.

3. The following data is provided:

a. Company Name: Daniel, Mann, Johnson & Mendenhall.

b. Local Address: Box 1-I, APO 96570.

c. Identification of US Citizen Employees: To be supplied after award of contract.

d. Number of US and ROK Employees:

| U.S. | - | 11 |
| ROK | - | 15 |

e. Reasons for Designation of an Invited Contractor: Open competitive bidding among local contractors is not practicable due to the following:

(1) Security considerations.

(2) Technical qualifications of the contractor involved.

f. Location of contract: Kwangju Air Base; Kunsan Air Base; Osan Air Base, and Taegu Air Base, Korea.

54

SUBJECT: Designation of US Invited Contractor under Article XV, Status of Forces Agreement

    g. Type of Contract: Architect-Engineering services.

    h. Length of Contract: Approximately 30 days.

    i. Sponsoring Component Command: Commander, Air Forces, Korea (Headquarters 6314th Support Wing (PACAF)).

FLOYD R. WALTZ, JR.
Colonel, United States Army
Assistant Chief of Staff, J 4

2

JOINT COMMITTEE
UNDER
THE REPUBLIC OF KOREA AND THE UNITED STATES
STATUS OF FORCES AGREEMENT

14 May 1968

MEMORANDUM FOR: The Joint Committee

SUBJECT: Designation of US Invited Contractor under Article XV,
Status of Forces Agreement

1. References:

    a. Paragraph 2, Article XV, Status of Forces Agreement.

    b. US Commerce Subcommittee Memorandum of Consultation, dated
9 May 1968, subject as above (Inclosure 1).

    c. ROK Commerce Subcommittee Memorandum of Consultation, dated
10 May 1968, subject as above (Inclosure 2).

2. The United States, after consultation with the ROK Commerce Subcommittee and after having duly considered their views, has designated
Trans-Asia Engineering Associates, Inc. as a US invited contractor for
execution of Contract #F62087-68-C-0096 for Architect and Engineering
services.

3. Pertinent data concerning US citizen employees will be provided to
the Joint Secretariat in the established periodic arrival and departure
format.

2 Incl
as

                    ROBERT J. FRIEDMAN
                    Lieutenant General
                    United States Air Force
                    United States Representative
                    Joint Committee

56

MINISTRY OF COMMERCE AND INDUSTRY
REPUBLIC OF KOREA
SEOUL, KOREA

10 May 1968

SUBJECT: Designation of US Invited Contractor under Article XV,
Status of Forces Agreement.

TO   : Chairman, US Commerce Subcommittee

1. References:

a. Paragraph 2, Article XV, Status of Forces Agreement.

b. US Commerce Subcommittee Memorandum of Consultation, Dated
9 May 1968, subject as above, pertaining to contract for architect-
engineering services in the Kwangju, Kunsan, and Osan Air Base construction projects.

2. The US memorandum, reference 1b above, has been reviewed and
the Government of the Republic of Korea fully understands the requirement for an invited contractor in this instance.

for Kil Yong Um
Chairman
ROK Commerce Subcommittee

57

REPUBLIC OF KOREA - UNITED STATES
COMMERCE SUBCOMMITTEE

9 May 1968

SUBJECT: Designation of US Invited Contractor under Article XV,
Status of Forces Agreement

ROK Chairman, Commerce Subcommittee

1. Reference: Paragraph 2, Article XV of the Status of Forces Agreement.

2. The Government of the Republic of Korea is informed through this written consultive process that the United States Forces, Korea, proposes to extend invited contractor status to the successful negotiated bidder among qualified US firms on the contract described in paragraph 3 below.

3. The following data is provided:

   a. Company Name: Trans-Asia Engineering Associates, Inc.

   b. Local Address: Building 1510, APO 96301.

   c. Identification of US Citizen Employees: To be supplied after award of contract.

   d. Number of US and ROK Employees:

                    U.S.   -   5
                    ROK   -   15

   e. Reasons for Designation of an Invited Contractor: Open competitive bidding among local contractors is not practicable due to the following:

   (1) Security considerations.

   (2) Technical qualifications of the contractor involved.

   f. Location of Contract: Kwangju Air Base, Kunsan Air Base, and Osan Air Base, Korea.

SUBJECT: Designation of US Invited Contractor under Article XV,
Status of Forces Agreement

g. Type of Contract: Architect-Engineering services.

h. Length of Contract: Approximately 45 days.

i. Sponsoring Component Command: Commander, Air Forces, Korea
(Headquarters 6314th Support Wing (PACAF)).

FLOYD R. WALTZ, JR.
Colonel, United States Army
US Chairman, Commerce Subcommittee

2

59

JOINT COMMITTEE
UNDER
THE REPUBLIC OF KOREA AND THE UNITED STATES
STATUS OF FORCES AGREEMENT

3 May 1968

MEMORANDUM FOR: The Joint Committee

SUBJECT: Designation of US Invited Contractor under Article XV,
Status of Forces Agreement

1. References:

    a. Paragraph 2, Artic le XV, Status of Forces Agreement.

    b. US Commerce Subcommittee Memorandum of Consultation, dated
30 April 1968, subject as above (Inclosure 1).

    c. ROK Commerce Subcommittee Memorandum of Consultation, dated
3 May 1968, subject as above (Inclosure 2).

2. The United States, after consultation with the ROK Commerce Subcommittee and after having duly considered their views, has designated
Vinnell Corporation as a US invited contractor for execution of
Contracts #DAAE13-67-C-0171, DA23-195-AMC-00772(T), DAJB11-68-C-0014,
and DAAE13-67-C-208 for the purpose of recruiting Korean personnel for
employment in South Vietnam.

3. Pertinent data concerning US citizen employees will be provided
to the Joint Secretariat in the established periodic arrival and
departure format.

2 Incl   ROBERT J. FRIEDMAN
as   Lieutenant General
                                    United States Air Force
                                    United States Representative
                                    Joint Committee

60

REPUBLIC OF KOREA - UNITED STATES
COMMERCE SUBCOMMITTEE

30 April 1968

SUBJECT: Designation of US Invited Contractor under Article XV,
Status of Forces Agreement

Chairman, ROK Commerce Subcommittee

1. Reference: Paragraph 2, Article XV of the Status of Forces Agreement.

2. The Government of the Republic of Korea is informed through this
written consultive process that the United States Forces, Korea, proposes to extend invited contractor status to the contractor described
in paragraph 3 below.

3. The following data is provided:

    a. Company Name: Vinnell Corporation.

    b. Local Address: 603 Annex Bldg., Room No. 602,
                         The Cho-Heung Bank
                         #14, 1-Ka, Namdaimun-Ro, Chung-Ku,
                         Seoul, Korea.

    c. Identification of US Citizen Employee: L. D. Good.

    d. Number of US and ROK Employees:

               U.S.   -   One.
               ROK   -   None.

    e. Reasons for Designation of an Invited Contractor: The Vinnell
Corporation will maintain and operate a Seoul, Korea personnel office
for the purpose of recruiting Korean personnel for employment in South
Vietnam and to handle the administrative and personnel problems. The
Vinnell Corporation employs approximately 3,000 Koreans in Vietnam.

    f. Location of Contract: The Vinnell Corporation is performing
the following US Government contracts in South Vietnam: DAAE13-67-C-0171,
DA23-195-AMC-00772(T), DAJB11-68-C-0014, and DAAE13-67-C-208.

6/

SUBJECT: Designation of US Invited Contractor under Article XV, Status of Forces Agreement

      g. <u>Type of Contract</u>: Cost reimbursement.

      h. <u>Length of Contract</u>: 30 September 1969.

      i. <u>Sponsoring Component Command</u>: CGUSAEIGHT.

4. The United States certifies that the Vinnell Corporation is present in the Republic of Korea solely for the purpose of executing contracts with the United States, for the benefit of the United States Armed Forces or other armed forces under the Unified Command receiving logistical support from the United States Forces.

5. The views of the Government of the Republic of Korea are earnestly solicited prior to United States selection and designation of an invited contractor to perform the work outlined above. You may be assured that your views will be considered carefully.

6. Your early reply will be greatly appreciated.

FLOYD R. WALTZ, JR.
Colonel, United States Army
US Chairman, Commerce Subcommittee

MINISTRY OF COMMERCE AND INDUSTRY
REPUBLIC OF KOREA
SEOUL, KOREA

3 May 1968

Subject: Designation of US Invited Contractor under Article XV, Status of Forces Agreement.

To   : Chairman, US Commerce Subcommittee

1. References:

   a. Paragraph 2, Article XV, Status of Forces Agreement.

   b. US Commerce Subcommittee Memorandum of Consultation, Dated 30 April 1968, subject as above, pertaining to the maintenance and operation a Seoul, Korea personnel office for the prupose of recruiting Korean personnel for employment in South Vietnam.

2. The US Memorandum, reference 1b above, has been reviewed and the Government of the Republic of Korea fully understands the requirement for an invited contractor in this instance.

For /Han Byung H/
Chairman
ROK Commerce Subcommittee

JOINT COMMITTEE
UNDER
THE REPUBLIC OF KOREA AND THE UNITED STATES
STATUS OF FORCES AGREEMENT

3 May 1968

MEMORANDUM FOR: The Joint Committee

SUBJECT: Designation of US Invited Contractor under Article XV, Status of Forces Agreement

1. References:

    a. Paragraph 2, Article XV, Status of Forces Agreement.

    b. US Commerce Subcommittee Memorandum of Consultation, dated 19 April 1968, subject as above (Inclosure 1).

    c. ROK Commerce Subcommittee Memorandum of Consultation, dated 3 May 1968, subject as above (Inclosure 2).

2. The United States, after consultation with the ROK Commerce Subcommittee and after having duly considered their views, has designated Barclay Overseas, Inc. as a US invited contractor for furnishing and delivering Minnesota Mining products of copying machines, thermofax brand copy paper, and other copying products to the U.S. Armed Forces in Korea, as well as providing necessary maintenance on the copying machines involved.

3. Pertinent data concerning US citizen employees will be provided to the Joint Secretariat in the established periodic arrival and departure format.

2 Incl
as

ROBERT J. FRIEDMAN
Lieutenant General
United States Air Force
United States Representative
Joint Committee

64

REPUBLIC OF KOREA - UNITED STATES
COMMERCE SUBCOMMITTEE

19 April 1968

SUBJECT: Designation of US Invited Contractor under Article XV,
Status of Forces Agreement

ROK Chairman, Commerce Subcommittee

1. Reference: Paragraph 2, Article XV of the Status of Forces Agreement.

2. The Government of the Republic of Korea is informed through this written consultative process that the United States Forces, Korea proposes to continue to extend invited contractor status to Barclay Overseas, Inc. on the contract described in paragraph 3 below.

3. The following data is provided:

a. <u>Company Name</u>: Barclay Overseas, Inc.

b. <u>Local Address</u>: #50-2, Susomun-dong, Sudaemun-ku, Seoul, Korea.

c. <u>Identification of U.S. employee</u>: Patrick E. O'Sullivan, Manager, UN Village, Apt. D-2, Seoul, Korea.

d. Number of U.S. employees   <u>1</u> .
   Number of ROK employees   <u>3</u> .

e. <u>Reasons for Designation of an Invited Contractor</u>: Unavailability of materials and services required by U.S. standards. The contractor is required to furnish and deliver Minnesota Mining products of copying machines, thermofax brand copy paper, and other copying products to the U.S. Armed Forces in Korea. They are also required to provide necessary maintenance on the copying machines involved.

f. <u>Location of contract</u>: Kimpo, Kunsan, and Osan Air Bases.
Also, all U.S. Army installations in Korea.

h. <u>Length of contract</u>: 6 April 1968 to 5 April 1969.

i. <u>Sponsoring Component Command</u>: Commander, Air Forces Korea.

65

SUBJECT: Designation of US Invited Contractor under Article XV,
Status of Forces Agreement.

4. The United States certifies that the named contractor is present
in the Republic of Korea solely for the purpose of executing a contract with the United States, for the benefit of the United States
Armed Forces or other Armed Forces under the Unified Command receiving
logistical support from the United States Forces.

5. The views of the Government of the Republic of Korea are earnestly
solicited prior to United States continuation of invited contractor
status to Barclay Overseas, Inc. to perform the work outlined above.
You may be assured that your views will be considered carefully.

6. Your early reply will be greatly appreciated.

JOHN T. HORROCKS
Colonel, U.S. Air Force
Alternate US Chairman,
Commerce Subcommittee

2

MINISTRY OF COMMERCE AND INDUSTRY
REPUBLIC OF KOREA
SEOUL, KOREA

3 May 1968

SUBJECT: Designation of US Invited Contractor under Article XV,
Status of Forces Agreement.

TO   : Chairman, US Commerce Subcommittee

1. References:

a. Paragraph 2, Article XV, Status of Forces Agreement.

b. US Commerce Subcommittee Memorandum of Consultation, Dated
19 April 1968, subject as above, pertaining to a contract for furnishing and delivering Minnesota Mining copying machine, thermofax brand
copy paper and other copying products to the U.S. Armed Forces in Korea.

2. The US memorandum, reference 1b above, has been reviewed and
the Government of the Republic of Korea fully understands the requirement for an invited contractor in this instance.

FOR Chairman
ROK Commerce Subcommittee

67

JOINT COMMITTEE
UNDER
THE REPUBLIC OF KOREA AND THE UNITED STATES
STATUS OF FORCES AGREEMENT

29 April 1968

MEMORANDUM TO: The Joint Committee

SUBJECT: Designation of US Invited Contractor under Article XV, Status of Forces Agreement

1. References:

    a. Paragraph 2, Article XV, Status of Forces Agreement.

    b. US Commerce Subcommittee Memorandum of Consultation, dated 29 March 1968, subject as above. (Incl 1)

    c. ROK Commerce Subcommittee Memorandum of Consultation, dated 2 April 1968, subject as above. (Incl 2)

2. The United States, after consultation with the ROK Commerce Subcommittee and after having duly considered their views, has designated Pacific Architects & Engineers, Inc. as a US Invited Contractor, for the execution of contract #DACA81-68-C-0051 for Architect-Engineer Services for Design of Miscellaneous Facilities and Related Work.

3. Pertinent data concerning U.S. citizen employees will be provided to the Joint Secretariat in the established periodic arrival and departure format.

2 Incl
as

ROBERT J. FRIEDMAN
Lieutenant General
United States Air Force
United States Representative
Joint Committee

68

MINISTRY OF COMMERCE AND INDUSTRY
REPUBLIC OF KOREA
SEOUL, KOREA

2 April 1968

SUBJECT: Designation of US Invited Contractor under Article XV,
Status of Forces Agreement.

TO   : Chairman, US Commerce Subcommittee

1. References:

   a. Paragraph 2, Article XV, Status of Forces Agreement.

   b. US Commerce Subcommittee Memorandum of Consultation,
dated 29 March 1968, subject as above, pertaining to contract for
Architect-Engineer Services for Design of Miscellaneous Facilities
and Related Work.

2. The US memorandum reference 1b above, has been reviewed and
the Government of the Republic of Korea fully understands the requirement for an invited contractor in this instance.

FOR / Han Byung Il
Chairman
ROK Commerce Subcommittee

69

REPUBLIC OF KOREA - UNITED STATES
COMMERCE SUBCOMMITTEE

29 March 1968

SUBJECT: Designation of US Invited Contractor under Article XV,
Status of Forces Agreement

ROK Chairman, Commerce Subcommittee

1. Reference: Paragraph 2, Article XV of the Status of Forces Agreement.

2. The Government of the Republic of Korea is informed through this
written consultive process that the United States Forces, Korea, proposes to extend invited contractor status to the successful negotiated
bidder among qualified US firms on the contract described in paragraph 3
below.

3. The following data is provided:

    a. Company Name: 1. Adrian Wilson Associates.
                     2. Daniel, Mann, Johnson & Mendenhall.
                     3. Pacific Architects & Engineers, Inc.

    b. Local Address: 1. JCA, 3ka-1, Yongsan-dong, Yongsan-ku,
                       Seoul, APO 96301.
                     2. Fuchu Air Station, Japan, APO 96525.
                     3. KMAG, APO 96302.

    c. Identification of US Citizen Employees: To be supplied on conclusion of negotiations.

    d. Number of US and ROK Employees: Number of US citizens and
Koreans is not known at this time and will be supplied upon conclusion
of negotiations.

    e. Reasons for Designation of an Invited Contractor: Open competitive bidding among local contractors is not practicable due to the
following:

    (1) Security considerations.

    (2) Limited technical qualifications of the contractors involved.

    f. Location of Contract: Various locations in Korea.

70

SUBJECT: Designation of US Invited Contractor under Article XV,
Status of Forces Agreement

    g. **Type of Contract:** Lump Sum Contract for Architect-Engineer
Services for Design of Miscellaneous Facilities and Related Work.

    h. **Length of Contract:** Approximately 6 months.

    i. **Sponsoring Component Command:** CGUSAEIGHT.

4. The United States certifies that the successful bidder or named
contractor is present in the Republic of Korea solely for the purpose
of executing contracts with the United States, for the benefit of the
United States Armed Forces or other armed forces under the Unified
Command receiving logistical support from the United States Forces.

5. The views of the Government of the Republic of Korea are earnestly
solicited prior to United States selection and designation of an invited
contractor to perform the work outlined above. You may be assured that
your views will be considered carefully.

6. Your early reply will be greatly appreciated.

                                 FLOYD R. WALTZ, JR.
                                 Colonel, United States Army
                                 US Chairman, Commerce Subcommittee

71

2

**JOINT COMMITTEE
UNDER
THE REPUBLIC OF KOREA AND THE UNITED STATES
STATUS OF FORCES AGREEMENT**

29 April 1968

MEMORANDUM TO: The Joint Committee

SUBJECT: Designation of US Invited Contractor under Article XV,
Status of Forces Agreement

1. References:

   a. Paragraph 2, Article XV, Status of Forces Agreement.

   b. US Commerce Subcommittee Memorandum of Consultation, dated
29 March 1968, subject as above. (Incl 1)

   a. ROK Commerce Subcommittee Memorandum of Consultation, dated
2 April 1968, subject as above. (Incl 2)

2. The United States, after consultation with the ROK Commerce Subcommittee and after having duly considered their views, has designated
Adrian Wilson Associates as a US Invited Contractor, for the execution
of contract #DACA81-68-C-0050 for Architect-Engineer Services for
Design of Miscellaneous Facilities and Related Work.

3. Pertinent data concerning U.S. citizen employees will be provided
to the Joint Secretariat in the established periodic arrival and
departure format.

2 Incl   ROBERT J. FRIEDMAN
as   Lieutenant General
                                United States Forces
                                United States Representative
                                Joint Committee

72

MINISTRY OF COMMERCE AND INDUSTRY
REPUBLIC OF KOREA
SEOUL, KOREA

2 April 1968

SUBJECT: Designation of US Invited Contractor under Article XV, Status of Forces Agreement.

TO   : Chairman, US Commerce Subcommittee

1. References:

    a. Paragraph 2, Article XV, Status of Forces Agreement.

    b. US Commerce Subcommittee Memorandum of Consultation, dated 29 March 1968, subject as above, pertaining to contract for Architect-Engineer Services for Design of Miscellaneous Facilities and Related Work.

2. The US memorandum reference 1b above, has been reviewed and the Government of the Republic of Korea fully understands the requirement for an invited contractor in this instance.

FOR /Han Byung Il

Chairman.
ROK Commerce Subcommittee

REPUBLIC OF KOREA – UNITED STATES
COMMERCE SUBCOMMITTEE

29 March 1968

SUBJECT: Designation of US Invited Contractor under Article XV,
Status of Forces Agreement

ROK Chairman, Commerce Subcommittee

1. Reference: Paragraph 2, Article XV of the Status of Forces Agreement.

2. The Government of the Republic of Korea is informed through this written consultive process that the United States Forces, Korea, proposes to extend invited contractor status to the successful negotiated bidder among qualified US firms on the contract described in paragraph 3 below.

3. The following data is provided:

    a. <u>Company Name</u>: 1. Adrian Wilson Associates.
                         2. Daniel, Mann, Johnson & Mendenhall.
                         3. Pacific Architects & Engineers, Inc.

    b. <u>Local Address</u>: 1. JCA, 3ka-1, Yongsan-dong, Yongsan-ku,
                            Seoul, APO 96301.
                         2. Fuchu Air Station, Japan, APO 96525.
                         3. KMAG, APO 96302.

    c. <u>Identification of US Citizen Employees</u>: To be supplied on conclusion of negotiations.

    d. <u>Number of US and ROK Employees</u>: Number of US citizens and Koreans is not known at this time and will be supplied upon conclusion of negotiations.

    e. <u>Reasons for Designation of an Invited Contractor</u>: Open competitive bidding among local contractors is not practicable due to the following:

    (1) Security considerations.

    (2) Limited technical qualifications of the contractors involved.

    f. <u>Location of Contract</u>: Various locations in Korea.

74

SUBJECT: Designation of US Invited Contractor under Article XV,
Status of Forces Agreement

    g. Type of Contract: Lump Sum Contract for Architect-Engineer Services for Design of Miscellaneous Facilities and Related Work.

    h. Length of Contract: Approximately 6 months.

    i. Sponsoring Component Command: CGUSAEIGHT.

4. The United States certifies that the successful bidder or named contractor is present in the Republic of Korea solely for the purpose of executing contracts with the United States, for the benefit of the United States Armed Forces or other armed forces under the Unified Command receiving logistical support from the United States Forces.

5. The views of the Government of the Republic of Korea are earnestly solicited prior to United States selection and designation of an invited contractor to perform the work outlined above. You may be assured that your views will be considered carefully.

6. Your early reply will be greatly appreciated.

FLOYD R. WALTZ, JR.
Colonel, United States Army
US Chairman, Commerce Subcommittee

2

JOINT ROK - US PRESS RELEASE
TWENTY-FIFTH ROK-US JOINT COMMITTEE MEETING
17 MAY 1968

The ROK-US Joint Committee approved 25 recommendations of its Facilities and Areas Subcommittee at its twenty-fifth meeting, held at the Capitol Building on Friday, 17 May. One of these Joint Committee actions involved US-ROK agreement on a list of all of the facilities and areas held by the US armed forces in the Republic of Korea, while 24 dealt with acquisition, release, and extension of temporary use of facilities and areas for the US armed forces.

The Republic of Korea Representative, Mr. YOON Ha Jong, Director of the Europe and America Bureau of the Foreign Ministry, presided at this meeting of the Joint Committee. The Joint Committee also assigned seven new tasks to the Facilities and Areas Subcommittee and noted designation of six US invited contractors.

The next meeting of the Joint Committee is scheduled to be held on Friday, 7 June, in the US SOFA Conference Room in Yongsan.

76

미공군기 추락에 관한 미국측 각서

　　한국 법무부에서는 사고 발생후 4, 5 일이 지나서 주한 미군 소청사무소로 부터 본 건 사고 처리를 신속 원만히하여둘 것을 요청받은바 있읍니다. 한국 법무부에서는 요청을 받은 즉시 사고발생지역을 관할하는 전주 지구 배상심의회와 관할 군청으로 하여금 피해자에게 조속히 배상신청을 하도록 종용하는 한편, 현지 검찰, 경찰 및 군청에 피해조사를 정확히 할 것을 지시한바 있읍니다. 그러나 협협에 기한 배상신청 절차를 모르는 피해자들은 서울에서 계업하고 있는 이응한 변호사에게 배상 신청권을 위임 하였고 동 변호사는 피해견적과 그 증빙을 갖추기 위하여 노력 하다가 68년 5월 14일에 야 배상 청구를 하였읍니다. 물론 동 변호사에 대하여도 배상 신청 촉구를 누차 하였읍니다. 현재 법무부에서는 현지 검찰과 경찰의 피해 조사 결과를 근거로 사건 처리를 하고 있으며 향후 10일 후에는 배상 결정 단계에 이르게 될 것입니다. 또한 피해자중 사망자에 대하여는 그전에라도 장례비의 사전 지급 조치를 취할 작정입니다.

　　　　　　　　　　　송무과　홍 사무관

미이 720~   196 8 . 5 . 27

수 신 : 배부처 참조

참 조 :

제 목 : 한.미 합동위원회 회의록 송부

　　1. 한.미간 군대지위협정에 의하여 196 8 . 5 . 17. 에

개최된 한.미 합동위원회 제 25 차 회의의 회의록을 별첨 송부하오니

참고 하시기 바랍니다.

　　2. 본 회의록은 한.미 양측의 합의에 의하여서만 공개할

수 있는 문서이오니 유념하시기 바랍니다.

첨부 : 합동위원회 제 25 차 회의록   부.   끝

외 무 부 장 관

3

배부처 : 법무부장관 (법무실장, 검찰국장), 국방부장관 (기획국장,

　　시설국장), 재무부장관 (세관국장, 세제국장),

　　상공부장관 (상역국장), 노동청장 (노정국장),

　　교통부장관 (항공국장), 내무부장관 (치안국장), 주미

　　주일, 주중, 주비대사   경제기획원 장관 (기획국장)

78

These minutes are considered as official documents pertaining to both
Governments and will not be released without mutual agreement.

**JOINT COMMITTEE
UNDER
THE REPUBLIC OF KOREA AND THE UNITED STATES
STATUS OF FORCES AGREEMENT**

MINUTES OF THE TWENTY-FIFTH MEETING

17 May 1968
Capitol Building
Republic of Korea
Seoul, Korea

1. The meeting was convened at 1500 hours by Mr. YOON Ha Jong,
the ROK Representative, who presided at the meeting. A copy of the
agenda is attached as Inclosure 1.

2. The following were in attendance:

ROK	US
Mr. YOON Ha Jong	LTG Robert J. Friedman, USAF
Mr. HUH Seung Joon	CAPT M. R. Massie, USN
Mr. SHIN Chung Sup	COL Walter V. Gresham, USAF
Mr. PARK Noh Soo	COL Herbert C. Hicks, Jr., USA
Mr. OH Myong Too	COL Gerald W. Davis, USA
Mr. WHANG Kong Riol	Mr. P. Wesley Kriebel, US Embassy
	Mr. Robert A. Kinney, USFK
	LTC Paul E. Jones, USAF

3. The ROK Representative called the meeting to order and invited
the US Representative to present four new tasks to the Facilities and
Areas Subcommittee.

4. The US Representative proposed the assignment of four additional
tasks to the Facilities and Areas Subcommittee, as follows:

a. Acquisition of a total of 16.455 acres of land in Paju-gun,
Kyonggi-do (Inclosure 2).

b. Conversion of 0.014 acre in Kwangju-gun, Kyonggi-do, currently held as a perpetual restrictive easement, to an exclusive use
basis (Inclosure 2).

c. Extension of Temporary Use Permit CAV-T-16 from 1 May
1968 to 30 April 1969 (Inclosure 2).

d. Conversion of 0.643 acre in Shihung-gun, Kyonggi-do, from
a perpetual restrictive easement to an exclusive use basis (Inclosure 3).

25th JC
17 May 68

These minutes are considered as official documents pertaining to both Governments and will not be released without mutual agreement.

5. The US Representative requested Joint Committee approval of the assignment of these four tasks to the Facilities and Areas Subcommittee and the ROK Representative concurred.

6. The ROK Representative presented for formal concurrence of the US Representative, three new tasks, to be assigned to the Facilities and Areas Subcommittee. The first two of the three tasks had already been signed by the two Representatives and assigned, as an exigency measure, to the Subcommittee. These two tasks were to prepare recommendations for the following requests (Inclosure 4):

     a. Release of a portion of SAC-715, Sections 2 and 3; 715-A; and a portion of Easement D, E, F, and G, which were required for an urban development project in the Special City of Seoul.

     b. Release of SAC-CS-198, located at Pajang-dong, Suwon, Kyonggi-do, in connection with an urban renewal project in the City of Suwon.

7. The ROK Representative proposed that these two tasks be included in the official record of the Joint Committee, and the US Representative concurred.

8. The ROK Representative stated that the third and last task related to the request for joint use of a railway side track at the Yongsan Railway Station (Inclosure 5). The ROK Representative proposed the formal assignment of this task to the Facilities and Areas Subcommittee, and the US Representative concurred.

9. The US Representative presented twenty-three recommendations of the Facilities and Areas Subcommittee, as follows:

     a. That the record of facilities and areas in use by the United States armed forces as of 9 February 1967 be approved (Inclosure 6). The US Representative commented that the determination of format and compilation of this record represents another outstanding achievement of the Facilities and Areas Subcommittee.

     b. The acquisition of the following land areas:

        (1) 5.07 acres at Hasangok-ni, Kyonggi-do (Inclosure 7).

        (2) 10.48 acres at Dongpa-ri, Kyonggi-do (Inclosure 8).

25th JC
17 May 68

2

These minutes are considered as official documents pertaining to both Governments and will not be released without mutual agreement.

      (3) 1.56 acres at Pobwon-ni, Kyonggi-do (Inclosure 8).

      (4) 0.0103 acre at Samok-ni, Kyonggi-do (Inclosure 9).

    c. The acquisition of a perpetual restrictive easement involving 0.16 acre of land at Majang-dong, Sungdong-ku, Seoul City (Inclosure 8).

    d. The acquisition of the following easements:

      (1) 1.1845 acres at 1004-6 Haemang-dong, Kunsan City and at 1501 Shinpung-ri, Cholla puk-do (Inclosure 9).

      (2) 1.0 acre of land at Tonggi-ri, Kyonggi-do (Inclosure 9).

      (3) 0.95 acre of existing road at Wonam-ni, Kangwon-do (Inclosure 10).

    e. The acquisition of temporary use permits for:

      (1) 59 acres of land at Toegyewon-ni, Kyonggi-do (Inclosure 11).

      (2) 173.943 acres of land at Kawol-li and Chuwol-li, Kyonggi-do (Inclosure 11).

      (3) 142.524 acres of land at Mapo-ri, Kyonggi-do (Inclosure 11).

      (4) 12,720 acres at various locations in Kimpo-gun, Kyonggi-do (Inclosure 10).

    f. The extension of the following Temporary Use Permits:

      (1) IC-T-38 (Inclosure 8).

      (2) 7X-T-3 (Inclosure 11).

      (3) 7X-IC-T-5 (Inclosure 11).

      (4) 7X-T-21 (Inclosure 10).

      (5) 7X-T-22 (Inclosure 10).

      (6) K-C-T-27 (Inclosure 10).

      (7) K-C-T-36 (Inclosure 10).

These minutes are considered as official documents pertaining to both Governments and will not be released without mutual agreement.

        (8) 7X-T-5 (Inclosure 10).

        (9) 7X-T-7 (Inclosure 10).

     g. The conversion of a portion of SAC-679B (23.50 acres) from an easement basis to an exclusive use basis (Inclosure 12).

    10. The US Representative proposed Joint Committee approval of these 23 recommendations of the Facilities and Areas Subcommittee. He commended this Subcommittee for having completed 90% of the 199 tasks it had been assigned prior to this twenty-fifth meeting. The ROK Representative concurred in the approval of these 23 recommendations, and also expressed the satisfaction of his Government for the good work of the Facilities and Areas Subcommittee.

    11. The ROK Representative presented two recommendations of the Facilities and Areas Subcommittee, as follows:

     a. The release of a portion of PAC-67, involving 1.2558 acres (Inclosure 13).

     b. The request for the release of a portion of SAC-685, involving 1.571 acres, has been withdrawn (Inclosure 14).

    12. The US Representative concurred in Joint Committee approval of these two recommendations of the Facilities and Areas Subcommittee.

    13. The US Representative presented memoranda to the Joint Committee informing the Republic of Korea Government of the designation of six new invited contractors under Article XV of the Status of Forces Agreement. After consultation with Republic of Korea Commerce Subcommittee personnel, the United States Forces, Korea, had designated the following as US invited contractors:

     a. Adrian Wilson Associates (Inclosure 15).

     b. Pacific Architects & Engineers, Inc. (Inclosure 16).

     c. Vinnell Corporation (Inclosure 17).

     d. Barclay Overseas, Inc. (Inclosure 18).

     e. Daniel, Mann, Johnson & Mendenhall (Inclosure 19).

     f. Trans-Asia Engineering Associates, Inc. (Inclosure 20).

25th JC

4   2138**17 May 68**

These minutes are considered as official documents pertaining to both Governments and will not be released without mutual agreement.

14.   The US Representative stated that pertinent data concerning employees of these invited contractors would be provided to the Government of Korea in accordance with mutually approved procedures.   The ROK Representative indicated that he was pleased to take note of and acknowledge US notification on the designation of these six USFK invited contractors.

15.   The US Representative noted for the record that the US SOFA Secretary had furnished the following information to the ROK SOFA Secretary, in accordance with Joint Committee decisions:

   a.   Twenty copies of a report listing arrivals, departures, and address changes of United States invited contractor personnel and their dependents, dated 27 April 1968.

   b.   Twenty copies of the report of United States armed forces personnel, the civilian component, invited contractors, and dependents entering or departing the Republic of Korea during the month of April 1968.

16.   The ROK Representative confirmed the receipt by the ROK SOFA Secretary of the documents as enumerated.

17.   The ROK Representative proposed that the next meeting of the Joint Committee be held at 1500 hours, on Friday, 7 June, in the US SOFA Conference Room, Yongsan.   He indicated that this was the usual three-week interval between meetings, and that it was being scheduled for Friday, 7 June, because the Korean Memorial Day was being observed on Thursday, 6 June.   The US Representative agreed that the next Joint Committee meeting be scheduled for 1500 hours, on Friday, 7 June.

18.   The ROK Representative indicated that copies of the draft text of the Joint Press Release, prepared and agreed upon by the two SOFA Secretaries (Inclosure 21), had been distributed beforehand.   He proposed adoption of the text as prepared, and the US Representative concurred.

19.   The meeting was adjourned at 1540 hours.

21 Inclosures

YOON HA JONG
REPUBLIC OF KOREA
REPRESENTATIVE

ROBERT J. FRIEDMAN
LIEUTENANT GENERAL
UNITED STATES AIR FORCE
UNITED STATES REPRESENTATIVE

25th JC
17 May 68

83   5

These minutes are considered as official documents pertaining to both Governments and ● not be released without mutu● greement.

AGENDA FOR THE TWENTY-FIFTH MEETING
OF THE ROK-US JOINT COMMITTEE
1500 HOURS, 17 MAY 1968, ROK CAPITOL BUILDING

I   Assignment of Additional Tasks to Facilities and Areas Subcommittee:

    1. Four tasks   -   US Presentation

    2. Three tasks   -   ROK Presentation

II   Recommendations of Facilities and Areas Subcommittee:

    1. Twenty-three recommendations   -   US Presentation

    2. Two recommendations   -   ROK Presentation

III   Memoranda on Designation of Six USFK Invited Contractors   -

       US Presentation

IV   Memoranda Presented to the ROK Government by the US, in the

       Implementation of the SOFA   -   US Presentation

V   Proposed Time of Next Meeting   -   1500 hours, Friday, 7 June,

       in the US SOFA Conference Room, Yongsan

VI   Agreement on Joint Press Release

VII   Adjourn

25th JC   (Incl 1)
17 May 68

84

These minutes are considered as official documents pertaining to both
Governments and will not be released without mutual agreement.

17 May 1968

MEMORANDUM FOR: Chairmen, Facilities & Areas Subcommittee

SUBJECT: Request for Acquisition of Real Estate and Extension
of Temporary Use Permit

1. SOFA provides, in Article II, paragraph 2, that the Governments
of the Republic of Korea and the United States may agree that
facilities and areas or portions thereof shall be returned to the
Republic of Korea or that additional facilities and areas may be
provided.

2. Pursuant to paragraph 1 above, it is requested that a recommendation be presented to the Joint Committee concerning a request for
the acquisition of a total of 16.455 acres of land at various locations
in Imjin-myon, Paju-gun, Kyonggi-do. Of this acreage, 3.76 acres
are required for exclusive use, and 12.695 acres of existing road
are required as an easement. The real estate is required as a
by-pass route for tracked vehicles.

3. Pursuant to paragraph 1 above, it is requested that a recommendation be presented to the Joint Committee concerning a request to
convert to an exclusive use basis 0.014 acre currently held as a
perpetual restrictive easement. The real estate is located at #142-1,
Hasangok-ni, Tongbu-myon, Kwangju-gun, Kyonggi-do. It is required
to construct a retaining wall to prevent erosion.

4. Pursuant to paragraph 1 above, it is requested that a recommendation
be presented to the Joint Committee concerning a request for extension of
Temporary Use Permit CAV-T-16, involving a total of 128,713.04 acres
of land. Of this acreage, 38,116.82 acres consist of arable land and
90,596.22 acres of non-arable land. The extension is requested from
1 May 1968 to 30 April 1969 for training purposes.

YOON HA JONG
Republic of Korea Representative

ROBERT J. FRIEDMAN
Lieutenant General
United States Air Force
United States Representative

85

25th JC (Incl 2)
17 May 68

These minutes are considered as official documents pertaining to both
Governments and ⬤ not be released without mutu⬤ greement.

**JOINT COMMITTEE
UNDER
THE REPUBLIC OF KOREA AND THE UNITED STATES
STATUS OF FORCES AGREEMENT**

17 May 1968

MEMORANDUM FOR: Chairmen, Facilities & Areas Subcommittee

SUBJECT: Request to Convert to an Exclusive Use Basis Land
Currently Held as a Perpetual Restrictive Easement

1. SOFA provides, in Article II, paragraph 2, that the Governments of the Republic of Korea and the United States may agree
that facilities and areas or portions thereof shall be returned to
the Republic of Korea or that additional facilities and areas
may be provided.

2. Pursuant to paragraph 1 above, it is requested that a recommendation be presented to the Joint Committee concerning a
request to convert to an exclusive use basis 0.643 acre of land
currently held as a perpetual restrictive easement (a portion of
SAC-685). The real estate is located at Bakdal-ni, Anyang-up,
Shihung-gun, Kyonggi-do. It is required to construct a helicopter
landing pad.

YOON HA JONG
Republic of Korea Representative

ROBERT J. FRIEDMAN
Lieutenant General
United States Air Force
United States Representative

25th JC (Incl 3)
17 May 68

86

JOINT COMMITTEE
UNDER
THE REPUBLIC OF KOREA AND THE UNITED STATES
STATUS OF FORCES AGREEMENT

6 May 1968

MEMORANDUM FOR: Chairmen, Facilities & Areas Subcommittee

SUBJECT: Requests for Release of Real Estate

1. SOFA provides, in Article II, paragraph 2, that the Governments of the Republic of Korea and the United States may agree that facilities and areas or portions thereof shall be returned to the Republic of Korea or that additional facilities and areas may be provided.

2. Pursuant to paragraph 1 above, it is requested that recommendations be presented to the Joint Committee concerning requests for the following releases:

   a. Release of a portion of SAC-715, Section 2, 3, and 715-A, and a portion of Easement D, E, F, and G located at Siheung, Yongdongpo-ku, Seoul. This real estate is required for urban development projects of the Special City of Seoul.

   b. Release of SAC-CS-198, located at Pajong-dong, Suwon, Kyonggi-do. This real estate is required for an urban development project of the city of Suwon.

YOON HA JONG
Republic of Korea Representative

ROBERT J. FRIEDMAN
Lieutenant General
United States Air Force
United States Representative

25th JC (Incl 4)
17 May 68

These minutes are considered as official documents pertaining to both
Governments and ⬛ not be released without mutu⬛greement.

JOINT COMMITTEE
UNDER
THE REPUBLIC OF KOREA AND THE UNITED STATES
STATUS OF FORCES AGREEMENT

17 May 1968

MEMORANDUM FOR: Chairmen, Facilities and Areas Subcommittee

SUBJECT: Request for Joint Use of a Railway Side Track

1. SOFA provides, in Article II, paragraph 2, that the Governments of
the Republic of Korea and the United States may agree that facilities
and areas or portions thereof shall be returned to the Republic of Korea
or that additional facilities and areas may be provided.

2. Pursuant to paragraph 1 above, it is requested that a recommendation be presented to the Joint Committee concerning a request for joint
use of a railway side track at the Yongsan Railway Station.

YOON HA JONG
Republic of Korea
Representative

ROBERT J. FRIEDMAN
Lieutenant General
United States Air Force
United States Representative

88

25th JC (Incl 5)
17 May 68

REPUBLIC OF KOREA – UNITED STATES
FACILITIES AND AREAS SUBCOMMITTEE

25 April 1968

MEMORANDUM FOR: THE JOINT COMMITTEE

1. Subcommittee members:

United States	Republic of Korea
COL I. M. Rice, Chairman	MG KIM Mook, Chairman
LTC J. B. Carrick, USAFCSK	Mr. SONG Yong Tai
LTC Robert E. Graf, J5, USFK	Mr. SHIN Chung Sup
MAJ James B. Hoodenpyle, USAF	Mr. LEE Soon Dong
LCDR Joe T. Patterson, J5, USNAG	Mr. LEE Kihl Choo
Mr. Francis K. Cook, J5, USFK	Mr. LEE Moon Sup
Mr. Richard Rose, USAEDFE	Mr. LEE Jong Do
Mrs. Betty H. Bowman, 8th Army	Mr. CHANG Kyong Shik
	Mr. CHA Sang Chun
	Mr. SEO Yong Kwan
	Mr. CHONG Young Hoon
	Mr. CHOI Chung Hwan
	Mr. NO Yong Goo
	Mr. PARK Noh Soo
	LTC KANG Jong Kuk
	Mr. KANG Hong Suk

2. Reference the Facilities and Areas Subcommittee memorandum to the Joint Committee, 23 March 1967, subject: Determination of the Format Involved in the Maintenance by the Joint Committee of Records of Facilities and Areas in Use by the U. S. Armed Forces (Reference Article II, para 1(b) of the SOFA).

3. Recommendation: It is recommended that the record of facilities and areas in use by the U. S. Armed Forces as of 9 February 1967 as enumerated on the attached Schedule of Facilities and Areas be approved.

89

25th JC (Incl 6)
17 May 68

4. Security Classification: Unclassified.

COLONEL I. M. RICE
Chairman, United States Component
Facilities and Areas Subcommittee

MAJOR GENERAL KIM Mook
Chairman, Republic of Korea Component
Facilities and Areas Subcommittee

APPROVED BY THE JOINT COMMITTEE ON
17 MAY 1968 AT TWENTY-FIFTH MEETING

YOON Ha Jong
Republic of Korea Representative

Robert J. Friedman
Lieutenant General
United States Air Force
United States Representative

2

25th JC (Incl 6)
17 May 68

These minutes are considered as official documents pertaining to both
Governments and w█ not be released without mutua█greement.

REPUBLIC OF KOREA - UNITED STATES
FACILITIES AND AREAS SUBCOMMITTEE

26 April 1968

MEMORANDUM FOR: THE JOINT COMMITTEE

1. Subcommittee members:

United States	Republic of Korea
COL I. M. Rice, Chairman	MG KIM Mook, Chairman
LTC J. B. Carrick, USAFCSK	Mr. SONG Yong Tai
LTC Robert E. Graf, J4, USFK	Mr. SHIN Chung Sup
MAJ James B. Hoodenpyle, USAF	Mr. LEE Soon Dong
Mr. Francis K. Cook, J5, USFK	Mr. LEE Kihl Choo
Mr. Richard Rose, USAEDFE	Mr. LEE Moon Sup
Mrs. Betty H. Bowman, 8th Army	Mr. LEE Jong Do
	Mr. CHANG Kyong Shik
	Mr. CHA Sang Chun
	Mr. KIM Byoung Chan
	Mr. CHONG Young Hoon
	Mr. CHOI Chung Hwan
	Mr. NO Yong Goo
	Mr. PARK Moh Soo
	LTC KANG Jong Kuk
	Mr. KANG Hong Suk

2. Subject of Recommendations: Requests for Acquisition of Real Estate
and Extension of Temporary Use Permits. (Reference Joint Committee
Memorandum, para 2, same subject, dated 14 March 1968).

3. Recommendations: The request for acquisition of 5.07 acres of non-
arable land located at Hasangok-ni, Tongbu-myon, Kwangju-gun, Kyonggi-do,
(of this total acreage, 3.732 acres of land are required for exclusive use,
0.89 acre of land is required for an easement, and 0.448 acre of an existing easement is required for conversion to exclusive use land) has been
accepted by the Ministry of National Defense. The real estate is required
for the expansion of Camp Colbern. The Ministry of National Defense and
the Far East District Engineer will be requested to prepare the necessary
documents. It is recommended that the Joint Committee, SOFA, approve
this acquisition.

25th JC (Incl 7)
17 May 68

91

4. Security Classification: Unclassified.

_____
COLONEL I. M. RICE
Chairman, United States Component
Facilities and Areas Subcommittee

_____
MAJOR GENERAL KIM Nook
Chairman, Republic of Korea Component
Facilities and Areas Subcommittee

**APPROVED BY THE JOINT COMMITTEE ON
17 MAY 1968 AT TWENTY-FIFTH MEETING**

_____
YOON HA JONG
Republic of Korea Representative

_____
ROBERT J. FRIEDMAN
Lieutenant General
United States Air Force
United States Representative

2

25th JC (Incl 7)
17 May 68

These minutes are considered as official documents pertaining to both Governments and ●●l not be released without mutu●● agreement.

25 April 1968

MEMORANDUM FOR: THE JOINT COMMITTEE

1. Subcommittee members:

United States	Republic of Korea
COL I. M. Rice, Chairman	MG KIM Mook, Chairman
LTC J. B. Carrick, USAFCSK	Mr. SONG Yong Tai
LTC Robert E. Graf, J4, USFK	Mr. SHIN Chung Sup
MAJ James B. Hoodenpyle, USAF	Mr. LEE Soon Dong
Mr. Francis K. Cook, J5, USFK	Mr. LEE Kihl Choo
Mr. Richard Rose, USAEDFE	Mr. LEE Moon Sup
Mrs. Betty H. Bowman, 8th Army	Mr. LEE Jong Do
	Mr. CHANG Kyong Shik
	Mr. CHA Sang Chun
	Mr. KIM Byoung Chan
	Mr. CHONG Young Hoon
	Mr. CHOI Chung Hwan
	Mr. NO Yong Goo
	Mr. PARK Moh Soo
	LTC KANG Jong Kuk
	Mr. KANG Hong Suk

2. Subject of Recommendations: Requests for Acquisition of Real Estate and Extension of Temporary Use Permits. (Reference Joint Committee Memorandum, paras 2a, b, d, and e, same subject, dated 4 April 1968).

3. Recommendations:

a. The request for acquisition of 10.48 acres of nonarable land located at Dongpa-ri, Chindong-myon, Changdan-gun, Kyonggi-do, has been accepted by the Ministry of National Defense. The real estate is required for the construction of troop housing. The Ministry of National Defense and the Far East District Engineer will be requested to prepare the necessary documents. It is recommended that the Joint Committee, SOFA, approve this acquisition.

25th JC (Incl 8)
17 May 68

93

b. The request for acquisition of 1.56 acres of land located at Pobwon-ni, Chonhyon-myon, Paju-gun, Kyonggi-do, has been accepted by the Ministry of National Defense. The real estate is required for construction of a military compound. The Ministry of National Defense and the Far East District Engineer will be requested to prepare the necessary documents. It is recommended that the Joint Committee, SOFA, approve this acquisition.

c. The request for acquisition of a perpetual restrictive easement, involving 0.16 acre of nonarable land located at Majang-dong, Sungdong-ku, Seoul City, has been accepted by the Ministry of National Defense. The real estate is required to provide security for and maintenance of a pipe line connecting two military installations. The Ministry of National Defense and the Far East District Engineer will be requested to prepare the necessary documents. It is recommended that the Joint Committee, SOFA, approve this acquisition.

d. The request for extension of temporary use permit IC-T-38, involving 11.41 acres of land located at Pujang-ni, Chonhyon-myon, Paju-gun, Kyonggi-do, from 1 April 1968 to 31 March 1969, has been accepted by the Ministry of National Defense. The real estate is required for continued use as an alert and field training area. It was acquired in 1965, and renewed on an annual basis. The Ministry of National Defense and the Far East District Engineer will be requested to prepare the necessary documents. It is recommended that the Joint Committee, SOFA, approve extension of this permit.

4. Security Classification: Unclassified.

_____   _____
COLONEL I. M. RICE   MAJOR GENERAL KIM Mook
Chairman, United States Component   Chairman, Republic of Korea Component
Facilities and Areas Subcommittee   Facilities and Areas Subcommittee

APPROVED BY THE JOINT COMMITTEE ON
17 MAY 1968 AT TWENTY-FIFTH MEETING

_____   _____
YOON HA JONG   ROBERT J. FRIEDMAN
Republic of Korea   2   Lieutenant General
Representative   United States Air Force
                                      United States Representative

25th JC (Incl 8)
17 May 68

REPUBLIC OF KOREA — UNITED STATES
FACILITIES AND AREAS SUBCOMMITTEE

26 April 1968

MEMORANDUM FOR: THE JOINT COMMITTEE

1. Subcommittee members:

United States	Republic of Korea
COL I. M. Rice, Chairman	MG KIM Mook, Chairman
LTC J. B. Carrick, USAFCSK	Mr. SONG Yong Tai
LTC Robert E. Graf, J4, USFK	Mr. SHIN Chung Sup
MAJ James B. Hoodenpyle, USAF	Mr. LEE Soon Dong
Mr. Francis K. Cook, J5, USFK	Mr. LEE Kihl Choo
Mr. Richard Rose, USAEDFE	Mr. LEE Moon Sup
Mrs. Betty H. Bowman, 8th Army	Mr. LEE Jong Do
	Mr. CHANG Kyong Shik
	Mr. CHA Sang Chun
	Mr. KIM Byoung Chan
	Mr. CHONG Young Hoon
	Mr. CHOI Chung Hwan
	Mr. NO Yong Goo
	Mr. PARK Moh Soo
	LTC KANG Jong Kuk
	Mr. KANG Hong Suk

2. Subject of Recommendations: Requests for Acquisition of Real Estate. (Reference Joint Committee Memorandum, same subject, dated 11 April 1968).

3. Recommendations:

a. The request for acquisition of 0.0103-acre of nonarable land located at Samok-ni, Imjin-myon, Paju-gun, Kyonggi-do, has been accepted by the Ministry of National Defense. The real estate is required for the erection of two observation towers to improve security. The Ministry of National Defense and the Far East District Engineer will be requested to prepare the necessary documents. It is recommended that the Joint Committee, SOFA, approve this acquisition.

25th JC (Incl 9)
17 May 68

b. The request for acquisition of an easement for 1.1845 acres of land located at 1004-6 Haemang-dong, Kunsan City, and at 1501 Shinpung-ri, Mi-myon, Okku-gun, Chollapuk-do, has been accepted by the Ministry of National Defense. The real estate is required to install POL pipe line between two military installations. The Ministry of National Defense and the Far East District Engineer will be requested to prepare the necessary documents It is recommended that the Joint Committee, SOFA, approve this acquisition.

c. The request for acquisition of an easement for 1.00 acre of land, consisting of 0.35 acre of stream bed and 0.65 acre of existing road located at Tonggi-ri, Kwangtan-myon, Paju-gun, Kyonggi-do, has been mutually agreed upon by the Ministry of National Defense and Eighth Army, in accordance with stipulations contained in the Kyonggi-do Governor's Instructions of 29 March 1968, attached. The real estate is required to construct a water pipe line connecting two military compounds. The Ministry of National Defense and the Far East District Engineer will be requested to prepare the necessary documents. It is recommended that the Joint Committee, SOFA, approve this acquisition.

4. Security Classification: Unclassified.

COLONEL I. M. RICE
Chairman, United States Component
Facilities and Areas Subcommittee

MAJOR GENERAL KIM Mook
Chairman, Republic of Korea Component
Facilities and Areas Subcommittee

1 Incl
as

APPROVED BY THE JOINT COMMITTEE ON
17 MAY 1968 AT TWENTY-FIFTH MEETING

YOON HA JONG
Republic of Korea
Representative

2

ROBERT J. FRIEDMAN
Lieutenant General
United States Air Force
United States Representative

25th JC (Incl 9)
17 May 68

These minutes are ____sidered as official documents pertaining to both Governments and w____not be released without mutual agreement.

Written Instruction

Kyonggi-Const No. 21

    Sunyu-Ri, Imchin-Myon, Paju-Gun, Kyonggi-Do
    2d Infantry Division, MND RE Representative
    Park Kyong Man

In accordance with Article 40 of Road Law, the request for use of road site dated 19 March 1968 is approved with the following stipulations.

1. Location: Between Sinsan-Ri and Bangchu-Ri, Kwangtan-Myon,
              Paju-Gun, Kyonggi-Do.

2. Acreage: 796 pyong

3. Purpose and period: Installation of underground water pipe line
                        (for ten (10) years)

4. Construction period: From 10 April to 30 June 1968.

5. The pipe line should be installed in road shoulder.

6. Man pwer (Labor) be utilized to dig out the roadsurface and traffic hindrance be prohibited.

7. Backfilling be accomplished with good soil and sand by labor after installation of pipe. The existing facilities be protected from the operation of heavy equipment.

8. If any road damages should occur from this project, it will be rehabilitated by using agency.

9. The cancellation of the approval will be possible if necessary by Road Management Office.

10. In case of above, road obtainer has a responsibility to rehabilitate the road and its necessary expense be made by using agency as per Road Management Office.

11. Within project area, a sign board indicating the followings be prepared.

    a. Date of approval and No.
    b. Location of acquired area.
    c. Period of acquisition.

                        29 March 1968

97

        GOVERNER OF KYONGGIDO, PARK KYONG MON

                        25th JC (Incl 1 to Incl 9)
                        17 May 68

These minutes are considered as official documents pertaining to both Governments and w█ not be released without mutua█ greement.

REPUBLIC OF KOREA - UNITED STATES
FACILITIES AND AREAS SUBCOMMITTEE

13 May 1968

MEMORANDUM FOR: THE JOINT COMMITTEE

1. Subcommittee members:

United States	Republic of Korea
COL I. M. Rice, Chairman	MG KIM Mook, Chairman
LTC J. B. Carrick, USAFCSK	Mr. SONG Yong Tai
LTC Robert E. Graf, J4, USFK	Mr. SHIN Chung Sup
MAJ James B. Hoodenpyle, USAF	Mr. LEE Soon Dong
Mr. Francis K. Cook, J5, USFK	Mr. LEE Kihl Choo
Mr. Richard Rose, USAEDFE	Mr. LEE Moon Sup
Mrs. Betty H. Bowman, 8th Army	Mr. LEE Jong Do
	Mr. CHANG Kyong Shik
	Mr. CHA Sang Chun
	Mr. KIM Byoung Chan
	Mr. CHONG Young Hoon
	Mr. CHOI Chung Hwan
	Mr. NO Yong Goo
	Mr. PARK Moh Soo
	LTC KANG Jong Kuk
	Mr. KANG Hong Suk

2. Subject of Recommendations: Requests for Acquisition of Real Estate, Acquisition of Temporary Use Permit, and Extension of Temporary Use Permits. (Reference Joint Committee Memorandum, paras 2, 3a, and 4a-f, same subject, dated 25 April 1968).

3. Recommendations:

a. The request for acquisition of an easement for 0.95 acre of existing road located at Wonam-ni, Tosung-myon, Kosung-gun, Kangwon-do, has been accepted by the Ministry of National Defense. The real estate is required to connect an airfield operations area with MSR S 24. The Ministry of National Defense and the Far East District Engineer will be requested to prepare the necessary documents. It is recommended that the Joint Committee, SOFA, approve this acquisition.

25th JC (Incl 10)
17 May 68

98

b. The request for acquisition of a temporary use permit for 12,720 acres of land located at various locations in Kimpo-myon, Kumdan-myon, Yangchon-myon, and Daekot-myon, Kimpo-gun, Kyonggi-do, required for the conduct of field exercises by the 7th US Division, from 29 April through 25 May 1968, has been accepted by the Ministry of National Defense. The Ministry of National Defense and the Far East District Engineer will be requested to prepare the necessary documents. It is recommended that the Joint Committee, SOFA, approve acquisition of this temporary use permit.

c. Request for extension of temporary use permit 7X-T-21, involving 123.6 acres of land for training purposes for the period 1 March 1968 through 28 February 1969, has been accepted by the Ministry of National Defense. The Ministry of National Defense and the Far East District Engineer will be requested to prepare the necessary documents. It is recommended that the Joint Committee, SOFA, approve extension of this permit.

d. Request for extension of temporary use permit 7X-T-22, involving 10,946 acres of land for training purposes for the period 1 February 1968 through 31 January 1969, has been accepted by the Ministry of National Defense. The Ministry of National Defense and the Far East District Engineer will be requested to prepare the necessary documents. It is recommended that the Joint Committee, SOFA, approve extension of this permit.

e. Request for extension of temporary use permit K-C-T-27, involving 30 acres of stream bed for training purposes for the period 15 May 1968 through 14 May 1969, has been accepted by the Ministry of National Defense. The Ministry of National Defense and the Far East District Engineer will be requested to prepare the necessary documents. It is recommended that the Joint Committee, SOFA, approve extension of this permit.

f. Request for extension of temporary use permit K-C-T-36, involving 365 acres of land for training purposes for the period 1 May 1968 through 30 April 1969, has been accepted by the Ministry of National Defense. The Ministry of National Defense and the Far East District Engineer will be requested to prepare the necessary documents. It is recommended that the Joint Committee, SOFA, approve extension of this permit.

g. Request for extension of temporary use permit 7X-T-5, involving 7,972 acres of land for training purposes for the period 16 May 1968 through 15 May 1969, has been accepted by the Ministry of National Defense. The Ministry of National Defense and the Far East District Engineer will be requested to prepare the necessary documents. It is recommended that the Joint Committee, SOFA, approve extension of this permit.

h. Request for extension of temporary use permit 7X-T-7, involving 486 acres of hilly and forested land for training purposes for the period 10 March 1968 through 9 March 1969, has been accepted by the Ministry of National Defense. The Ministry of National Defense and the Far East District Engineer will be requested to prepare the necessary documents. It is recommended that the Joint Committee, SOFA, approve extension of this permit.

99

2

These minutes are considered as official documents pertaining to both Governments and w █ not be released without mutua █ greement.

4. Security Classification: Unclassified.

_____
COLONEL I. M. RICE
Chairman, United States Component
Facilities and Areas Subcommittee

_____
for MAJOR GENERAL KIM Hook
Chairman, Republic of Korea Component
Facilities and Areas Subcommittee

APPROVED BY THE JOINT COMMITTEE ON
17 MAY 1968 AT TWENTY-FIFTH MEETING

_____
YOON HA JONG
Republic of Korea
Representative

_____
ROBERT J. FRIEDMAN
Lieutenant General
United States Air Force
United States Representative

3

25th JC (Incl 10)
17 May 68

REPUBLIC OF KOREA – UNITED STATES
FACILITIES AND AREAS SUBCOMMITTEE

25 April 1968

MEMORANDUM FOR: THE JOINT COMMITTEE

1. Subcommittee members:

United States	Republic of Korea
COL I. M. Rice, Chairman	MG KIM Mook, Chairman
LTC J. B. Carrick, USAFCSK	Mr. SONG Yong Tai
LTC Robert E. Graf, J4, USFK	Mr. SHIN Chung Sup
MAJ James B. Hoodenpyle, USAF	Mr. LEE Soon Dong
Mr. Francis K. Cook, J5, USFK	Mr. LEE Kihl Choo
Mr. Richard Rose, USAEDFE	Mr. LEE Moon Sup
Mrs. Betty H. Bowman, 8th Army	Mr. LEE Jong Do
	Mr. CHANG Kyong Shik
	Mr. CHA Sang Chun
	Mr. KIM Byoung Chan
	Mr. CHONG Young Hoon
	Mr. CHOI Chung Hwan
	Mr. NO Yong Goo
	Mr. PARK Moh Soo
	LTC KANG Jong Kuk
	Mr. KANG Hong Suk

2. Subject of Recommendations: Requests for Acquisition of Real Estate and Extension of Temporary Use Permits. (Reference Joint Committee Memorandum, same subject, dated 11 April 1968).

3. Recommendations:

a. The request for acquisition of a temporary use permit for a total of 59 acres of land, consisting of 25 acres of river bed and 34 acres of wooded land located at Toegyewon-ni, Pyollae-myon, Yangju-gun, Kyonggi-do, for the period 9-10 April 1968, has been accepted by the Ministry of National Defense. The real estate is required to conduct an operational readiness test. The Ministry of National Defense and the Far East District Engineer will be requested to prepare the necessary documents. It is recommended that the Joint Committee, SOFA, approve this acquisition.

101

These minutes are considered as official documents pertaining to both Governments and ●●l not be released without mutu●● agreement.

b. The request for acquisition of a temporary use permit for 173.943 acres of river bed located at Kawol-li, and Chuwol-li, Choksong-myon, Paju-gun, Kyonggi-do, for the period 1 May 1968 to 30 April 1969, has been accepted by the Ministry of National Defense. The real estate is required for the conduct of firing tests and for training. The Ministry of National Defense and the Far East District Engineer will be requested to prepare the necessary documents. It is recommended that the Joint Committee, SOFA, approve acquisition of this temporary use permit.

c. The request for acquisition of a temporary use permit for 142.524 acres of river bed located at Napo-ri, Chongong-myon, Yonchon-gun, Kyonggi-do, for the period 1 May 1968 to 30 April 1969, has been accepted by the Ministry of National Defense. The real estate is required for the conduct of firing tests and for training. The Ministry of National Defense and the Far East District Engineer will be requested to prepare the necessary documents. It is recommended that the Joint Committee, SOFA, approve acquisition of this temporary use permit.

d. The request for extension of temporary use permit 7X-T-3, involving 287 acres of forested land, from 14 April 1968 to 13 April 1969, has been accepted by the Ministry of National Defense. The real estate is required for continued use as a field training area. The Ministry of National Defense and the Far East District Engineer will be requested to prepare the necessary documents. It is recommended that the Joint Committee, SOFA, approve extension of this permit.

e. The request for extension of temporary use permit 7X-IC-T-5, involving 400 acres of forested land, from 14 April 1968 to 13 April 1969, has been accepted by the Ministry of National Defense. The real estate is required for continued use as a field training area. The Ministry of National Defense and the Far East District Engineer will be requested to prepare the necessary documents. It is recommended that the Joint Committee, SOFA, approve extension of this permit.

4. Security Classification: Unclassified.

_____
COLONEL I. M. RICE
Chairman, United States Component
Facilities and Areas Subcommittee

_____
for MAJOR GENERAL KIM Mook
Chairman, Republic of Korea Component
Facilities and Areas Subcommittee

APPROVED BY THE JOINT COMMITTEE ON
17 MAY 1968 AT TWENTY-FIFTH MEETING

_____
YOON HA JONG
Republic of Korea Representative

_____
ROBERT J. FRIEDMAN
Lieutenant General
United States Air Force
United States Representative

2

25th JC (Incl 11)
17 May 68

102

These minutes are considered as official documents pertaining to both Governments and will not be released without mutual agreement.

REPUBLIC OF KOREA - UNITED STATES
FACILITIES AND AREAS SUBCOMMITTEE

14 May 1968

MEMORANDUM FOR: THE JOINT COMMITTEE

1. Subcommittee members:

United States	Republic of Korea
COL I. M. Rice, Chairman	MG KIM Mook, Chairman
LTC J. B. Carrick, USAFCSK	Mr. SONG Yong Tai
LTC Robert E. Graf, J4, USFK	Mr. SHIN Chung Sup
MAJ James B. Hoodenpyle, USAF	Mr. LEE Soon Dong
Mr. Francis K. Cook, J5, USFK	Mr. LEE Kihl Choo
Mr. Richard Rose, USAEDFE	Mr. LEE Moon Sup
Mrs. Betty H. Bowman, 8th Army	Mr. LEE Jong Do
	Mr. CHANG Kyong Shik
	Mr. CHA Sang Chun
	Mr. KIM Byoung Chan
	Mr. CHONG Young Hoon
	Mr. CHOI Chung Hwan
	Mr. NO Yong Goo
	Mr. PARK Moh Soo
	LTC KANG Jong Kuk
	Mr. KANG Hong Suk

2. Subject of Recommendation: Request for Conversion of Real Estate to Exclusive Use. (Reference Joint Committee Memorandum, same subject, dated 14 March 1968).

3. Recommendation: The request for conversion of a portion of SAC-679B, located at Shindong-ni, Shinbuk-myon, Chunsung-gun, Kangwon-do, consisting of 23.50 acres of land from a perpetual restrictive easement basis to an exclusive use basis, has been accepted by the Ministry of National Defense. This conversion is required to establish a buffer area along the existing perimeter fence and for future erosion control. In addition, the area is required for construction of facilities for a Republic of Korea security guard assigned at the site. The Ministry of National Defense and the Far East District Engineer will be requested to prepare the necessary documents. It is recommended that the Joint Committee, SOFA, approve this conversion.

103.

25th JC (Incl 12)
17 May 68

4. Security Classification: Unclassified.

_____
COLONEL I. M. RICE
Chairman, United States Component
Facilities and Areas Subcommittee

_____
MAJOR GENERAL KIM Mook
Chairman, Republic of Korea Component
Facilities and Areas Subcommittee

APPROVED BY THE JOINT COMMITTEE ON
17 MAY 1968 AT TWENTY-FIFTH MEETING

_____
YOON HA JONG
Republic of Korea Representative

_____
ROBERT J. FRIEDMAN
Lieutenant General
United States Air Force
United States Representative

2

104

25th JC (Incl 12)
17 May 68

REPUBLIC OF KOREA - UNITED STATES
FACILITIES AND AREAS SUBCOMMITTEE

26 April 1968

MEMORANDUM FOR: THE JOINT COMMITTEE

1. Subcommittee members:

United States	Republic of Korea
COL I. M. Rice, Chairman	MG KIM Mook, Chairman
LTC J. B. Carrick, USAFCSK	Mr. SONG Yong Tai
LTC Robert E. Graf, J4, USFK	Mr. SHIN Chung Sup
MAJ James B. Hoodenpyle, USAF	Mr. LEE Soon Dong
Mr. Francis K. Cook, J5, USFK	Mr. LEE Kihl Choo
Mr. Richard Rose, USAEDFE	Mr. LEE Moon Sup
Mrs. Betty H. Bowman, 8th Army	Mr. LEE Jong Do
	Mr. CHANG Kyong Shik
	Mr. CHA Sang Chun
	Mr. KIM Byoung Chan
	Mr. CHONG Young Hoon
	Mr. CHOI Chung Hwan
	Mr. NO Yong Goo
	Mr. PARK Moh Soo
	LTC KANG Jong Kuk
	Mr. KANG Hong Suk

2. Subject of Recommendations: Request for Release of Real Estate.
(Reference Joint Committee Memorandum, same subject, dated 11 April 1968).

3. Recommendations: The request for release of a portion of PAC-67, involving 1.2558, has been accepted by the Ministry of National Defense. The Ministry of National Defense and the Far East District Engineer will be requested to prepare the necessary documents. It is recommended that the Joint Committee, SOFA approve this release.

25th JC (Incl 13)
17 May 68

105

4. Security Classification: Unclassified.

_____
COLONEL I. M. RICE
Chairman, United States Component
Facilities and Areas Subcommittee

_____
MAJOR GENERAL KIM Mook
Chairman, Republic of Korea Component
Facilities and Areas Subcommittee

APPROVED BY THE JOINT COMMITTEE ON
17 MAY 1968 AT TWENTY-FIFTH MEETING

_____
YOON HA JONG
Republic of Korea Representative

_____
ROBERT J. FRIEDMAN
Lieutenant General
United States Air Force
United States Representative

2

25th JC (Incl 13)
17 May 68

These minutes are considered as official documents pertaining to both
Governments and will not be released without mutual agreement.

REPUBLIC OF KOREA - UNITED STATES
FACILITIES AND AREAS SUBCOMMITTEE

29 April 1968

MEMORANDUM FOR: THE JOINT COMMITTEE

1. Subcommittee members:

United States	Republic of Korea
COL I. M. Rice, Chairman	MG KIM Mook, Chairman
LTC J. B. Carrick, USAFCSK	Mr. SONG Yong Tai
LTC Robert E. Graf, J4, USFK	Mr. SHIN Chung Sup
MAJ James B. Hoodenpyle, USAF	Mr. LEE Soon Dong
Mr. Francis K. Cook, J5, USFK	Mr. LEE Kihl Choo
Mr. Richard Rose, USAEDFE	Mr. LEE Moon Sup
Mrs. Betty H. Bowman, 8th Army	Mr. LEE Jong Do
	Mr. CHANG Kyong Shik
	Mr. CHA Sang Chun
	Mr. KIM Byoung Chan
	Mr. CHONG Young Hoon
	Mr. CHOI Chung Hwan
	Mr. NO Yong Goo
	Mr. PARK Moh Soo
	LTC KANG Jong Kuk
	Mr. KANG Hong Suk

2. Subject of Recommendations: Requests for Release of Real
Estate. (Reference Joint Committee Memorandum, para 2f, same subject,
dated 30 November 1967.

3. Recommendations:

Request for release of a portion of SAC-685, containing 1.571
acres at No. 39-1 Suhyang-ri, Sunghwan-myon, Chunwon-gun, Chungchongnam-
do. Memorandum recommending approval of this release was submitted to
the Joint Committee, 26 December 1967. Release was approved by the
Joint Committee on 18 January 1968. Subsequently, it was determined
that retention of the area is required. Retention of the facility has
been accepted by the Ministry of National Defense. It is therefore
recommended that no further action be taken on this task.

25th JC (Incl 14)
17 May 68

4. Security Classification: Unclassified.

signature

COLONEL I. M. RICE
Chairman, United States Component
Facilities and Areas Subcommittee

signature

MAJOR GENERAL KIM Mook
Chairman, Republic of Korea Component
Facilities and Areas Subcommittee

**APPROVED BY THE JOINT COMMITTEE ON
17 MAY 1968 AT TWENTY-FIFTH MEETING**

signature

YOON HA JONG
Republic of Korea Representative

signature

ROBERT J. FRIEDMAN
Lieutenant General
United States Air Force
United States Representative

2

25th JC (Incl
17 May 68

JOINT COMMITTEE
UNDER
THE REPUBLIC OF KOREA AND THE UNITED STATES
STATUS OF FORCES AGREEMENT

29 April 1968

MEMORANDUM TO: The Joint Committee

SUBJECT: Designation of US Invited Contractor under Article XV, Status of Forces Agreement

1. References:

    a. Paragraph 2, Article XV, Status of Forces Agreement.

    b. US Commerce Subcommittee Memorandum of Consultation, dated 29 March 1968, subject as above. (Incl 1)

    c. ROK Commerce Subcommittee Memorandum of Consultation, dated 2 April 1968, subject as above. (Incl 2)

2. The United States, after consultation with the ROK Commerce Subcommittee and after having duly considered their views, has designated Adrian Wilson Associates as a US Invited Contractor, for the execution of contract #DACA81-68-C-0050 for Architect-Engineer Services for Design of Miscellaneous Facilities and Related Work.

3. Pertinent data concerning U.S. citizen employees will be provided to the Joint Secretariat in the established periodic arrival and departure format.

2 Incl
as

ROBERT J. FRIEDMAN
Lieutenant General
United States Forces
United States Representative
Joint Committee

25th JC (Incl 15)
17 May 68

109

These minutes are considered as official documents pertaining to both
Governments and wil●●ot be released without mutual●●reement.

REPUBLIC OF KOREA - UNITED STATES
COMMERCE SUBCOMMITTEE

29 March 1968

SUBJECT: Designation of US Invited Contractor under Article XV,
Status of Forces Agreement

ROK Chairman, Commerce Subcommittee

1. Reference: Paragraph 2, Article XV of the Status of Forces Agreement.

2. The Government of the Republic of Korea is informed through this
written consultive process that the United States Forces, Korea, proposes to extend invited contractor status to the successful negotiated
bidder among qualified US firms on the contract described in paragraph 3
below.

3. The following data is provided:

  a. Company Name: 1. Adrian Wilson Associates.
                     2. Daniel, Mann, Johnson & Mendenhall.
                     3. Pacific Architects & Engineers, Inc.

  b. Local Address: 1. JCA, 3ka-1, Yongsan-dong, Yongsan-ku,
                          Seoul, APO 96301.
                      2. Fuchu Air Station, Japan, APO 96525.
                      3. KMAG, APO 96302.

    c. Identification of US Citizen Employees: To be supplied on con-
clusion of negotiations.

    d. Number of US and ROK Employees: Number of US citizens and
Koreans is not known at this time and will be supplied upon conclusion
of negotiations.

    e. Reasons for Designation of an Invited Contractor: Open com-
petitive bidding among local contractors is not practicable due to the
following:

    (1) Security considerations.

    (2) Limited technical qualifications of the contractors involved.

    f. Location of Contract: Various locations in Korea.

25th JC (Incl 1 to Incl 15)
17 May 68

110

SUBJECT: Designation of US Invited Contractor under Article XV,
          Status of Forces Agreement

    g. <u>Type of Contract</u>: Lump Sum Contract for Architect-Engineer Services for Design of Miscellaneous Facilities and Related Work.

    h. <u>Length of Contract</u>: Approximately 6 months.

    i. <u>Sponsoring Component Command</u>: CGUSAEIGHT.

4. The United States certifies that the successful bidder or named contractor is present in the Republic of Korea solely for the purpose of executing contracts with the United States, for the benefit of the United States Armed Forces or other armed forces under the Unified Command receiving logistical support from the United States Forces.

5. The views of the Government of the Republic of Korea are earnestly solicited prior to United States selection and designation of an invited contractor to perform the work outlined above. You may be assured that your views will be considered carefully.

6. Your early reply will be greatly appreciated.

                              FLOYD R. WALTZ, JR.
                              Colonel, United States Army
                              US Chairman, Commerce Subcommittee

2

These minutes are considered as official documents pertaining to both Governments and will not be released without mutual agreement.

MINISTRY OF COMMERCE AND INDUSTRY
REPUBLIC OF KOREA
SEOUL, KOREA

2 April 1968

SUBJECT: Designation of US Invited Contractor under Article XV, Status of Forces Agreement.

TO : Chairman, US Commerce Subcommittee

1. References:

    a. Paragraph 2, Article XV, Status of Forces Agreement.

    b. US Commerce Subcommittee Memorandum of Consultation, dated 29 March 1968, subject as above, pertaining to contract for Architect-Engineer Services for Design of Miscellaneous Facilities and Related Work.

2. The US memorandum reference 1b above, has been reviewed and the Government of the Republic of Korea fully understands the requirement for an invited contractor in this instance.

For /Han Byung Il
Chairman
ROK Commerce Subcommittee

25th JC (Incl 2 to Incl 15)
17 May 68

These minutes are considered as official documents pertaining to both Governments and will not be released without mutual agreement.

**JOINT COMMITTEE
UNDER
THE REPUBLIC OF KOREA AND THE UNITED STATES
STATUS OF FORCES AGREEMENT**

29 April 1968

MEMORANDUM TO: The Joint Committee

SUBJECT: Designation of US Invited Contractor under Article XV,
Status of Forces Agreement

1. References:

a. Paragraph 2, Article XV, Status of Forces Agreement.

b. US Commerce Subcommittee Memorandum of Consultation, dated
29 March 1968, subject as above. (Incl 1)

c. ROK Commerce Subcommittee Memorandum of Consultation, dated
2 April 1968, subject as above. (Incl 2)

2. The United States, after consultation with the ROK Commerce Subcommittee and after having duly considered their views, has designated
Pacific Architects & Engineers, Inc. as a US Invited Contractor, for
the execution of contract #DACA81-68-C-0051 for Architect-Engineer
Services for Design of Miscellaneous Facilities and Related Work.

3. Pertinent data concerning U.S. citizen employees will be provided
to the Joint Secretariat in the established periodic arrival and
departure format.

2 Incl
as

ROBERT J. FRIEDMAN
Lieutenant General
United States Air Force
United States Representative
Joint Committee

25th JC (Incl 16)
17 May 68

REPUBLIC OF KOREA - UNITED STATES
COMMERCE SUBCOMMITTEE

29 March 1968

SUBJECT: Designation of US Invited Contractor under Article XV, Status of Forces Agreement

ROK Chairman, Commerce Subcommittee

1. Reference: Paragraph 2, Article XV of the Status of Forces Agreement.

2. The Government of the Republic of Korea is informed through this written consultive process that the United States Forces, Korea, proposes to extend invited contractor status to the successful negotiated bidder among qualified US firms on the contract described in paragraph 3 below.

3. The following data is provided:

    a. <u>Company Name</u>: 1. Adrian Wilson Associates.
                         2. Daniel, Mann, Johnson & Mendenhall.
                         3. Pacific Architects & Engineers, Inc.

    b. <u>Local Address</u>: 1. JCA, 3ka-1, Yongsan-dong, Yongsan-ku, Seoul, APO 96301.
                         2. Fuchu Air Station, Japan, APO 96525.
                         3. KMAG, APO 96302.

    c. <u>Identification of US Citizen Employees</u>: To be supplied on conclusion of negotiations.

    d. <u>Number of US and ROK Employees</u>: Number of US citizens and Koreans is not known at this time and will be supplied upon conclusion of negotiations.

    e. <u>Reasons for Designation of an Invited Contractor</u>: Open competitive bidding among local contractors is not practicable due to the following:

    (1) Security considerations.

    (2) Limited technical qualifications of the contractors involved.

    f. <u>Location of Contract</u>: Various locations in Korea.

25th JC (Incl 1 to Incl 16)
17 May 68

114

These minutes are considered as official documents pertaining to both
Governments and will not be released without mutual agreement.

29 March 1968

SUBJECT: Designation of US Invited Contractor under Article XV,
Status of Forces Agreement

g. Type of Contract: Lump Sum Contract for Architect-Engineer
Services for Design of Miscellaneous Facilities and Related Work.

h. Length of Contract: Approximately 6 months.

i. Sponsoring Component Command: CGUSAEIGHT.

4. The United States certifies that the successful bidder or named
contractor is present in the Republic of Korea solely for the purpose
of executing contracts with the United States, for the benefit of the
United States Armed Forces or other armed forces under the Unified
Command receiving logistical support from the United States Forces.

5. The views of the Government of the Republic of Korea are earnestly
solicited prior to United States selection and designation of an invited
contractor to perform the work outlined above. You may be assured that
your views will be considered carefully.

6. Your early reply will be greatly appreciated.

FLOYD R. WALTZ, JR.
Colonel, United States Army
US Chairman, Commerce Subcommittee

115

25th JC (Incl 1 to Incl 16)
17 May 68

2

These minutes are considered as official documents pertaining to both Governments and will not be released without mutual agreement.

MINISTRY OF COMMERCE AND INDUSTRY
REPUBLIC OF KOREA
SEOUL, KOREA

2 April 1968

SUBJECT: Designation of US Invited Contractor under Article XV, Status of Forces Agreement.

TO : Chairman, US Commerce Subcommittee

1. References:

    a. Paragraph 2, Article XV, Status of Forces Agreement.

    b. US Commerce Subcommittee Memorandum of Consultation, dated 29 March 1968, subject as above, pertaining to contract for Architect-Engineer Services for Design of Miscellaneous Facilities and Related Work.

2. The US memorandum reference 1b above, has been reviewed and the Government of the Republic of Korea fully understands the requirement for an invited contractor in this instance.

For /Han Byung Il
Chairman
ROK Commerce Subcommittee

116

25th JC (Incl 2 to Incl 16)
17 May 68

MINISTRY OF COMMERCE AND INDUSTRY
REPUBLIC OF KOREA
SEOUL, KOREA

3 May 1968

Subject: Designation of US Invited Contractor under Article XV, Status of Forces Agreement.

To   : Chairman, US Commerce Subcommittee

1. References:

    a. Paragraph 2, Article XV, Status of Forces Agreement.

    b. US Commerce Subcommittee Memorandum of Consultation, Dated 30 April 1968, subject as above, pertaining to the maintenance and operation a Seoul, Korea personnel office for the prupose of recruiting Korean personnel for employment in South Vietnam.

2. The US Memorandum, reference 1b above, has been reviewed and the Government of the Republic of Korea fully understands the requirement for an invited contractor in this instance.

For   Chairman
          ROK Commerce Subcommittee

25th JC (Incl 2 to Incl 17)
17 May 68

30 April 1968

SUBJECT: Designation of US Invited Contractor under Article XV, Status of Forces Agreement

    g. **Type of Contract:** Cost reimbursement.

    h. **Length of Contract:** 30 September 1969.

    i. **Sponsoring Component Command:** CGUSAEIGHT.

4. The United States certifies that the Vinnell Corporation is present in the Republic of Korea solely for the purpose of executing contracts with the United States, for the benefit of the United States Armed Forces or other armed forces under the Unified Command receiving logistical support from the United States Forces.

5. The views of the Government of the Republic of Korea are earnestly solicited prior to United States selection and designation of an invited contractor to perform the work outlined above. You may be assured that your views will be considered carefully.

6. Your early reply will be greatly appreciated.

FLOYD R. WALTZ, JR.
Colonel, United States Army
US Chairman, Commerce Subcommittee

118

25th JC (Incl 1 to Incl 17)
17 May 68

2

30 April 1968

SUBJECT: Designation of US Invited Contractor under Article XV,
Status of Forces Agreement

Chairman, ROK Commerce Subcommittee

1. Reference: Paragraph 2, Article XV of the Status of Forces Agreement.

2. The Government of the Republic of Korea is informed through this
written consultive process that the United States Forces, Korea, proposes to extend invited contractor status to the contractor described
in paragraph 3 below.

3. The following data is provided:

    a. Company Name: Vinnell Corporation.

    b. Local Address: 603 Annex Bldg., Room No. 602,
    The Cho-Heung Bank
    #14, 1-Ka, Namdaimun-Ro, Chung-Ku,
    Seoul, Korea.

    c. Identification of US Citizen Employee: L. D. Good.

    d. Number of US and ROK Employees:

        U.S.   -   One.
        ROK   -   None.

    e. Reasons for Designation of an Invited Contractor: The Vinnell
Corporation will maintain and operate a Seoul, Korea personnel office
for the purpose of recruiting Korean personnel for employment in South
Vietnam and to handle the administrative and personnel problems. The
Vinnell Corporation employs approximately 3,000 Koreans in Vietnam.

    f. Location of Contract: The Vinnell Corporation is performing
the following US Government contracts in South Vietnam: DAAE13-67-C-0171,
DA23-195-AMC-00772(T), DAJB11-68-C-0014, and DAAE13-67-C-208.

25th JC (Incl 1 to Incl 17)
17 May 68

These minutes are considered as official documents pertaining to both
Governments and will not be released without mutual agreement.

**JOINT COMMITTEE
UNDER
THE REPUBLIC OF KOREA AND THE UNITED STATES
STATUS OF FORCES AGREEMENT**

3 May 1968

MEMORANDUM FOR: The Joint Committee

SUBJECT: Designation of US Invited Contractor under Article XV,
Status of Forces Agreement

1. References:

    a. Paragraph 2, Artic le XV, Status of Forces Agreement.

    b. US Commerce Subcommittee Memorandum of Consultation, dated
30 April 1968, subject as above (Inclosure 1).

    c. ROK Commerce Subcommittee Memorandum of Consultation, dated
3 May 1968, subject as above (Inclosure 2).

2. The United States, after consultation with the ROK Commerce Subcommittee and after having duly considered their views, has designated
Vinnell Corporation as a US invited contractor for execution of
Contracts #DAAE13-67-C-0171, DA23-195-AMC-00772(T), DAJB11-68-C-0014,
and DAAE13-67-C-208 for the purpose of recruiting Korean personnel for
employment in South Vietnam.

3. Pertinent data concerning US citizen employees will be provided
to the Joint Secretariat in the established periodic arrival and
departure format.

2 Incl
as

ROBERT J. FRIEDMAN
Lieutenant General
United States Air Force
United States Representative
Joint Committee

25th JC (Incl 17)
17 May 68

JOINT COMMITTEE
UNDER
THE REPUBLIC OF KOREA AND THE UNITED STATES
STATUS OF FORCES AGREEMENT

3 May 1968

MEMORANDUM FOR: The Joint Committee

SUBJECT: Designation of US Invited Contractor under Article XV,
Status of Forces Agreement

1. References:

a. Paragraph 2, Article XV, Status of Forces Agreement.

b. US Commerce Subcommittee Memorandum of Consultation, dated
19 April 1968, subject as above (Inclosure 1).

c. ROK Commerce Subcommittee Memorandum of Consultation, dated
3 May 1968, subject as above (Inclosure 2).

2. The United States, after consultation with the ROK Commerce Subcommittee and after having duly considered their views, has designated
Barclay Overseas, Inc. as a US invited contractor for furnishing and
delivering Minnesota Mining products of copying machines, thermofax
brand copy paper, and other copying products to the U.S. Armed Forces
in Korea, as well as providing necessary maintenance on the copying
machines involved.

3. Pertinent data concerning US citizen employees will be provided to
the Joint Secretariat in the established periodic arrival and departure
format.

2 Incl
as

ROBERT J. FRIEDMAN
Lieutenant General
United States Air Force
United States Representative
Joint Committee

25th JC (Incl 18)
17 May 68

121

These minutes are considered as official documents pertaining to both Governments and will not be released without mutual agreement.

REPUBLIC OF KOREA - UNITED STATES
COMMERCE SUBCOMMITTEE

19 April 1968

SUBJECT: Designation of US Invited Contractor under Article XV,
Status of Forces Agreement

ROK Chairman, Commerce Subcommittee

1. Reference: Paragraph 2, Article XV of the Status of Forces Agreement.

2. The Government of the Republic of Korea is informed through this written consultative process that the United States Forces, Korea proposes to continue to extend invited contractor status to Barclay Overseas, Inc. on the contract described in paragraph 3 below.

3. The following data is provided:

a. Company Name: Barclay Overseas, Inc.

b. Local Address: #50-2, Susomun-dong, Sudaemun-ku, Seoul, Korea.

c. Identification of U.S. employee: Patrick E. O'Sullivan, Manager, UN Village, Apt. D-2, Seoul, Korea.

d. Number of U.S. employees   1 .
   Number of ROK employees   3 .

e. Reasons for Designation of an Invited Contractor: Unavailability of materials and services required by U.S. standards. The contractor is required to furnish and deliver Minnesota Mining products of copying machines, thermofax brand copy paper, and other copying products to the U.S. Armed Forces in Korea. They are also required to provide necessary maintenance on the copying machines involved.

f. Location of contract: Kimpo, Kunsan, and Osan Air Bases. Also, all U.S. Army installations in Korea.

h. Length of contract: 6 April 1968 to 5 April 1969.

i. Sponsoring Component Command: Commander, Air Forces Korea.

25th JC (Incl 1 to Incl 18)
17 May 68

SUBJECT: Designation of US Invited Contractor under Article XV,
          Status of Forces Agreement.

4. The United States certifies that the named contractor is present
in the Republic of Korea solely for the purpose of executing a contract with the United States, for the benefit of the United States
Armed Forces or other Armed Forces under the Unified Command receiving
logistical support from the United States Forces.

5. The views of the Government of the Republic of Korea are earnestly
solicited prior to United States continuation of invited contractor
status to Barclay Overseas, Inc. to perform the work outlined above.
You may be assured that your views will be considered carefully.

6. Your early reply will be greatly appreciated.

JOHN T. HORROCKS
Colonel, U.S. Air Force
Alternate US Chairman,
Commerce Subcommittee

123

2

These minutes are considered as official documents pertaining to both Governments and will not be released without mutual agreement.

MINISTRY OF COMMERCE AND INDUSTRY
REPUBLIC OF KOREA
SEOUL, KOREA

3 May 1968

SUBJECT: Designation of US Invited Contractor under Article XV, Status of Forces Agreement.

TO   : Chairman, US Commerce Subcommittee

    1. References:

        a. Paragraph 2, Article XV, Status of Forces Agreement.

        b. US Commerce Subcommittee Memorandum of Consultation, Dated 19 April 1968, subject as above, pertaining to a contract for furnishing and delivering Minnesota Mining copying machine, thermofax brand copy paper and other copying products to the U.S. Armed Forces in Korea.

    2. The US memorandum, reference 1b above, has been reviewed and the Government of the Republic of Korea fully understands the requirement for an invited contractor in this instance.

FOR Chairman
ROK Commerce Subcommittee

25th JC (Incl 2 to Incl 18)
17 May 68

124

JOINT COMMITTEE
UNDER
THE REPUBLIC OF KOREA AND THE UNITED STATES
STATUS OF FORCES AGREEMENT

14 May 1968

MEMORANDUM FOR: The Joint Committee

SUBJECT: Designation of US Invited Contractor under Article XV, Status of Forces Agreement

1. References:

   a. Paragraph 2, Article XV, Status of Forces Agreement.

   b. US Commerce Subcommittee Memorandum of Consultation, dated 9 May 1968, subject as above (Inclosure 1).

   c. ROK Commerce Subcommittee Memorandum of Consultation, dated 10 May 1968, subject as above (Inclosure 2).

2. The United States, after consultation with the ROK Commerce Sub-committee and after having duly considered their views, has designated Daniel, Mann, Johnson & Mendenhall as a US invited contractor for execution of Contract #F62087-68-C-0095 for Architect and Engineering services.

3. Pertinent data concerning US citizen employees will be provided to the Joint Secretariat in the established periodic arrival and departure format.

2 Incl
as

ROBERT J. FRIEDMAN
Lieutenant General
United States Air Force
United States Representative
Joint Committee

125

25th JC (Incl 19)
17 May 68

REPUBLIC OF KOREA - UNITED STATES
COMMERCE SUBCOMMITTEE

9 May 1968

SUBJECT: Designation of US Invited Contractor under Article XV,
Status of Forces Agreement

ROK Chairman, Commerce Subcommittee

1. Reference: Paragraph 2, Article XV of the Status of Forces Agreement.

2. The Government of the Republic of Korea is informed through this written consultive process that the United States Forces, Korea, proposes to extend invited contractor status to the successful negotiated bidder among qualified US firms on the contract described in paragraph 3 below.

3. The following data is provided:

   a. Company Name: Daniel, Mann, Johnson & Mendenhall.

   b. Local Address: Box 1-I, APO 96570.

   c. Identification of US Citizen Employees: To be supplied after award of contract.

   d. Number of US and ROK Employees:

            U.S.   -   11
            ROK   -   15

   e. Reasons for Designation of an Invited Contractor: Open competitive bidding among local contractors is not practicable due to the following:

      (1) Security considerations.

      (2) Technical qualifications of the contractor involved.

   f. Location of contract: Kwangju Air Base; Kunsan Air Base; Osan Air Base, and Taegu Air Base, Korea.

25th JC (Incl 1 to Incl 19)
17 May 68

9 May 1968

SUBJECT: Designation of US Invited Contractor under Article XV,
Status of Forces Agreement

    g. <u>Type of Contract</u>: Architect-Engineering services.

    h. <u>Length of Contract</u>: Approximately 30 days.

    i. <u>Sponsoring Component Command</u>: Commander, Air Forces, Korea
(Headquarters 6314th Support Wing (PACAF)).

FLOYD R. WALTZ, JR.
Colonel, United States Army
Assistant Chief of Staff, J 4

127

2

These minutes are considered as official documents pertaining to both Governments and will not be released without mutual agreement.

MINISTRY OF COMMERCE AND INDUSTRY
REPUBLIC OF KOREA
SEOUL, KOREA

19 May 1968

SUBJECT: Desingation of US Invited Contractor under Article XV, Status of Forces Agreement.

TO   :   Chairman, US Commerce Subcommittee

1. References:

    a. Paragraph 2, Article XV, Status of Forces Agreement.

    b. US Commerce Subcommittee Memorandum of Consultation, Dated 9 May 1968, subject as above, pertaining to contract for architect-engineering service in the Kwangju, Kunsan, Osan and Taegu Air Base construction projects.

2. The US memorandum, reference 1b above, has been reviewed and the Government of the Republic of Korea fully understands the requirement for an invited contractor in this instance.

for Kil Yong Um
Chairman
ROK Commerce Subcommittee

128

25th JC (Incl 2 to Incl 19)
17 May 68

JOINT COMMITTEE
UNDER
THE REPUBLIC OF KOREA AND THE UNITED STATES
STATUS OF FORCES AGREEMENT

14 May 1968

MEMORANDUM FOR: The Joint Committee

SUBJECT: Designation of US Invited Contractor under Article XV,
Status of Forces Agreement

1. References:

a. Paragraph 2, Article XV, Status of Forces Agreement.

b. US Commerce Subcommittee Memorandum of Consultation, dated
9 May 1968, subject as above (Inclosure 1).

c. ROK Commerce Subcommittee Memorandum of Consultation, dated
10 May 1968, subject as above (Inclosure 2).

2. The United States, after consultation with the ROK Commerce Subcommittee and after having duly considered their views, has designated
Trans-Asia Engineering Associates, Inc. as a US invited contractor for
execution of Contract #F62087-68-C-0096 for Architect and Engineering
services.

3. Pertinent data concerning US citizen employees will be provided to
the Joint Secretariat in the established periodic arrival and departure
format.

2 Incl
as

ROBERT J. FRIEDMAN
Lieutenant General
United States Air Force
United States Representative
Joint Committee

25th JC (Incl 20)
17 May 68

129

REPUBLIC OF KOREA - UNITED STATES
COMMERCE SUBCOMMITTEE

9 May 1968

SUBJECT: Designation of US Invited Contractor under Article XV, Status of Forces Agreement

ROK Chairman, Commerce Subcommittee

1. Reference: Paragraph 2, Article XV of the Status of Forces Agreement.

2. The Government of the Republic of Korea is informed through this written consultive process that the United States Forces, Korea, proposes to extend invited contractor status to the successful negotiated bidder among qualified US firms on the contract described in paragraph 3 below.

3. The following data is provided:

  a. Company Name: Trans-Asia Engineering Associates, Inc.

  b. Local Address: Building 1510, APO 96301.

  c. Identification of US Citizen Employees: To be supplied after award of contract.

  d. Number of US and ROK Employees:

          U.S.   -   5
          ROK   -   15

  e. Reasons for Designation of an Invited Contractor: Open competitive bidding among local contractors is not practicable due to the following:

    (1) Security considerations.

    (2) Technical qualifications of the contractor involved.

  f. Location of Contract: Kwangju Air Base, Kunsan Air Base, and Osan Air Base, Korea.

130

25th JC (Incl 1 to Incl 20)
17 May 68

SUBJECT: Designation of US Invited Contractor under Article XV, Status of Forces Agreement

g. Type of Contract: Architect-Engineering services.

h. Length of Contract: Approximately 45 days.

i. Sponsoring Component Command: Commander, Air Forces, Korea (Headquarters 6314th Support Wing (PACAF)).

FLOYD R. WALTZ, JR.
Colonel, United States Army
US Chairman, Commerce Subcommittee

131

2

These minutes are c●sidered as official documents ●taining to both Governments and wil●not be released without mutual ●reement.

MINISTRY OF COMMERCE AND INDUSTRY
REPUBLIC OF KOREA
SEOUL, KOREA

10 May 1968

SUBJECT: Designation of US Invited Contractor under Article XV, Status of Forces Agreement.

TO : Chairman, US Commerce Subcommittee

1. References:

    a. Paragraph 2, Article XV, Status of Forces Agreement.

    b. US Commerce Subcommittee Memorandum of Consultation, Dated 9 May 1968, subject as above, pertaining to contract for architect-engineering services in the Kwangju, Kunsan, and Osan Air Base construction projects.

2. The US memorandum, reference 1b above, has been reviewed and the Government of the Republic of Korea fully understands the requirement for an invited contractor in this instance.

for Kil Yong Um
Chairman
ROK Commerce Subcommittee

132

These minutes are considered as official documents pertaining to both Governments and will not be released without mutual agreement.

JOINT ROK - US PRESS RELEASE
TWENTY-FIFTH ROK-US JOINT COMMITTEE MEETING
17 MAY 1968

The ROK-US Joint Committee approved 25 recommendations of its Facilities and Areas Subcommittee at its twenty-fifth meeting, held at the Capitol Building on Friday, 17 May. One of these Joint Committee actions involved US-ROK agreement on a list of all of the facilities and areas held by the US armed forces in the Republic of Korea, while 24 dealt with acquisition, release, and extension of temporary use of facilities and areas for the US armed forces.

The Republic of Korea Representative, Mr. YOON Ha Jong, Director of the Europe and America Bureau of the Foreign Ministry, presided at this meeting of the Joint Committee. The Joint Committee also assigned seven new tasks to the Facilities and Areas Subcommittee and noted designation of six US invited contractors.

The next meeting of the Joint Committee is scheduled to be held on Friday, 7 June, in the US SOFA Conference Room in Yongsan.

25th JC (Incl 21)
17 May 68

133

대한민국 외무부
공보관실

보 도 자 료

─   호   이 기사는 제공처인 외무부를
년 월 일 시 분 발표   밝히고 보도할수 있음

한.미 합동위원회 제25차 회의 공동발표문

1968. 5. 17. (금) 15:00시
외무부 회의실

한.미 합동위원회는 5월 17일 (금) 중앙청에서 개최된 제25차 회의에서 시설구역 분과위원회의 건의 25건을 승인했다. 이중 1건은 주한 미군이 사용중인 전 시설과 구역의 목록에 관한 한.미간의 합의 에 관한 것이고 나머지 24건은 시설과 구역의 취득, 반환 및 임시 사용 연장에 관한 것이다.

대한민국 대표 외무부 구미국장이 동 회의를 주재하였다.

또한 합동위원회는 시설구역 분과위원회에 7건의 신규과제를 부여하고 6명의 미국 초청계약자 지명을 승인하였다.

차기 합동위원회 회의는 6월 7일 (금요일) 용산 SOFA 회의실 에서 열릴 예정이다.

134

ㄹ. 제 26 차. 1968. 6·5

135

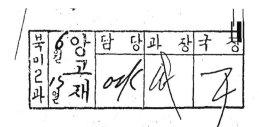

JOINT COMMITTEE
UNDER
THE REPUBLIC OF KOREA AND THE UNITED STATES
STATUS OF FORCES AGREEMENT

___ June 1968

MEMORANDUM TO: Chairmen, Criminal Jurisdictions Subcommittee

SUBJECT   : Situation in the vicinity of Osan Air Base.

1. Reference is made to the minute of the twenty-sixth *meeting* of
the Joint Committee ~~meeting~~, which was specifically called to
discuss the situation in the vicinity of Osan Air Base.

2. It is requested that you will review the conditions
prevailing in the vicinity of Osan Air Base, especially in the
town commonly known as "Chicol Village" (Sinchang-ni, Songtan-up,
Pyongtaek-gun, Kyonggi-do) and recommend to the Joint Committee
appropriate actions that might be found necessary.

Robert J. Friedman   Yoon Ha Jong
Lieutenant General   Republic of Korea Representative
United States Air Force
United States Representative

136

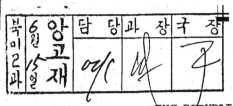

JOINT COMMITTEE
UNDER
THE REPUBLIC OF KOREA AND THE UNITED STATES
STATUS OF FORCES AGREEMENT

_____ June 1968

MEMORANDUM TO: Chairmen, Transportation Subcommittee

SUBJECT   :   Drivers' licenses of the members of the United States
                   armed forces, the civilian component, and their
                   dependents

1. Paragraph 1, Article XXIV of the Status of Forces Agreement

provides that the Republic of Korea shall accept as valid, without

a driving test or fee, the driving permit or license or military

driving permit issued by the United States, or political subdivision

thereof, to a member of the United States armed forces, the civilian

component, and their dependents.

2. Such driving permit or license needs to be converted

into a form recognizable by controlling officials of the Republic

of Korea.

3. It is requested that you recommend to Joint Committee

the format and the procedures of issuing such format.

_____   _____
Robert J. Friedman   Yoon Ha Jong
Lieutenant General   Republic of Korea Representative
United States Air Force
United States Representative

13기

한.미 군대지위협정 한.미 합동위원회
제26차 회의 (긴급 회의)

1968. 6. 5.

한국대표 발언 자료

138

오산지구 치안 현황

1. 지역내 한.미 각종 수사 기관장은 월례회의를 개최하여 긴밀한 협조를 유지하고 있다.

2. 일반 경찰관서가 정원미달인 실정에 불구하고 오산 관할지서 (송탄지서) 는 정원 10명에 비하여 미군당국 요청에 따라 현재 13명의 인원을 배치 하고 있으며, 헌병대 및 OSI 파견 경관도 2명을 증배하여 5명을 배치 하고 있다.

3. 현지 경찰 당국은 조직적인 폭력 또는 범죄단체가 있다는 징조를 상금 인지한바 없고, 미측 당국에서도 그러한 사실을 지적한바 없었다.

4. 현지 경찰은 항시 폭력배 및 우범자 동태를 조사 파악하고 있는바, 동 지역의 위안부 (약 1,000명)을 상대로 초객원 (pimp)활동을 하는자 약 69명 및 신흥 폭력배 91명등 계 약 160명의 우범자가 있으나 이미 언급한바와 같이 범죄 조직이 있다는 징후는 없다.

5. 폭력사건 발생 현황을 보면 1967년 1월 부터 5월 사이의 발생건 수 169건에 비하여 금년 5월 7까지의 발생 건수는 156건으로 약 10%의 감소 경향을 보여주고 있다.

6. 미군관계 도난 사건은 67년 1-5월 발생건수 27건에 비하여 금년 동기 33건으로 약간 증가하기는 하였으나 반면 작년 동 기간 발생건 중 해결건수가 6건에 불과한데 반하여 금년에는 33건중 23건을 수사 완결하고 있다.

7. 금년중 미군관계 중요 도난 사건은 4건인바 그중 1건은 범인 일부를 이미 체포 하였고 잔여 미결건에 대하여 각각 전담 형사 4명을 배치하여 수사 진행중.

8. 3월 20일 미군인 4명을 상대로한 강도사건은 사건 위일 범인 3명을 체포하였다.

9. K-55   기지 침입절도방지를 위한 협조요청에 대하여는 매일 야간에 경찰관 1명과 방범대원 4명을 배치외가 순찰을 실시하고 있음.

140

1. 노상 청객 행위자 단속요망

현 황

K-55 기지 주변에 윤락여성수가 1,100명 가량으로 그중 청객 상습행위자수가 약 50여명임.

조 치

지서방법 단속 근무자 매일 4명과 부녀회 (위안부 자치회) 감찰8명이 합동으로 수시 단속 또는 본서에서 매주 1회 내근자동원 송탄지구에 대한 일제단속을 실시하는 관계로 최근 노상 청객행위자가 감소되고 있다.

가. 단속상황

구분 대비	단속건수	처리건수	처리내용						비고
			구류	벌금	과료	귀가	직업알선	입교	
계	226	185	88	8	89	21		20	
67. 5.	85	65	53		12	15		5	
68. 5.	141	120	35	8	77	6		15	
대비	+56	+55	-18	+8	+65	-9		+10	

2. 기지내 불법침입자 단속 요망

K-55 기지에 배치된 경찰관 4명과 미군헌병의 합동 순찰로 단속하고 있다.

가. 기지 불법침입자 처리상황

년도 구분 대비	총 건수	처리결과					비고
		구류	과료	훈방	입건	이첩	
계	28	13	8	4	1	1	
67. 5.	15	9	3	2		1	1명은 담배값으로 람정수
68. 5.	13	4	5	3	1		훈방: 1명은 농아자
대비	-2	-5	+2	+1	+1	-1	1명은 미군친지 와출입

141

搜査主管

1. K-55 周변에 暴力輩가 亂舞한 事實

가. 組織暴力배로서 計劃的으로 亂舞하는 경향은 없고 우발적으로 청객하는 펨프 등의 행패가 有할뿐임

나. 1968. 3. 20. 23:30分경에 私服인 新場里 所在 K-55 入口 路上 美軍헌병 4名을 기절 할거 불능케 하고 衣類및 現金을 강취 事件이 發生 피의자 홍 등 외 3名을 緊急拘束 送致

2. 暴力輩의 組織 狀況

가. 組織暴力은 全無하고

나. 非組織暴力 우범자가 A級 2名 B級 12名 C級 27名 其他(新規) 27名 計 69名

다. 暴力再犯 우려자 91名

총계 160名

3. 不良輩들의 職業分布 狀況

無職者(펨프및 前科者) 80%

其他 20%

142

ㄴ. K-55 部隊 盜難事件 發生狀況

發生 日時	場 所	被害品	措 置
1. 68. 3.17	K-55 某地域	美軍 권총7정	전담제...ㅗ요
13:40~14:40	T-30가호건물	실탄 및 권총彈	으메치수사中
2. 68. 4.16	K-55 某地域	美軍 권총8	1무건기송치비검
~11:00~	숙소관리처창고	점外 18점	자수시킴
3. 68. 5.1.	K-55 基地	美軍 담푸루	全단제...ㅗ요
12:00	802工兵隊	적心(七)	메치수사中
4. 68. 5.6	K-55 基地	절차中在	〃
16:45	점근주차장	1台	〃

평택싱찰서

143

一般暴力事

區分 年度	發生	檢擧	人員	조치			
				군속	비군속	이첩	즉심
67年度	464	424	723	96	627		
69.6月현재	169	134	202	23	179		
68. ″	156	106	179	34	145		
대비	-13	-28	-23	+11	-34		

一般盜犯

區分 年度	發生	檢擧	人員	被害額	회수액	조치		
						군속	비군속	이첩
67年度	713	483	333	2.079.007	4.311.483	264	69	
69.6月현	728	230	146	9.059.032	1.773.333	119	27	
68. ″	195	141	115	1.448.702	575.080	83	29	3
대비	-163	-89	-31	+3.610.670	+3.801.747	+36	+2	+3

外國人盜犯

區分 年度	發生	檢擧	人員	被害額	회수액	군속	비군속	이첩
67年度	28	47	46	8.112.424	2.216.333	21	27	
69.6月	27	6	103	3.819.927	604.200	23	4	
68.5月	33	23	23	10.168.950	4.224.985	12	11	
대비	+6	+17	+16	+6.349.083	+3.619.785	+9	+7	

평택경찰서

144

密貿易事犯

区分	檢擧	人員	金 額	起訴	不起訴	이첩
1967年度	41	36	530.8PU	-	11	25
67年 5月	12	16	98.340-		3	13
68年 5月	64	64	424.595	3	18	42
대 비	+52	+48	+326.255	+3	+16	+29

外 國 換管理法

区分	檢擧	人員	金 額	起訴	不起訴	이첩
1967年度	4	4			4	
67年 5月	2	2	5弗		2	
68年 5月	5	4	685弗	1	3	
대 비	+3	+2	+680	+1	+1	

麻藥法

区分	檢擧	人員	金 額	起訴	不起訴	이첩
1967年度	3	4	26.980	3	1	
67年 5月	2	2	無	2		
68年 5月	1	1	아까징 102 아리낭 담배	1		
대비	-1	-1		-1		

平澤警察署

美軍側의 要請事項

內容	措置
1. 美軍基地周邊 支署및 美OP M.P隊에 兵力 增配 要請	1. 松炭支署 TO上의 10名의 警察官 배치를 현재 증원 13名으로 배치하고 美OP 및 헌병대내 파견 경찰반 3名을 2名을 증배 5名으로 配置
2. 基地周邊 경비원 배치	2. 基地주변에 서독 機同所를 設置 警官 2名을 배치 하였으나 97년대 兵力이 배치 된으로因하여 인상 措置 하였음
3. 以北基地侵入 점도 防止를 爲한 警察官配置	3. 夜間에 警察官 1名에 防犯隊 4名을 配置 외곽 순찰中임.

평택경찰서

外殘業組 為山支部 爭議內容 :

5.10 12:00   K-55 美空軍 基地內의 BX 從
業員 本想금外 10%에 위하여 出入
래스 回收 (理由 美 O.S.I. 副官 MAR-
TIN은 BX 從業員들이 67.12.25 增부터
物品을 規定대로 販賣하지 않은 님x
하는 店에게 근미츤츨 받은 일때
하였다. 호피스 후렁크런에게 해고통보)

5.__ 12:30   基地 周辺 출근處에서 BX
從業員이 모여 協商 하였으나 결
정을 보지 못함.

5.14 17:00   다시 모여 BX 승소는 烏山
支部에 建設하여 노사 회의를 開催
토록 合致

5.23 8:00   松菜은 新場里 所在 朴오x
식당에서 中,次 運営委員会를
開催 (28에中 20名 참석) 美측금에
노사 회의를 要求 했으나 아무런
반응이 없으므로. 5.24 ~ 5.31 202
爭議 비밀 投票를 實施키로 合致

5.31 13:00   同会 投票겼다. 從業員 167.0內

平澤警察署
147

찬 1196 표의 投票 可 1157 총 13
무효 11

6.3 10:20 投炭을 新場里 所在 香湖屋에
서 第2次 喜拾奄含室 開催 (28명중
18명 참석)

① 6.4. 07:00 부터 노조원 출근은 에이
마틴을 추방하라는 홍래를 달은 취
영한다.

② 繼續是 반응이 없으면 6.14 17:00
부터 지기를 한다

6.4. 07:00 부터 組合員이 마틴을 추방하
라는 홍래를 달은 출근 하므로 미헌
병대에서 출입지 못하도록 제지

6.4. 08:00 約 500명의 從業員이 正門 周邊
에 운집 (가장 6라 정문해앞 김사복
20명 출근 사이 이엔 방지와 彼
리수송)

6.4. 10:00 約 1000명이 正門 周邊 운집
한면도록 08:10~09:30 203.5 [?]
용근 사령부에서 회의 개최

15. ① BX 종업원 시병순 완전한 원한

평택경찰서

분장으로 協調選으로 입각하여
處理를 받는다
ⓔ 종업원이 캐스를 찾어 안할지는
事象선에 인게되며 以前은 수사
와 處理를 받는다
15:45~17:10 BX 사우실에서 BX
호텔서 후랭크린바 위기 노조 조합
장 金永櫂와 간부 3명이 協議
ⓔ 6.11 까지 BX 종업원 11시까지 취
하에 덜떤 폭키시키고 수사를 받어
나또 處理한다
ⓔ 協議내용은 6.5 야:30 에기
서신 통보를 라며 부장취사가 시정
되지 않으면 6.14 기하에 즉한
후랭을 붙사한다
17:15 원래 金從業소는 흥세를
대면 노業취업에 들어 갔음

149

외기노조와의 분쟁관계

참고: 1) 5.10. OSI Capt. Martin   해고통보

— 구두 지시에도 불구하고 (본인들은 그러한 지시를 받은바
없다고 주장) 재한량 이상을 판매하는 대신 고객으로 부터
구전을 받는다는 일방적 주장— 에 의하여 PX 종업원
11명의 출입증 회수

2) 5.28. 외기노조 지부 운영위원회

3) 5.31. 쟁의가부 투표

가 1167 부 13 무효 16

4) 6. 4. Martin   을 추방하라는 흉패착용, 흉패 착용자는
출입금지, 일부 흉패를 떼고 취업.

1. 오산외기 노조의 쟁의에 관하여는 노동청이 조사한 내용으로는 상급
노조측에 관계노동 법령, 협정위반 사유를 발견할 수 없었고 또한 현재
양 당사자간에 해결과정에 있다 하므로 현 단계로서는 군대지위협정 소정
조정기능을 발동하거나 합동위원회가 개입할 단계로는 간주하지 않는다.

2. 6.4. 일시 조업중단에 관하여는 그것이 파업이 아니고 미군측이 합법적
시위를 제기하기 위하여 출입을 금지한데 기인한 조업중단이었음을 지적한다.

3. 흉장 패용에 관하여는 그것이 합법적 시위로 인정된 2개의 선례가 있음에
유의한다.

150

These minutes are considered as official documents pertaining to both Governments and will not be released without mutual agreement.

JOINT COMMITTEE
UNDER
THE REPUBLIC OF KOREA AND THE UNITED STATES
STATUS OF FORCES AGREEMENT

MINUTES OF THE TWENTY-SIXTH MEETING

5 June 1968
Headquarters
U.S. Forces, Korea
Seoul, Korea

1. The meeting was convened at 1500 hours by Lieutenant General Robert J. Friedman, the US Representative, who presided at the meeting.

2. The following were in attendance:

ROK	US
Mr. YOON Ha Jong	LTG Robert J. Friedman, USAF
Mr. LEE Sung Jung	CAPT M. R. Massie, USN
Mr. KIM Sung Jae	COL Herbert C. Hicks, Jr., USA
Mr. HUH Seung Joon	COL Gerald W. Davis, USA
Mr. SHIN Chung Sup	Mr. P. Wesley Kriebel, US Embassy
Mr. OH Myong Too	Mr. Robert A. Kinney, USFK
Mr. HONG Duk Sik	LTC Paul E. Jones, USAF

3. General Friedman thanked the ROK officials and expressed his deep appreciation for their responding so quickly to his request for a special Joint Committee meeting, knowing how busy they were. He stated that the number of ROK officials present was indicative of the good relations between the two components of the Joint Committee and the officials of the Governments of the Republic of Korea and of the United States. The US Representative indicated he would not have called a special meeting except for a serious situation which had developed at Osan Air Base.

4. The US Representative invited the ROK Representative to introduce the ROK officials. The ROK Representative stated that in support
of the US Representative's opening statement, he would like to emphasize that the US-ROK Joint Committee is one body, working toward a
common objective..... what concerns the US component also concerns
the ROK component, and the ROK Government. Mr. Yoon introduced
Mr. KIM Sung Jae, the new Director of the Bureau of Prosecution of
the Ministry of Justice, who replaced Mr. KIM Il Doo on the Joint Committee. He also introduced Mr. HONG Duk Sik, Chief of the Investigation Guidance Section of the Korean National Police.

5. The US Representative presented a statement on the situation
at the Osan Air Base which is attached as Inclosure 1.

6. The ROK Representative stated that the ROK officials had
listened very carefully to the statement made by the US Representative.
He stated that the ROK Government had great concern over the anxiety
which the US authorities had over conditions at Chicol Village, near
Osan Air Base. Because of common defense of the ROK by the armed
forces of the US and ROK, the ROK Government shares the US anxiety.
He stated that he wished to state that the ROK Government will take
all appropriate measures to correct the situation. The ROK Government has already taken certain actions to help correct the situation.
Regarding the statement of the US Representative about the lack of an
effective civil government and only a nominal police force, the ROK
Representative commented that neither local government nor police

152

2

force was as ineffective as it had been described. The Chicol Village

is under the administration of the county office at Pyongtaek and police

officers are stationed at Sin-chang-ni, Songtan-up. The ROK Repre-

sentative indicated that his preliminary investigation confirmed that

close liaison has been maintained between US-ROK law enforcement

agencies ever since the Korean War. He indicated that the police assigned

to Songtan-up had recently been raised from 10 to 13 and the ROK police

detachment assigned to OSI had been raised from 3 to 5. The ROK

Representative indicated that the ROK police organization had this

area under close observation and control, and was aware of trends

among criminal elements in this area. The ROK Representative noted

that there was a ten percent increase in the number of thefts and lar-

cenies in this area in 1968 over 1967. For example, in the first five

months of 1967, there were 27 cases of larceny and burglaries involv-

ing US property, while there were 33 such cases in the first five months

of 1968. However, in 1967, in six of the 27 cases arrests were made,

while in 1968, arrests were made in 23 of the 33 cases. The ROK

Representative indicated that, if the US component desired, the ROK

Government is ready to supply statistics for these matters to the US

component. He stated that during 1968, there were only four important

theft cases. One of these cases had been settled and the other three

still were under investigation. On 19 March 1968, four US personnel

were robbed and the following day three suspects were arrested.

(53

3

7. The ROK Representative pointed out that there had been no complaints by US law enforcement officials at the regular monthly meetings of police officials at Osan. These facts and figures are presented not to defend ROK law enforcement agencies, but to help US officials to fully understand the situation there. The ROK Representative stated that he could not accept that there existed general lawlessness or organized criminal elements at Osan. However, since US officials brought this up, it will be investigated and corrective action taken as required. The last part of the US Representative's statement mentioned labor troubles. We have preliminary reports from both ROK police and labor officials. There was the firing of eleven USFK Korean National personnel for alleged misconduct. The personnel thought the firings were unfair and appealed to their union. The local chapter of the union voted 95% to make this a labor dispute under labor relations procedures. There was certain action by USFK Korean national employees but it is believed this was simply a labor demonstration. If there is any clear evidence of instigation by subversive elements, such elements will be convicted. If this is simply a labor relations problem, it will be handled by the Joint Committee labor relations procedures. The ROK interests are the same as those of the US. There will be a more complete investigation of the situation, and the Joint Committee Labor Subcommittee should be able to handle the situation. The ROK and US labor relations officials should investigate the situation. The ROK Representative indicated he had

4

tried to clarify the position of officials of the ROK Government on certain

points. He again emphasized the ROK Government shared the anxiety of

the US over the general situation and would investigate.

8. The US Representative thanked the ROK Representative for his

estimate of the situation. He accepted the ROK proposal to investigate

the situation and help to find a solution which would preclude a recur-

rence of such problems. He also noted the ROK Representative's offer

to furnish ROK Government statistics and other facts on this situation,

which he would accept. He also expressed the hope that the ROK Repre-

sentative's estimate of the situation at Chicol Village was a more accurate

assessment of the situation than that presented by the US. He pointed

out that the fact remains that over considerable periods of time, situa-

tions similar to the current one have arisen but not resolved at local

level. Only when referred to central government had a solution been

reached. He stated he would like to note for the record the support

the US has received from certain ROK Government officials. ROK

Police Director Kim had responded on every occasion when called up

to augment the local police at Chicol Village. His assistance had not

only been immediate but most effective. However, as he indicated when

higher elements in the police organization had departed the area, the

situation tended to revert to the previously unsatisfactory state. He

stated that the situation at Osan could not be labeled as primarily a

labor dispute. It was rather, the manifestation of a much deeper and

155

5

more serious problem. The ROK and US, as the US Representative understands it, both want to stamp out, once and for all, illegal and blackmarket operations. All are working in concert to solve this problem. The situation which gave rise to the present problem was, at least in part, the result of a US effort to expose and break up a smuggling ring. Despite the determination of both our Governments to stamp out smuggling, a representative of the US organization was threatened with his life. It was on this basis that the assistance of the ROK Government authorities has been requested to help local authorities at Osan to deal with the situation. The US Representative stated that he did not intend to infer that this situation at Osan was Communist instigated but meant to point out that the situation is the kind Communists try to exploit and capitalize upon, and make the problems of both Governments more difficult. The US Representative stated that he knew this was a complex and difficult problem and that it would not be resolved today. He stated that he felt both Governments had much to do in mutual efforts and that the problem would be worked out.

9. It was agreed that the ROK and US authorities would cooperate closely in resolving this situation and that the Criminal Jurisdiction Subcommittee be assigned the task of looking into this problem and recommending appropriate actions to the Joint Committee. It was agreed there would be no press release.

6

10. The meeting was adjourned at 1630 hours.

1 Inclosure

ROBERT J. FRIEDMAN   YOON HA JONG
LIEUTENANT GENERAL   REPUBLIC OF KOREA
UNITED STATES AIR FORCE   REPRESENTATIVE
UNITED STATES REPRESENTATIVE

157

7

STATEMENT BY US REPRESENTATIVE AT THE SPECIAL MEETING OF THE JOINT COMMITTEE, WEDNESDAY, 5 JUNE 1968

1. At the request of the Commander of the United States Forces, Korea, I have called this special session of the Republic of Korea - United States Joint Committee, to bring to the attention of the officials of the Government of the Republic of Korea the serious security situation which has developed in the vicinity of the Osan Air Base. This problem is presented to the Republic of Korea - United States Joint Committee because it is directly related to the provisions of several articles of the Republic of Korea - United States Status of Forces Agreement, and because, if not dealt with effectively at Osan, could spread to other key defense installations in the Republic of Korea.

2. Immediately adjoining the large Osan Air Base, which has an extremely important role in the defense of the Republic of Korea, is Sin-chang-ni, Songtan-up, Pyongtaek-gun -- commonly known as "Chicol Village." Although this area has a population of approximately 50,000 Koreans, it has no organized government as such, and only a nominal police force. Chicol Village grew up with the development of the Osan Air Force Base. Almost all of the people in Chicol Village obtain their livelihood either in legitimate ways relating to the presence of the Air Base and its American personnel or from illegal and black-market operations and organized crime feeding on the area. Organized criminal elements in Chicol Village have become an increasingly serious

26th JC (Incl i)
5 June 68

158

security threat. These criminal elements engage in many types of illegal activity, e.g., blackmarketing, thievery, prostitution, smuggling, narcotics, customs violations, etc. We will readily admit that some United States personnel have dealings with such criminal elements, but we are doing everything possible to exercise control over our own personnel.

3. North Korean intelligence and subversive agencies are known to be attempting to operate among criminal elements in the Republic of Korea. The presence of such large, well-organized criminal groups in the immediate vicinity of the headquarters of the Air Forces, Korea, offers the North Korean communist regime a lucrative target for exploitation, against the security interests of the Governments of both the Republic of Korea and of the United States. These criminal elements, operating in an environment where no civil government exists to maintain any control over the situation, exert a highly adverse effect on the security and combat readiness of the air defense structure of the Republic of Korea.

4. United States Air Force authorities have concentrated available assets in an effort to counter this security threat. They have achieved some success in recent months in the detection and apprehension of organized criminal elements. Such successes as have been realized were the result of increased physical security, intensive investigation, and appeals for cooperation to local, provincial, and national Republic

2

26th JC (Incl 1)
5 Jun 68

of Korea Government officials. However, these successful operations against criminal elements operating from Chicol Village have precipitated sharp reactions from criminals in the area. These criminal elements have been exhibiting increased defiance of all law and order and have threatened and intimidated United States Air Force personnel who are attempting to deal with the situation. Reports of threats to kill United States Air Force special investigators have been received. Korean criminal elements have supplied false and misleading information to Korean newspapers, and libelous articles against such United States Air Force personnel have appeared in Seoul newspapers. Intimidation, harassment, and defiance of United States Air Force security personnel has now extended to USFK's Korean employees. Picket lines were set up outside the gate at Osan Air Base on Tuesday, 4 June. These Korean demonstrators would not permit the USFK's Korean employees to enter the Base unless they wore a distinctive yellow badge which denounced United States Air Force law enforcement personnel and told them to "go home."

    5. Article XXV of the ROK-US Status of Forces Agreement provides that:

> "The United States and the Republic of Korea will cooperate
> in taking such steps as may, from time to time, be necessary
> to ensure the security of the United States armed forces, the

26th JC (Incl 1)
5 Jun 68

3

members thereof, the civilian component, the persons who are present in the Republic of Korea pursuant to Article XV, their dependents and their property. The Government of the Republic of Korea agrees to seek such legislation and to take such other action as may be necessary to ensure the adequate security and protection within its territory of installations, equipment, property, records, and official information of the United States and, consistent with Article XXII, to ensure the punishment of offenders under the applicable laws of the Republic of Korea. "

6. The Government of the United States believes that a situation has developed in the immediate vicinity of the Osan Air Base that is a serious threat to the accomplishment of the mission of the United States Forces at Osan and to the security of the Republic of Korea. The criminal elements in Chicol Village have become increasingly bold, and through threats, intimidation and direct actions, are attempting to defy all constituted authority and Republic of Korea laws. For example, on 4 June such elements instigated activities which disrupted the orderly operation of the Air Base. USFK's Korean employees have been duped into actions which are clearly in violation of the Republic of Korea - United States Status of Forces Agreement. Because these criminal elements appear to be attempting to try to capitalize by every

161   4

26th JC (Incl 1)
5 Jun 68

possible means, including labor disputes, to intimidate United States authorities at Osan, it is important to emphasize that the United States Forces, Korea has fair and impartial procedures for adjudicating any legitimate grievance of its Korean employees. Vigorous investigations of the situation relating to dismissal of certain Osan Base Exchange employees for thievery are underway. As is well known, Article XVII of the Status of Forces Agreement provides for orderly hOK-US Joint Committee procedures to resolve any labor dispute "which cannot be settled through the grievance or labor relations procedures of the United States armed forces..." It is the joint responsibility of our two Governments to implement this Article effectively, and not to permit criminal elements to try to incite USFK's Korean employees to disruptive tactics or other illegal actions which are contrary to ROK law and the ROK-US Status of Forces Agreement. Such tactics by these illegal elements, if successful, could only benefit the North Korean communist regime and further undermine respect for law and order in the vicinity of this vital defense installation.

7. The Government of the United States earnestly requests the cooperation of the Republic of Korea in dealing with this serious threat to our mutual security interests. The Government of the Republic of Korea has been waging a concerted campaign against blackmarketing, smuggling, and other illegal activities in the Republic. These efforts

26th JC (Incl 1)
5 Jun 68

162

5

are to be commended, and the United States authorities pledge their

support to such activities. In this connection, the United States author-

ities believe that the organized criminal elements in the Osan area

present an immediate and urgent challenge to the Republic of Korea

authorities. It is urgently recommended that the Government of the

Republic of Korea take steps to organize an effective civil government,

with adequate police force, at Chicol Village. These problems con-

cern not only the ROK-US Joint Committee, and the Ministries of Home

Affairs and Health and Social Affairs, but also the Republic of Korea

security forces in the various ministries and special agencies. The

US authorities have recommended to the ROK authorities the establish-

ment of a new Subcommittee of the Joint Committee, to deal with

problems relating to security, blackmarketing, and law enforcement.

The United States authorities are prepared to cooperate closely with

the Government of the Republic of Korea to eliminate such situations,

as now prevail in the vicinity of the Osan Air Base. Immediate action

is needed to restore law and order and to remove the threat to combat

readiness of US and ROK defense forces. Illegal activities at Osan are

detrimental not only to the security of the Republic of Korea but also to

its economy and to its economic growth. Criminal elements which have

demonstrated contempt for both the Government of the Republic of Korea

and the ROK-US Status of Forces Agreement must be dealt with effectively

and sternly.

26th JC (Incl 1)

6   5 Jun 68

163

외 무 부

미이 720-

196 8 . 6 . 24.

수 신 : 배부처 참조

참 조 :

제 목 : 한.미 합동위원회 회의록 송부

　　　1. 한.미간 군대지위협정에 의하여 196 8 . 6 . 5 . 에
개최된 한.미 합동위원회 제 26 차 회의의 회의록을 별첨 송부하오니
참고 하시기 바랍니다.

　　　2. 본 회의록은 한.미 양측의 합의에 의하여서만 공개할
수 있는 문서이오니 유념하시기 바랍니다.

　　　첨부 : 합동위원회 제 26 차 회의록

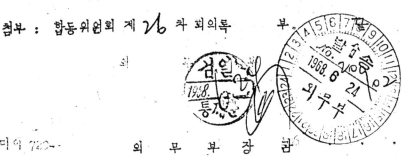

외 무 부 장 관

배부처 : 법무부장관 (법무실장, 검찰국장), 국방부장관 (기획국장,
　　　　시설국장), 재무부장관 (세관국장, 세제국장),
　　　　상공부장관 (상역국장), 노동청장 (노정국장),
　　　　교통부장관 (항공국장), 내무부장관 (치안국장), 주미.
　　　　주일, 주중, 주비대사 경제기획원장관 (개개개획총장)

164

These minuntes ♥♥ onsidered as official docum♥♥ pertaining to both
Governments an♥♥ll not be released without m♥♥ agreement.

JOINT COMMITTEE
UNDER
THE REPUBLIC OF KOREA AND THE UNITED STATES
STATUS OF FORCES AGREEMENT

MINUTES OF THE TWENTY-SIXTH MEETING

> 5 June 1968
> Headquarters
> U. S. Forces, Korea
> Seoul, Korea

1. The meeting was convened at 1500 hours by Lieutenant General Robert J. Friedman, the US Representative, who presided at the meeting.

2. The following were in attendance:

ROK	US
Mr. YOON Ha Jong	LTG Robert J. Friedman, USAF
Mr. LEE Sung Jung	CAPT M. R. Massie, USN
Mr. KIM Sung Jae	COL Herbert C. Hicks, Jr., USA
Mr. HUH Seung Joon	COL Gerald W. Davis, USA
Mr. SHIN Chung Sup	Mr. P. Wesley Kriebel, US Embassy
Mr. OH Myong Too	Mr. Robert A. Kinney, USFK
Mr. HONG Duk Sik	LTC Paul E. Jones, USAF

3. General Friedman thanked the ROK officials and expressed his deep appreciation for their responding so quickly to his request for a special Joint Committee meeting, knowing how busy they were. He stated that the number of ROK officials present was indicative of the good relations between the two components of the Joint Committee and the officials of the Governments of the Republic of Korea and of the United States. The US Representative indicated he would not have called a special meeting except for a serious situation which had developed at Osan Air Base.

4. The US Representative invited the ROK Representative to introduce the ROK officials. Mr. Yoon introduced Mr. KIM Sung Jae, the new Director of the Bureau of Prosecution of the Ministry of Justice, who replaced Mr. KIM Il Doo on the Joint Committee. He also introduced Mr. HONG Duk Sik, Chief of the Investigation Guidance Section of the Korean National Police.

> 26th JC
> 5 Jun 68

165

5. The ROK Representative stated that in support of the US Representative's opening statement, he would like to emphasize that the US-ROK Joint Committee is one body, working toward a common objective. What concerns the US component also concerns the ROK component, and the ROK Government.

6. The US Representative presented a statement on the situation at the Osan Air Base, which is attached as Inclosure 1.

7. The US Representative also presented to the ROK Representative copies of a file consisting of 25 letters from the United States Forces, Korea to various ROK Governmental agencies and authorities, outlining USFK measures to address the problems relating to smuggling, theft, and blackmarketing. This transfer of documents was accompanied by a statement that maximum mutual cooperation would be continuing to address this serious problem.

8. The ROK Representative stated that the ROK officials had listened very carefully to the statement made by the US Representative. He had no doubt that there were grounds for the concern of the US authorities over conditions at Chicol Village, near Osan Air Base. He stated that the ROK Government shared this concern because of common defense of the security of the Republic of Korea by the armed forces of the US and the ROK, and that the ROK Government would certainly take all appropriate measures that might be found necessary after full investigation of the situation. Regarding the reference of the US Representative concerning the lack of an effective local civil government and the existence of only a nominal police force in the area, etc., the ROK Representative commented that neither the local government nor the police force were as ineffective as had been described. Chicol Village is under the administrative jurisdiction of the Pyongtaek county office and the area is covered by the police sub-station at Songtan-up. The ROK Representative's preliminary inquiries disclosed that close liaison had been maintained among US-ROK law enforcement agencies, and that regular monthly meetings had been held between relevant police authorities and special investigation agencies of the two countries in the area. Despite the fact that ROK police organizations are generally understaffed due to recent organization of mobile police task forces following the infiltration in Seoul of agents on January 21, 1968, the number of policemen assigned to the Songtan Sub-station was increased to thirteen, exceeding the T/O authorized strength of ten. The ROK police detachment assigned to OSI had been raised from three to five, in compliance with US requests. The ROK police organization had this area under close observation and control, keeping tabs on delinquent or crime-prone elements, which number around 160. The ROK

166

2

26th JC
5 Jun 68

These minutes are ⬤⬤idered as official documents ⬤⬤aining to both Governments and will not be released without mutual agreement.

police had not detected any indication of an organized syndicate, nor had it previously received any report or complaint from US agencies about such organized crimes. The ROK police organization has been keeping a close watch on criminal trends in the area. For example, during first five months of 1968, there were 156 assault cases, which compared with 169 cases for the same period of 1967, a reduction of 10 percent. With regard to larceny and burglary cases involving the property of the US Government or US personnel, there were 33 cases during the first five months of this year, as compared to 27 cases for the same period of 1967, indicating an increase. On the other hand, only six of the 27 cases were solved and arrests made in 1967, while 23 of the 33 cases have been solved in 1968, which indicate an improving efficiency of the investigative efforts. There have been four important theft cases thus far in 1968. The culprit has been apprehended in one of these cases and for each of the remaining three cases, four detectives had been detailed for solution. As to a robbery committed against four US personnel on 20 March, three suspects were arrested the following day. The ROK Representative indicated that, if the US component so desired, these and other related statistics will be made available to the US side.

9. The ROK Representative emphasized that he presented these facts and figures not to defend ROK law enforcement agencies but simply to show facts which preliminary inquiries disclosed. The ROK Representative concluded that he could not see that there existed general lawlessness or organized criminal elements at Osan. He again pointed out that there had been no complaints by US law enforcement officials at the regular monthly meetings of police officials at Osan or on any other occasions. However, he felt the need for a full investigation and proposed that the matter be referred to the Criminal Jurisdiction Subcommittee for its review and recommendations.

10. The ROK Representative stated that if there is any clear evidence of communist instigation or the involvement of subversive elements, there are sufficient means to crush such elements and defeat the attempt at any time.

11. Regarding labor disturbance aspects of the situation, the ROK Representative explained that as far as Korean authorities could determine, there had been no instances of action on the part of the local Union which were considered in violation of relevant legislation or agreements. According to a preliminary report, there were eleven USFK Korean personnel dismissed for alleged misconduct. The individuals concerned thought the dismissals unfair and appealed to their Union. The local chapter of the Union voted on 31 May by a majority of more than 95 percent

167

3

26th JC
5 Jun 68

These minutes are considered as official documents pertaining to both Governments and will not be released without mutual agreement.

to make this issue a labor dispute under labor relations procedures. The interruption of work which occurred on 4 June was not a strike or refusal to work initiated by the Union; rather, the refusal of the US Air Base authorities at the base entrance to admit those wearing badges inscribing a slogan caused the involuntary interruption. It is noted that on two occasions a precedent was established to recognize the practice of wearing badges while on work as a legitimate demonstration. The ROK Representative stated that as it was understood that this dispute was in the process of solution, he saw no need for the SOFA mechanism or the Joint Committee to intervene at this moment. Nevertheless, he fully shared the concern of the US authorities over these labor disturbances at the Osan Air Base.

12.   The US Representative thanked the ROK Representative for his estimate of the situation. He accepted the ROK proposal to assign the Criminal Jurisdiction Subcommittee the task of investigating the situation and to recommending actions which would preclude a recurrence of such problems. He also noted the ROK Representative's offer to furnish additional ROK Government statistics and other facts on this situation, which he gladly accepted. He also expressed the hope that the ROK Representative's estimate of the situation at Chicol Village was a more accurate assessment than that presented in the US statement. He pointed out, however, that the fact remained that over considerable periods of time, situations similar to the current one had arisen at Osan and were not resolved at the local level. Only when the problem was referred to the national government level had an improvement of the situation been achieved. He stated he would like to note for the record the support the US has received from certain ROK Government officials. ROK Police Director Kim had responded on every occasion when requested to augment the local police at Chicol Village. His assistance had not only been immediate but most effective. The US Representative indicated, however, that when higher level elements in the police organization subsequently departed the area, the situation tended to revert to the previously unsatisfactory state. The US Representative agreed that the situation at Osan could not be labeled as primarily a labor dispute. The labor aspects of the situation were a manifestation of a much deeper and more serious problem.

13.   The US Representative stated that he understood that both the ROK and US wanted to stamp out, once and for all, illegal and blackmarket operations and all were working in concert to solve this problem. The situation which gave rise to the present problem was, at least in part, the result of a US effort to expose and break up a smuggling ring. Despite the determination of both our Governments to stamp out smuggling and thefts, a representative of the US investigative organization was threatened

168

4

26th JC
5 Jun 68

These minutes are ██ sidered as official documents pertaining to both
Governments and ██ not be released without mutu ██ reement.

with his life. It was on the basis of such factors that the assistance of the
ROK Government national-level authorities had been requested to help
local authorities at Osan to deal with the situation. The US Representative stated that he did not intend to infer that the situation at Osan was
Communist-instigated but that he did want to point out that the situation
there was the kind the Communists tried to exploit and capitalize upon,
to make the problems of both the ROK and US Governments more difficult. The US Representative stated that he knew this was a complex and
difficult problem and that it could not be resolved at this Joint Committee
meeting. He stated that he felt both Governments were prepared to work
together on this problem, and that with such close cooperation the problem could be worked out.

14. It was agreed that the ROK and US authorities would cooperate
closely in resolving this problem and that the Criminal Jurisdiction
Subcommittee would be assigned the task of studying this problem and
recommending appropriate actions to correct the situation. It was
agreed there would be no press release on this Joint Committee meeting.

15. The meeting was adjourned at 1630 hours.

1 Inclosure

YOON HA JONG
REPUBLIC OF KOREA
REPRESENTATIVE

ROBERT J. FRIEDMAN
LIEUTENANT GENERAL
UNITED STATES AIR FORCE
UNITED STATES REPRESENTATIVE

169

5

26th JC
5 Jun 68

These minutes are considered as official documents pertaining to both Governments and will not be released without mutual agreement.

with his life. It was on the basis of such factors that the assistance of the ROK Government national-level authorities had been requested to help local authorities at Osan to deal with the situation. The US Representative stated that he did not intend to infer that the situation at Osan was Communist-instigated but that he did want to point out that the situation there was the kind the Communists tried to exploit and capitalize upon, to make the problems of both the ROK and US Governments more difficult. The US Representative stated that he knew this was a complex and difficult problem and that it could not be resolved at this Joint Committee meeting. He stated that he felt both Governments were prepared to work together on this problem, and that with such close cooperation the problem could be worked out.

14. It was agreed that the ROK and US authorities would cooperate closely in resolving this problem and that the Criminal Jurisdiction Subcommittee would be assigned the task of studying this problem and recommending appropriate actions to correct the situation. It was agreed there would be no press release on this Joint Committee meeting.

15. The meeting was adjourned at 1630 hours.

1 Inclosure

YOON HA JONG
REPUBLIC OF KOREA
REPRESENTATIVE

ROBERT J. FRIEDMAN
LIEUTENANT GENERAL
UNITED STATES AIR FORCE
UNITED STATES REPRESENTATIVE

170

5

26th JC
5 Jun 68

These minutes are considered as official documents pertaining to both Governments and will not be released without mutual agreement.

STATEMENT BY US REPRESENTATIVE AT THE SPECIAL MEETING OF THE JOINT COMMITTEE, WEDNESDAY, 5 JUNE 1968

1. At the request of the Commander of the United States Forces, Korea, I have called this special session of the Republic of Korea - United States Joint Committee, to bring to the attention of the officials of the Government of the Republic of Korea the serious security situation which has developed in the vicinity of the Osan Air Base. This problem is presented to the Republic of Korea - United States Joint Committee because it is directly related to the provisions of several articles of the Republic of Korea - United States Status of Forces Agreement, and because, if not dealt with effectively at Osan, could spread to other key defense installations in the Republic of Korea.

2. Immediately adjoining the large Osan Air Base, which has an extremely important role in the defense of the Republic of Korea, is Sin-chang-ni, Songtan-up, Pyongtaek-gun -- commonly known as "Chicol Village." Although this area has a population of approximately 50,000 Koreans, it has no organized government as such, and only a nominal police force. Chicol Village grew up with the development of the Osan Air Force Base. Almost all of the people in Chicol Village obtain their livelihood either in legitimate ways relating to the presence of the Air Base and its American personnel or from illegal and black-market operations and organized crime feeding on the area. Organized criminal elements in Chicol Village have become an increasingly serious

26th JC (Incl 1)

security threat. These criminal elements engage in many types of illegal activity, e.g., blackmarketing, thievery, prostitution, smuggling, narcotics, customs violations, etc. We will readily admit that some United States personnel have dealings with such criminal elements, but we are doing everything possible to exercise control over our own personnel.

3. North Korean intelligence and subversive agencies are known to be attempting to operate among criminal elements in the Republic of Korea. The presence of such large, well-organized criminal groups in the immediate vicinity of the headquarters of the Air Forces, Korea, offers the North Korean communist regime a lucrative target for exploitation, against the security interests of the Governments of both the Republic of Korea and of the United States. These criminal elements, operating in an environment where no civil government exists to maintain any control over the situation, exert a highly adverse effect on the security and combat readiness of the air defense structure of the Republic of Korea.

4. United States Air Force authorities have concentrated available assets in an effort to counter this security threat. They have achieved some success in recent months in the detection and apprehension of organized criminal elements. Such successes as have been realized were the result of increased physical security, intensive investigation, and appeals for cooperation to local, provincial, and national Republic

2

26th JC (Incl 1)
5 Jun 68

of Korea Government officials. However, these successful operations

against criminal elements operating from Chicol Village have precipi-

tated sharp reactions from criminals in the area. These criminal

elements have been exhibiting increased defiance of all law and order

and have threatened and intimidated United States Air Force personnel

who are attempting to deal with the situation. Reports of threats to

kill United States Air Force special investigators have been received.

Korean criminal elements have supplied false and misleading informa-

tion to Korean newspapers, and libelous articles against such United

States Air Force personnel have appeared in Seoul newspapers. Intimi-

dation, harassment, and defiance of United States Air Force security

personnel has now extended to USFK's Korean employees. Picket lines

were set up outside the gate at Osan Air Base on Tuesday, 4 June. These

Korean demonstrators would not permit the USFK's Korean employees to

enter the Base unless they wore a distinctive yellow badge which denounced

United States Air Force law enforcement personnel and told them to "go

home."

    5. Article XXV of the ROK-US Status of Forces Agreement provides

that:

> "The United States and the Republic of Korea will cooperate
>
> in taking such steps as may, from time to time, be necessary
>
> to ensure the security of the United States armed forces, the

26th JC (Incl 1)
5 Jun 68

173

3

members thereof, the civilian component, the persons who are present in the Republic of Korea pursuant to Article XV, their dependents and their property. The Government of the Republic of Korea agrees to seek such legislation and to take such other action as may be necessary to ensure the adequate security and protection within its territory of installations, equipment, property, records, and official information of the United States and, consistent with Article XXII, to ensure the punishment of offenders under the applicable laws of the Republic of Korea. "

6. The Government of the United States believes that a situation has developed in the immediate vicinity of the Osan Air Base that is a serious threat to the accomplishment of the mission of the United States Forces at Osan and to the security of the Republic of Korea. The criminal elements in Chicol Village have become increasingly bold, and through threats, intimidation and direct actions, are attempting to defy all constituted authority and Republic of Korea laws. For example, on 4 June such elements instigated activities which disrupted the orderly operation of the Air Base. USFK's Korean employees have been duped into actions which are clearly in violation of the Republic of Korea - United States Status of Forces Agreement. Because these criminal elements appear to be attempting to try to capitalize by every

possible means, including labor disputes, to intimidate United States authorities at Osan, it is important to emphasize that the United States Forces, Korea has fair and impartial procedures for adjudicating any legitimate grievance of its Korean employees. Vigorous investigations of the situation relating to dismissal of certain Osan Base Exchange employees for thievery are underway. As is well known, Article XVII of the Status of Forces Agreement provides for orderly ROK-US Joint Committee procedures to resolve any labor dispute "which cannot be settled through the grievance or labor relations procedures of the United States armed forces..." It is the joint responsibility of our two Governments to implement this Article effectively, and not to permit criminal elements to try to incite USFK's Korean employees to disruptive tactics or other illegal actions which are contrary to ROK law and the ROK-US Status of Forces Agreement. Such tactics by these illegal elements, if successful, could only benefit the North Korean communist regime and further undermine respect for law and order in the vicinity of this vital defense installation.

7. The Government of the United States earnestly requests the cooperation of the Republic of Korea in dealing with this serious threat to our mutual security interests. The Government of the Republic of Korea has been waging a concerted campaign against blackmarketing, smuggling, and other illegal activities in the Republic. These efforts

26th JC (Incl 1)
5 Jun 68

175

5

are to be commended, and the United States authorities pledge their support to such activities. In this connection, the United States authorities believe that the organized criminal elements in the Osan area present an immediate and urgent challenge to the Republic of Korea authorities. It is urgently recommended that the Government of the Republic of Korea take steps to organize an effective civil government, with adequate police force, at Chicol Village. These problems concern not only the ROK-US Joint Committee, and the Ministries of Home Affairs and Health and Social Affairs, but also the Republic of Korea security forces in the various ministries and special agencies. The US authorities have recommended to the ROK authorities the establishment of a new Subcommittee of the Joint Committee, to deal with problems relating to security, blackmarketing, and law enforcement. The United States authorities are prepared to cooperate closely with the Government of the Republic of Korea to eliminate such situations, as now prevail in the vicinity of the Osan Air Base. Immediate action is needed to restore law and order and to remove the threat to combat readiness of US and ROK defense forces. Illegal activities at Osan are detrimental not only to the security of the Republic of Korea but also to its economy and to its economic growth. Criminal elements which have demonstrated contempt for both the Government of the Republic of Korea and the ROK-US Status of Forces Agreement must be dealt with effectively and sternly.

176

26th JC (Incl 1)
5 Jun 68

6

3. 제 2 7 차. 1968. 6. 7

177

한.미 합동위원회 제27차 회의 의제

1968. 6. 7. 15:00시

미8군 SOFA 회의실

1. 시설구역 분과위원회 추가과제 부여 - 미측 설명 8건

2. 시설구역 분과위원회 건의

　가. 한국측 설명 2건

　나. 미측 설명 4건

3. 시설구역 분과위원회 운영 절차에 관한 합동위원회에 대한 각서 — 한국측 설명

4. 제16조 제1항 해석에 관한 합동위원회에 대한 각서 — 미측설명

5. 미국 초청계약자 지명에 관한 각서 — 미측 설명

6. SOFA 시행상 미측이 한국 정부에 제출하는 각서 — 미측 설명

7. 차기회의 — 1968. 7. 3. (水) 15:00시 중앙청 회의실

8. 공동발표문 채택

9. 폐 회

178

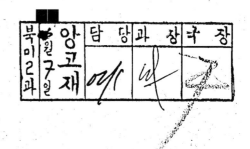

한. 미군대지위협정 한.미 합동위원회
제 27 차 회의

1968. 6. 7.

대한민국 대표 발언취지 (안)

179

(의제 1 - 시설구역 분과위원회 신규과제부여)

미국대표 설명 - 8건

(미국대표 시설구역 분과위원회에 부여할 8개의 신규과제를 설명하고
합동위원회 승인을 제안)

감사합니다.

대한민국 대표는 지금 미국대표께서 설명하신 8건의 신규과제를
시설구역 분과위원회에 부여하는데 동의하는 바입니다.

180

(의제 2 - 시설구역 분과위원회 건의)

　　1.　한국측 설명 - 2건

　　　(미국대표 동 분과위원회 건의 2건을 한국 대표가 설명할 것을 요청)

　　감사합니다.

　　시설구역 분과위원회는 국방부 및 미8군이 합의한 조건의 이행을 전제로
PAC-10　의 일부 약 1.634 에이커의 취득 해제를 건의하고 있읍니다.
시설구역 분과위원회의 두번째의 건의는 합동위원회가 금년 2월 21일
부여한 과제인 ASCOM-375　　　　의 일부 1.716 에이커의 취득
해제요청에 관한 것입니다. 본 건 해제요청 토지는 한국 해군 통신시설
건설 목적으로 소요된 것으로서 동 통신 시설의 건설이 동 지역내 기타
통신시설 운영에 장애가 될 것이므로 현 실정하에서는 동 계획 추진이
불가하다는 결론에 도달하여 본 건 해제신청의 철회를 건의하고 있읍니다.
대한민국 대표는 지금 설명한 2건의 시설구역 분과위원회 건의에 대한
합동위원회 승인을 제안하는 바입니다.

　　(미국대표 동의표시)

　　감사합니다.

2.　미국측 설명 - 4건

　　　(미국대표 4건의 건의를 설명하고 이에 대한 합동위원회 승인을 제안)

|8|

감사합니다.

대한민국 대표는 임진면 소재 토지 취득에 관한 특별 조건을 포함하여 지금 설명하신 4건의 시설 구역 분과위원회 건의 채택에 동의하는 바입니다.

182

(의제 3 - 운영규정에 관한 각서)

(미국대표 한국 대표의 설명을 청함.)

감사합니다.

대한민국 대표는 시설구역 분과위원회 운영 절차에 관하여 공식 각서를 제출합니다.

합동위원회는 제1차 회의에서 채택한 각 분과위원회 운영규정 및 제5차 회의에서 채택한 시설구역 분과위원회 운영규정에서 등 분과위원회는 합동위원회가 회부한 사항 또는 과제에 한하여 이를 취급한다는 원칙을 정하였으며 동 분과위원회 발족이래 이 원칙이 엄격히 준수되어 왔읍니다.

연이나 과거 1년 유여의 경험에 의하여 동 분과위원회에 부여되는 과제의 거의 전부가 개개부동산에 대한 취득, 해제, 임시사용허가의 연장, 재구분등이고 또한 공식과제 부여에 앞서 어차피 동 분과위원회의 사전 심사가 필요하였으며 따라서 합동위원회의 공식 과제 부여는 형식적 절차에 불과하다는 결론에 도달하게 되었읍니다.

이러한 고려에 입각하여 사무 간소화를 위하여 다음과 같은 원칙을 합동위원회가 채택할 것을 제안하는 바입니다.

1) 시설구역 분과위원회는 개개 부동산에 관한 각종 요청에 관하여는 합동위원회의 과제부여없이 의견 또는 건의를 합동위원회에 제출할 수 있다.

2) 의견 차이가 있은 경우에는 상방이 합동위원회에 문제를 제기하여 그의 결정을 청하는 권리를 유보한다.

3) 동 분과위원회는 합동위원회가 특정과제를 부여하지 않는한 일반 정책 또는 절차에 관한 사항을 취급하지 않는다.

183

　　　　시설구역 분과위원회가 합동위원회의 하부 기관이므로 그 업무에 있어
합동위원회의 일반적 감독을 받아야 함은 자명한 일이며 전기한 분과
위원회 권한 한계에 관한 원칙에 대해서는 공공용역 분과위원회에 관하여
이미 예외가 설치되었음을 상기합니다. 이러한 전제하에 시설구역
분과위원회 운영규정에 관한 전기 제안에 대하여 미국 대표의 동의를
청하는 바입니다.

　　　　(미국 대표 응답)

184

(의제 4 - 제16조 1항 해석에 관한 합동위원회 앞 각서)

(미국대표 설명)

　　미국측 각서와 이에 대한 미국대표의 명료한 설명을 감사합니다.

　　본 건은 이미 양 관계당국간에 장기간 논의되어 왔으며 한국측의
일반적 견해에 대하여는 상공부 당국과의 공문 교환 및 기타 비공식
논의를 통하여 미국측이 이미 숙지하고 있는 것으로 믿읍니다.

　　한국 대표는 즉석에서 미국 측 각서에 대한 공식 회답을 할 준비를
갖추지 못하였으므로 추후 회의에서 한국측 견해를 표시하는 권리를
유보하고 본 건에 관한 오늘 토의는 일단 종결할 것을 제의합니다.

(미국측 동의 표시)

185

(의 제 5 - 초청계약자 지명에 관한 각서)

(미측 설명)

감사합니다.

한국 대표는 Daniel, Mann, Johnson & Mendenhall, Adrian
Wilson Associates및 Trans-Asia Engineering Associates, Inc.
에 대한 초청계약자 지명 통고의 접수를 확인하고, 아울러 동 지명에
있어 합동위원회가 정한 접차를 완전히 이행하였음을 확인하는 바입니다.

186

(의 제6 - 군대지위협정 시행상 미측이 한국측에 전달한 문서)

(미국대표 한국측에 전달한 문서를 열거)

한국측에 전달한 문서를 일일히 열거해 주신데 대하여 감사합니다.

한국 대표는 한국측 사무국이 지금 열거하신 문서를 접수 하였음을

확인하는 바입니다.

187

(의 제 7 - 다음회의 예정)

   (미국대표는 다음회의를 7월 3일 (수) 15시 중앙청 회의실 에서
개최할 것을 제의)

   지금 제안하신 일시는 적절한 것으로 생각되므로 동의하는 바입니다.
   이 기회에 종전에 3주 간격으로 정기회의를 개최하고 있었으나
추후에는 특별한 사유가 없는한 4주 간격으로 정기회의를 개최한다는
원칙을 정할 것을 제의하는 바입니다.

   (미국대표 동의 표시)

188

(의제 8 - 공동발표문 채택)

(미국 대표 양측 간사가 작성한 발표문 채택을 제의)

한국 대표는 동 문안 채택에 동의합니다.

189

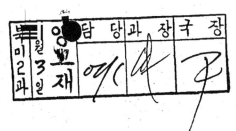

JOINT COMMITTEE
UNDER
THE REPUBLIC OF KOREA AND THE UNITED STATES
STATUS OF FORCES AGREEMENT

7 June 1968

MEMORANDUM TO: The Joint Committee

SUBJECT   : Operating Procedures for the Facilities
                  and Areas Subcommittee

        1. Reference is made to the following passages of
the Joint Committee decisions:

        a. Procedures for operation of the ROK-US
Joint Committee Subcommittees.(Inclosure 5, Minutes of
the First Meeting)

                " 1. . . . Subcommittees will give advice
        and make recommendations only on those matters
        specifically referred to them by the Joint Committee."

        b. Facilities and Areas Subcommittee procedures.
(Inclosure 2, Minutes of the Fifth Meeting)

                "III. Order of Business

                2. Unless otherwise directed by the Joint
        Committee, the Facilities and Areas Subcommittee
        will address only matters referred to it by the
        Joint Committee."

                "IV. Conduct of Business

                1. The Facilities and Areas Subcommittee
        will act only on tasks assigned by the Joint
        Committee"

        2. The principle adopted by the Joint Committee
and referred to in the proceding paragraph has been
strictly adhered to for the operation of the Facilities
and Areas Subcommittee since its inauguration. However,
it is noted that almost all of the tasks assigned to
the Subcommittee concern acquisition, extension of
temporary use permit, release or reclassification of
individual real estate, that before formal assignment

190-

of such tasks prescreening by the Subcpmmittee was
necessary, and that consequently the assignment of such
tasks by the Joint Committee is a mere formality.
It is also recalled that on several occasions the Joint
Committee was obliged to follow exigency procedures due
to urgency of some actions.

3. Therefore it is pro_sed that the following principle
be adopted by the Joint Committee in order to simplify
the procedures:

a. The Facilities and Areas Subcommittee may
submit to the Joint Committee its views and recommendations
on requests concerned with individual real estate without
being formally assigned a task.

b. In case of disagreement both sides reserve
the right to bring the matter to the Joint Committee for
its decision.

c. The Subcommittee will not act on matters of
general policy or procedures unless a specific task was
assigned by the Joint Committee.

Yoon Ha Jong
Republic of Korea
Representative

JOINT COMMITTEE
UNDER
THE REPUBLIC OF KOREA AND THE UNITED STATES
STATUS OF FORCES AGREEMENT

MINUTES OF THE TWENTY-SEVENTH MEETING

7 June 1968
Headquarters
U.S. Forces, Korea
Seoul, Korea

1. The meeting was convened at 1500 hours by Lieutenant General Robert J. Friedman, the US Representative, who presided at the meeting. A copy of the agenda is attached as Inclosure 1.

2. The following were in attendance:

ROK	US
Mr. YOON Ha Jong	LTG Robert J. Friedman, USAF
Mr. LEE Sun Jung	CAPT M. R. Massie, USN
Mr. KIM Sung Jae	COL Herbert C. Hicks, Jr., USA
Mr. HUH Seung Joon	COL Gerald W. Davis, USA
Mr. SHIN Chung Sup	Mr. P. Wesley Kriebel, US Embassy
Mr. OH Myong Too	Mr. Robert A. Kinney, USFK
	LTC Paul E. Jones, USAF

3. The US Representative called the meeting to order and proposed assignment of eight new tasks to the Facilities and Areas Subcommittee. These involved (Inclosure 2):

    a. Acquisition of 1.19 acres at Kanghwa-gun, Kyonggi-do.

    b. Acquisition of 1.16 acres with seven buildings and three facilities at Hannam-dong, Yongsan-ku, Seoul.

    c. Acquisition of 1.98 acres at #322 Chung-dong, Tongnae-ku, Pusan.

    d. Acquisition of 0.8 acre at Howon-dong, Uijongbu, Kyonggi-do.

    e. Acquisition of 0.23 acre at Kanung-dong, Uijongbu, Kyonggi-do.

    f. Acquisition of 62.23 acres at Yongtae-ri, Wolong-myon, Paju-gun, Kyonggi-do.

27th JC
7 Jun 68

These minutes are considered as official documents pertaining to both Governments and will not be released without mutual agreement.

     g. Acquisition of an easement for 0.85 acre near Pangchung-ni, Kwangtan-myon, Paju-gun, Kyonggi-do.

     h. Extension of Temporary Use Permit, CAV-T-9, from 7 May 1968 to 6 May 1969.

    4. The ROK Representative concurred in the assignment of these eight new tasks to the Facilities and Areas Subcommittee.

    5. The ROK Representative presented two recommendations of the Facilities and Areas Subcommittee. These involved:

     a. The withdrawal of a request for release of a portion of ASCOM-375, involving 1.716 acres, which was assigned as a task on 21 February 1968 (Inclosure 3).

     b. The release of a portion of PAC-10, involving approximately 1.634 acres, (Inclosure 4), subject to the fulfillment of conditions agreed upon by the Ministry of National Defense and the Eighth US Army.

    6. The US Representative concurred in Joint Committee approval of these two recommendations of the Facilities and Areas Subcommittee.

    7. The US Representative presented four recommendations of the Facilities and Areas Subcommittee, as follows:

     a. The acquisition of 0.18 acre of land of Kumo-dong, Uijongbu, Kyonggi-do (Inclosure 5).

     b. The acquisition of 16.455 acres of land at various locations in Imjin-myon, Paju-gun, Kyonggi-do (Inclosure 6).

     c. The conversion to an exclusive use basis 0.014 acre currently held as a perpetual restrictive easement in Kwangju-gun, Kyonggi-do (Inclosure 6).

     d. The extension of Temporary Use Permit CAV-T-16 (Inclosure 6).

    8. The US Representative proposed Joint Committee approval of these four recommendations of the Facilities and Areas Subcommittee and the ROK Representative concurred.

    9. The ROK Representative submitted a written memorandum on the subject of operating procedures for the Facilities and Areas Subcommittee

2

27th JC
7 Jun 68

These minutes ●● considered as official docu●● pertaining to both Governments and will not be released without mutual agreement.

(Inclosure 7). He stated that the Joint Committee adopted at its first meeting "Procedures for Operation of the US-ROK Joint Committee Subcommittees," and adopted at its fifth meeting Facilities and Areas Subcommittee Procedures. These procedures established the principle that the Subcommittee acts only on matters or tasks referred to it by the Joint Committee, a principle strictly adhered to since inauguration of the Subcommittee. However, it had been noted from experience of more than a year, that nearly all of the tasks assigned to the Subcommittee relate to acquisition, extension of temporary use permit, release or reclassification of individual property, and that in any case, pre-screening by the Subcommittee was necessary before assignment of such tasks, and therefore formal assignment of tasks had been mere formality. Based on these considerations, it was proposed that the following principle be adopted by the Joint Committee in order to simplify the procedures:

a. The Facilities and Areas Subcommittee may submit to the Joint Committee its views and recommendations on requests relating to individual real estate without being formally assigned a task.

b. In case of disagreement, both sides reserve the right to bring the matter to the Joint Committee for decision.

c. The Subcommittee will not act on matters of general policy or procedures unless a specific task thereon was assigned by the Joint Committee.

10. The ROK Representative noted that the Subcommittee being a subsidiary organ of the Joint Committee, it goes without saying that the Subcommittee remains under general supervision of the Joint Committee, and recalled that an exception to the limitative principle of subcommittee authority had already been made with regard to the Utilities Subcommittee. He requested concurrence of the US Representative to the foregoing proposal concerning operating procedures for the Facilities and Areas Subcommittee.

11. The US Representative thanked the ROK Representative and stated he was pleased to receive the memorandum from the ROK Representative concerning modification of operating procedures for the Facilities and Areas Subcommittee. He stated it was mutually agreed that steps to simplify this Subcommittee's procedures and increase its efficiency of operation in every way possible are desirable, and it is believed that the proposal of the Republic of Korea Representative has considerable merit. The Facilities and Areas Subcommittee operations have been among the most effective of any Subcommittee, and it has been accepted that there may be further actions to simplify its procedures with the passage of

3

27th JC
7 Jun 68

These minutes are considered as official documents pertaining to both
Governments and will not be released without mutual agreement.

time. The US Representative proposed that the memorandum presented
by the ROK Representative be reviewed by the ROK and US SOFA Secretaries in coordination with the ROK and US Secretaries of the Facilities
and Areas Subcommittees. Further, he proposed that these personnel
develop mutually agreed recommendations concerning simplification of
Facilities and Areas Subcommittee procedures, for consideration by
the Joint Committee at the earliest Joint Committee-meeting. The ROK
Representative indicated his concurrence.

12. The US Representative presented a memorandum on the subject
of "Interpretation of Article XVI, paragraph 1, of the US-ROK Status of
Forces Agreement" (Inclosure 8). This memorandum, which had been
distributed to the Republic of Korea component prior to the meeting,
quoted the relevant passage of the Agreement which reads:

> "The United States may contract for any materials,
> supplies, equipment and services (including con-
> struction work) to be furnished or undertaken in
> the Republic of Korea for purposes of, or author-
> ized by, this Agreement, without restriction as to
> choice of contractor, supplier or person who pro-
> vides such services. "

13. The US Representative stated that he believed that under the
foregoing provision of Article XVI, United States armed forces may
contract "without restriction" in Korea with any Korean contractor
or firm duly licensed by the Government of the Republic of Korea to
do business in Korea. ‹It is believed that ROK Law 979, which provides
that Korean contractors and businessmen must obtain a special license,
in addition to any standard license, to do business with the United States
armed forces in Korea was contrary to the provisions of the Status of
Forces Agreement› In this connection, attention was called to paragraph 2 of Article XXIX which provides that:

> "The Government of the Republic of Korea shall
> undertake to seek from its legislature all legis-
> lative and budgetary action necessary to give
> effect to the provisions of this Agreement."

14. The US Representative stated that it was in the mutual interests
of both the Governments of the United States and the Republic of Korea
and of benefit to their mutual defense responsibilities, to have maximum
competition in local procurement by the United States armed forces in
Korea. It was recognized that paragraph 2 of Article XVI stipulated
that procurement by the United States armed forces "which may have

195

4

27th JC
7 Jun 68

These minutes ●● considered as official docum●● pertaining to both Governments and will not be released without mutual agreement.

an adverse affect on the economy of the Republic of Korea shall be procured in coordination with, and, when desirable, through or with the assistance of, the competent authorities of the Republic of Korea." The US Representative stated that the United States armed forces had been and will continue to be, ready to implement such provisions as well as the provisions of Agreed Minute 2 which read:

> "The problem of a satisfactory settlement of difficulties with respect to procurement contracts arising out of differences between economic laws and business practices of the Republic of Korea and the United States will be studied by the Joint Committee or other appropriate representatives."

15. The US Representative said he trusted that the Government of the Republic of Korea would accept this interpretation of Article XVI of the Status of Forces Agreement and take appropriate action to fulfill its obligations under paragraph 2 of Article XXIX of the SOFA.

16. The ROK Representative thanked the US Representative for the memorandum and his presentation. The ROK Representative, after pointing out that the subject had long been discussed between the pertinent authorities of the two countries and that the general views of the Korean side are well known to the US authorities, regretted not being prepared to make a formal reply to the memorandum immediately at this meeting. He stated that a formal position would be conveyed at a later meeting.

17. The US Representative presented memoranda to the Joint Committee informing the Republic of Korea Government of the designation of three new invited contractors under Article XV of the Status of Forces Agreement. After consultation with Republic of Korea Commerce Subcommittee personnel, the United States Forces, Korea, designated as US invited contractors Adrian Wilson Associates (Inclosure 9); Trans-Asia Engineering Associates, Inc. (Inclosure 10); and Daniel, Mann, Johnson, & Mendenhall (Inclosure 11). Pertinent data concerning employees of these invited contractors will be provided to the Government of the Republic of Korea in accordance with mutually approved procedures.

18. The ROK Representative stated he was pleased to acknowledge the US notification on designations of Daniel, Mann, Johnson & Mendenhall; Adrian Wilson Associates; and Trans-Asia Engineering Associates, Inc., as invited contractors, and also confirmed that agreed procedures for consultation were duly observed in these designations.

5

27th JC
7 Jun 68

These minutes are considered as official documents pertaining to both Governments and will not be released without mutual agreement.

19. The US Representative noted for the record that the US SOFA Secretary furnished the following information to the ROK SOFA Secretary, in accordance with the Joint Committee decisions:

    a. Five copies of reports on the US armed forces disposition of cases for the month of April 1968.

    b. Twenty copies of a report listing arrivals, departures, and address changes of US invited contractors and their dependents, dated 31 May 1968. The ROK Representative explained that he was happy to confirm the receipt by the ROK SOFA Secretary of the documents as enumerated.

20. The US Representative proposed that the next meeting of the Joint Committee be held on Wednesday, 3 July, at 1500 hours, in the Republic of Korea Capitol Building.

21. The ROK Representative stated that the time and date proposed for the next meeting seemed most appropriate, and that he was most happy to accept the proposal.

22. The US Representative proposed acceptance of the joint press release for the twenty-seventh Joint Committee meeting, as prepared by the ROK and US SOFA Secretaries (Inclosure 12). The ROK Representative agreed to adopt the proposed press release as drafted.

23. The US Representative stated that before the meeting adjourned, he wished to express his sincere regret that the Eighth US Army member of the US component, Colonel Herbert C. Hicks, Jr., will be departing Korea before the next scheduled Joint Committee meeting. Both the US and ROK Representatives thanked Colonel Hicks for his substantial contributions to the Joint Committee during his service with the Committee ever since it was first organized early in 1967.

24. The meeting was adjourned at 1545 hours.

12 Inclosures

YOON HA JONG
REPUBLIC OF KOREA
REPRESENTATIVE

ROBERT J. FRIEDMAN
LIEUTENANT GENERAL
UNITED STATES AIR FORCE
UNITED STATES REPRESENTATIVE

6

27th JC
7 Jun 68

AGENDA FOR THE TWENTY-SEVENTH MEETING
OF THE ROK-US JOINT COMMITTEE
1500 HOURS, 7 JUNE 1968, US SOFA CONFERENCE ROOM

I   Assignment of Additional Tasks to Facilities and Areas Subcommittee:

Eight tasks   -   US Presentation

II   Recommendations of Facilities and Areas Subcommittee:

1. Two recommendations   -   ROK Presentation

2. Four recommendations   -   US Presentation

III   Memorandum to Joint Committee on Operating Procedures for

Facilities and Areas Subcommittee   -   ROK Presentation

IV   Memorandum to Joint Committee on Interpretation of Paragraph 1,

Article XVI   -   US Presentation

V   Memoranda on Designation of USFK Invited Contractors   -

US Presentation

VI   Memoranda Presented to the ROK Government by the US, in the

Implementation of the SOFA   -   US Presentation

VII   Proposed Time of Next Meeting - 1500 hours, Wednesday, 3 July 1968,

in the ROK Capitol Building

VIII   Agreement on Joint Press Release

IX   Adjourn

|98

**JOINT COMMITTEE
UNDER
THE REPUBLIC OF KOREA AND THE UNITED STATES
STATUS OF FORCES AGREEMENT**

7 June 1968

MEMORANDUM FOR: Chairmen, Facilities & Areas Subcommittee

SUBJECT: Requests for Acquisition of Real Estate and Extension
of a Temporary Use Permit

1. SOFA provides, in Article II, paragraph 2, that the Governments of the Republic of Korea and the United States may agree that facilities and areas or portions thereof shall be returned to the Republic of Korea or that additional facilities and areas may be provided.

2. Pursuant to paragraph 1 above, it is requested that recommendations be presented to the Joint Committee concerning requests for the following acquisitions:

a. Acquisition of 1.19 acres of non-arable land at San, 152, 262-1, Lim Bukun-ni, Hajum-myon, Kanghwa-gun, Kyonggi-do. This land is required for the erection of a security fence around the existing STRATCOM communications site.

b. Acquisition of 1.16 acres of land with seven buildings and three facilities at Hannam-dong, Yongsan-ku, Seoul. This land and facilities are needed for expansion of the 8th Army Retreat Center.

c. Acquisition of 1.98 acres of cultivated land at #322 Chung-dong, Tongnae-ku, Pusan City. The land is required for a storage area.

d. Acquisition of 0.8 acre of non-arable land at Howon-dong, Uijongbu-si, Kyonggi-do. This property is required for expansion of Hill 651 Compound (IC-203).

e. Acquisition of 0.23 acre of non-arable land at Kanung-dong, Uijongbu-si, Kyonggi-do. This property is required for the expansion of Camp Albany Compound (IC-164).

f. Acquisition of 62.23 acres of land located at Yongtae-ri, Wolong-myon, Paju-gun, Kyonggi-do. This land is required for the consolidation of the 2nd Supply and Transportation Battalion at one location.

g. Acquisition of an easement for 0.85 acre of non-arable land located near the village of Pangchung-ni, Kwangtan-myon, Paju-gun, Kyonggi-do. This easement is required for accomplishment of an erosion control project adjacent to route 1B of Compound N-1, 7th Infantry Division Artillery.

3. Pursuant to paragraph 1 above, it is requested that a recommendation be presented to the Joint Committee concerning the extension of Temporary Use Permit, CAV-T-9, consisting of 145 acres of land from 7 May 1968 to 6 May 1969. This land is required for continued use as a field training area.

YOON HA JONG
Republic of Korea Representative

ROBERT J. FRIEDMAN
Lieutenant General
United States Air Force
United States Representative

2

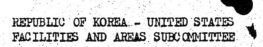

REPUBLIC OF KOREA - UNITED STATES
FACILITIES AND AREAS SUBCOMMITTEE

29 May 1968

MEMORANDUM FOR: THE JOINT COMMITTEE

1. Subcommittee members:

United States	Republic of Korea
COL I. M. Rice, Chairman	MG KIM Mook, Chairman
LTC J. B. Carrick, USAFCSK	Mr. SONG Yong Tai
LTC Robert E. Graf, J4, USFK	Mr. SHIN Chung Sup
MAJ James B. Hoodenpyle, USAF	Mr. LEE Soon Dong
Mr. Francis K. Cook, J5, USFK	Mr. LEE Kihl Choo
Mr. Richard Rose, USAEDFE	Mr. LEE Moon Sup
Mrs. Betty H. Bowman, 8th Army	Mr. LEE Jong Do
	Mr. CHANG Kyong Shik
	Mr. CHA Sang Chun
	Mr. KIM Byoung Chan
	Mr. CHONG Young Hoon
	Mr. CHOI Chung Hwan
	Mr. NO Yong Goo
	Mr. PARK Moh Soo
	LTC KANG Jong Kuk
	Mr. KANG Hong Suk

2. Subject of Recommendation: Request for Release of Real Estate
(Reference para 2g, Joint Committee Memorandum, same subject, dated
21 February 1968).

3. Recommendation: This is a request for release of a portion of
ASCOM-375, containing 1.716 acres of land at Mansuk-dong, Inchon City,
for construction of signal communication facilities for the Republic of
Korea Navy. The Ministry of National Defense and the Eighth U.S.Army
have agreed that release of the proposed site is not feasible at this
time since location of the ROK Navy transmitter system would hamper the
operation of other electrical equipment on the same area. A copy of the
resolution is attached. It is therefore recommended that this request
for release be withdrawn.

4. Security Classification:

   Unclassified.

COLONEL I. M. RICE
Chairman, United States Component
Facilities and Areas Subcommittee

MAJOR GENERAL KIM Mook
Chairman, Republic of Korea Component
Facilities and Areas Subcommittee

1 Incl
as

2

RESOLUTION OF
THE JOINT WORKING GROUP
TASK NO. 160

THE JOINT WORKING GROUP

HAVING REGARD to its Task No. 160, concerning the request for release of 2,100 pyong of land on Wolmi-Do (Acquisition ASCOM 375) for construction of a ROK Naval Defense Transmitter System (See Appendix #1),

RECOGNIZING that the objective set forth in Task No. 160 should be achieved by a mutually agreeable proposal and by constructive efforts on the part of parties hereto,

DEEPLY CONSCIOUS of the ultimate need and necessity of construction of ROK Naval Defense Transmitter System along the coastal area of the Inchon Port to maintain its defense posture,

HAVING RECEIVED the "Special Reports" of OL 28, First Combat Evaluation Group, US Air Force, and AADCP #2, APO 96571, U.S. Army, which was based on the technical information and data provided by the ROK Naval technicians and engineers (See Appendix #2 & #3),

ASSUMING that the location of the ROK Navy transmitter system on proposed site would hamper the operation of other electronic equipment on the same area,

AGREES that the release of proposed site on Wolmido referred to in its Task No. 160 is not feasible at this time.

LEE, SUN-SIK
Commander, ROKN
Chairman for ROK Component

DATE: 26 April -68

CHARLES N. THOMAS
LTC, TC
Chairman for U.S. Component

DATE: 26 Apr 1968

Incl 1

203

REPUBLIC OF KOREA - UNITED STATES
FACILITIES AND AREAS SUBCOMMITTEE

29 May 1968

MEMORANDUM FOR: THE JOINT COMMITTEE

1. Subcommittee Members:

United States	Republic of Korea
COL I. M. Rice, Chairman	MG KIM Mook, Chairman
LTC J. B. Carrick, USAFCSK	Mr. SONG Yong Tai
LTC Robert E. Graf, J4, USFK	Mr. SHIN Chung Sup
MAJ James B. Hoodenpyle, USAF	Mr. LEE Soon Dong
Mr. Francis K. Cook, J5, USFK	Mr. LEE Kihl Choo
Mr. Richard Rose, USAEDFE	Mr. LEE Moon Sup
Mrs. Betty H. Bowman, 8th Army	Mr. LEE Jong Do
	Mr. CHANG Kyong Shik
	Mr. CHA Sang Chun
	Mr. KIM Byoung Chan
	Mr. CHONG Young Hoon
	Mr. CHOI Chung Hwan
	Mr. NO Yong Goo
	Mr. PARK Moh Soo
	LTC KANG Jong Kuk
	Mr. KANG Hong Suk

2. Subject of Recommendation: Request for Release of Real Estate
(Reference para 2e, Joint Committee Memorandum, same subject, dated
21 February 1968.

3. Recommendation: A portion of PAC-10 (SP#48) consisting of approximately
1.634 acres of land located at Pumildong, Pusan City, for an urban development project can be released by USFK subject to the fulfillment of the
conditions of release as have been mutually agreed upon by the Ministry
of National Defense and the Eighth US Army. The Ministry of National
Defense and the Far East District Engineer will be requested to prepare
the necessary documents. It is recommended that the Joint Committee, SOFA,
approve this release.

204

4. Security Classification:

   Unclassified.

COLONEL I. M. RICE
Chairman, United States Component
Facilities and Areas Subcommittee

MAJOR GENERAL KIM Mook
Chairman, Republic of Korea Component
Facilities and Areas Subcommittee

1 Incl
Conditions for Partial Release
of Acquisition PAC-10 (SP #48)

2

CONDITIONS FOR PARTIAL RELEASE
OF
ACQUISITION PAC-10, SP #48

48 보급지역 취득 부동산 (PAC-10)의 부분 이양에

관한 조건 사항

206

CONDITIONS FOR PARTIAL RELEASE
OF
ACQUISITION PAC-10, SP #48

48보급지의 취득 부동산 (PAC- 10)의 부분 이양에 관한 조건사항

1. PURPOSE: a. The Purpose of this Mutually Agreeable Proposal is
   목적   상호 동의된 본 제안서의 목적은 부산시내에

to set forth certain conditions for the recommended release of approximately
위치한 주한 미군 48 보급지의 약 2,000평을 이양하는데 필요한

2,000 pyongs of United States Forces, Korea (USFK) Supply Point (SP) Number
몇가지 조건을 설정함에 있음.

48 sited within the City of Pusan.

   b. This proposal was drafted in response to a Republic of Korea (ROK)
       초안된 본 제안서는 대한민국측의 상기 부동산 (취득 부동산

request for release of this real estate (part of Acquisition PAC-10). This
PAC - 10의 일부분) 이양 요청에 의하여 작성되었음. 이 지역은

area is needed for use in connection with a Pusan City highway development
부산시 도로 확장 계획에 필요함.

plan.

2. AUTHORITY: US Component authorization for preparation of this proposal
    권능   본 제안서 준비를 위임케 한 미국측 공문서는

is contained in Ltr, Hqs, Eighth United States Army Depot Command and Eight
다음과 같다. 1968년 3월 11일부 미8군 후방사령부 및 보급사령부발

United States Army Rear, cite EADC-SVE, Subject, Appointment of a Joint
공동, 주제 "한미 합동 실무자 회의 임명 소집 – 사업 번호 158".

Working Group - Task No. 158, dated 11 March 1968 (Incl #1).
   (별지 제 1)

3. PREPARATION: This proposal was developed through efforts of the Joint
    준비   본 제안서는 한국정부 (부산시)및 부산 미군사령부

Working Group with membership representing both ROK Government (City of Pusan)
양측 대표들로 구성된 합동 실무자 회의의 노력으로 작성되었음.

and USFK sited at Pusan, Korea. Joint Working Group was established by

합동 실무자 회의는   미 8군   합동위원회의   시설 및 구역

Facilities and Areas Subcommittee (FASC), Joint Committee, Eighth United

분과위원회가 한국 정부와   절충하여 선정 되었음.

States Army, in coordination with ROK Government.

4. PROPOSAL: The USFK will release to the City of Pusan the Northwest

   제안   주한미군은   별지 제2 도면 16-09-96에 표시된

portion of SP #48, as indicated on attached drawing #16-09-96 Sheet #1

   48보급지점의 북서 지역 부분을 부산시에 이양 할거임.

(Incl #2).

5. CONDITIONS: Release of land, per para 4 above, is predicated upon the

   조건   상기 제 4항목에 기재된 토지 이양은 다음 여러

following conditions:

   조건에 근거를 두고 실시됨.

   a. That a certain parcel of land in vicinity of Pusan will be acquisi-

      부산에 인접한 한 토지구역을 주한미군이 취득케 하여

tioned to the USFK for use as a Property Disposal Office (PDO) Holding Area.

   미군 재산처리처 재산 직접소로 사용케 할거임.   주한미군이

The real estate desired by USFK is located within the boundaries of Area B,

   요망한 상기 부동산은 부동산 취득번호 PAC-25의 일부분 구역 "B" 의

Acquisition No PAC-25 Partial. A USFK request has been initiated for

   경계선내에 위치함. 주한미군은 상기한 부동산 취득 요청 수속을 이미

acquisition of proposed property.

   받고 있음.

   b. That the City of Pusan shall perform the following at no expense to

      부산시는 미국 정부의 비용 부담없이 다음 사항을

the United States Government:

   수행할거임.

   (1) Construct a new concrete block security wall along the Northwest

      48 보급지점의 북서 경계선에 연하여 콘크리트 부로그

Boundary of SP #48. The new wall shall be built to the same height, thickness

   경비용 담벽을 신설함거임. 신설한 담벽의 높이, 두께 및 재료는

2

POSS

and materials as the existing wall. Additionally, it will be installed
현존한 담벽과 똑 같아야 함. 더 나아가서 도면 16-09-96

with a barbed wire barrier at the top as shown on attached drawings
제 2지 (별지 3)에 표시한 것과 마찬가지로 담벽위에 철조망을

#16-09-96 Sheet 2 (Incl #3).
설정할것임.

(2) Relocate the Supply Point Northwest Gate, in the existing security
현존한 담벽에 접해있는 보급 지점 북서문을 주한 미군

wall, to a new location designated by USFK Representatives. In accomplishing
대표가 지정한 새로운 장소에 재 배치할것임. 새 콘크리트 기둥을

this relocation, new concrete gate posts shall be constructed.
신축함으로써 동 재배치는 완수 될것임.

(3) Construct a 20' X 60' concrete block building for use as a PDO
변소 시설을 설치한 20' x 60' 콘크리트 부로크 건물 함동을

administrative office to include installed latrine facilities. This cons-
건립할상 (재산 처리처 사무심용). 동 건축은 도면 16-09-96

truction will be in accordance with specifications outlined on the attached
제 3지 (별지 4)에 표시한 시방서에 의하여 시공할것임. 동 건물은

Drawing #16-09-96 Sheet #3 (Incl #4). The new structure will be in lieu
재 배치가 불가능한 건물 1474 (현재의 재산처리처 행정사무실) 된

of existing buildings #1474 (Current PDO administrative Office) and #1479
1479 (현존한 재산처리처 변소 시설) 대신으로 건립 되는것임.

(existing PDO latrine facility) which cannot be relocated.

(4) Relocate Buildings #1487 (PDO Warehouse) and #1488 (PDO Korean
건물 1487 (재산 처리처 창고) 된 1488 (재산 처리처

National Lounge) to a new site as shown on attached Drawing #16-09-96
한국인 휴게실) 을 도면 16-09-96 제 1지 (별지 2)에 표시한 새로운

Sheet #1 (Incl #2).
장소에 재배치할상.

(5) Construct a suitable size septic tank for the new latrine facility
새 변소 시설은 주둔 하수구에 연결될 하수도 파이프 된

with effluent piping which will discharge into a main sewer system.
알맞는 크기의 하수 정화요 탱크 (한개)를 건축할것임.

(6) Extend existing water mains to the new latrine facility located
현존한 상수도관을 새로 지울 재산 처리처 행정사무실 건물내에

within the new PDO administrative building.
위치한 새로운 변소 시설까지 연장시설할사.

(7) Remove that portion of the present water mains now extending to
현재, 건물 1479 까지 뻗쳐고 있는 현존 상수도관의

Building #1479 as prescribed by USFK representatives.
그 부분을 주한미군 대표가 제거할사.
지시하는데로

(8) Provide a storm drainage system for proper runoff of water from
48 보급지점내에 위치한 재산처리처 구역에서 알맞게

the Property Disposal Area, within Supply Point #48.
배수될수 있는 비상용 배수 장치를 구비할사.

c. That the United States Government will:
미국 정부는 다음 사항을 실행할사.

(1) Relocate the security lights, poles and transmission lines along
상기한 5b (1) 항목에 기재된 경계선 담벽부분에 연하여

that portion of the boundary fence indicated in sub-para 5b(1) above.
있는 보안등 및 전선줄을 재 배치할사.

(2) Wire all USFK buildings that are relocated or constructed by
부산시측이 새로운 장소에 재 배치했거나 건축한 모든

the City of Pusan at their new locations.
건물에 전선줄을 닳것.

6. ADDITIONAL STIPULATIONS: a. The USFK will remove the following equip-
추가 규정   주한 미군은 양도될 구역내에 있는

ment and facilities from the area to be released:
다음과 같은 장비 및 시설을 제거할사.

(1) Building #1472.
건물 1472

(2) Oil Storage Tank.
유류 저장 탱크

(3) Hot Water Heater.
물 히타

(4) All electric fixtures and switches within existing buildings.
현존한 건물속에 있는 모든 전기 비품 및 수윗치

4

2|03088

(5) Selective plumbing and piping fixtures except latrine facilities.
변소 시설을 제외한 시설의 선택 된 프랍브 및 파이프 비품.

b. The USFK will abandon existing buildings #1474 and #1479. Removal
주한 미균은 현존한 건물 1474 및 1479를 포기할것임.

and disposal of these structures is at discretion of the City of Pusan.
동 건물의 제거 및 처리는 부산시의 재량에 맡김.

7. PRIORITIES: The PDO administrative office structure must be constructed
우선권   새로운 경비용 담벽을 건립하기전에 재산 처리처

and existing Buildings #1487 and #1488 relocated before the new security
행정 사무실 건물을 건축할것이며 또한 현존한 건물 1487 및 1488을

wall is erected. Further in the interest of SP #48 security, the new wall
재 배치할사. 더 나아가서 48 보급지점 보안을 위해서 새로운 담벽은

must be constructed before the existing wall is removed.
현존한 담벽을 제거하기전에 건립할사.

8. RESPONSIBILITY: The City of Pusan shall assume responsibility for any
책임   부산시는 위에 기재한 건축 혹은 재배치를

injuries to personnel or damages to property occuring during the construc-
하는 동안 발생하는 인명 및 재산 피해에 대한 책임을 질것임.

tion or relocation activities outlined above.

9. REVISION: This proposal may be revised by mutual consent of both
수정   본 제안서는 상방의 상호 합의에 의하여 수정

parties concerned. Such revisions must be submitted in writing and pro-
될수도 있음. 수정 상항은 반드시 서면상으로 제출하되 타당한

perly authenticated.
신빈성이 있어야 함.

10. AUTHENTICATION: When signed by the chairman, ROK, and the chairman,
인증   본제안서는 한미 합동 실무자 획의의 양측 의장이

USFK, Joint Working Group, this document represents the mutually Agreeable
서명하는 즉시 48 보급 지점 취득 부동산에 대한 상호 동의가 성립,

5

Proposal for partial release of Acquisition PAC-10, SP #48
되었음을 나타냄.

Signed this _____15th_____ of _____MAY_____ 1968 in the City of Pusan,
서명   1968년 대한민국 부산시

Republic of Korea.

Mr. LEE, CHANG TAL   WARREN J. WEBER
Republic of Korea   LTC, TC
Joint Working Group   United States of America
이 창 달   Joint Working Group
합동·실무자 회의   워렌 제이 웨버
대한민국측 대표   중령 수송 병과
                                            합동·실무자 회의
                                            미국측 대표

4 Incl
1. Ltr frm EADC/EAR
2. SP #48 Instal Map
3. Wall Barrier SP #48
4. Drawing of Proposed Bldg #1474

4. 첨부 서류
1. 미후방기지 및 보급 사령부 공문서
2. 48보급지 서설자도
3. 48보급지 담벽 경계선
4. 제안된 건물 1474의 도면

6

REPUBLIC OF KOREA - UNITED STATES
FACILITIES AND AREAS SUBCOMMITTEE

29 May 1968

MEMORANDUM FOR: THE JOINT COMMITTEE

1. Subcommittee members:

United States

COL I. M. Rice, Chairman
LTC J. B. Carrick, USAFCSK
LTC Robert E. Graf, J4, USFK
MAJ James B. Hoodenpyle, USAF
Mr. Francis K. Cook, J5, USFK
Mr. Richard Rose, USAEDFE
Mrs. Betty H. Bowman, 8th Army

Republic of Korea

MG KIM Mook, Chairman
Mr. SONG Yong Tai
Mr. SHIN Chung Sup
Mr. LEE Soon Dong
Mr. LEE Kihl Choo
Mr. LEE Moon Sup
Mr. LEE Jong Do
Mr. CHANG Kyong Shik
Mr. CHA Sang Chun
Mr. KIM Byoung Chan
Mr. CHONG Young Hoon
Mr. CHOI Chung Hwan
Mr. NO Yong Goo
Mr. PARK Moh Soo
LTC KANG Jong Kuk
Mr. KANG Hong Suk

2. Subject of Recommendation: Requests for Acquisition of Real Estate
and Extension of Temporary Use Permit (Reference para 2c, same subject,
Joint Committee Memorandum, dated 4 April 1968).

3. Recommendation: The request for acquisition of 0.18 acre of mountainous
land located at Kumo-dong, Uijongbu-si, Kyonggi-do, has been accepted by the
Ministry of National Defense. The real estate is required for the erection
of a microwave reflector. The Ministry of National Defense and the Far East
District Engineer will be requested to prepare the necessary documents.
It is recommended that the Joint Committee, SOFA, approve this acquisition.

4. Security Classification:

   Unclassified.

COLONEL I. M. RICE
Chairman, United States Component
Facilities and Areas Subcommittee

MAJOR GENERAL KIM Mook
Chairman, Republic of Korea Component
Facilities and Areas Subcommittee

REPUBLIC OF KOREA – UNITED STATES
FACILITIES AND AREAS SUBCOMMITTEE

29 May 1968

MEMORANDUM FOR: THE JOINT COMMITTEE

1. Subcommittee members:

United States   Republic of Korea

COL I. M. Rice, Chairman   MG KIM Mook, Chairman
LTC J. B. Carrick, USAFCSK   Mr. SONG Yong Tai
LTC Robert E. Graf, J4, USFK   Mr. SHIN Chung Sup
MAJ James B. Hoodenpyle, USAF   Mr. LEE Kihl Choo
Mr. Francis K. Cook, J5, USFK   Mr. LEE Moon Sup
Mr. Richard Rose, USAEDFE   Mr. LEE Jong Do
Mrs. Betty H. Bowman, 8th Army   Mr. CHANG Kyong Shik
                                      Mr. CHA Sang Chun
                                      Mr. KIM Byoung Chan
                                      Mr. CHONG Young Hoon
                                      Mr. CHOI Chung Hwan
                                      Mr. NO Yong Goo
                                      Mr. PARK Moh Soo
                                      LTC KANG Jong Kuk
                                      Mr. KANG Hong Suk
                                      Mr. LEE Soon Dong

2. Subject of Recommendations: Request for Acquisition of Real Estate
and Extension of Temporary Use Permit (Reference Joint Committee Memorandum,
same subject, dated 17 May 1968).

3. Recommendations:

    a. Request for acquisition of a total of 16.455 acres of land at
various locations in Imjin-myon, Paju-gun, Kyonggi-do (3.76 acres for
exclusive use and 12.695 acres of existing road as an easement) has been
accepted by the Ministry of National Defense with the stipulation that
before initiation of road construction, the 2nd Inf Div Post Engineer and
the 36th Engineer Group will coordinate with the MND Real Estate Representative to preclude any damage to adjacent property. The real estate is

required for a by-pass route for tracked vehicles. The Ministry of
National Defense and the Far East District Engineer will be requested
to prepare the necessary documents. It is recommended that the Joint
Committee, SOFA, approve this acquisition.

b. The request to convert to an exclusive use basis 0.014 acre currently
held as a perpetual restrictive easement, located at #142-1 Hasangok-ni,
Tongbu-myon, Kwangju-gun, Kyonggi-do, has been accepted by the Ministry of
National Defense. This real estate is required to construct a retaining
wall to prevent erosion. The Ministry of National Defense and the Far East
District Engineer will be requested to prepare the necessary documents.
It is recommended that the Joint Committee, SOFA, approve this acquisition.

c. Request for extension of temporary use permit CAV-T-16, involving
a total of 128,713.04 acres of land (38,116.82 acres consist of arable land
and 90,596.22 acres of non-arable land) from 1 May 1968 to 30 April 1969
for training purposes has been accepted by the Ministry of National Defense.
The Ministry of National Defense and the Far East District Engineer will be
requested to prepare the necessary documents. It is recommended that the
Joint Committee, SOFA, approve extension of this permit.

4. Security Classification: Unclassified.

COLONEL I. M. RICE
Chairman, United States Component
Facilities and Areas Subcommittee

MAJOR GENERAL KIM Mook
Chairman, Republic of Korea Component
Facilities and Areas Subcommittee

2

JOINT COMMITTEE
UNDER
THE REPUBLIC OF KOREA AND THE UNITED STATES
STATUS OF FORCES AGREEMENT

7 June 1968

MEMORANDUM TO: The Joint Committee

SUBJECT   :   Operating Procedures for the Facilities
                  and Areas Subcommittee

        1.   Reference is made to the following passages
of the Joint Committee decisions:

        a.   Procedures for operation of the ROK-US
Joint Committee Subcommittees. (Inclosure 5, Minutes of
the First Meeting)

            " 1 . . . Subcommittees will give advice
        and make recommendations only on these matters
        specifically referred to them by the Joint
        Committee."

        b.   Facilities and Areas Subcommittee procedures.
(Inclosure 2, Minutes of the Fifth Meeting)

        " III.   Order of Business

        2.   Unless otherwise directed by the Joint
        Committee, the Facilities and Areas Subcommittee
        will address only matters referred to it by
        the Joint Committee."

        "IV.   Conduct of Business

        1.   The Facilities and Areas Subcommittee
        will act only on tasks assigned by the Joint
        Committee."

        2.   The principle adopted by the Joint Committee
and referred to in the proceeding paragraph has been

strictly adhered to for the operation of the Facilities
and Areas Subcommittee since its inauguration. However,
it is noted that almost all of the tasks assigned to
the Subcommittee concern with acquisition, extension of
temporary use permit, release or reclassification of
individual real estate, that before formal assignment
of such tasks prescreening by the Subcommittee was
necessary, and that consequently the assignment of such
tasks by the Joint Committee is a mere formality.
It is also recalled that on several occasions the Joint
Committee was obliged to follow exisgency procedures due
to urgency of some actions.

    3. Therefore it is proposed that the following
principle be adopted by the Joint Committee in order to
simplify the procedures:

    a. The Facilities and Areas Subcommittee may
submit to the Joint Committee its views and recommendations
on requests concerned with individual real estate without
being formally assigned a task.

    b. In case of disagreement both sides reserve
the right to bring the matter to the Joint Committee for
its decision.

    c. The Subcommittee will not act on matters
of general policy or procedures unless a specific task
thereon was assigned by the Joint Committee.

Yoon Ha Jong
Republic of Korea
Representative

7 June 1968

MEMORANDUM TO: Joint Committee

SUBJECT: Interpretation of Article XVI, Paragraph 1, of the
US-ROK SOFA

1. Paragraph 1, Article XVI, provides that "The United States may
contract for any materials, supplies, equipment and services
(including construction work) to be furnished or undertaken in the
Republic of Korea for purposes of, or authorized by, this Agreement, without restriction as to choice of contractor, supplier or
person who provides such services..."

2. The first sentence of paragraph 1, Article XVI, clearly gives
the United States unrestricted right to contract in the Republic of
Korea. Specifically, it is believed that under Article XVI of the
Status of Forces Agreement, a Korean contractor who is duly
licensed by the Government of the Republic of Korea to do business
in Korea is not required to obtain a special license to do business
with the United States armed forces in Korea. In this connection,
it is our opinion that the restrictions on freedom of US selection
of Korean contractors contained in ROK Law 979 are inconsistent
with the purpose and language of paragraph 1, Article XVI.

3. As paragraph 2 of Article XVI indicates, only that procurement
by the US armed forces which may have an adverse effect on the
economy of the Republic of Korea is legally required to be procured
in coordination with, and, when desirable, through or with the
assistance of, the competent authorities of the Republic of Korea.

4. The United States believes that it is in the mutual interests of
both the Governments of the Republic of Korea and of the United
States to have maximum competition in local procurement actions
by the US armed forces in Korea. It is clear that paragraph 1,

219

Article XVI, provides the US with the right of competitive bidding "without restriction," and that this would contribute to free competition in local procurement and promote the joint ROK-US defense of the Republic of Korea.

5.   We believe that the Government of the Republic of Korea should accept the above interpretation in paragraph 4 regarding Article XVI, paragraph 1, and should take appropriate action with regard to Law 979 in view of its obligations under paragraph 2 of Article XXIX.

ROBERT J. FRIEDMAN
Lieutenant General
United States Air Force
United States Representative

2

JOINT COMMITTEE
UNDER
THE REPUBLIC OF KOREA AND THE UNITED STATES
STATUS OF FORCES AGREEMENT

28 May 1968

MEMORANDUM FOR: The Joint Committee

SUBJECT: Designation of US Invited Contractor under Article XV, Status of Forces Agreement

1. References:

    a. Paragraph 2, Article XV, Status of Forces Agreement.

    b. US Commerce Subcommittee Memorandum of Consultation, dated 23 May 1968, subject as above (Inclosure 1).

    c. ROK Commerce Subcommittee Memorandum of Consultation, dated 25 May 1968, subject as above (Inclosure 2).

2. The United States, after consultation with the ROK Commerce Sub-committee and after having duly considered their views, has designated Trans-Asia Engineering Associates, Inc. as a US invited contractor for execution of Contract #F62087-68-C-0101 for Architect and Engineering services.

3. Pertinent data concerning US citizen employees will be provided to the Joint Secretariat in the established periodic arrival and departure format.

2 Incl
as

ROBERT J. FRIEDMAN
Lieutenant General
United States Air Force
United States Representative
Joint Committee

MINISTRY OF COMMERCE AND INDUSTRY
REPUBLIC OF KOREA
SEOUL, KOREA

25 May 1968

SUBJECT: Designation of US Invited Contractor under Article XV, Status of Forces Agreement.

TO : Chairman, US Commerce Subcommittee.

1. References:

a. Paragraph 2, Article XV, Status of Forces Agreement.

b. US Commerce Subcommittee Memorandum of Consultation, Dated 23 May 1968, subject as above, pertaining to contract for architect-engineering services in the Kunsan and Osan Air Base construction projects.

2. The US memorandum, reference 1b above, has been reviewed and the Government of the Republic of Korea fully understands the requirement for an invited contractor in this instance.

Chairman
ROK Commerce Subcommittee

REPUBLIC OF KOREA - UNITED STATES
COMMERCE SUBCOMMITTEE

23 May 1968

SUBJECT: Designation of US Invited Contractor under Article XV,
Status of Forces Agreement

ROK Chairman, Commerce Subcommittee

1. Reference: Paragraph 2, Article XV of the Status of Forces Agreement.

2. The Government of the Republic of Korea is informed through this written consultive process that the United States Forces, Korea, proposes to extend invited contractor status to the qualified US firm on the contract described in paragraph 3 below.

3. The following data is provided:

a. Company Name: Trans-Asia Engineering Associates, Inc.

b. Local Address: Building 1510, APO 96301.

c. Identification of US Citizen Employees: To be supplied after award of contract.

d. Number of US and ROK Employees:

U.S. - 5
ROK - 20

e. Reasons for Designation of an Invited Contractor: Open competitive bidding among local contractors is not practicable due to the following:

(1) Security considerations.

(2) Technical qualifications of the contractor involved.

f. Location of Contract: Kunsan Air Base and Osan Air Base, Korea.

SUBJECT: Designation of US Invited Contractor under Article XV,
           Status of Forces Agreement

   g.   <u>Type of Contract</u>: Architect-Engineering services.

   h.   <u>Length of Contract</u>: Approximately 30 days.

   i.   <u>Sponsoring Component Command</u>: Commander, Air Forces, Korea.
(Headquarters, 6314th Support Wing (PACAF)).

                              FLOYD R. WALTZ, JR.
                              Colonel, United States Army
                              US Chairman, Commerce Subcommittee

214

2

JOINT COMMITTEE
UNDER
THE REPUBLIC OF KOREA AND THE UNITED STATES
STATUS OF FORCES AGREEMENT

28 May 1968

MEMORANDUM FOR: The Joint Committee

SUBJECT: Designation of US Invited Contractor under Article XV,
Status of Forces Agreement

1. References:

   a. Paragraph 2, Article XV, Status of Forces Agreement.

   b. US Commerce Subcommittee Memorandum of Consultation, dated
23 May 1968, subject as above (Inclosure 1).

   c. ROK Commerce Subcommittee Memorandum of Consultation, dated
23 May 1968, subject as above (Inclosure 2).

2. The United States, after consultation with the ROK Commerce Sub-
committee and after having duly considered their views, has designated
Adrian Wilson Associates as a US invited contractor for execution of
Contract #F62087-68-C-0102 for Architect and Engineering services.

3. Pertinent data concerning US citizen employees will be provided to
the Joint Secretariat in the established periodic arrival and departure
format.

2 Incl
as

ROBERT J. FRIEDMAN
Lieutenant General
United States Air Force
United States Representative
Joint Committee

MINISTRY OF COMMERCE AND INDUSTRY
REPUBLIC OF KOREA
SEOUL, KOREA

25 May 1968

SUBJECT: Designation of US Invited Contractor under Article XV, Status of Forces Agreement.

TO   : Chairman, US Commerce Subcommittee.

1. References:

    a. Paragraph 2, Article XV, Status of Forces Agreement.

    b. US Commerce Subcommittee Memorandum of Consultation, Dated 23 May 1968, subject as above, pertaining to contract for architect-engineering services in the Kwang-Ju, Taegu, and Osan Air Base construction projects.

    2. The US memorandum, reference 1b above, has been reviewed and the Government of the Republic of Korea fully understands the requirement for an invited contractor in this instance.

For /Han Byung 2l
Chairman
ROK Commerce Subcommittee

REPUBLIC OF KOREA - UNITED STATES
COMMERCE SUBCOMMITTEE

23 May 1968

SUBJECT: Designation of US Invited Contractor under Article XV,
Status of Forces Agreement

ROK Chairman, Commerce Subcommittee

1. Reference: Paragraph 2, Article XV of the Status of Forces Agreement.

2. The Government of the Republic of Korea is informed through this written consultive process that the United States Forces, Korea, proposes to extend invited contractor status to the qualified US firm on the contract described in paragraph 3 below.

3. The following data is provided:

   a. Company Name: Adrian Wilson Associates.

   b. Local Address: 136-2 Itaewon-Dong, Yongsan-Ku, Seoul, Korea.

   c. Identification of US Citizen Employees: To be supplied after award of contract.

   d. Number of US and ROK Employees:

                    U.S. - 8
                    ROK   - 20

   e. Reasons for Designation of an Invited Contractor: Open competitive bidding among local contractors is not practicable due to the following:

   (1) Security considerations.

   (2) Technical qualifications of the contractor involved.

   f. Location of Contract: Kwang-Ju, Taegu, and Osan Air Bases, Korea.

SUBJECT: Designation of US Invited Contractor under Article XV, Status of Forces Agreement

g. Type of Contract: Architect-Engineering services.

h. Length of Contract: Approximately 30 days.

i. Sponsoring Component Command: Commander, Air Forces, Korea. (Headquarters, 6314th Support Wing (PACAF)).

FLOYD R. WALTZ, JR.
Colonel, United States Army
US Chairman, Commerce Subcommittee

2

JOINT COMMITTEE
UNDER
THE REPUBLIC OF KOREA AND THE UNITED STATES
STATUS OF FORCES AGREEMENT

28 May 1968

MEMORANDUM FOR: The Joint Committee

SUBJECT: Designation of US Invited Contractor under Article XV,
Status of Forces Agreement

1. References:

    a. Paragraph 2, Article XV, Status of Forces Agreement.

    b. US Commerce Subcommittee Memorandum of Consultation, dated
23 May 1968, subject as above (Inclosure 1).

    c. ROK Commerce Subcommittee Memorandum of Consultation, dated
25 May 1968, subject as above (Inclosure 2).

2. The United States, after consultation with the ROK Commerce Subcommittee and after having duly considered their views, has designated
Daniel, Mann, Johnson & Mendenhall as a US invited contractor for
execution of Contract #F62087-68-C-0100 for Architect and Engineering
services.

3. Pertinent data concerning US citizen employees will be provided to
the Joint Secretariat in the established periodic arrival and departure
format.

2 Incl
as

ROBERT J. FRIEDMAN
Lieutenant General
United States Air Force
United States Representative
Joint Committee

229

MINISTRY OF COMMERCE AND INDUSTRY
REPUBLIC OF KOREA
SEOUL, KOREA

25 May 1968

SUBJECT: Designation of US Invited Contractor under Article XV, Status of Forces Agreement.

TO   : Chairman, US Commerce Subcommittee

1. References:

a. Paragraph 2, Article XV, Status of Forces Agreement.

b. US Commerce Subcommittee Memorandum of Consultation, Dated 23 May 1968, subject as above, pertaining to contract for architect-engineering services in the Suwon and Osan Air Base construction projects.

2. The US memorandum, reference 1b above, has been reviewed and the Government of the Republic of Korea fully understands the requirement for an invited contractor in this instance.

For Chairman
ROK Commerce Subcommittee

23 May 1968

SUBJECT: Designation of US Invited Contractor under Article XV,
Status of Forces Agreement

ROK Chairman, Commerce Subcommittee

1. Reference: Paragraph 2, Article XV of the Status of Forces Agreement.

2. The Government of the Republic of Korea is informed through this written consultive process that the United States Forces, Korea, proposes to extend invited contractor status to the qualified US firm on the contract described in paragraph 3 below.

3. The following data is provided:

    a. Company Name: Daniel, Mann, Johnson and Mendenhall.

    b. Local Address: Box 11, APO 96570.

    c. Identification of US Citizen Employees: To be supplied after award of contract.

    d. Number of US and ROK Employees:

                    U.S. - 12
                    ROK   - 15

    e. Reasons for Designation of an Invited Contractor: Open competitive bidding among local contractors is not practicable due to the following:

    (1) Security considerations.

    (2) Technical qualifications of the contractor involved.

    f. Location of Contract: Suwon and Osan Air Bases, Korea.

SUBJECT: Designation of US Invited Contractor under Article XV,
Status of Forces Agreement

g. <u>Type of Contract</u>: Architect-Engineering services.

h. <u>Length of Contract</u>: Approximately 30 days.

i. <u>Sponsoring Component Command</u>: Commander, Air Forces, Korea.
(Headquarters, 6314th Support Wing (PACAF)).

FLOYD R. WALTZ, JR.
Colonel, United States Army
US Chairman, Commerce Subcommittee

2

JOINT ROK - US PRESS RELEASE
TWENTY-SEVENTH ROK-US JOINT COMMITTEE MEETING
7 JUNE 1968

The ROK-US Joint Committee discussed simplification of operating

procedures of its Facilities and Areas Subcommittee at its twenty-seventh

meeting on 7 June 1968.

The Joint Committee also accepted six recommendations of its

Facilities and Areas Subcommittee, relating to the acquisition and

release of facilities and areas by the US armed forces in Korea.   The

Joint Committee also assigned eight new tasks to its Facilities and

Areas Subcommittee at this meeting, which was held in the US SOFA

Conference Room in Yongsan.

The US Representative, Lieutenant General Robert J. Friedman,

presided at this Joint Committee meeting.   The Joint Committee

scheduled its next meeting for 3 July at the ROK Capitol Building.

외   무

미이 720~   196 8 . 6 . 21 .

수 신 : 배부처 참조

참 조 :

제 목 : 한.미 합동위원회 회의록 송부

　　　　1. 한.미간 군대지위협정에 의하여 196 8 . 6 . 7 .에
재최됨 한.미 합동위원회 제 27 차 회의의 회의록을 별첨 송부하오니
참고 하시기 바랍니다.

　　　　2. 본 회의록은 한.미 양측의 합의에 의하여서만 공개할
수 있는 문서이오니 유념하시기 바랍니다.

　　첨부 : 합동위원회 제 27 차 회의록　　부

　　　　　　　　　　외 무 부 장 관

배부처 : 법무부장관 (법무실장, 검찰국장), 국방부장관 (기획국장,
　　시설국장), 재무부장관 (세관국장, 세제국장),
　　상공부장관 (상역국장), 노동청장 (노정국장),
　　교통부장관 (항공국장) 내무부장관 (치안국장), 주미
　　주일, 주중, 주비대사　경제기획원장관 (경제기획국장)

234

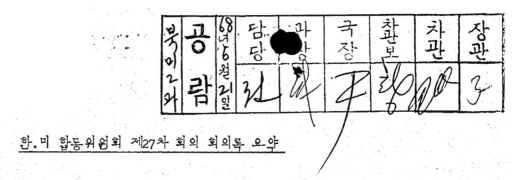

한.미 합동위원회 제27차 회의 회의록 요약

1968. 6. 7.
미군사령부 회의실

1. 시설구역 분과위원회 신규 과제부여 및 건의처리

신규과제부여			건 의		
종 별	건수	면적(에이커)	종 별	건 수	면 적 (에이커)
취 득	6	67.59	취득	2	16.635
지역권취득	1	0.85	사용권변경	1	0.014
임시사용허가연장	1		임시사용허가연장	1	
반 환	1	1.634			
건의취소	1	1.716			

2. 시설구역 분과위원회 운영규정 개정

가. 합동위원회에 의한 과제부여 없이도 저개부동산에 대한 건의를 할수 있다.

나. 합의 불성립시 합동위원회에 결정을 요구할 수 있는 권리 유보。

다. 합동위원회의 요구 없이는 전반적 정책이나 절차를 처리할 수 없다.

3. 협정 제16조 제1항 해석 문제

법률 제979조 "군납 촉진에 관한 임시 조치법"중 "주한 미군과 사업 계약을
체결코저 하는 자는 면허를 요한다" 는 조항은 협정 제16조 제1항의
"계약자, 공급자 또는 용역 제공자의 선택에 관하여 제한을 받지 않고"
라는 조항에 위배되는바 협정 제29조에 따라 국내법을 개정해야 한다.

These minutes are considered as official documents pertaining to both Governments and will not be released without mutual agreement.

JOINT COMMITTEE
UNDER
THE REPUBLIC OF KOREA AND THE UNITED STATES
STATUS OF FORCES AGREEMENT

MINUTES OF THE TWENTY-SEVENTH MEETING

7 June 1968
Headquarters
U.S. Forces, Korea
Seoul, Korea

1. The meeting was convened at 1500 hours by Lieutenant General Robert J. Friedman, the US Representative, who presided at the meeting. A copy of the agenda is attached as Inclosure 1.

2. The following were in attendance:

ROK	US
Mr. YOON Ha Jong	LTG Robert J. Friedman, USAF
Mr. LEE Sun Jung	CAPT M. R. Massie, USN
Mr. KIM Sung Jae	COL Herbert C. Hicks, Jr., USA
Mr. HUH Seung Joon	COL Gerald W. Davis, USA
Mr. SHIN Chung Sup	Mr. P. Wesley Kriebel, US Embassy
Mr. OH Myong Too	Mr. Robert A. Kinney, USFK
	LTC Paul E. Jones, USAF

3. The US Representative called the meeting to order and proposed assignment of eight new tasks to the Facilities and Areas Subcommittee. These involved (Inclosure 2):

a. Acquisition of 1.19 acres at Kanghwa-gun, Kyonggi-do.

b. Acquisition of 1.16 acres with seven buildings and three facilities at Hannam-dong, Yongsan-ku, Seoul.

c. Acquisition of 1.98 acres at #322 Chung-dong, Tongnae-ku, Pusan.

d. Acquisition of 0.8 acre at Howon-dong, Uijongbu, Kyonggi-do.

e. Acquisition of 0.23 acre at Kanung-dong, Uijongbu, Kyonggi-do.

f. Acquisition of 62.23 acres at Yongtae-ri, Wolong-myon, Paju-gun, Kyonggi-do.

27th JC
7 Jun 68

These minutes are considered as official documents pertaining to both Governments and will not be released without mutual agreement.

       g. Acquisition of an easement for 0.85 acre near Pangchung-ni, Kwangtan-myon, Paju-gun, Kyonggi-do.

       h. Extension of Temporary Use Permit, CAV-T-9, from 7 May 1968 to 6 May 1969.

    4. The ROK Representative concurred in the assignment of these eight new tasks to the Facilities and Areas Subcommittee.

    5. The ROK Representative presented two recommendations of the Facilities and Areas Subcommittee. These involved:

       a. The withdrawal of a request for release of a portion of ASCOM-375, involving 1.716 acres, which was assigned as a task on 21 February 1968 (Inclosure 3).

       b. The release of a portion of PAC-10, involving approximately 1.634 acres, (Inclosure 4), subject to the fulfillment of conditions agreed upon by the Ministry of National Defense and the Eighth US Army.

    6. The US Representative concurred in Joint Committee approval of these two recommendations of the Facilities and Areas Subcommittee.

    7. The US Representative presented four recommendations of the Facilities and Areas Subcommittee, as follows:

       a. The acquisition of 0.18 acre of land of Kumo-dong, Uijongbu, Kyonggi-do (Inclosure 5).

       b. The acquisition of 16.455 acres of land at various locations in Imjin-myon, Paju-gun, Kyonggi-do (Inclosure 6).

       c. The conversion to an exclusive use basis 0.014 acre currently held as a perpetual restrictive easement in Kwangju-gun, Kyonggi-do (Inclosure 6).

       d. The extension of Temporary Use Permit CAV-T-16 (Inclosure 6).

    8. The US Representative proposed Joint Committee approval of these four recommendations of the Facilities and Areas Subcommittee and the ROK Representative concurred.

    9. The ROK Representative submitted a written memorandum on the subject of operating procedures for the Facilities and Areas Subcommittee

2

      27th JC
      7 Jun 68

These minutes are considered as official documents pertaining to both Governments and will not be released without mutual agreement.

(Inclosure 7). He stated that the Joint Committee adopted at its first meeting "Procedures for Operation of the US-ROK Joint Committee Subcommittees," and adopted at its fifth meeting Facilities and Areas Subcommittee Procedures. These procedures established the principle that the Subcommittee acts only on matters or tasks referred to it by the Joint Committee, a principle strictly adhered to since inauguration of the Subcommittee. However, it had been noted from experience of more than a year, that nearly all of the tasks assigned to the Subcommittee relate to acquisition, extension of temporary use permit, release or reclassification of individual property, and that in any case, pre-screening by the Subcommittee was necessary before assignment of such tasks, and therefore formal assignment of tasks had been mere formality. Based on these considerations, it was proposed that the following principle be adopted by the Joint Committee in order to simplify the procedures:

    a. The Facilities and Areas Subcommittee may submit to the Joint Committee its views and recommendations on requests relating to individual real estate without being formally assigned a task.

    b. In case of disagreement, both sides reserve the right to bring the matter to the Joint Committee for decision.

    c. The Subcommittee will not act on matters of general policy or procedures unless a specific task thereon was assigned by the Joint Committee.

    10. The ROK Representative noted that the Subcommittee being a subsidiary organ of the Joint Committee, it goes without saying that the Subcommittee remains under general supervision of the Joint Committee, and recalled that an exception to the limitative principle of subcommittee authority had already been made with regard to the Utilities Subcommittee. He requested concurrence of the US Representative to the foregoing proposal concerning operating procedures for the Facilities and Areas Subcommittee.

    11. The US Representative thanked the ROK Representative and stated he was pleased to receive the memorandum from the ROK Representative concerning modification of operating procedures for the Facilities and Areas Subcommittee. He stated it was mutually agreed that steps to simplify this Subcommittee's procedures and increase its efficiency of operation in every way possible are desirable, and it is believed that the proposal of the Republic of Korea Representative has considerable merit. The Facilities and Areas Subcommittee operations have been among the most effective of any Subcommittee, and it has been accepted that there may be further actions to simplify its procedures with the passage of

3

These minutes are considered as official documents pertaining to both Governments and will not be released without mutual agreement.

time. The US Representative proposed that the memorandum presented by the ROK Representative be reviewed by the ROK and US SOFA Secretaries in coordination with the ROK and US Secretaries of the Facilities and Areas Subcommittees. Further, he proposed that these personnel develop mutually agreed recommendations concerning simplification of Facilities and Areas Subcommittee procedures, for consideration by the Joint Committee at the earliest Joint Committee meeting. The ROK Representative indicated his concurrence.

12. The US Representative presented a memorandum on the subject of "Interpretation of Article XVI, paragraph 1, of the US-ROK Status of Forces Agreement" (Inclosure 8). This memorandum, which had been distributed to the Republic of Korea component prior to the meeting, quoted the relevant passage of the Agreement which reads:

> "The United States may contract for any materials, supplies, equipment and services (including construction work) to be furnished or undertaken in the Republic of Korea for purposes of, or authorized by, this Agreement, without restriction as to choice of contractor, supplier or person who provides such services. "

13. The US Representative stated that he believed that under the foregoing provision of Article XVI, United States armed forces may contract "without restriction" in Korea with any Korean contractor or firm duly licensed by the Government of the Republic of Korea to do business in Korea. It is believed that ROK Law 979, which provides that Korean contractors and businessmen must obtain a special license, in addition to any standard license, to do business with the United States armed forces in Korea was contrary to the provisions of the Status of Forces Agreement. In this connection, attention was called to paragraph 2 of Article XXIX which provides that:

> "The Government of the Republic of Korea shall undertake to seek from its legislature all legislative and budgetary action necessary to give effect to the provisions of this Agreement. "

14. The US Representative stated that it was in the mutual interests of both the Governments of the United States and the Republic of Korea and of benefit to their mutual defense responsibilities, to have maximum competition in local procurement by the United States armed forces in Korea. It was recognized that paragraph 2 of Article XVI stipulated that procurement by the United States armed forces "which may have

4

27th JC
7 Jun 68

an adverse affect on the economy of the Republic of Korea shall be procured in coordination with, and, when desirable, through or with the assistance of, the competent authorities of the Republic of Korea." The US Representative stated that the United States armed forces had been and will continue to be, ready to implement such provisions as well as the provisions of Agreed Minute 2 which read:

> "The problem of a satisfactory settlement of difficulties with respect to procurement contracts arising out of differences between economic laws and business practices of the Republic of Korea and the United States will be studied by the Joint Committee or other appropriate representatives."

15. The US Representative said he trusted that the Government of the Republic of Korea would accept this interpretation of Article XVI of the Status of Forces Agreement and take appropriate action to fulfill its obligations under paragraph 2 of Article XXIX of the SOFA.

16. The ROK Representative thanked the US Representative for the memorandum and his presentation. The ROK Representative, after pointing out that the subject had long been discussed between the pertinent authorities of the two countries and that the general views of the Korean side are well known to the US authorities, regretted not being prepared to make a formal reply to the memorandum immediately at this meeting. He stated that a formal position would be conveyed at a later meeting.

17. The US Representative presented memoranda to the Joint Committee informing the Republic of Korea Government of the designation of three new invited contractors under Article XV of the Status of Forces Agreement. After consultation with Republic of Korea Commerce Sub-committee personnel, the United States Forces, Korea, designated as US invited contractors Adrian Wilson Associates (Inclosure 9); Trans-Asia Engineering Associates, Inc. (Inclosure 10); and Daniel, Mann, Johnson, & Mendenhall (Inclosure 11). Pertinent data concerning employees of these invited contractors will be provided to the Government of the Republic of Korea in accordance with mutually approved procedures.

18. The ROK Representative stated he was pleased to acknowledge the US notification on designations of Daniel, Mann, Johnson & Mendenhall; Adrian Wilson Associates; and Trans-Asia Engineering Associates, Inc., as invited contractors, and also confirmed that agreed procedures for consultation were duly observed in these designations.

5

27th JC
7 Jun 68

These minutes are considered as official documents pertaining to both Governments an⬤ill not be released without m⬤l agreement.

19. The US Representative noted for the record that the US SOFA Secretary furnished the following information to the ROK SOFA Secretary, in accordance with the Joint Committee decisions:

a. Five copies of reports on the US armed forces disposition of cases for the month of April 1968.

b. Twenty copies of a report listing arrivals, departures, and address changes of US invited contractors and their dependents, dated 31 May 1968. The ROK Representative explained that he was happy to confirm the receipt by the ROK SOFA Secretary of the documents as enumerated.

20. The US Representative proposed that the next meeting of the Joint Committee be held on Wednesday, 3 July, at 1500 hours, in the Republic of Korea Capitol Building.

21. The ROK Representative stated that the time and date proposed for the next meeting seemed most appropriate, and that he was most happy to accept the proposal.

22. The US Representative proposed acceptance of the joint press release for the twenty-seventh Joint Committee meeting, as prepared by the ROK and US SOFA Secretaries (Inclosure 12). The ROK Representative agreed to adopt the proposed press release as drafted.

23. The US Representative stated that before the meeting adjourned, he wished to express his sincere regret that the Eighth US Army member of the US component, Colonel Herbert C. Hicks, Jr., will be departing Korea before the next scheduled Joint Committee meeting. Both the US and ROK Representatives thanked Colonel Hicks for his substantial contributions to the Joint Committee during his service with the Committee ever since it was first organized early in 1967.

24. The meeting was adjourned at 1545 hours.

12 Inclosures

YOON HA JONG
REPUBLIC OF KOREA
REPRESENTATIVE

ROBERT J. FRIEDMAN
LIEUTENANT GENERAL
UNITED STATES AIR FORCE
UNITED STATES REPRESENTATIVE

6

27th JC
7 Jun 68

These minutes are considered as official documents pertaining to both Governments and will not be released without mutual agreement.

AGENDA FOR THE TWENTY-SEVENTH MEETING
OF THE ROK-US JOINT COMMITTEE
1500 HOURS, 7 JUNE 1968, US SOFA CONFERENCE ROOM

I   Assignment of Additional Tasks to Facilities and Areas Subcommittee:

    Eight tasks - US Presentation

II   Recommendations of Facilities and Areas Subcommittee:

    1. Two recommendations - ROK Presentation

    2. Four recommendations - US Presentation

III   Memorandum to Joint Committee on Operating Procedures for

    Facilities and Areas Subcommittee - ROK Presentation

IV   Memorandum to Joint Committee on Interpretation of Paragraph 1,

    Article XVI - US Presentation

V   Memoranda on Designation of USFK Invited Contractors -

    US Presentation

VI   Memoranda Presented to the ROK Government by the US, in the

    Implementation of the SOFA - US Presentation

VII   Proposed Time of Next Meeting - 1500 hours, Wednesday, 3 July 1968,

    in the ROK Capitol Building

VIII   Agreement on Joint Press Release

IX   Adjourn

27th JC (Incl 1)
7 Jun 68

**JOINT COMMITTEE
UNDER
THE REPUBLIC OF KOREA AND THE UNITED STATES
STATUS OF FORCES AGREEMENT**

7 June 1968

MEMORANDUM FOR: Chairmen, Facilities & Areas Subcommittee

SUBJECT: Requests for Acquisition of Real Estate and Extension
             of a Temporary Use Permit

1. SOFA provides, in Article II, paragraph 2, that the Governments of the Republic of Korea and the United States may agree that facilities and areas or portions thereof shall be returned to the Republic of Korea or that additional facilities and areas may be provided.

2. Pursuant to paragraph 1 above, it is requested that recommendations be presented to the Joint Committee concerning requests for the following acquisitions:

  a. Acquisition of 1.19 acres of non-arable land at San, 152, 262-1, Lim Bukun-ni, Hajum-myon, Kanghwa-gun, Kyonggi-do. This land is required for the erection of a security fence around the existing STRATCOM communications site.

  b. Acquisition of 1.16 acres of land with seven buildings and three facilities at Hannam-dong, Yongsan-ku, Seoul. This land and facilities are needed for expansion of the 8th Army Retreat Center.

  c. Acquisition of 1.98 acres of cultivated land at #322 Chung-dong, Tongnae-ku, Pusan City. The land is required for a storage area.

  d. Acquisition of 0.8 acre of non-arable land at Howon-dong, Uijongbu-si, Kyonggi-do. This property is required for expansion of Hill 651 Compound (IC-203).

  e. Acquisition of 0.23 acre of non-arable land at Kanung-dong, Uijongbu-si, Kyonggi-do. This property is required for the expansion of Camp Albany Compound (IC-164).

  f. Acquisition of 62.23 acres of land located at Yongtae-ri, Wolong-myon, Paju-gun, Kyonggi-do. This land is required for the consolidation of the 2nd Supply and Transportation Battalion at one location.

243

27th JC (Incl 2)
7 Jun 68

These minutes ● considered as official docum●● s pertaining to both
Governments and will not be released without mutual agreement.

g. Acquisition of an easement for 0.85 acre of non-arable land
located near the village of Pangchung-ni, Kwangtan-myon, Paju-gun,
Kyonggi-do. This easement is required for accomplishment of an
erosion control project adjacent to route 1B of Compound N-1, 7th
Infantry Division Artillery.

3. Pursuant to paragraph 1 above, it is requested that a recommendation be presented to the Joint Committee concerning the extension of
Temporary Use Permit, CAV-T-9, consisting of 145 acres of land
from 7 May 1968 to 6 May 1969. This land is required for continued
use as a field training area.

YOON HA JONG
Republic of Korea Representative

ROBERT J. FRIEDMAN
Lieutenant General
United States Air Force
United States Representative

27th JC (Incl 2)
7 Jun 68

2

REPUBLIC OF KOREA - UNITED STATES
FACILITIES AND AREAS SUBCOMMITTEE

29 May 1968

MEMORANDUM FOR: THE JOINT COMMITTEE

1. Subcommittee members:

United States	Republic of Korea
COL I. M. Rice, Chairman	MG KIM Mook, Chairman
LTC J. B. Carrick, USAFCSK	Mr. SONG Yong Tai
LTC Robert E. Graf, J4, USFK	Mr. SHIN Chung Sup
MAJ James B. Hoodenpyle, USAF	Mr. LEE Soon Dong
Mr. Francis K. Cook, J5, USFK	Mr. LEE Kihl Choo
Mr. Richard Rose, USAEDFE	Mr. LEE Moon Sup
Mrs. Betty H. Bowman, 8th Army	Mr. LEE Jong Do
	Mr. CHANG Kyong Shik
	Mr. CHA Sang Chun
	Mr. KIM Byoung Chan
	Mr. CHONG Young Hoon
	Mr. CHOI Chung Hwan
	Mr. NO Yong Goo
	Mr. PARK Moh Soo
	LTC KANG Jong Kuk
	Mr. KANG Hong Suk

2. Subject of Recommendation: Request for Release of Real Estate (Reference para 2g, Joint Committee Memorandum, same subject, dated 21 February 1968).

3. Recommendation: This is a request for release of a portion of ASCOM-375, containing 1.716 acres of land at Mansuk-dong, Inchon City, for construction of signal communication facilities for the Republic of Korea Navy. The Ministry of National Defense and the Eighth U.S.Army have agreed that release of the proposed site is not feasible at this time since location of the ROK Navy transmitter system would hamper the operation of other electrical equipment on the same area. A copy of the resolution is attached. It is therefore recommended that this request for release be withdrawn.

27th JC (Incl 3)
7 Jun 68

4. Security Classification:

Unclassified.

_____
COLONEL I. M. RICE
Chairman, United States Component
Facilities and Areas Subcommittee

_____
MAJOR GENERAL KIM Mook
Chairman, Republic of Korea Component
Facilities and Areas Subcommittee

1 Incl
as

**APPROVED BY THE JOINT COMMITTEE ON
7 JUNE 1968 AT TWENTY-SEVENTH MEETING**

_____
YOON HA JONG
Republic of Korea Representative

_____
ROBERT J. FRIEDMAN
Lieutenant General
United States Air Force
United States Representative

27th JC (Incl 3)
7 Jun 68

2

546 주한미군지위협정(SOFA) 한·미 합동위원회 1

These minutes a●●considered as official docume●● pertaining to both
Governments and will not be released without mutual agreement.

RESOLUTION OF
THE JOINT WORKING GROUP
TASK NO. 160

THE JOINT WORKING GROUP

HAVING REGARD to its Task No. 160, concerning the request for
release of 2,100 pyong of land on Wolmi-Do (Acquisition ASCOM 375)
for construction of a ROK Naval Defense Transmitter System (See
Appendix #1),

RECOGNIZING that the objective set forth in Task No. 160 should
be achieved by a mutually agreeable proposal and by constructive efforts
on the part of parties hereto,

DEEPLY CONSCIOUS of the ultimate need and necessity of construction
of ROK Naval Defense Transmitter System along the coastal area of the
Inchon Port to maintain its defense posture,

HAVING RECEIVED the "Special Reports" of OL 28, First Combat
Evaluation Group, US Air Force, and AADCP #2, APO 96571, U.S. Army,
which was based on the technical information and data provided by the
ROK Naval technicians and engineers (See Appendix #2 & #3),

ASSUMING that the location of the ROK Navy transmitter system on
proposed site would hamper the operation of other electronic equipment
on the same area,

AGREES that the release of proposed site on Wolmido referred to in
its Task No. 160 is not feasible at this time.

LEE, SUN-SIK
Commander, ROKN
Chairman for ROK Component

DATE: 26 April -68

CHARLES N. THOMAS
LTC, TC
Chairman for U.S. Component

DATE: 26 Apr 1968

Incl 1

24門

27th JC (Incl 1 to Incl 3)
7 Jun 68

These minutes are considered as official documents pertaining to both Governments an███ill not be released without mu███l agreement.

REPUBLIC OF KOREA - UNITED STATES
FACILITIES AND AREAS SUBCOMMITTEE

29 May 1968

MEMORANDUM FOR: THE JOINT COMMITTEE

1. Subcommittee Members:

United States	Republic of Korea
COL I. M. Rice, Chairman	MG KIM Mook, Chairman
LTC J. B. Carrick, USAFCSK	Mr. SONG Yong Tai
LTC Robert E. Graf, J4, USFK	Mr. SHIN Chung Sup
MAJ James B. Hoodenpyle, USAF	Mr. LEE Soon Dong
Mr. Francis K. Cook, J5, USFK	Mr. LEE Kihl Choo
Mr. Richard Rose, USAEDFE	Mr. LEE Moon Sup
Mrs. Betty H. Bowman, 8th Army	Mr. LEE Jong Do
	Mr. CHANG Kyong Shik
	Mr. CHA Sang Chun
	Mr. KIM Byoung Chan
	Mr. CHONG Young Hoon
	Mr. CHOI Chung Hwan
	Mr. NO Yong Goo
	Mr. PARK Moh Soo
	LTC KANG Jong Kuk
	Mr. KANG Hong Suk

2. Subject of Recommendation: Request for Release of Real Estate (Reference para 2e, Joint Committee Memorandum, same subject, dated 21 February 1968.

3. Recommendation: A portion of PAC-10 (SR#48) consisting of approximately 1.634 acres of land located at Pumildong, Pusan City, for an urban development project can be released by USFK subject to the fulfillment of the conditions of release as have been mutually agreed upon by the Ministry of National Defense and the Eighth US Army. The Ministry of National Defense and the Far East District Engineer will be requested to prepare the necessary documents. It is recommended that the Joint Committee, SOFA, approve this release.

27th JC (Incl 4)
7 Jun 68

4. Security Classification:

   Unclassified.

_____ _____
COLONEL I. M. RICE /s/ MAJOR GENERAL KIM Mook
Chairman, United States Component Chairman, Republic of Korea Component
Facilities and Areas Subcommittee Facilities and Areas Subcommittee

1 Incl
Conditions for Partial Release
of Acquisition PAC-10 (SP #48)

APPROVED BY THE JOINT COMMITTEE ON
7 JUNE 1968 AT TWENTY-SEVENTH MEETING

_____ _____
YOON HA JONG ROBERT J. FRIEDMAN
Republic of Korea Representative Lieutenant General
 United States Air Force
 United States Representative

           27th JC (Incl 4)
           7 Jun 68

2

These minutes are considered as official documents pertaining to both Governments and will not be released without mutual agreement.

CONDITIONS FOR PARTIAL RELEASE
OF
ACQUISITION PAC-10, SP #48

48 보급지의 취득 부동산 (PAC-10)의 부분 이양에
관한 조건 사항

27th JC (Incl 1 to Incl 4)
7 Jun 68

These minutes a⬤considered as official docume⬤ pertaining to both Governments and will not be released without mutual agreement.

CONDITIONS FOR PARTIAL RELEASE
OF
ACQUISITION PAC-10, SP #48

48보급지의 취득 부동산 (PAC- 10)의 부분 이양에 관한 조건사항

1. PURPOSE: a. The Purpose of this Mutually Agreeable Proposal is
   목적   상호 동의된 본 제안서의 목적은 부산시내에

to set forth certain conditions for the recommended release of approximately
위치한 주한 미군 48 보급지의 약 2,000평을 이양하는데 필요한

2,000 pyongs of United States Forces, Korea (USFK) Supply Point (SP) Number
몇가지 조건을 설정함에 있음.

48 sited within the City of Pusan.

   b. This proposal was drafted in response to a Republic of Korea (ROK)
       초안된 본 제안서는 대한민국측의 상기 부동산 (취득 부동산

request for release of this real estate (part of Acquisition PAC-10). This
PAC - 10의 일부분) 이양 요청에 의하여 작성되었음. 이 지역은

area is needed for use in connection with a Pusan City highway development
부산시 도로 확장 계획에 필요함.

plan.

2. AUTHORITY: US Component authorization for preparation of this proposal
   권능   본 제안서 준비를 위임케 한 미국측 공문서는

is contained in Ltr, Hqs, Eighth United States Army Depot Command and Eight
   다음과 같다. 1968년 3월 11일부 미8군 후방사령부 및 보급사령부발

United States Army Rear, cite EADC-SVE, Subject, Appointment of a Joint
   공문, 주제 "한미 합동 실무자 회의 임명 소집 — 사업 번호 158".

Working Group - Task No. 158, dated 11 March 1968 (Incl #1).
   (별지 제 1)

3. PREPARATION: This proposal was developed through efforts of the Joint
   준비   본 제안서는 한국정부 (부산시) 및 부산 미군사령부

Working Group with membership representing both ROK Government (City of Pusan)
   양측 대표들로 구성된 합동 실무자 회의의 노력으로 작성되었음.

27th JC (Incl 1 to Incl 4)
7 Jun 68

and USFK sited at Pusan; Korea. Joint Working Group was established by
합동 실무자 회의는 미 8군 합동위원회의 시설 및 구역

Facilities and Areas Subcommittee (FASC), Joint Committee, Eighth United
분과위원회가 한국 정부와 절충하여 선정 되었음.

States Army, in coordination with ROK Government.

4. PROPOSAL: The USFK will release to the City of Pusan the Northwest
제안 주한미군은 별지 제2 도면 16-09-96에 표시된

portion of SP #48, as indicated on attached drawing #16-09-96 Sheet #1
48보급지점의 북서 지역 부분을 부산시에 이양 할것임.

(Incl #2).

5. CONDITIONS: Release of land, per para 4 above, is predicated upon the
조건 상기 제 4항목에 기재된 토지 이양은 다음 여러

following conditions:
조건에 근거를 두고 실시됨.

a. That a certain parcel of land in vicinity of Pusan will be acquisi-
부산에 인접한 한 토지구역을 주한미군이 취득게 하여

tioned to the USFK for use as a Property Disposal Office (PDO) Holding Area.
미군 재산처리처 재산 직접소로 사용게 할것임. 주한미군이

The real estate desired by USFK is located within the boundaries of Area B,
요망한 상기 부동산은 부동산 취득번호 PAC-25의 일부분 구역 "B" 의

Acquisition No PAC-25 Partial. A USFK request has been initiated for
경계선내에 위치함. 주한미군은 상기한 부동산 취득 요청 수속을 이미

acquisition of proposed property.
받고 있음.

b. That the City of Pusan shall perform the following at no expense to
부산시는 미국 정부의 비용 부담없이 다음 사항을

the United States Government:
수행할것임.

(1) Construct a new concrete block security wall along the Northwest
48 보급지점의 북서 경계선에 연하여 콩크리트 부로크

Boundary of SP #48. The new wall shall be built to the same height, thickness
경비용 담벽을 신설할것임. 신설한 담벽의 높이, 두께 및 재료는

2

and materiels as the existing wall. Additionally, it will be installed
현존한 담벽과 꼭 같어야 함. 더 나아가서 도면 16-09-96

with a barbed wire barrier at the top as shown on attached drawings
제 2지 (별지 3)에 표시한 것과 마찬가지로 담벽위에 철조망을

#16-09-96 Sheet 2 (Incl #3).
설정할것임.

(2) Relocate the Supply Point Northwest Gate, in the existing security
현존한 담벽에 접해있는 보급 지점 북서문을 주한 미군

wall, to a new location designated by USFK Representatives. In accomplishing
대표가 지정한 새로운 장소에 재 배치할것임. 새 콩크리트 기둥을

this relocation, new concrete gate posts shall be constructed.
신축함으로서 동 재배치는 완수 됫것임.

(3) Construct a 20' X 60' concrete block building for use as a PDO
변소 시설을 설치한 20' x 60' 콩크리트 부로크 건물 한동을

administrative office to include installed latrine facilities. This cons-
건립할사 (재산 처리처 사무실용). 등 건축은 도면 16-09-95

truction will be in accordance with specifications outlined on the attached
제 3지 (별지 4)에 표시한 시방서에 의하여 시공할것임. 동 건물은

Drawing #16-09-96 Sheet #3 (Incl #4). The new structure will be in lieu
재 배치가 불가능한 건물 1474 (현재의 재산처리처 행정사무실) 뒬

of existing buildings #1474 (Current PDO Administrative Office) and #1479
1479 (현존한 재산처리처 변소 시설) 대신으로 건립 되는것임.

(Existing PDO latrine facility) which cannot be relocated.

(4) Relocate Buildings #1487 (PDO Warehouse) and #1488 (PDO Korean
건물 1487 (재산 처리처 창고) 뒬 1488 (재산 처리처

National Lounge) to a new site as shown on attached Drawing #16-09-96
한국인 휴게실) 을 도면 16-09-96 제 1지 (별지 2)에 표시한 새로운

Sheet #1 (Incl #2).
장소에 재배치할사.

(5) Construct a suitable size septic tank for the new latrine facility
새 변소 시설은 수득 하수구에 연결될 하수도 파이프 뒬

with effluent piping which will discharge into main sewer system.
알맞는 크기의 하수 정화용 탱크 (한개)를 설치할것임.

(6) Extend existing water mains to the new latrine facility located
현존한 상수도관을 새로 지울 재산 처리처 행정사무실 건물내에

within the new PDO administrative building.
위치한 새로운 변소 시설까지 연장시설할사.

(7) Remove that portion of the present water mains now extending to
현재, 건물 1479 까지 뻗치고 있는 현존 상수도관의

Building #1479 as prescribed by USFK representatives.
그 부분을 주한미군 대표가 지시하는데로 제거할사.

(8) Provide a storm drainage system for proper runoff of water from
48 보급지점내에 위치한 재산처리처 구역에서 알맞게

the Property Disposal Area, within Supply Point #48.
배수될수 있는 비상용 배수 장치를 구비할사,

c. That the United States Government will:
미국 정부는 다음 사항을 실행할사.

(1) Relocate the security lights, poles and transmission lines along
상기한 5b (1) 항목에 기재된 경계선 담벽부분에 연하여

that portion of the boundary fence indicated in sub-para 5b(1) above.
있는 보안등 및 전선줄을 재 배치할사.

(2) Wire all USFK buildings that are relocated or constructed by
부산시측이 새로운 장소에 재 배치했거나 건축한 모든

the City of Pusan at their new locations.
건물에 전선줄을 닿저.

6. ADDITIONAL STIPULATIONS: a. The USFK will remove the following equip-
추가 규정   주한 미군은 양도될 구역내에 있는

ment and facilities from the area to be released:
다음과 같은 장비 및 시설을 제거할사.

(1) Building #1472.
건물 1472

(2) Oil Storage Tank.
유류 저장 탱크

(3) Hot Water Heater.
물 히타

(4) All electric fixtures and switches within existing buildings.
현존한 건물속에 있는 모든 전기 비품 및 수월치

4

These minutes a●●considered as official docume●●s pertaining to both
Governments and will not be released without mutual agreement.

    (5) Selective plumbing and piping fixtures except latrine facilities.
    변소 시설을 제외한 시설의 선택 된 프람브 및 파이프 비품.

   b. The USFK will abandon existing buildings #1474 and #1479. Removal
   주한 미균은 현존한 건물 1474 및 1479를 포기할거임.

and disposal of these structures is at discretion of the City of Pusan.
동 건물의 제거 및 처리는 부산시의 재량에 맡김.

7. PRIORITIES: The PDO administrative office structure must be constructed
   우선권   새로운 경비용 담벽을 건립하기전에 재산 처리처

and existing Buildings #1487 and #1488 relocated before the new security
행정 사무실 건물을 건축할것이며 또한 현존한 건물 1487 및 1488을

wall is erected. Further in the interest of SP #48 security, the new wall
재 배치할사. 더 나아가서 48 보급지점 보안을 위해서 새로운 담벽은

must be constructed before the existing wall is removed.
현존한 담벽을 제거하기전에 건립할사.

8. RESPONSIBILITY: The City of Pusan shall assume responsibility for any
   책임   부산시는 위에 기재한 건축 혹은 재배치를

injuries to personnel or damages to property occuring during the construc-
하는 동안 발생하는 인명 및 재산 피해에 대한 책임을 질것임.

tion or relocation activities outlined above.

9. REVISION: This proposal may be revised by mutual consent of both
   수정   본 제안서는 쌍방의 상호 합의에 의하여 수정

parties concerned. Such revisions must be submitted in writing and pro-
될수도 있음. 수정 상향은 반드시 서면상으로 제출하되 타당한

perly authenticated.
신빈성이 있어야 함.

10. AUTHENTICATION: When signed by the chairman, ROK, and the chairman,
   인증   본제안서는 한미 합동 실무자 회의의 양측 의장이

USFK, Joint Working Group, this document represents the mutually Agreeable
서명하는 즉시 48 보급 지점 취득 부동산에 대한 상호 동의가 성립,

5

27th JC (Incl 1 to Incl 4)
7 Jun 68

Proposal for partial release of Acquisition PAC-10, SP #48
되었음을 나타냄.

Signed this _____15th_____ of _____MAY_____ 1968 in the City of Pusan,
서명   1968년 대한민국 부산시

Republic of Korea.

Mr. LEE, CHANG TAL   WARREN J. WEBER
Republic of Korea   LTC, TC
Joint Working Group   United States of America
이 창 달   Joint Working Group
합동·실무자 회의   워렌 제이 웨버
대한민국측 대표   종령 수송 병과
                                      합동·실무자 회의
                                      미국측 대표

4 Incl
1. Ltr frm EADC/EAR
2. SP #48 Instal Map
3. Wall Barrier SP #48
4. Drawing of Proposed Bldg #1474

4. 첨부 서류
1. 미후방기자 및 보급 사령부 공문서
2. 48보급지 서설지도
3. 48보급지 담벽 경계선
4. 제안된 건물 1474의 도면

6

256

8

These minutes are considered as official documents pertaining to both Governments and will not be released without mutual agreement.

REPUBLIC OF KOREA - UNITED STATES
FACILITIES AND AREAS SUBCOMMITTEE

29 May 1968

MEMORANDUM FOR: THE JOINT COMMITTEE

1. Subcommittee members:

United States	Republic of Korea
COL I. M. Rice, Chairman	MG KIM Mook, Chairman
LTC J. B. Carrick, USAFCSK	Mr. SONG Yong Tai
LTC Robert E. Graf, J4, USFK	Mr. SHIN Chung Sup
MAJ James B. Hoodenpyle, USAF	Mr. LEE Soon Dong
Mr. Francis K. Cook, J5, USFK	Mr. LEE Kihl Choo
Mr. Richard Rose, USAEDFE	Mr. LEE Moon Sup
Mrs. Betty H. Bowman, 8th Army	Mr. LEE Jong Do
	Mr. CHANG Kyong Shik
	Mr. CHA Sang Chun
	Mr. KIM Byoung Chan
	Mr. CHONG Young Hoon
	Mr. CHOI Chung Hwan
	Mr. NO Yong Goo
	Mr. PARK Moh Soo
	LTC KANG Jong Kuk
	Mr. KANG Hong Suk

2. Subject of Recommendation: Requests for Acquisition of Real Estate and Extension of Temporary Use Permit (Reference para 2c, same subject, Joint Committee Memorandum, dated 4 April 1968).

3. Recommendation: The request for acquisition of 0.18 acre of mountainous land located at Kumo-dong, Uijongbu-si, Kyonggi-do, has been accepted by the Ministry of National Defense. The real estate is required for the erection of a microwave reflector. The Ministry of National Defense and the Far East District Engineer will be requested to prepare the necessary documents. It is recommended that the Joint Committee, SOFA, approve this acquisition.

27th JC (Incl 5)
7 Jun 68

These minutes are considered as official documents pertaining to both Governments and will not be released without mutual agreement.

0340

4. Security Classification:

Unclassified.

COLONEL I. M. RICE
Chairman, United States Component
Facilities and Areas Subcommittee

MAJOR GENERAL KIM Mook
Chairman, Republic of Korea Component
Facilities and Areas Subcommittee

APPROVED BY THE JOINT COMMITTEE ON
7 JUNE 1968 AT TWENTY-SEVENTH MEETING

YOON HA JONG
Republic of Korea Representative

ROBERT J. FRIEDMAN
Lieutenant General
United States Air Force
United States Representative

2

27th JC (Incl 5)
7 Jun 68

REPUBLIC OF KOREA - UNITED STATES
FACILITIES AND AREAS SUBCOMMITTEE

29 May 1968

MEMORANDUM FOR: THE JOINT COMMITTEE

1. Subcommittee members:

United States	Republic of Korea
COL I. M. Rice, Chairman	MG KIM Mook, Chairman
LTC J. B. Carrick, USAFCSK	Mr. SONG Yong Tai
LTC Robert E. Graf, J4, USFK	Mr. SHIN Chung Sup
MAJ James B. Hoodenpyle, USAF	Mr. LEE Kihl Choo
Mr. Francis K. Cook, J5, USFK	Mr. LEE Moon Sup
Mr. Richard Rose, USAEDFE	Mr. LEE Jong Do
Mrs. Betty H. Bowman, 8th Army	Mr. CHANG Kyong Shik
	Mr. CHA Sang Chun
	Mr. KIM Byoung Chan
	Mr. CHONG Young Hoon
	Mr. CHOI Chung Hwan
	Mr. NO Yong Goo
	Mr. PARK Moh Soo
	LTC KANG Jong Kuk
	Mr. KANG Hong Suk
	Mr. LEE Soon Dong

2. Subject of Recommendations: Request for Acquisition of Real Estate and Extension of Temporary Use Permit (Reference Joint Committee Memorandum, same subject, dated 17 May 1968).

3. Recommendations:

a. Request for acquisition of a total of 16.455 acres of land at various locations in Imjin-myon, Paju-gun, Kyonggi-do (3.76 acres for exclusive use and 12.695 acres of existing road as an easement) has been accepted by the Ministry of National Defense with the stipulation that before initiation of road construction, the 2nd Inf Div Post Engineer and the 36th Engineer Group will coordinate with the MND Real Estate Representative to preclude any damage to adjacent property. The real estate is

27th JC (Incl 6)
7 Jun 68

259

required for a by-pass route for tracked vehicles. The Ministry of National Defense and the Far East District Engineer will be requested to prepare the necessary documents. It is recommended that the Joint Committee, SOFA, approve this acquisition.

b. The request to convert to an exclusive use basis 0.014 acre currently held as a perpetual restrictive easement, located at #142-1 Hasangok-ni, Tongbu-myon, Kwangju-gun, Kyonggi-do, has been accepted by the Ministry of National Defense. This real estate is required to construct a retaining wall to prevent erosion. The Ministry of National Defense and the Far East District Engineer will be requested to prepare the necessary documents. It is recommended that the Joint Committee, SOFA, approve this acquisition.

c. Request for extension of temporary use permit CAV-T-16, involving a total of 128,713.04 acres of land (38,116.82 acres consist of arable land and 90,596.22 acres of non-arable land) from 1 May 1968 to 30 April 1969 for training purposes has been accepted by the Ministry of National Defense. The Ministry of National Defense and the Far East District Engineer will be requested to prepare the necessary documents. It is recommended that the Joint Committee, SOFA, approve extension of this permit.

4. Security Classification: Unclassified.

COLONEL I. M. RICE
Chairman, United States Component
Facilities and Areas Subcommittee

MAJOR GENERAL KIM Mook
Chairman, Republic of Korea Component
Facilities and Areas Subcommittee

**APPROVED BY THE JOINT COMMITTEE ON
7 JUNE 1968 AT TWENTY-SEVENTH MEETING**

YOON HA JONG
Republic of Korea Representative

ROBERT J. FRIEDMAN
Lieutenant General
United States Air Force
United States Representative

2

27th JC (Incl 6)
7 Jun 68

JOINT COMMITTEE
UNDER
THE REPUBLIC OF KOREA AND THE UNITED STATES
STATUS OF FORCES AGREEMENT

7 June 1968

MEMORANDUM TO: The Joint Committee

SUBJECT : Operating Procedures for the Facilities
and Areas Subcommittee

1. Reference is made to the following passages
of the Joint Committee decisions:

a. Procedures for operation of the ROK-US
Joint Committee Subcommittees. (Inclosure 5, Minutes of
the First Meeting)

" 1 . . . Subcommittees will give advice
and make recommendations only on these matters
specifically referred to them by the Joint
Committee."

b. Facilities and Areas Subcommittee procedures.
(Inclosure 2, Minutes of the Fifth Meeting)

" III. Order of Business

2. Unless otherwise directed by the Joint
Committee, the Facilities and Areas Subcommittee
will address only matters referred to it by
the Joint Committee."

"IV. Conduct of Business

1. The Facilities and Areas Subcommittee
will act only on tasks assigned by the Joint
Committee."

2. The principle adopted by the Joint Committee
and referred to in the proceeding paragraph has been

27th JC (Incl 7)
7 Jun 68

strictly adhered to for the operation of the Facilities
and Areas Subcommittee since its inauguration. However,
it is noted that almost all of the tasks assigned to
the Subcommittee concern with acquisition, extension of
temporary use permit, release or reclassification of
individual real estate, that before formal assignment
of such tasks prescreening by the Subcommittee was
necessary, and that consequently the assignment of such
tasks by the Joint Committee is a mere formality.
It is also recalled that on several occasions the Joint
Committee was obliged to follow exisgency procedures due
to urgency of some actions.

    3. Therefore it is proposed that the following
principle be adopted by the Joint Committee in order to
simplify the procedures:

        a. The Facilities and Areas Subcommittee may
submit to the Joint Committee its views and recommendations
on requests concerned with individual real estate without
being formally assigned a task.

        b. In case of disagreement both sides reserve
the right to bring the matter to the Joint Committee for
its decision.

        c. The Subcommittee will not act on matters
of general policy or procedures unless a specific task
thereon was assigned by the Joint Committee.

Yoon Ha Jong
Republic of Korea
Representative

These minutes a●●considered as official docume●●pertaining to both
Governments and will not be released without mutual agreement.

JOINT COMMITTEE
UNDER
THE REPUBLIC OF KOREA AND THE UNITED STATES
STATUS OF FORCES AGREEMENT

7 June 1968

MEMORANDUM TO: Joint Committee

SUBJECT: Interpretation of Article XVI, Paragraph 1, of the
US-ROK SOFA

1. Paragraph 1, Article XVI, provides that "The United States may
contract for any materials, supplies, equipment and services
(including construction work) to be furnished or undertaken in the
Republic of Korea for purposes of, or authorized by, this Agreement, without restriction as to choice of contractor, supplier or
person who provides such services..."

2. The first sentence of paragraph 1, Article XVI, clearly gives
the United States unrestricted right to contract in the Republic of
Korea. Specifically, it is believed that under Article XVI of the
Status of Forces Agreement, a Korean contractor who is duly
licensed by the Government of the Republic of Korea to do business
in Korea is not required to obtain a special license to do business
with the United States armed forces in Korea. In this connection,
it is our opinion that the restrictions on freedom of US selection
of Korean contractors contained in ROK Law 979 are inconsistent
with the purpose and language of paragraph 1, Article XVI.

3. As paragraph 2 of Article XVI indicates, only that procurement
by the US armed forces which may have an adverse effect on the
economy of the Republic of Korea is legally required to be procured
in coordination with, and, when desirable, through or with the
assistance of, the competent authorities of the Republic of Korea.

4. The United States believes that it is in the mutual interests of
both the Governments of the Republic of Korea and of the United
States to have maximum competition in local procurement actions
by the US armed forces in Korea. It is clear that paragraph 1,

27th JC (Incl 8)
7 Jun 68

263

Article XVI, provides the US with the right of competitive bidding "without restriction," and that this would contribute to free competition in local procurement and promote the joint ROK-US defense of the Republic of Korea.

5. We believe that the Government of the Republic of Korea should accept the above interpretation in paragraph 4 regarding Article XVI, paragraph 1, and should take appropriate action with regard to Law 979 in view of its obligations under paragraph 2 of Article XXIX.

ROBERT J. FRIEDMAN
Lieutenant General
United States Air Force
United States Representative

2

These minutes are considered as official documents pertaining to both
Governments and will not be released without mutual agreement.

JOINT COMMITTEE
UNDER
THE REPUBLIC OF KOREA AND THE UNITED STATES
STATUS OF FORCES AGREEMENT

28 May 1968

MEMORANDUM FOR: The Joint Committee

SUBJECT: Designation of US Invited Contractor under Article XV,
Status of Forces Agreement

1. References:

    a. Paragraph 2, Article XV, Status of Forces Agreement.

    b. US Commerce Subcommittee Memorandum of Consultation, dated
23 May 1968, subject as above (Inclosure 1).

    c. ROK Commerce Subcommittee Memorandum of Consultation, dated
23 May 1968, subject as above (Inclosure 2).

2. The United States, after consultation with the ROK Commerce Sub-
committee and after having duly considered their views, has designated
Adrian Wilson Associates as a US invited contractor for execution of
Contract #F62087-68-C-0102 for Architect and Engineering services.

3. Pertinent data concerning US citizen employees will be provided to
the Joint Secretariat in the established periodic arrival and departure
format.

2 Incl
as

ROBERT J. FRIEDMAN
Lieutenant General
United States Air Force
United States Representative
Joint Committee

27th JC (Incl 9)
7 Jun 68

These minutes are considered as official documents pertaining to both Governments and will not be released without mutual agreement.

REPUBLIC OF KOREA - UNITED STATES
COMMERCE SUBCOMMITTEE

23 May 1968

SUBJECT: Designation of US Invited Contractor under Article XV, Status of Forces Agreement

ROK Chairman, Commerce Subcommittee

1. Reference: Paragraph 2, Article XV of the Status of Forces Agreement.

2. The Government of the Republic of Korea is informed through this written consultive process that the United States Forces, Korea, proposes to extend invited contractor status to the qualified US firm on the contract described in paragraph 3 below.

3. The following data is provided:

   a. Company Name: Adrian Wilson Associates.

   b. Local Address: 136-2 Itaewon-Dong, Yongsan-Ku, Seoul, Korea.

   c. Identification of US Citizen Employees: To be supplied after award of contract.

   d. Number of US and ROK Employees:

      U.S. - 8
      ROK - 20

   e. Reasons for Designation of an Invited Contractor: Open competitive bidding among local contractors is not practicable due to the following:

      (1) Security considerations.

      (2) Technical qualifications of the contractor involved.

   f. Location of Contract: Kwang-Ju, Taegu, and Osan Air Bases, Korea.

27th JC (Incl 1 to Incl 9)
7 Jun 68

SUBJECT: Designation of US Invited Contractor under Article XV,
          Status of Forces Agreement

    g. Type of Contract: Architect-Engineering services.

    h. Length of Contract: Approximately 30 days.

    i. Sponsoring Component Command: Commander, Air Forces, Korea.
(Headquarters, 6314th Support Wing (PACAF)).

FLOYD R. WALTZ, JR.
Colonel, United States Army
US Chairman, Commerce Subcommittee

2

MINISTRY OF COMMERCE AND INDUSTRY
REPUBLIC OF KOREA
SEOUL, KOREA

25 May 1968

SUBJECT: Designation of US Invited Contractor under Article XV, Status of Forces Agreement.

TO   : Chairman, US Commerce Subcommittee.

    1. References:

        a. Paragraph 2, Article XV, Status of Forces Agreement.

        b. US Commerce Subcommittee Memorandum of Consultation, Dated 23 May 1968, subject as above, pertaining to contract for architect-engineering services in the Kwang-Ju, Taegu, and Osan Air Base construction projects.

    2. The US memorandum, reference 1b above, has been reviewed and the Government of the Republic of Korea fully understands the requirement for an invited contractor in this instance.

For /Han Byung Il
Chairman
ROK Commerce Subcommittee

27th JC (Incl 2 to Incl 9)
7 Jun 68

These minutes are considered as official documents pertaining to both Governments and will not be released without mutual agreement.

JOINT COMMITTEE
UNDER
THE REPUBLIC OF KOREA AND THE UNITED STATES
STATUS OF FORCES AGREEMENT

28 May 1968

MEMORANDUM FOR: The Joint Committee

SUBJECT: Designation of US Invited Contractor under Article XV, Status of Forces Agreement

1. References:

   a. Paragraph 2, Article XV, Status of Forces Agreement.

   b. US Commerce Subcommittee Memorandum of Consultation, dated 23 May 1968, subject as above (Inclosure 1).

   c. ROK Commerce Subcommittee Memorandum of Consultation, dated 25 May 1968, subject as above (Inclosure 2).

2. The United States, after consultation with the ROK Commerce Subcommittee and after having duly considered their views, has designated Trans-Asia Engineering Associates, Inc. as a US invited contractor for execution of Contract #F62087-68-C-0101 for Architect and Engineering services.

3. Pertinent data concerning US citizen employees will be provided to the Joint Secretariat in the established periodic arrival and departure format.

2 Incl
as

ROBERT J. FRIEDMAN
Lieutenant General
United States Air Force
United States Representative
Joint Committee

27th JC (Incl 10)
7 Jun 68

269

REPUBLIC OF KOREA - UNITED STATES
COMMERCE SUBCOMMITTEE

23 May 1968

SUBJECT: Designation of US Invited Contractor under Article XV, Status of Forces Agreement

ROK Chairman, Commerce Subcommittee

1. Reference: Paragraph 2, Article XV of the Status of Forces Agreement.

2. The Government of the Republic of Korea is informed through this written consultive process that the United States Forces, Korea, proposes to extend invited contractor status to the qualified US firm on the contract described in paragraph 3 below.

3. The following data is provided:

　　a. Company Name: Trans-Asia Engineering Associates, Inc.

　　b. Local Address: Building 1510, APO 96301.

　　c. Identification of US Citizen Employees: To be supplied after award of contract.

　　d. Number of US and ROK Employees:

　　　　　　　　　U.S.　-　5
　　　　　　　　　ROK　-　20

　　e. Reasons for Designation of an Invited Contractor: Open competitive bidding among local contractors is not practicable due to the following:

　　　(1) Security considerations.

　　　(2) Technical qualifications of the contractor involved.

　　f. Location of Contract: Kunsan Air Base and Osan Air Base, Korea.

27th JC (Incl 1 to Incl 10)
7 Jun 68

SUBJECT: Designation of US Invited Contractor under Article XV, Status of Forces Agreement

 g. <u>Type of Contract</u>: Architect-Engineering services.

 h. <u>Length of Contract</u>: Approximately 30 days.

 i. <u>Sponsoring Component Command</u>: Commander, Air Forces, Korea. (Headquarters, 6314th Support Wing (PACAF)).

FLOYD R. WALTZ, JR.
Colonel, United States Army
US Chairman, Commerce Subcommittee

2

These minutes are considered as official documents pertaining to both Governments and ███ill not be released without mu███l agreement:

MINISTRY OF COMMERCE AND INDUSTRY
REPUBLIC OF KOREA
SEOUL, KOREA

25 May 1968

SUBJECT: Designation of US Invited Contractor under Article XV, Status of Forces Agreement.

TO   : Chairman, US Commerce Subcommittee.

1. References:

a. Paragraph 2, Article XV, Status of Forces Agreement.

b. US Commerce Subcommittee Memorandum of Consultation, Dated 23 May 1968, subject as above, pertaining to contract for architect-engineering services in the Kunsan and Osan Air Base construction projects.

2. The US memorandum, reference 1b above, has been reviewed and the Government of the Republic of Korea fully understands the requirement for an invited contractor in this instance.

Chairman
ROK Commerce Subcommittee

27th JC (Incl 2 to Incl 10)
7 Jun 68

These minutes are considered as official documents pertaining to both Governments and will not be released without mutual agreement.

**JOINT COMMITTEE
UNDER
THE REPUBLIC OF KOREA AND THE UNITED STATES
STATUS OF FORCES AGREEMENT**

28 May 1968

MEMORANDUM FOR: The Joint Committee

SUBJECT: Designation of US Invited Contractor under Article XV, Status of Forces Agreement

1. References:

    a. Paragraph 2, Article XV, Status of Forces Agreement.

    b. US Commerce Subcommittee Memorandum of Consultation, dated 23 May 1968, subject as above (Inclosure 1).

    c. ROK Commerce Subcommittee Memorandum of Consultation, dated 25 May 1968, subject as above (Inclosure 2).

2. The United States, after consultation with the ROK Commerce Sub-committee and after having duly considered their views, has designated Daniel, Mann, Johnson & Mendenhall as a US invited contractor for execution of Contract #F62087-68-C-0100 for Architect and Engineering services.

3. Pertinent data concerning US citizen employees will be provided to the Joint Secretariat in the established periodic arrival and departure format.

2 Incl
as

ROBERT J. FRIEDMAN
Lieutenant General
United States Air Force
United States Representative
Joint Committee

27th JC (Incl 11)
7 Jun 68

These minutes are considered as official documents pertaining to both Governments and will not be released without mutual agreement.

REPUBLIC OF KOREA - UNITED STATES
COMMERCE SUBCOMMITTEE

23 May 1968

SUBJECT: Designation of US Invited Contractor under Article XV, Status of Forces Agreement

ROK Chairman, Commerce Subcommittee

1. Reference: Paragraph 2, Article XV of the Status of Forces Agreement.

2. The Government of the Republic of Korea is informed through this written consultive process that the United States Forces, Korea, proposes to extend invited contractor status to the qualified US firm on the contract described in paragraph 3 below.

3. The following data is provided:

   a. Company Name: Daniel, Mann, Johnson and Mendenhall.

   b. Local Address: Box 11, APO 96570.

   c. Identification of US Citizen Employees: To be supplied after award of contract.

   d. Number of US and ROK Employees:

                    U.S.   -   12
                    ROK   -   15

   e. Reasons for Designation of an Invited Contractor: Open competitive bidding among local contractors is not practicable due to the following:

   (1) Security considerations.

   (2) Technical qualifications of the contractor involved.

   f. Location of Contract: Suwon and Osan Air Bases, Korea.

27th JC (Incl 1 to Incl 11)
7 Jun 68

SUBJECT: Designation of US Invited Contractor under Article XV, Status of Forces Agreement

g. <u>Type of Contract</u>: Architect-Engineering services.

h. <u>Length of Contract</u>: Approximately 30 days.

i. <u>Sponsoring Component Command</u>: Commander, Air Forces, Korea. (Headquarters, 6314th Support Wing (PACAF)).

FLOYD R. WALTZ, JR.
Colonel, United States Army
US Chairman, Commerce Subcommittee

2

These minutes are considered as official documents pertaining to both Governments an● ●●l not be released without mu●●l agreement.

MINISTRY OF COMMERCE AND INDUSTRY
REPUBLIC OF KOREA
SEOUL, KOREA

25 May 1968

SUBJECT: Designation of US Invited Contractor under Article XV, Status of Forces Agreement.

TO   : Chairman, US Commerce Subcommittee

1. References:

a. Paragraph 2, Article XV, Status of Forces Agreement.

b. US Commerce Subcommittee Memorandum of Consultation, Dated 23 May 1968, subject as above, pertaining to contract for architect-engineering services in the Suwon and Osan Air Base construction projects.

2. The US memorandum, reference 1b above, has been reviewed and the Government of the Republic of Korea fully understands the requirement for an invited contractor in this instance.

For /Jan Byung Il
Chairman
ROK Commerce Subcommittee

These minutes a█████nsidered as official docume██pertaining to both
Governments and will not be released without mutual agreement.

JOINT ROK - US PRESS RELEASE
TWENTY-SEVENTH ROK-US JOINT COMMITTEE MEETING
7 JUNE 1968

The ROK-US Joint Committee discussed simplification of operating procedures of its Facilities and Areas Subcommittee at its twenty-seventh meeting on 7 June 1968.

The Joint Committee also accepted six recommendations of its Facilities and Areas Subcommittee, relating to the acquisition and release of facilities and areas by the US armed forces in Korea. The Joint Committee also assigned eight new tasks to its Facilities and Areas Subcommittee at this meeting, which was held in the US SOFA Conference Room in Yongsan.

The US Representative, Lieutenant General Robert J. Friedman, presided at this Joint Committee meeting. The Joint Committee scheduled its next meeting for 3 July at the ROK Capitol Building.

27th JC (Incl 12)
7 Jun 68

보 도 자 료

─ 호

년 월 일 시 분 발표

이 기사는 제공처인 외무부를
밝히고 보도할수 있음

한.미 합동위원회 제27차 회의

공동 발표문

1968. 6.7. 15:00시

미8군 SOFA 회의실

한.미 합동위원회는 1968년 6월 7일 제27차 회의를 열고
시설구역 분과위원회 운영절차의 간소화에 관한 토의를 했다.

또한 동 합동위원회는 용산 미8군 회의실에서 열린 동 회의
에서 주한 미군에 의한 시설과 구역의 취득 및 반환에 관한
시설구역 분과위원회의 건의 6건을 채택하고 동 분과위원회에 신규
과제 8건을 부여하였다.

미국대표 프리드만 중장이 동 회의를 주재하였다.

차기 회의는 7월 3일 중앙청 회의실에서 개최될 예정이다.

The ROK-US Joint Committee discussed simplification
of operating procedures of its Facilities and Areas
Subcommittee at its twenty-seventh meeting on 7 June 1968.

The Joint Committee also accepted six recommendations
of its Facilities and Areas Subcommittee, relating to the
acquisition and release of facilities and areas by the
US armed forces in Korea. The Joint Committee also
assigned eight new tasks to its Facilities and Areas
Subcommittee at this meeting, which was held in the US
SOFA Conference Room in Yongsan.

The US Representative, Lieutenant General Robert J.
Friedman, presided at this Joint Committee meeting.
The Joint Committee scheduled its next meeting for
3 July at the ROK Capitol Building.

외교문서 비밀해제: 주한미군지위협정(SOFA) 24

주한미군지위협정(SOFA) 한 · 미 합동위원회 1

초판인쇄 2024년 03월 15일
초판발행 2024년 03월 15일

지은이 한국학술정보(주)
펴낸이 채종준
펴낸곳 한국학술정보(주)
주 소 경기도 파주시 회동길 230(문발동)
전 화 031-908-3181(대표)
팩 스 031-908-3189
홈페이지 http://ebook.kstudy.com
E-mail 출판사업부 publish@kstudy.com
등 록 제일산-115호(2000. 6. 19)

ISBN 979-11-7217-035-6 94340
        979-11-7217-011-0 94340 (set)